Perspectives on Gulf Coast Prehistory

Ripley P. Bullen Monographs
in Anthropology and History
Number 5
The Florida State Museum

Ripley P. Bullen Monographs
in Anthropology and History

Jerald T. Milanich, general editor

Number 1. *Tacachale: Essays on the Indians of Florida and South-eastern Georgia during the Historic Period,* edited by Jerald T. Milanich and Samuel Proctor (1978).

Number 2. *Aboriginal Subsistence Technology on the Southeastern Coastal Plain during the Late Prehistoric Period,* by Lewis H. Larson (1980).

Number 3. *Cemochechobee: Archaeology of a Mississippian Ceremonial Center on the Chattahoochee River,* by Frank T. Schnell, Vernon J. Knight, Jr., and Gail S. Schnell (1981).

Number 4. *Fort Center: An Archaeological Site in the Lake Okeechobee Basin,* by William H. Sears, with contributions by Elsie O'R. Sears and Karl T. Steinen (1982).

Perspectives on Gulf Coast Prehistory

Edited by Dave D. Davis

University Presses of Florida
University of Florida Press/Florida State Museum
Gainesville

UNIVERSITY PRESSES OF FLORIDA is the central agency for scholarly publishing of the State of Florida's university system, producing books selected for publication by the faculty editorial committees of Florida's nine public universities: Florida A&M University (Tallahassee), Florida Atlantic University (Boca Raton), Florida International University (Miami), Florida State University (Tallahassee), University of Central Florida (Orlando), University of Florida (Gainesville), University of North Florida (Jacksonville), University of South Florida (Tampa), University of West Florida (Pensacola).

Orders for books published by all member presses of University Presses of Florida should be addressed to University Presses of Florida, 15 NW 15th Street, Gainesville, FL 32603.

Library of Congress Cataloging in Publication Data
Main entry under title:

Perspectives on Gulf Coast prehistory.

(Ripley P. Bullen monographs in anthropology and history; no. 5)
Papers from a conference on Gulf Coast archaeology, held Mar. 23–24, 1981, at Avery Island, La.
Bibliography: p.
Includes index.
1. Indians of North America—Southern States—Antiquities—Congresses.   2. Southern States—Antiquities—Congresses.   3. Indians of North America—Gulf States—Antiquities—Congresses.   4. Gulf States—Antiquities—Congresses.   I. Davis, Dave D.   II. Series.
E78.S65P47   1984   976'.01   84–3686
ISBN 0–8130–0756–9 (alk. paper)

Contents

Contributors

Lawrence E. Aten, National Park Service, U.S. Department of the Interior, Washington, D.C.

David S. Brose, Cleveland Museum of Natural History, Cleveland.

Ian W. Brown, Peabody Museum, Harvard University, Cambridge.

Jefferson Chapman, Department of Anthropology, University of Tennessee, Knoxville.

Ann S. Cordell, Department of Anthropology, Florida State Museum, Gainesville.

Dave D. Davis, Department of Anthropology, Tulane University, New Orleans.

Sherwood M. Gagliano, Coastal Environments, Inc., Baton Rouge.

Marco Giardino, Department of Anthropology, Tulane University, New Orleans.

Jon L. Gibson, Center for Archaeological Studies, University of Southwestern Louisiana, Lafayette.

Dale Greenwell, South Mississippi Archaeological Research Group, Biloxi.

James B. Griffin, Museum of Anthropology, University of Michigan, Ann Arbor.

William G. Haag, Department of Geography and Anthropology, Louisiana State University, Baton Rouge.

Stephen H. Hale, Department of Anthropology, University of Florida, Gainesville.

Vernon J. Knight, Jr., Office of Archaeological Research, University of Alabama, Tuscaloosa.

Rochelle A. Marrinan, Department of Anthropology, Florida State University, Tallahassee.

Jerald T. Milanich, Department of Anthropology, Florida State Museum, Gainesville.

Robert W. Neuman, Department of Geography and Anthropology, Louisiana State University, Baton Rouge.

J. Richard Shenkel, Department of Geography and Anthropology, University of New Orleans, New Orleans.

Stephen Williams, Peabody Museum, Harvard University, Cambridge.

Preface

THIS volume resulted from a conference on Gulf coast archaeology held at Avery Island, Louisiana, on March 23–24, 1981. The conference was a response to a feeling, shared by a growing number of archaeologists, that prehistoric cultural events and processes on the Gulf coast were sufficiently different from those of the interior river valleys to warrant examination of the coast as a region. Southeastern archaeology has, for the most part, traditionally had a riverine orientation. Many of the Southeast's regional chronologies, and many of our perspectives on prehistoric cultural change derive from archaeological research on large sites in the interior alluvial valleys. Archaeologists working in coastal areas have often been surprised by the lack of fit between their results and the models of prehistory produced by work in the interior.

Research in the coastal zone has continued to produce indications of substantial along-coast similarities during various periods of prehistory. Some of these similarities were undoubtedly due to contact among prehistoric coastal peoples; others reflect parallel adaptations to comparable environmental conditions. Now, few archaeologists want to argue that the Gulf coast should be regarded as a cultural area in its own right. Nor has anyone suggested that the influence of cultural developments in the interior river valleys was unimportant in coastal prehistory. The purpose of the conference was, quite simply, to focus on *one dimension* of coastal archaeology that deserved systematic consideration, namely, the significance of being coastal.

In recognition of the paucity of excavated Paleo-Indian and Archaic sites on the Gulf coast, the scope of the conference was further confined to the Woodland and Mississippian periods of prehistory. It was not our purpose to define either of the latter two terms very strictly; we were generally interested in coastal prehistory from about the time that ceramics began to be frequently made (about 1000 or 500 B.C.) through the early years of European settlement (about A.D. 1750).

The conference was sponsored by Tulane University and hosted by Mr. and Mrs. Edward M. Simmons of Avery Island. The facilities made available to us on Avery Island are especially conducive to interchange of ideas among a relatively small group of conferees. With this consideration (as well as logistical factors) in mind, the list of invited participants was limited to fourteen individuals. This limitation meant that it was impossible to represent all of the interesting coastal archaeological research that has been done in recent years. The necessity to exclude some excellent coastal archaeology (and some coastal archaeologists) from the conference is in no way a commentary upon the significance of any coastal research. Happily, the limitation on the number of participants achieved the intended goal of promoting intensive interchange among the conferees in the informal context of a small group.

The list of conference participants reflects an effort to balance three considerations: (1) to cover as much of the geographic and temporal range of coastal Woodland and Mississippian prehistory as possible, while (2) representing a broad cross section of research topics and theoretical perspectives and (3) providing an external "check" from some archaeologists whose principal research interests are in the interior sections of the Southeast. Therefore, what the reader will find in these pages is not a comprehensive treatment of Gulf coast prehistory but rather a sample of the substantive research and theoretical approaches in current Gulf coast archaeology.

The conference participants were Lawrence Aten (Heritage Conservation and Recreation Service, Washington, D.C.), David Brose (Cleveland Museum of Natural History), Ian Brown (Harvard University), Dave Davis (Tulane University), Sherwood Gagliano (Coastal Environments, Inc., Baton Rouge, Louisiana), Marco Giardino (Tulane University), Jon Gibson (University of Southwestern Louisiana), James Griffin (University of Michigan), William Haag (Louisiana State University), V. James Knight (University of Alabama), Jerald Milanich (Florida State Museum), Robert Neuman (Louisiana State University), J. Richard Shenkel (University of New Orleans), and Stephen Williams (Harvard University). Professors Griffin and Haag served as discussants; all other participants presented papers, most of which were revised and contributed to this volume. I am also delighted to be able to include here Dale Greenwell's overview of the archaeology of coastal Mississippi; far too little has been written about this archaeologically important area.

Papers were presented on the first day of the conference in a meeting which was open to the archaeological community and the general public. The second day was devoted to two roundtable discussion sessions by the participants. The first of these sessions was a wide-ranging discussion of problems in coastal archaeology; the second, ably chaired by James Griffin, was a structured discussion of Gulf coast culture history. An edited transcript of that second discussion appears as the final chapter in this volume.

It is my pleasure to acknowledge the interest and support of Exxon U.S.A., which contributed substantially toward the expenses of the conference. Exxon's genuine interest in supporting a better understanding of the heritage of the Gulf coast states made the conference possible.

Mr. and Mrs. Edward Simmons provided an excellent setting for the conference and worked diligently to minimize logistical problems and to create a relaxed atmosphere in which to carry out our work. I am sure that I speak for all the participants in recording our sincere gratitude to the Simmons family.

Finally, I cannot leave the reader with the impression that this was the first conference on the archaeology of the Gulf coast. That recognition belongs to a meeting in Texas in 1971 under the organizational guidance of Lawrence Aten and Charles Bollich. The spirit of the Avery Island meeting was the same that had guided the first conference: to explore broadly our current knowledge of prehistoric chronology and cultural change in this archaeologically interesting area and to chart better the significant substantive problems in Gulf coast prehistory.

1

Geoarchaeology of the Northern Gulf Shore

Sherwood M. Gagliano

If there is any value in considering the Gulf coast as an area distinct from interior regions, it derives from the distinctive nature of coastal environments. Gagliano, a longtime proponent of closer integration of geological and archaeological data, develops here an overview of the unique features of coastal habitats. Distinguishing between ecosystems and the larger natural systems of which they are parts, Gagliano outlines the broad evolution of natural systems on the northern Gulf coast. From an analytical point of view, human groups interact with natural systems at several hierarchical levels or scales. Gagliano discusses four types of aboriginal settlement-subsistence patterns in relation to scales of variation in natural systems on the Gulf coast.

This synthesis of factors affecting coastal man-land relationships is in essence a plea for a broad perspective. Gagliano's emphasis upon the evolutionary characteristics of coastal systems provides a framework for understanding the interplay of man and environment in the coastal zone.

Geoarchaeological approach

IN any examination of the relationships between humans and the landscape (man-land relationships), it becomes evident that people

1

are opportunists. From the earliest hunter-gatherers to the present, there have been situations of opportunity to sustain certain life types. The provision of food, water, appropriate shelter, and general security is basic. In addition, opportunities for trade, intergroup contact, ceremony, and other social amenities are sought or at least accepted.

Sites providing situations of opportunity have not been equally distributed quantitatively, qualitatively, or temporally; so humans have been forced to modify settlement patterns, adjust their style of life, or migrate in response to environmental or cultural pressure. However, given a situation of great opportunity, sites have been occupied even in the face of high probability of natural disaster, site instability, and outside threat by other peoples.

Modern planners have rediscovered the advantages of conducting human activities in harmony with natural processes and have attempted to formalize landscape analysis as a basis for planning. This is usually achieved by conducting an environmental baseline study in an area where some new development is planned. The baseline study serves to identify situational or environmental "opportunities" and "constraints" as they relate to the proposed development, and they are used as the basis for selecting a suitable location or site for the proposed activity, as well as in establishing design criteria. Good statements of this approach are made by Ian L. McHarg (1969) in *Design With Nature*, and by W. M. Marsh (1978) in *Environmental Analysis: For Land Use and Site Planning*. The same basic methodology is employed in the now familiar "Environmental Impact Statement" (EIS) resulting from the National Environmental Policy Act of 1969.

Archaeologists can use the EIS or environmental planning methodology in order to understand better why people were conducting certain activities at particular places in the past. The archaeologist can examine site locations, artifacts, and ecofacts from the viewpoint of situational opportunities and constraints. As these conditions may have changed considerably since the time that the site was occupied, they must often be reconstructed from landforms, sedimentary deposits, soils, faunal and floral remains, and other paleoenvironmental indicators. Cultural situations frequently are related to cultural mix, potential for intergroup contact, phasing of cultural change, and social structure. It is possible to examine the archaeological record to understand better the particular situation of environment and culture at any specific place or time. Conversely, an understanding of the particular environmental situation in the vicinity of a site at the time of occupancy will contribute significantly to interpretation of the archaeological record.

This holistic view of the archaeological record in reference to an ever-changing environmental setting can be approached through what has come to be known as geoarchaeology. As the name implies, it combines geology and archaeology, but as both tend to be interdisciplinary it is really a combination of the earth sciences, biological sciences, and archaeology. The term is used here in an even broader sense and includes consideration of archaeological data in the context of processes and forms related to natural systems and ecosystems. Few situations are as ideally suited to such a viewpoint as coastal zones, where there is often the fortunate combination of ample opportunity for human utilization (resulting in a rich archaeological record) and rapid environmental change.

Karl W. Butzer (1971) in *Environment and Archaeology* has done much to formalize this approach. Following his lead, Gladfelter (1977), Hassan (1979), and others have effectively pointed out that there has generally been parallel development in method and theory between archaeology, the earth science disciplines (geology and geomorphology), and ecology. George Rapp and John A. Gifford (1982) have discussed the emergence of this interdisciplinary approach, which they call geological archaeology. It is also interesting to note that the Geological Society of America now has an Archaeological Geology Division. Other related natural science/archaeology approaches include archaeological chemistry and zooarchaeology.

Geoarchaeology has a long tradition in the northern Gulf region and continues to emerge as a viable field of research. This trend is seen by numerous excellent studies in the contributing disciplines. Some workers have ventured across discipline boundaries and have related archaeological data to the natural setting or have used such data to enhance the interpretation of geological and environmental change. Of course, it hasn't always been recognized that this was "geoarchaeology," since the term has only recently come into general use.

Perhaps the earliest practitioner of geoarchaeology in the northern Gulf region, and one of the fathers of the hybrid discipline in America, was E. H. Sellards. His work at the Vero site on the Atlantic coast of Florida (1916, 1917) is, strictly speaking, beyond the boundaries of the Gulf area, but it has definite bearing on the region. His report that human skeletal remains from the site were associated with Pleistocene vertebrate fossils (refuted by Aleš Hrdlička [1917, 1918]) was an important geological argument for the antiquity of man in the New World. Rouse (1951) reevaluated the Vero site and concluded that the human remains were intrusive, but studies by Weigel (1962) seem to have reconfirmed Sellards's interpretation and date the material as Paleo-Indian.

In a 1940 paper, Sellards described artifacts and Pleistocene vertebrate fossils from sites in the Mission River drainage along the west Texas coast. The sites were associated with the Berclair terrace, interpreted by Sellards as a riverine equivalent of the late Pleistocene coastal Beaumont terrace. Work along Mission River combined excavated archaeological and paleontological data with geological and geomorphic interpretations and led to the conclusion that the artifacts from the lower levels of the excavated sections were of the same age as the extinct Pleistocene animal remains. An equally important implication was that at least parts of the Beaumont terrace, a widespread feature in the northern Gulf region, were much younger than most geological contemporaries of Sellards believed. Sellards was far ahead of his time, and his insight into the interrelationships of geologic and archaeological data can only now be fully appreciated.

In Louisiana, archaeology has traditionally been allied with geography and geology. In the 1930s, a fertile research milieu developed in the School of Geology at Louisiana State University under the leadership of Henry V. Howe. The group included Richard J. Russell, a coastal and alluvial morphologist, Harold N. Fisk, a quaternary geologist, Fred B. Kniffen, a cultural geographer, and Clair A. Brown, a plant ecologist and taxonomist (from the Department of Botany). These people and their students launched an aggressive research attack on the Mississippi River valley and delta, which provided a firm foundation for understanding the processes that shaped the natural landscape and man's relationship to it. Among the many published works of this group, a few classics should be cited: C. A. Brown (1936, 1938), H. N. Fisk (1938a, 1938b, 1944), H. V. Howe et al. (1935), F. B. Kniffen (1936), and R. J. Russell (1936). It was in this setting that the young James A. Ford began his professional career in archaeology and in which his early ideas incubated. The influence of this group on Ford is evidenced in his early works (Ford 1936, 1951; Ford and Willey 1940) and was apparently extended to his colleagues in the lower Mississippi valley surveys (Phillips, Ford, and Griffin 1951); Ford, Phillips, and Haag 1955; Phillips 1970).

In the Mississippi River deltaic plain the man-land approach was first demonstrated by Fred B. Kniffen (1936) and was expanded upon by William G. McIntire (1958, 1959) and Roger T. Saucier (1963, 1974, 1981). In a 1962 article, William G. Haag discussed the effects of Pleistocene glaciation on the changes in position of shorelines and coastal and riverine landforms and the relationship of these changes to the archaeological record. Haag made special reference to the northern Gulf of Mexico region. The author and his colleagues at Coastal Environments, Inc. have continued to apply and refine the approach (Gagliano 1963, 1967, 1979; Gagliano, Weinstein, and Burden 1975; Coastal Environments, Inc. 1977; Gagliano et al. 1979, 1980, 1982; Weinstein et al. 1979; Weinstein 1981). Much of the current research in the Mississippi River deltaic plain utilizes a geoarchaeological approach to a greater or lesser degree. Examples include, but are not limited to, Jon Gibson (1982), J. Richard Shenkel (n.d.), and Brian J. Duhe (1981).

In the early 1950s, Harold N. Fisk left LSU for a position as geological research director for a major oil company in Houston, Texas. About the same time, Rufus J. LeBlanc and Hugh A. Bernard also took positions with petroleum companies in Houston. This initiated a round of Quaternary geological research along the Texas coast (Fisk 1959; Bernard and LeBlanc 1965; Bernard et al. 1970). Lawrence Aten was the first to integrate Quaternary geology and archaeology in the southeast Texas coast area. An undergraduate paper written by Aten in 1966 on the late Quaternary geology of the lower Trinity delta provided the framework upon which he and his colleagues built in subsequent years (Aten 1966a, 1966b). Working in the Trinity River delta at the head of Galveston Bay, Harry J. Shafer (1966), Richard J. Ambler (1973), Tom D. Dillehay (1975), Kathleen Gilmore (1974), Lawrence Aten (1967), and others from the University of Texas have integrated site excavation data into the paleoecology of the changing Trinity delta. The approach has been applied to neighboring areas of the southeast coast of Texas and southwestern Louisiana (Aten 1971; Beavers 1978; Shelley 1981). A synthesis of much of this work can be found in Aten's 1979 work on the Indians of the upper Texas coast.

In the literature pertaining to coastal Mississippi and Alabama there are occasional cross-references between archaeological and geological data, but a strong geoarchaeological approach has never developed. One interesting exception is a paper by Nicholas Holmes and Bruce Trickey (1974) in which an attempt was made to correlate the elevation of midden deposits found in the delta of the Tombigbee and Alabama rivers with late Quaternary sea level fluctuations.

In Florida, excellent examples of geoarchaeology can be found in research conducted at the site level, but integration of data into a larger framework of paleogeographic change seems to be rare. Outstanding applications of the geoarchaeological approach at the site level are found in the work of Carl Clausen and his colleagues at the Little Salt Springs and Warm Mineral Springs sites (Sheldon and Cameron 1976; Clausen et al. 1979). Underwater excavations on ledges in these sinkholes have yielded materials from a sequence that extends back at least 13,000 years. Geomorphic, geological, and geochemical data have been used to interpret the history of change within and around the sinkholes.

Albert C. Goodyear, Mark J. Brooks, Lyman O. Warren, and Sam B. Upchurch have used a geoarchaeological approach to investigate submerged prehistoric sites in the Tampa Bay area of Florida. Goodyear, Brooks, and Warren have recovered Paleo-Indian and Archaic artifacts and fossils dredged from the drowned sites (Goodyear and Warren 1972; Goodyear, Upchurch, and Brooks 1980), while Upchurch has studied the geological occurrence of chert, which was a major factor of site distribution in the bay area (Upchurch 1980). Some of the sites clearly were occupied during periods of lower sea stand.

Characteristics of natural systems

Natural systems are defined by recurring patterns of flow of energy and materials on, or near, the earth's surface (fig. 1.1). These energy flows or fluxes are most commonly in the form of fluid movement (water, ice, wind, etc.) but may also be through chemical processes. Energy flow is the integrating factor that defines the natural system. Energy fluxes are recurring or cyclic within a given geographic area and through a given time interval. Thus, the whole earth's surface may be divided into a specific number of natural systems. Or, as stated by Chorley and Kennedy (1971:1), the world "can be viewed as comprising sets of interlinked systems at various scales and of varying complexity, which are nested into each other to form a systems hierarchy (i.e., of subsystems, systems, super-systems, etc.)."

As illustrated in figure 1.1, a coastal system is a zone of interaction between terrestrial and marine processes. All systems of the northern Gulf region interface with riverine and marine systems. The character of each is determined by the kinds and intensities of processes active within it.

Although they may be intimately related, a distinction can be made

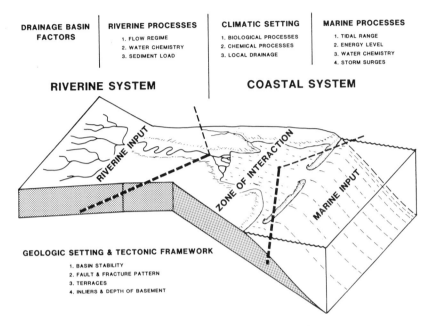

DRAINAGE BASIN FACTORS	RIVERINE PROCESSES	CLIMATIC SETTING	MARINE PROCESSES
	1. FLOW REGIME	1. BIOLOGICAL PROCESSES	1. TIDAL RANGE
	2. WATER CHEMISTRY	2. CHEMICAL PROCESSES	2. ENERGY LEVEL
	3. SEDIMENT LOAD	3. LOCAL DRAINAGE	3. WATER CHEMISTRY
			4. STORM SURGES

RIVERINE SYSTEM   **COASTAL SYSTEM**

RIVERINE INPUT

ZONE OF INTERACTION

MARINE INPUT

GEOLOGIC SETTING & TECTONIC FRAMEWORK
1. BASIN STABILITY
2. FAULT & FRACTURE PATTERN
3. TERRACES
4. INLIERS & DEPTH OF BASEMENT

Fig. 1.1. Major factors influencing a coastal system.

between a natural system and an ecological system or ecosystem. The ecosystem includes interactions between living organisms and the natural system. Odum (1971) defines an ecosystem as an area that includes living organisms and nonliving substances interacting to produce an exchange of materials between living and nonliving parts.

While ecosystems are dependent upon matter and energy, emphasis is on their use to build biological structures or biomass and biological reproduction. An ecosystem must maintain necessary internal energy levels for the biological aspects of the system to be in balance. Natural systems drive ecosystems. However, natural systems have existed in the past without any biological components, and they apparently exist on other planets without biological components.

Natural systems functioned on earth before life appeared. Wind-driven systems operate on the moon and on the planets. Mariner 9 photographs of Mars have revealed sinuous channels with many tributaries that closely resemble terrestrial stream channels. These have been interpreted as streams formed by the flow of water in the recent geologic past of Mars.

When viewed in a geological perspective, it is found that natural systems may be active or relict. Active systems are those that are functioning today and can be observed and measured. In relict systems, there is physical evidence of former repetitive movement of energy and materials in a given geographic area, but these flows no longer occur. For example, shallow marine deposits in cliff face exposures in the arid West provide evidence that a system that once occupied that area and was driven by marine processes has been replaced by a completely different one. Thus, natural systems can die. This process is of interest because archaeological sites may be associated with relict systems.

Evidence that the loci of natural systems can move or migrate is found in coastal plain and continental shelf areas around the world, where there have been significant shifts in the positions of coastal systems during the Quaternary epoch in response to changes in sea level induced by continental glaciation.

Boundaries of natural systems may expand or contract in response to process change. An expanding coastal system may become more environmentally complex, with increasing habitat diversity. This change may lead in turn to greater biological productivity and greater opportunity for human utilization and, at a given level of technology, greater human carrying capacity. Sometimes less productive systems expand at the expense of more productive ones, and these relationships are reversed. Periods of expansion and stability of systems with high biological productivity are optimal for human habitation and use.

Contraction in size of systems or changes in process parameters may result in a reduction or loss of easily exploitable renewable resources. For example, an increase in aridity may cause a shrinking in areal extent of forest and wetland habitat types that support certain assemblages of plants, fish, and wildlife that are readily exploitable for food and fiber. Complete loss of these habitat types may result in extinction of individual species or even whole assemblages of plants and animals.

Systems may also be altered or destroyed as a result of human impact. Human-induced changes in natural systems during prehistoric times resulted most commonly from impact on biological components, an upsetting of ecosystem balance by exploitation of fauna or flora. However, humans have also altered the flow of energy and materials, which may greatly change the character of a natural system. An example of such alteration is found in the irrigation and cultivation of arid lands by prehistoric peoples of the Peruvian coastal desert, which increased biological productivity of the system. An opposite situation is found in the manipulation of modern rivers in the United States for navigation and drainage, which has reduced renewable resource yield of both the river systems and the coastal systems with which they interface.

Distribution of the earth's renewable resources at any one time is directly related to kinds and conditions of natural systems and the ecosystems that they drive and support. Nonrenewable resource distribution (fossil fuels, ore deposits, salt, etc.) may be related to present systems but more commonly can be referred to some relict system that occupied the same geographic area that is occupied now by an active system. The focus here is on renewable resource values and landscape opportunities of active coastal systems.

Systems of the northern Gulf region

Within the active shore zone of the northern Gulf of Mexico there are fourteen coastal systems that have been in their present position since the beginning of the late Holocene stage (fig. 1.2). From east to west they are:

Florida Keys: carbonate island and bay coast
Ten Thousand Islands: mangrove coast
Central Florida: barrier and bay coast
Big Bend: drowned karst coast
Apalachicola delta: deltaic coast
West Florida–Alabama: barrier and bay coast
Mobile Bay: barrier and bay coast
Mississippi Sound: barrier, sound, and bay coast
Mississippi delta: deltaic coast
Cheniere Plain: marsh and lake coast
Galveston Bay: barrier and bay coast
Brazos-Colorado delta: deltaic coast
West Texas: barrier, lagoon, and bay coast
Rio Grande delta: deltaic coast

These systems, stretching across 16° of longitude and 7° of latitude, show considerable diversity in climate, geological setting, and processes (fig. 1.3). Differences are reflected in turn by biotic and abiotic features, such as distribution of vegetation communities and land-

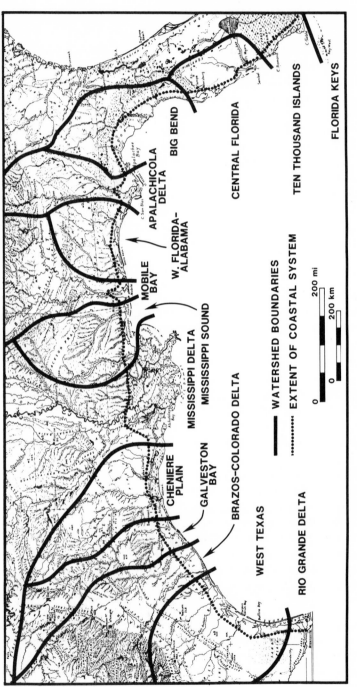

Fig. 1.2. Natural coastal systems of the northern Gulf of Mexico that have been active during the late Holocene epoch. The coastal systems are intimately linked to the watersheds of streams that discharge into the shore zone.

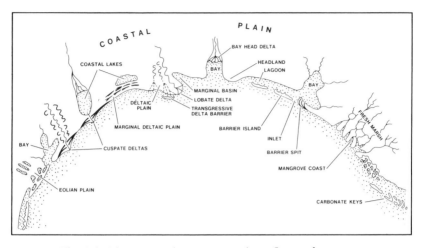

Fig. 1.3. Diagrammatic representation of coastal systems.

forms. These differences give each a distinctive character, with its own assemblage of landforms, fauna, and flora (fig. 1.4–1.6).

Each system also had its own history of change through the Holocene stage. Each has responded to fluctuations in sea level and climate, and each has gone through one or more successions of change in landforms and habitat types. For a sector-by-sector discussion of the coastal morphology and Quaternary geology of the region, the reader is referred to Shepard and Wanless (1971).

As shown in figure 1.1, the coastal systems are linked to the watersheds of the streams that discharge into them. In this broader sense they may be viewed as part of what Chorley and Kennedy (1971) call cascading systems, a chain of systems having spatial magnitude and geographical location and dynamically linked by a cascade of energy.

The fourteen coastal systems of the northern Gulf have provided the stages upon which cultural changes have unfolded, and their environmental characteristics are the backdrops and stage settings. Their characteristics have undoubtedly tempered cultural events. For these reasons study of man-land relationships within the system context is a fundamental part of regional cultural consideration.

System dynamics

Long-term trends

Changes in kind, intensity, and duration of processes are reflected in the system landscape. Resulting changes in habitat types, landforms,

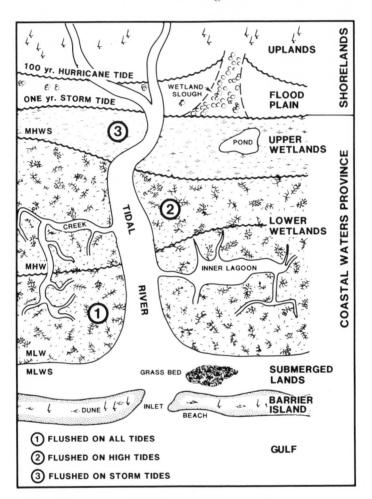

Fig. 1.4. Landforms and habitats of a hypothetical mangrove coastal system in southwest Florida (after Clark 1977).

and so on in turn directly affect renewable resource productivity and suitability of the system for human activity at a given level of technology. Process changes may also drive ecological successions that evolve through orderly stages. Dynamic changes can be thought of in terms of a hierarchical series based on duration and intensity. At the highest level are those that unfold over long periods of time (thousands or tens of thousands of years) and are due to worldwide or regional events. Such events as eustatic sea-level fluctuations and climatic

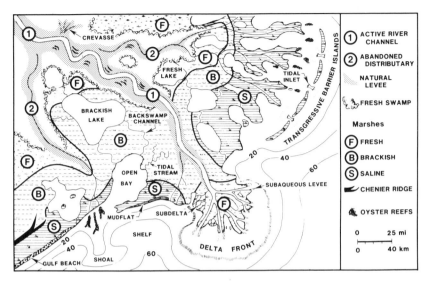

Fig. 1.5. Idealized delta system showing distribution and surface relationships of landforms and related habitats.

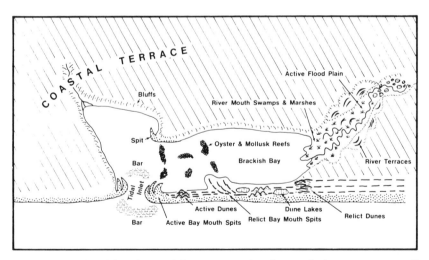

Fig. 1.6. Idealized barrier and bay system showing typical arrangement of landforms and habitats.

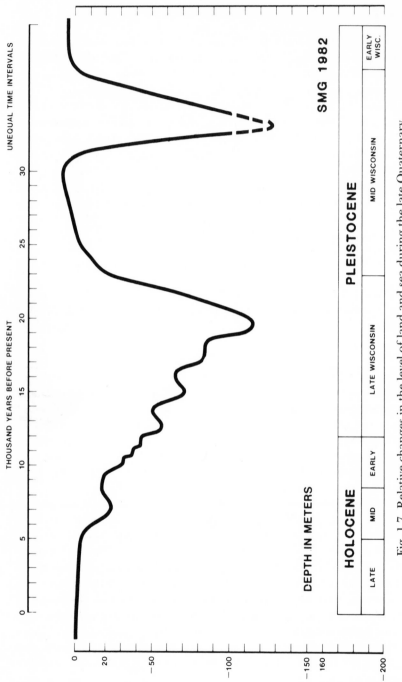

Fig. 1.7. Relative changes in the level of land and sea during the late Quaternary.

change fall into this category. Figures 1.7 and 1.8 summarize changes in sea level and other long-term events for the northern Gulf region during the late Quaternary.

Examples of the profound effects that changes in climate and sea level have had on coastal systems can be found for the past 12,000 years. The sea level had been rising at a rapid rate for several thousand years prior to 10,000 B.P. Relict shore trends on the continental shelf attributed to this interval of rapid rise suggest short-term halts, or reductions in rate of rise, that may have lasted for a few hundred years each. Peat deposits that have been dated from this interval suggest that conditions were wetter than at present. It is also significant that the remains of large, extinct Pleistocene vertebrates (Pleistocene megafauna) are common from deposits of this interval. River valleys carved during the late Wisconsin low sea stand began to be inundated and drowned along reaches that presently lie in the inner shelf and active shore zone. Paleo-Indian artifacts have been found in some of these areas that are occupied by the present shore zone, usually in situations where the position of the present coastal system is coincident with the position of a coastal system that was active during the Paleo-Indian interval.

At about 9500 B.P., the rise in sea level halted, initiating a minor "still stand" that lasted until about 8000 B.P. This interval was a significant time in the coastal zone from the standpoint of the geological and archaeological record. Dated peat deposits and bone beds suggest that wet conditions persisted and that the Pleistocene megafauna were still represented. Inundation of the entrenched stream valleys became more pronounced. While Late Paleo-Indian and Early Archaic artifacts are found in the presently active coastal zone, a true coastal site from these periods remains to be identified.

The interval between about 8000 and 6500 B.P. was a time of severe environmental change which resulted in great stresses to the occupants of the region. Conditions became considerably drier than during the preceding period and were even drier than those that presently exist. Stream discharge was greatly reduced. Sea level dropped 5 to 10 meters below the level of the previous period. Floodplain forests, coastal wetlands, and estuarine habitats, which had expanded during the previous wet interval, diminished in extent and disappeared in many areas as a result of stream entrenchment and drier climatic conditions. Thus, there was a reduction in both diversity and extent of the coastal habitats that were richest in renewable resource values.

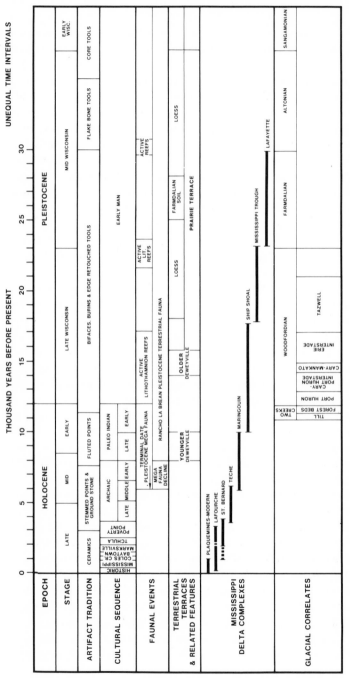

Fig. 1.8. Some late Quaternary geological events and the cultural sequence from the Mississippi River deltaic area.

Conditions in the Rio Grande delta, West Texas, and even the Brazos-Colorado delta (fig. 1.2), became very arid. Great aeolian sand sheets became active in the West Texas section of the Gulf margin. In the eastern Gulf, arid conditions predominated throughout peninsular Florida. Water levels in karst sinkholes were lowered significantly, vegetation became sparse, and dune fields formed. Evidence of more arid conditions in the central Gulf area is found in caliche development in coastal terrace soils and in relict stream scars that are smaller than those formed during the preceding period. It was during this interval that the last survivors of the Pleistocene megafauna became extinct, probably due, at least in part, to reduction in the habitats that supported these animal assemblages.

The archaeological record reflects these changes. In the active shore zone, evidence of early Archaic peoples is virtually absent. While there may have been a reduction in human populations, it is also likely that the zone of favorable habitats shifted seaward and much of the record lies submerged in the shallow shelf area. There are suggestions of this shifting from the Central Florida and Big Bend areas, where drowned sites have been reported.

From about 6,500 to 5,000 years ago was a time of rapid sea-level rise. The climate may have remained dry. Inundation of river valleys by an encroaching sea again occurred. The modern barrier islands began to form. Few archaeological sites inhabited during this time are known from the active shore zone.

By about 4,500 years ago, the sea had reached its present level. In fact, there is some geomorphic evidence to suggest that it may have been somewhat higher than its present level for a short period. The most important consideration, however, is that this time marks the beginning of the late Holocene stillstand. While minor fluctuations of sea level and minor variations of climate have occurred during the last 4,500 years, conditions in comparison to the preceding intervals have been stable. It is during the late Holocene that systems in the active shore zone have become well defined. Because stable conditions have persisted through a relatively long time period, the shoreline has gradually prograded, coastal morphology has become more complex, and coastal habitats have become diversified and have increased in aerial extent, all of which in turn has caused an increase in the biological productivity of coastal systems. It is during this stable interval that late Archaic and Formative cultures of the Gulf region developed and that more than 90 percent of the archaeological sites in the presently active shore zone were inhabited.

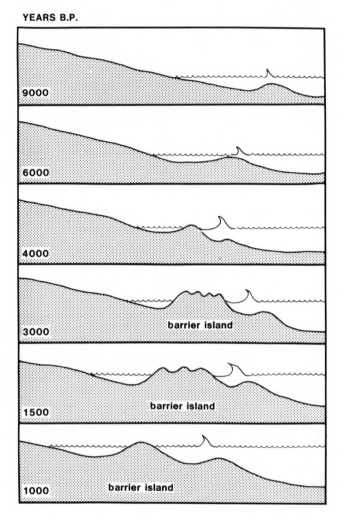

9000

6000

4000

barrier island
3000

barrier island
1500

barrier island
1000

Fig. 1.9. Most of the Gulf coast barrier islands evolved during the late Holocene (beginning about 5000 B.P.) as sea level approached its present stand. About 3,000 years ago there was a period when great surpluses of sand were available to be reworked by shoreline processes, and the barriers became more complex. In recent decades there seems to be much less sand available, and most of the islands are eroding and moving landward (after Dolan, Hayden, and Lins 1980).

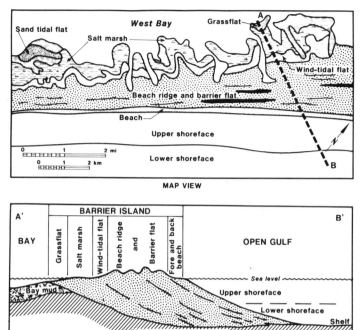

Fig. 1.10. Landforms, habitats, and sedimentary facies of Galveston Island (cross section after Bernard et al. 1970, modified by Fisher et al. 1972).

⌐ In a review article on barrier islands, Dolan, Hayden, and Lins (1980) have shown the evolutionary development of Atlantic and Gulf coast barrier islands during the late Holocene (figs. 1.9 and 1.10). The islands generally began to emerge about 5,000 years ago. About 3,000 years ago, barrier islands received great surpluses of sand that caused them to accrete. This accretion was followed by a period of gradual deterioration and decline, and in modern decades the islands are eroding and noticeably moving landward. Stated in another way, this sequence of changes, driven first by sea-level rise and stability and then by sediment nourishment, caused the islands to become larger and more complex (in terms of morphology and habitat), to reach a peak of development, and then to deteriorate and decline.

Most of the bays of the northern Gulf formed as drowned river valleys, or rias. The valleys were carved by streams during pre-Holocene periods of lower sea stand. Each bay has passed through a series of

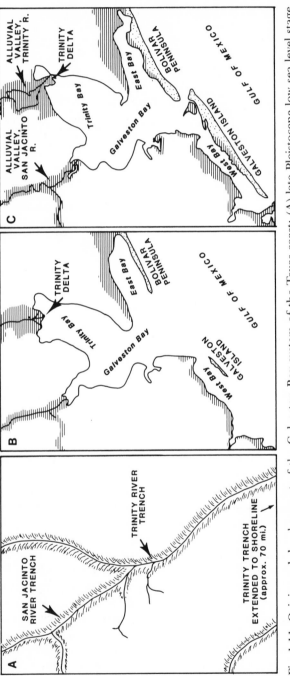

Fig. 1.11. Origin and development of the Galveston Bay system of the Texas coast: (A) late Pleistocene low sea level stage, ca. 20,000 years B.P.; (B) mid-Holocene rising sea level stage, ca. 5000 B.P.; (C) late Holocene stillstand, ca. 2000 B.P. (after LeBlanc and Hodgson 1959).

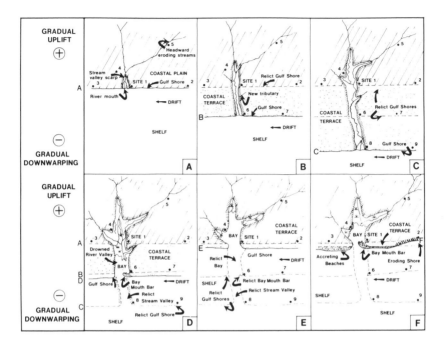

Fig. 1.12. Hypothetical sequence of landform development during a "ria cycle." (Sea level fluctuations associated with the cycle are shown in fig. 1.13.) Typical site locations are indicated by numbers (after Coastal Environments, Inc. 1977).

evolutionary stages (ria cycle), which has had a profound effect upon the environmental succession and man-land relationships. This evolutionary process is well illustrated by Galveston Bay as seen in figure 1.11. During the Holocene rise of sea level, river valleys became progressively drowned. Since sea level reached its present stand about 4,500 years ago, the bays have been enlarged somewhat by shoreline erosion and their morphology has become more complex, with the addition of such features as bayhead deltas, bay mouth–bar spit complexes, shoreline spits, and accretion features. Mudflats and marshes have been added locally around the bay margins, and shell reefs and beds have developed within the bays. In some instances former bays have been completely filled by deltaic sediment, as in the case of the Rio Grande, the Brazos, the Mississippi, the Pearl, and the Apalachicola rivers.

An idealized ria cycle is illustrated in figures 1.12 and 1.13. Such cycles have occurred on several scales during the last 30,000 years and

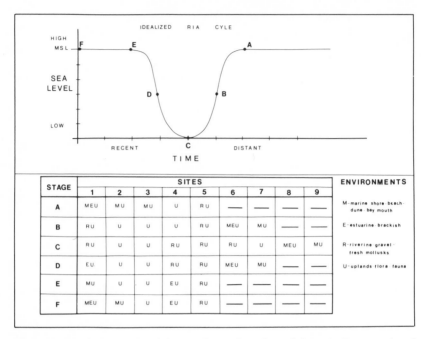

Fig. 1.13. Idealized sea level fluctuations of a "ria cycle" (*top*). (For associated changes in coastal landforms, see fig. 1.12.) The matrix (*bottom*) indicates changes in environments or habitats in the vicinity of the sites shown in fig. 1.12, which occur as the "ria cycle" unfolds (after Coastal Environments, Inc. 1977).

have left a distinctive record within the northern Gulf region. A complete understanding of the ria cycle is particularly important in understanding the changes that have occurred in the active coastal systems during the Holocene.

Cyclic changes

Changes that recur with a frequency of hundreds or thousands of years and progress through a predictable sequence of events are important characteristics of many coastal systems. Perhaps the best example is the habit of upstream diversion in the Mississippi River delta, which initiates cycles of lobate delta building and deterioration. Delta cycles progress through stages of growth followed by stages of deterioration which drive an environmental succession. This succession in turn is responsible for much of the biological productivity of the deltaic area.

A similar phenomenon, but with shorter duration, is related to subdelta development along the lower reaches of the active trunk channel of the river (figs. 1.14 and 1.15). Subdeltas typically have life cycles of 100 to 150 years and drive environmental successions that change opportunity for human utilization. Settlement patterns in the active area of the Mississippi River deltaic plain have been greatly influenced by these subdelta developments (Gagliano 1979).

Another short-duration cycle is associated with the development and decline of oxbow cutoff lakes in the upper deltaic plain and alluvial valley of the Mississippi River (see fig. 1.16; Weinstein et al.

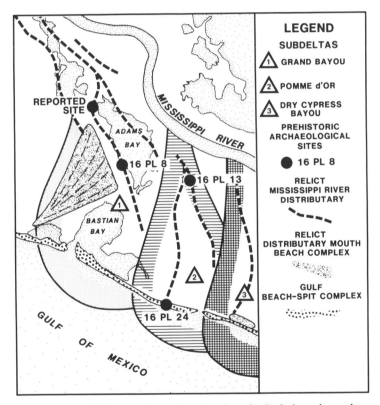

Fig. 1.14. Subdeltas and associated archaeological sites along the lower reaches of the Mississippi River. The Buras Mound site (16PL13) is a late Mississippian village located in the Pomme d'Or subdelta. Site 16PL24 is a beach deposit representing a satellite or special activity site originally located near the distal end of one of the subdelta distributaries. The Pomme d'Or subdelta is believed to have been active from about A.D. 1500 until A.D. 1650 (after Gagliano 1979).

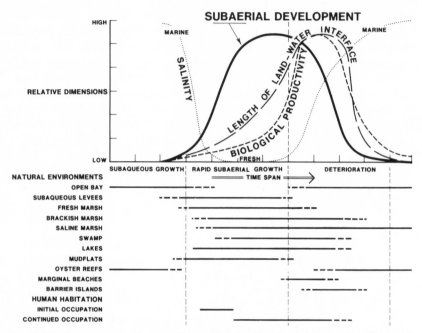

Fig. 1.15. Environmental succession of an idealized subdelta cycle. The typical subdelta cycle usually unfolds in about 100–150 years. Associated with the cyclic character of delta building is a sequence of landform and habitat changes. These changes in turn influence the character of human utilization and exploitation (after Coastal Environments, Inc. 1977).

1979; Weinstein 1981). Infilling of large alluvial valley deltaic plain lakes by lacustrine delta-building processes drives still another environmental succession that is cyclic in character.

Recurring annual changes in processes related to solar radiation and earth mechanics are common to all coastal systems. These are evident in such things as fish and wildlife migration, flood cycles, coastal storms, tidal and wave energy variation, and the growth and maturity of plant foods and materials.

Variations in primary productivity and food chains

It is generally recognized that coastal areas are rich in fish, wildlife, and plant resources, and this abundance and accessibility of foodstuffs and fibers has always attracted peoples with a hunting-fishing-gathering economic base. Ecological research has not only confirmed what has long been apparent, but ecologists have developed techniques for qualitative and quantitative analysis that are useful in attaining a better understanding of man-land relationships. All coastal systems are not equally well endowed with abundantly available natural foodstuffs. There is significant variation in biological productivity, and this variation can be examined in reference to the basic food chains operating within shore zone ecosystems. For example, the estuarine ecosystem is considered to be among the most productive on earth. Development of estuarine habitats varies from system to system along the northern Gulf. One measure of this variation is the modern com-

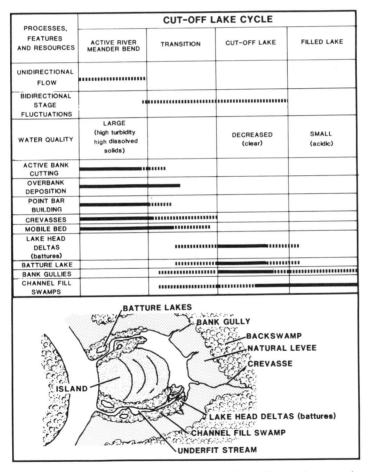

Fig. 1.16. Life cycle of an oxbow or cutoff lake illustrating associated landforms and water bodies (after Weinstein et al. 1979).

mercial fish harvest from the deltaic coast of Louisiana (typically more than 25 percent of the total annual fish harvest of the United States). Louisiana produces not only more fish per year than any other state but more than twice as much as Alaska, its closest competitor. This abundance is attributed to a broad and complex estuarine zone resulting from the Mississippi delta system and the processes that drive that system.

Comparisons of the estuarine food chains of the mangrove area of the Florida coast, the marsh and overflow swamps of coastal Louisiana, and the hypersaline lagoons of the Texas coast show that the bulk of the biomass may be concentrated in different species. It may be more readily accessible at a given level of technology within one food chain than within another. Thus, it is conceivable that a coastal system could have high biological productivity and produce a great annual yield of biomass, but this biomass may not be readily accessible to people living there if their technology is inadequate to harvest or to utilize key species, or both.

Hierarchical levels of man-land relationships

In exploring man-land relationships it is useful to view the problem from different levels of perspective (Gladfelter 1977). The highest resolution is the physical evidence from the site itself (artifacts, ecofacts, site stratigraphy, geometry, sedimentology, etc.). The second level is the relationship between site and landform or habitat: What is the physical relationship between the site and its geometry and the landform upon which it is situated? and what is the relationship between site and habitats in the vicinity of that landform? At a third level the site is viewed in terms of the subsystem, a definable part of the major natural system. It may be at a scale that represents the exploitable area of a given group, wherein the relationships of site groups and activities represented at sites within the group can be examined in the context of the subsystem. The fourth level is that of the major natural system, a level at which settlement patterns should be considered in reference to the "geomorphic grain" of the system and areas of cultural influence viewed within a time perspective can be considered. The hierarchical approach can be expanded to include all systems within the active shore zone as well as neighboring systems, such as river basins.

Site level
Some basic definitions are appropriate at the first level. An archaeological site may be defined as a place where there is physical evidence

of some past human activity. Evidence may include all or some artifacts, structures, features, ecofacts, and archaeological deposits. Artifacts are objects that show convincing evidence of human authorship.

Ecofacts, the remains of plants and animals, occur commonly in archaeological sites and may be particularly abundant and well preserved in coastal sites. Archaeological deposits consisting predominantly of ecofacts may be hundreds of meters in length and 5 or more meters thick. Ecofacts may be confined to individual strata, such as bone beds or shell lenses. They may also occur as inclusions within a site matrix of sand, silt, clay, or other clastic detritus.

Ecofacts are the realm of the zooarchaeologist and the paleobotanist. As they represent remains of fauna or flora that constituted a part of the diet or were otherwise utilized by the site inhabitants, they may contribute significantly to an understanding of past economic activities. Calculations of population size have been made for coastal shell middens (Byrd 1976b), and seasonality of occupation has been determined from studies of annual growth rings of shellfish (Aten 1981), deer antler, and seed remains. Ecofacts are also of primary importance in providing samples for radiometric dating.

In addition to their use in dating and cultural interpretation, ecofacts are also of exceptional value in establishing environmental conditions in the vicinity of the site during its occupation, as sites often contain concentrated samples of ecofacts gleaned from neighboring environments by inhabitants. Shellfish, for example, are sensitive indicators of salinity, water temperature, turbidity, and other process factors that define environments and subenvironments. Interpretations of such material from coastal sites provide an excellent basis for reconstruction of paleoenvironmental conditions.

Three common categories of ecofacts are found within the northern Gulf: bones of fish, birds, and animals; shells of pelecypods and gastropods (the freshwater clam *Unio* sp., the brackish water clam *Rangia cuneata*, shells of the oyster *Crassostrea virginica*, etc.); and plant materials (wood, grass, seeds, pollen). As demonstrated by McIntire (1958), changes in species of molluscs represented by shells within the vertical sequence of a coastal archaeological site may be used in the interpretation of ecological change.

Archaeological deposits are the sediments that accumulate in an area of activity or habitation and that show indications of human process. Such deposits may be partially or wholly composed of artifacts or ecofacts or both, but they usually have some component of "natural" detrital clastic sediment. Archaeological deposits are three-dimensional; they have a specific geometry. They may exhibit internal stratification and have sedimentological characteristics that distinguish them from natural deposits. These characteristics provide important clues to the kinds of human processes that occurred at the site (Gagliano et al. 1982).

Archaeological deposits must also be considered in reference to the landform with which the site is associated. Because of the dynamic processes active within the coastal setting, such deposits frequently become incorporated into natural sedimentary deposits. Archaeological materials are often found on, or within, deposits of natural levees, beaches, dunes, and other depositional landforms.

Figure 1.17 depicts some common relationships found between archaeological deposits and those of natural levees and associated environments in the Mississippi River deltaic plain. Note in figure 1.17 that deposits identified as (A) are interbedded with those of the natural levee, indicating that the site was occupied while the distributary was active. Archaeological materials at (B) are interbedded with backswamp clays and peats. They may have accumulated either while the distributary was active or after it had been abandoned. Such accumulations are usually deposited in standing water and may contain well-preserved perishable artifacts and ecofacts. The archaeological deposits on top of the natural levee surface (C) accumulated after the distributary had been abandoned as an active course of the parent river system. In this position are usually found the major midden deposits of intensive occupation areas, burials, etc. Archaeological materials interbedded in the channel fill (D) obviously accumulated after the distributary had been abandoned. Such material may be reworked.

In subsiding areas, entire sites may be slowly covered with sediment. This burial preserves the site and is a rather common occurrence in the Mississippi River deltaic plain and other Gulf coast estuaries. Such sites are the deltaic equivalent of Pompeii, being slowly buried by a rain of organic sediment and clay. Excellent preservation can be anticipated. A typical subsided site situation is illustrated in figure 1.18.

Beach deposits can be defined as reworked lag left after erosion of a coastal midden. When the midden is destroyed, the finer-grained material of the matrix is winnowed out by waves and currents. Integrity of the site from the standpoint of stratigraphy and geometry is destroyed, and only a mixed jumble of the coarsest components may be left. Lag deposits typically include wave-rounded shell and artifacts. Beach deposits are often thrown back on marshy shores where they form a thin veneer of shell and other site debris (fig. 1.19). Ar-

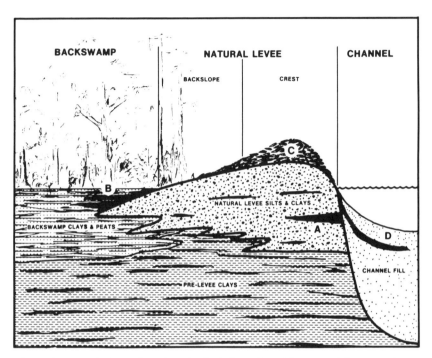

Fig. 1.17. Association of archaeological deposits with natural levee and related deposits: (A) midden deposits interbedded with natural levee sediment; (B) midden deposits interbedded with backswamp clays and peats; (C) archaeological deposits on natural levee surfaces; (D) archaeological deposits interbedded with channel fill deposits (after Gagliano et al. 1980).

Fig. 1.18. Shell mound on a subsided natural levee ridge enveloped by marsh and mud.

chaeological material from beach deposits does have scientific value. Even though it has been displaced and reworked, it is usually in the general vicinity of the eroded site and may contain valuable information regarding utilized fauna, as well as artifacts that may indicate site age and activity. Study of beach deposits in conjunction with historic data concerning site size and geometry, or geologic data, or both, may allow a reasonable reconstruction of the character of a destroyed site.

In coastal areas archaeological material is frequently encountered in dredge spoil deposits. These are remnants of archaeological sites that have been displaced by mechanical means, either by hydraulic dredging or some type of bucket dredging (fig. 1.20). Spoil deposits are usually found relatively close to the site from which they were derived. They may be in various conditions of mixture or reworking. For example, soil deposits dredged through the hydraulic technique may be completely winnowed and mixed. On the other hand, spoil deposits thrown up by a bucket dredge may exhibit large, relatively undisturbed samples of the site content. In many instances, remnants of the site's stratigraphy may be preserved and the soil lumps may contain faunal, floral, and artifact samples. Data from this type of soil deposit are exceptionally useful and demand careful attention.

Landform level

In dynamic coastal situations the changes in positions of shorelines and streams are accompanied by shifts in settlement pattern and land use. Consequently the distribution of archaeological sites is closely related to the distribution of the active and relict landforms and associated habitats (stream banks, beaches, margins of estuaries, dune lakes, and important ecotones). The landform is the product of intensity and kinds of processes active in coastal systems. Process is reflected in such measurable variables as sediment characteristics, geomorphic form, vegetation, soil, and human utilization. The simple truth that the form of the feature mirrors the processes that shaped it is the key to interpretation. Interpretation, then, depends largely upon an understanding of process-form relationships and effective use of natural analogs. The landform is the basic element of landscape analysis. While each landform type may have a wide distribution throughout the shore zone, it can be demonstrated that certain assemblages serve to identify natural systems and subsystems.

The landform is said to be active if its character and form are changing and responding to active processes, but the form and other characteristics may be preserved after the shaping processes have ceased

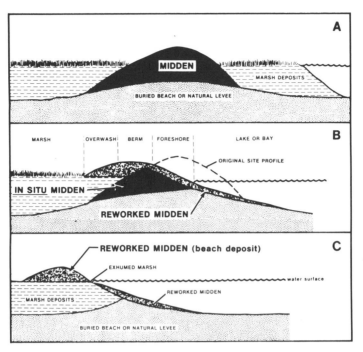

Fig. 1.19. Progressive shoreline erosion of a coastal midden. The end product is a beach deposit (after Gagliano et al. 1980).

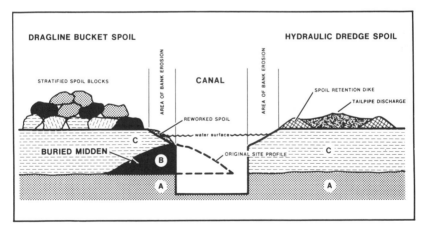

Fig. 1.20. Idealized section of midden deposits that have been revealed by dredging. On the left are stratified spoil blocks containing relatively undisturbed samples of the midden and other deposits within the section. Hydraulic dredge spoil on the right has been completely disturbed, but artifacts and ecofacts can be found concentrated in the tailpipe discharge zone (after Gagliano et al. 1980).

and the landform is said to be relict. Some relict landforms may be reactivated after being dormant for a period of time. For example, along some sectors of the Gulf coast the position of the present shoreline is coincident with the position of the mid-Wisconsin Farmdalian shoreline, and Farmdalian beaches and dunes have been reactivated after having been dormant for 20,000 years or more.

Specific relationships between site and landform (attitude of site geometry in reference to overall landform geometry), the question of whether the landform was active or relict at the time of site occupancy, and initial occupation of the site are all relevant considerations at this level. Initial occupation of the site establishes the minimum age of the landform, which may be particularly important for landforms that were occupied while they were active; initial occupation may mark the stage in their development at which they were first suitable for human occupation or use. Subsequent occupational history of a site may indicate the time or times after initial occupation when conditions were favorable.

A simple case of site-landform relationships is found in places where shoreline progradation has occurred over a period of time and a series of relict shorelines has been left behind the active one. Basic relationships in such a situation are shown in figure 1.21. As shown, the stream mouth has been a favored habitation place through time; sites are found not only at the present stream mouth but also at its former locations. Some site occupations may have continued even after the stream mouth shifted as a result of progradation; however, it is the initial occupation that most closely approximates the age of the features upon which the site is located. Sequential maps showing initial occupation sites are useful in geoarchaeological interpretation.

The record may be more difficult to decipher where a set of prograded relict shorelines has been truncated by a later shoreline as illustrated in figure 1.22. Artifacts and ecofacts from sites associated with the initial relict shorelines may be left as beach deposits along the later shoreline. A knowledge of geomorphic processes and dating of the shorelines may be an aid in establishing a clear sequence of occupation.

Subsystem level

Relationships among sites, landforms, and habitats at the subsystem level provide important clues to environmental resource use. Consider the situation shown in figure 1.23. The cross section is through a typical Gulf coast subsystem that includes a coastal plain upland, an

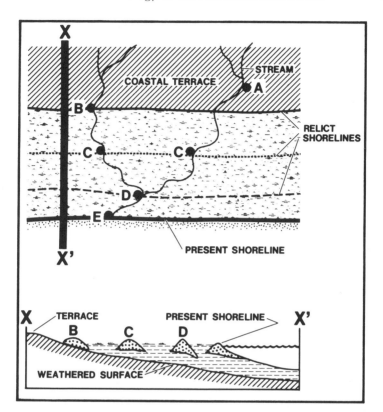

Fig. 1.21. Distribution of initial occupation sites in a prograding beach sequence: (A) oldest; (E) youngest (after Coastal Environments, Inc. 1977).

estuarine area, a barrier island, and adjacent shallow marine areas. Three sites are shown in the hypothetical section, each of which is related to an active or relict landform and each of which has related archaeological deposits. At the site level, there are both surficial archaeological deposits that identify the site and buried deposits associated with either active or relict landforms. In cases of active landforms, archaeological deposits have become incorporated into the sediment sequence as a result of natural deposits and process (B_1 and C_1); in the case of the relict landform, the archaeological deposits are intrusive into older sediments as a result of human process (A_1).

Sites are located in places that provide a strategic advantage for exploitation of habitats associated with the landforms and water bodies. The extent to which habitats can be exploited then becomes a func-

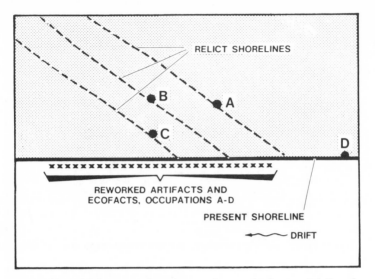

Fig. 1.22. Initial occupation sites and reworked material (beach deposits) on truncated shorelines: (A) oldest; (D) youngest (after Coastal Environments, Inc. 1977).

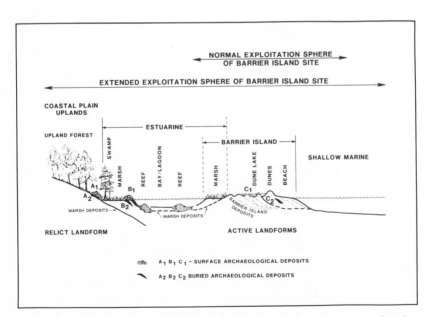

Fig. 1.23. Hypothetical cross section of barrier and bay subsystem showing site-landform relationships.

tion of transportation time to the exploited area. In this hypothetical situation, if the barrier island is considered a feasible place for permanent or semipermanent habitation, the normal exploitation sphere for the barrier island habitation site is generally restricted by the distances that can be easily traversed on foot or by small boat within a day. This sphere would certainly include the beach dune, lake, and marsh environments of the body of the island, as well as the shallow marine environments and estuarine environments of the bay.

The exploitation sphere of the barrier island site may be extended through longer trips, which may result in special-activity sites. These sites may be in strategic locations for access to neighboring habitats, but the locations may not be suitable for permanent or semipermanent habitation. Limiting factors or constraints are likely to include susceptibility to flooding and seasonality of the resource being exploited. What is typically found at the subsystem level is a complex of sites, with one site representing a permanent or semipermanent habitation place and smaller satellite sites, or special activity sites, scattered about in surrounding areas.

Thus, we can start with two simple models, as shown in figure 1.24, for site distribution in reference to coastal resources. The first is the normal exploitation sphere (A) in close proximity to a permanent or semipermanent habitation site. The second is a permanent or semipermanent site with satellite, special-activity sites (B) giving access to other habitats. Other patterns were undoubtedly utilized in the coastal zone: one depicts the familiar annual round (C) in which people moved from inland areas to the coast on a seasonal basis; the other represents a periodic movement of a permanent or semipermanent habitation site with satellite activity areas (D). The motivation for movement may be cultural patterns, resource depletion, or changes in environmental conditions, as discussed. Obviously, combinations of these factors may have occurred.

Systems level

The perspective at the systems level must be a composite of subsystem synthesis. However, it usually has the added complication of a much greater time depth. It must combine, then, long-term trends, cyclic trends, relationships to the food chain, and all of the cultural responses and independent cultural variables that may occur within the system area over a long period of time. Synthesis at this level is obviously difficult and is dependent upon input from all other levels of analysis. Even with incomplete data, the geoarchaeological methodol-

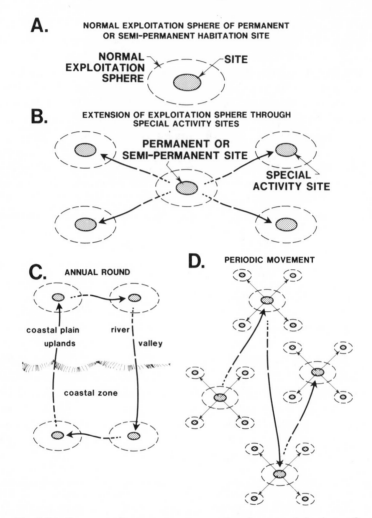

Fig. 1.24. Some settlement patterns related to exploitation of coastal resources at the subsystem level.

ogy applied with the system as a framework may lead to clear understanding of man-land relationships and usually identifies fruitful areas for additional research.

The Mississippi River deltaic plain again provides examples of man-land relationships at the systems level. A clear pattern of preferred site locations has emerged from work in the deltaic plain. The most common site situations are shown diagramatically in figure 1.25. Per-

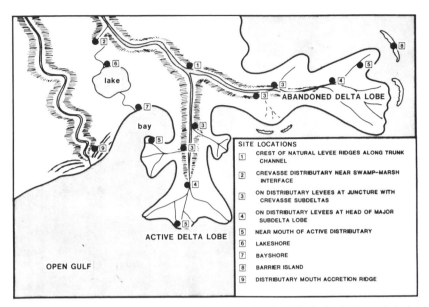

Fig. 1.25. Preferred prehistoric site locations in the Mississippi River deltaic plain (after Gagliano et al. 1980).

haps the most frequent location of major sites is at the juncture of river distributaries. There are several reasons for these preferred locations. Transportation within the delta during prehistoric times was water oriented: the trunk channel provided a major artery of transportation, lesser distributaries provided access into fringing backswamp and interdistributary basin environments that were particularly rich in fish and wildlife resources.

From a dynamic standpoint, areas of delta building and retreat occur because of periodic upstream river diversion and attack of marine forces on abandoned delta lobes. Riverbank and delta lobe site relationships are illustrated in figure 1.26. Sites are located primarily along natural levee ridges of trunk channels and distributaries. While the period of initial occupation of sites associated with an abandoned river course or delta lobe may approximate the time when it was active, habitation may have continued after the system ceased to function as an active delta lobe. In some instances the habitation sequence may be out of phase with the delta sequence. An explanation for these relationships is found in the cyclic nature of the delta building and the environmental succession that unfolds as the cycle progresses (see fig. 1.15).

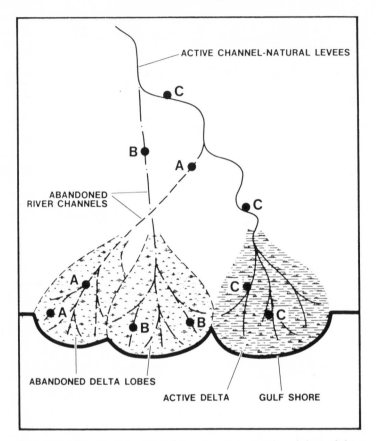

Fig. 1.26. Distribution of initial occupation sites in a lobate delta:
(A) oldest; (C) youngest (after Coastal Environments, Inc. 1977).

After the delta lobe becomes abandoned as the result of an upstream
river diversion, the delta landmass is subjected to marine processes
and erosion and reshaping begins. This process is called the deterioration or transgressive phase of delta building. Eroded and reworked
sites are frequently found in the distal ends of transgressive delta
lobes as illustrated in figure 1.27. Artifacts and ecofacts from eroded
sites that were once on natural levee ridges of distributaries may be
redistributed as beach deposits along the fronts of, and incorporated
within the sands of, transgressive barrier islands that develop during
the deterioration stage of the delta cycle.

Figure 1.28 summarizes the complex relationships between forma-

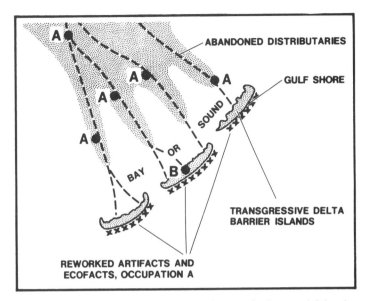

Fig. 1.27. Initial occupation sites and reworked material in the deterioration phase of a delta cycle: (A) oldest; (B) youngest (after Coastal Environments, Inc. 1977).

tion of the Mississippi River deltaic plain landmass and sequential settlement from the Middle Archaic period through historic times.

Summary

Natural systems provide a useful framework for studying human activity in reference to the landscape through time. Boundaries of the systems are delineated by energy flows and their characteristics defined by mapping the kinds and extents of landforms (both relict and active) and associated habitat types. By viewing the landforms and habitat types as a reflection of active process, the dynamics of the system can be better understood.

Coastal systems are dynamic, constantly undergoing change. The change is a reflection of variation in magnitude and duration of process. Some changes are long term, occurring over many thousands of years; others are cyclic, occurring within time ranges varying from a few thousand years to seasonal events. Changes are usually orderly, conforming to systematic and predictable patterns. Changes usually result in an environmental succession at the system or subsystem level.

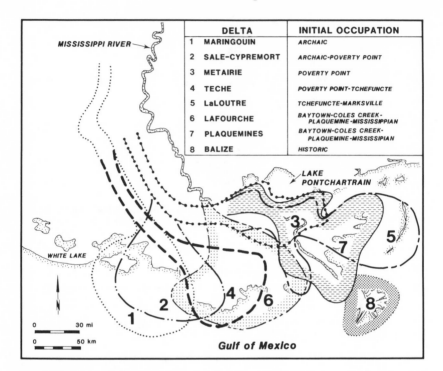

	DELTA	INITIAL OCCUPATION
1	MARINGOUIN	ARCHAIC
2	SALE–CYPREMORT	ARCHAIC-POVERTY POINT
3	METAIRIE	POVERTY POINT
4	TECHE	POVERTY POINT-TCHEFUNCTE
5	LaLOUTRE	TCHEFUNCTE-MARKSVILLE
6	LAFOURCHE	BAYTOWN-COLES CREEK-PLAQUEMINE-MISSISSIPPIAN
7	PLAQUEMINES	BAYTOWN-COLES CREEK-PLAQUEMINE-MISSISSIPIAN
8	BALIZE	HISTORIC

Fig. 1.28. Major delta complexes and archaeological site associations in the Mississippi River deltaic plain.

Archaeological data must be viewed within the systems framework, not only within a hierarchical time framework but also at hierarchical levels of scale. The greatest resolution is at the site level. Landforms and subsystems provide intermediate levels. General synthesis is accomplished at the system level.

While culture is not dictated by environment, the environment does provide the physical framework and resource base upon which culture operates and, therefore, is a key parameter in archaeological interpretation. The distribution of archaeological sites in the coastal zone of the northern Gulf of Mexico is intimately related to the characteristics of the natural systems. Site locations are related to the character of landforms and neighboring habitats at the time of occupations. Activities at a given site may be related to changes in culture and technology as well as to changes in processes and habitat conditions.

2

Early Woodland in Coastal Louisiana

J. Richard Shenkel

The history of archaeological investigations of the Early Woodland Tche-functe culture in Louisiana mirrors in many ways the study of other southeastern prehistoric cultures. The concept and initial descriptions of Tchefuncte were formalized in the 1940s, and since then our knowl-edge has continued to grow. The "new archaeology" has brought new emphases to the discipline, and our understanding of Tchefuncte now includes criteria other than time and space parameters and descriptions of ceramic and lithic artifacts.

In this chapter, Shenkel builds on the early work of James A. Ford and George Quimby to provide an overview of the Tchefuncte culture. Rely-ing on new data provided by a number of researchers and on his own work at Big and Little Oak Island, Shenkel examines the archaeological evidence for Tchefuncte, including such phenomena as economic adap-tation and social organization. The provocative results of this synthesis illustrate the kinds of questions archaeologists working in the Gulf coast region are asking.

IN this discussion of the Early Woodland period in coastal Louisiana, Early Woodland is taken to mean, following Griffin (1967), that pe-riod of time following the Late Archaic and preceding the Middle

Woodland. The Late Archaic in Louisiana is identified as Poverty Point; the Middle Woodland is called Marksville, and it has many cultural affinities to classic Hopewell of Illinois and Ohio. The name by which Early Woodland Louisiana archaeological culture is generally known is Tchefuncte, after the original name of a Louisiana State Park in which the type site is located. What makes it Early Woodland is that it is more or less contemporary with other post-Archaic and pre-Middle Woodland archaeological cultures which are characterized by the addition of ceramics to an otherwise Archaic artifact assemblage.

The original definition of Tchefuncte was by Ford and Quimby (1945); their work remains today the single most comprehensive publication on the subject. Their report was based on excavations conducted under the auspices of the Louisiana State Archaeological Survey, a project of the Works Progress Administration in the late 1930s, as well as an early 1930s project sponsored by the Civil Works Administration. Participating in these early investigations were Gordon R. Willey, Preston Holder, Edwin Doran, Robert S. Neitzel, Walter Beecher, Carlyle Smith, and C. L. Johnson. The first publication dealing with material of the period was J. Richard Czajkowski (1934), a preliminary report of the archaeology of the Little Woods sites, a CWA project on the south shore of Lake Pontchartrain in what is now a developed suburban area of New Orleans. The Ford and Quimby monograph incorporated material from the reexcavation of the Little Woods sites and from the excavations of Big Oak Island near the southeastern shore of Lake Pontchartrain, the Tchefuncte middens on the northeastern shore of Lake Pontchartrain, and the Lafayette Mounds near Lafayette, Louisiana, on the floodplain of the Vermilion River. Also included in this original definition was the Copell site on Pecan Island in southwestern Louisiana, a site which, due to its aceramic nature, is now considered to be Archaic.

During the 1950s and 1960s, a series of archaeological investigations undertaken in coastal Louisiana was directed primarily at increasing our understanding of the changing Mississippi River delta and its associated geomorphic features. In this case, the archaeological chronology developed by Ford and his colleagues a decade earlier was a tool applied to another discipline. Through such works as McIntire (1958) and Saucier (1963), our knowledge of the relationship between Indian settlement patterns and the development of various Mississippi River deltas was increased considerably.

Two main concentrations of sites of the Tchefuncte period were noted during this work. The first, recognized earlier by Ford and

Quimby, with a few sites added by McIntire and Saucier, was around the shores of Lake Pontchartrain. The second was around Calcasieu, Grand and White lakes, and Vermilion Bay in southwestern Louisiana.

Since the late 1960s there has been renewed interest in the Tchefuncte period. Jon Gibson and his associates at the University of Southwestern Louisiana have excavated a 1 percent sample from five Tchefuncte sites in the Vermilion River basin and have collected data from at least six others (Gibson 1976a, 1976b). Robert Neuman and Kathleen Byrd have investigated Tchefuncte components at Week's Island on the eastern end of Vermilion Bay (Byrd 1974) and at Bayou Jasmine near the western end of Lake Pontchartrain. Philip Rivet (1973) undertook a reappraisal of the original Tchefuncte ceramic typology in light of the type-variety espoused by Phillips (1970) for the material excavated from the Tchefuncte type site. Shenkel, initially with Gibson and later independently, conducted three seasons of excavations on the Big Oak and Little Oak Island sites on the southeastern shore of Lake Pontchartrain (Shenkel 1974, 1976, 1979, 1980, n.d.; Shenkel and Gibson 1974; Shenkel and Holley 1975). Richard Weinstein and Philip Rivet analyzed a Tchefuncte component from the Beau Mire site, not far from Baton Rouge and just beyond the edge of the coastal plain (Weinstein and Rivet 1978).

These projects had several goals, the primary one a refinement of the original reconstruction by Ford and Quimby, utilizing the type-variety system to clarify the cultural-historical relationships among the various localities in which Tchefuncte has been identified. Other elements of more recent work involve settlement patterning and cultural ecology.

Much of the information uncovered during the last decade has not yet been published in final form. The only full site report widely available is the Beau Mire report by Weinstein and Rivet (1978). The other references are master's theses, papers read at meetings, preliminary reports, and contract reports.

The collections, notes, and records of the several investigations of the Tchefuncte culture are housed principally in three institutions. The largest collections are at Louisiana State University in Baton Rouge and consist of the material collected during WPA and geomorphological periods of investigation. Also included are the Week's Island, Beau Mire, and Bayou Jasmine collections. The recently excavated materials from the Oak Islands as well as small collections from several other Tchefuncte sites in the Pontchartrain basin are located at the University of New Orleans. Extensive collections from the Vermilion River basin, as well as noncoastal Tchefuncte materials from the Catahoula Lake area, reside at the University of Southwestern Louisiana in Lafayette.

Despite all of the research that has been done, there is no general agreement about the specific chronological limits of the Tchefuncte culture. Radiocarbon dates from various Tchefuncte contexts range from 520 B.C. ± 65 (Shenkel 1974) to A.D. 495 ± 720 (Byrd 1974). In a complete listing and analysis of the available dates in good contexts, I have suggested that a reasonable time span for the Tchefuncte would be between about 600 B.C. and 100 B.C. (Shenkel 1980). Webb (1977) sees a probable demise of the Poverty Point culture at about 700 B.C., and certain Marksville characteristics are definitely present by about 100 B.C. in good stratigraphic position overlying pure Tchefuncte contexts. Additional dates from more stratigraphic contexts would certainly help, but, at this point, it is likely that neither end of this proposed continuum will vary by more than 100 years.

In their original definition, Ford and Quimby described Tchefuncte as primarily a hunting, fishing, and gathering culture consisting of small groups of people living an essentially Archaic way of life. The significant difference between Archaic and Tchefuncte is the addition of ceramics and burial mounds to the overall cultural assemblage. In most respects, this assessment is little changed by recent work. Byrd has added the possibility of limited horticulture with the recovery of squash seeds from the Morton Shell Mound on Week's Island (Byrd 1974), and Griffin maintains that the Tchefuncte are not to be counted among the Mound Builders (Griffin 1979). Both of these topics will be considered here in greater detail.

What recent work has accomplished is a more precise rendering of the original picture. By the increasing specificity of both archaeological questions and investigative techniques, the impressionistic framework of the 1940s has been filled in with an ever-increasing richness of quantitative detail. This elaboration of information focuses on a number of problem areas, including ceramic typology and the associated cultural-historical relationships, other material culture, settlement and subsistence patterns, and social organization.

There are two distinct aspects of the Tchefuncte. Some sites are located on the coastal plain and exhibit a definite coastal adaptation with the exploitation of the brackish water clam, *Rangia cuneata*, and fishes (e.g., Weeks Island [Byrd 1974] and the sites around Lake Pontchartrain [Saucier 1963]). Other sites and site clusters located inland from the coastal plain do not exhibit typical coastal characteristics, such as the sites around Lafayette, Beau Mire, and Catahoula Lake, among others. The precise nature of the inland Tchefuncte adaptation is not well understood because of a lack of quantified stratigraphic data. However, due to the work of Byrd and Shenkel, the coastal Tchefuncte adaptation is better interpreted and has implications for understanding much of the remainder of Louisiana coastal prehistory. The upland and coastal plain aspects of the Tchefuncte are unified by a general similarity observable in the ceramic technology and typology and, to a far lesser extent, in lithic materials.

The remainder of this chapter is two main parts. The first is a brief description of the excavations and data recovered from Big Oak and Little Oak islands near the southeastern shore of Lake Pontchartrain in eastern New Orleans. This description will serve as a basis for considering cultural-historical relationships of the Tchefuncte, their social organization, and the coastal adaptation that they developed.

Excavations of the Oak Islands

When the Oak Island sites were occupied, they were located directly on the southeastern shore of Lake Pontchartrain. The lake had been recently formed by the closing of a coastal embayment by a growing delta of the Mississippi River. During the period of occupation, the lake was brackish, maintaining saltwater interchange through several passes to the Gulf of Mexico on its eastern end. However, as the delta continued to grow, the amount of saltwater diminished until, by about 50 B.C., the lake was completely fresh. It was at this time that the Tchefuncte sites along the lake edges were abandoned. Indians came back to the shores of the lake several hundred years later, after the river switched channels; the combined effects of erosion and coastal subsidence deteriorated the abandoned delta, and saltwater intrusion again turned the lake brackish.

Big Oak Island is the larger of the two Oak Island sites, with about 8,000 m² exposed above the surrounding marsh. A 1 percent nonlinear random sample composed of 19 2-meter by 2-meter units, and 24 nonrandom, discontinuous linear, and other selected 2-meter by 2-meter units, was excavated to provide the data base for this site. Big Oak is a classic Louisiana shell midden, reaching 4 meters in depth. Three distinct components were found. The lowest occupation was a dense, concentrated lens of aoxic peaty muck resting directly on top of a natural alluvial clay surface. This basal component did not contain shell refuse, but the artifact content was high and was pure Tchefuncte. This stratum was reached in only 14 of the units due to problems with the midden depth and the water table. A radiocarbon assay dated this component to 520 B.C.

Lying above the basal level is a thick noncultural zone of shell beach deposit. Above that is another cultural zone, this time composed of massive dumps of collected *Rangia cuneata* shells with numerous artifacts and animal bone included in the matrix. The majority of the ceramics are pure Tchefuncte with a small percentage of sandy-tempered Mandeville or Alexander ceramic types. This second cultural zone has been dated by several radiocarbon assays to 300–200 B.C.

On a relatively restricted area of the site, the Tchefuncte midden is overlain by a mixed component containing ceramic types attributed to both Tchefuncte and Marksville. This upper shell midden is dated to 90 B.C.

In a small area at the highest portion of the site is a mass burial or ossuary consisting of the disturbed remains of at least 50 bundled individuals of all ages and both sexes. Included with these burials were numerous artifacts of Marksville affinity such as beads of exotic materials, *Busycon* cups, and broken ceramic vessels, two of which exhibit a raptorial bird motif. A date of 55 B.C. was obtained from this feature, and it is likely that the burials represent the last cultural event at the Big Oak site prior to its abandonment (Shenkel 1984).

Little Oak Island is quite different from Big Oak. It is located exactly 2,000 meters east of its larger neighbor. It is circular in shape and covers about 600 m². Excavated material was from a stratified nonlinear random sample covering 2.18 percent of the site. In addition to the random sample, two areas were expanded to expose large areas of compacted earthen floors with postmold patterns to add a further 1.5 percent to the site coverage.

The stratigraphy of Little Oak is far less complex than that of Big Oak. The entire site lies on a natural shell beach devoid of cultural material other than intrusive postmolds and burials. The occupation level is a thin earth midden above the shell. This occupation was extremely intense, leaving a large quantity of artifacts and food bone remains. This component was dated to 215 B.C. and is therefore considered to be exactly contemporaneous with the massive Tchefuncte shell midden occupation on neighboring Big Oak Island.

In summary, the two Oak Island sites contain three Tchefuncte components. Two are earth middens with dense artifact concentrations and are probably multifunction villages. The third is a massive shell midden occupied at the same time as one of the earth middens with the shell midden having a much lower artifact concentration. After the Tchefuncte occupations, we have a mixed, or perhaps transitional, Tchefuncte-Marksville shell midden occupation at the Big Oak site.

Ceramics

Perhaps the aspect of material culture of the Tchefuncte that has received the greatest amount of attention in recent years is the ceramic industry. This attention is due, in part, to the widespread adoption of the type-variety system of ceramic analysis as proposed by Phillips (1970) and to the recognition that Tchefuncte represents the beginnings of the major utilization of ceramics in the lower Mississippi valley. To be sure, a small quantity of ceramics is known from preceding Poverty Point contexts, including fiber-tempered wares identified as Wheeler, sand-tempered wares identified as Alexander, and nontempered wares identified as St. Johns (Webb 1977). I strongly suggest that all of these are trade wares and are not of local manufacture. Also present in these Poverty Point contexts are small quantities of rather typical Tchefuncte ceramics, but it is not clear whether they are contemporaneous with the actual Poverty Point occupations or are later. In any event, the amount of pottery found in these Poverty Point contexts is miniscule. The manufacture and use of ceramics do not become significant factors until the Tchefuncte period.

The basic ware of the Tchefuncte is a temperless or grog-tempered ceramic with small quantities of sand and vegetable fiber accidentally included. It is differentiated from the ceramics of the succeeding Baytown periods by the fact that it exhibits a contorted or laminated appearance in cross section and is generally poorly fired. Given these diagnostic traits, it is the only grog-tempered ware in the lower Mississippi valley sequence to have its own plainware designation. All of the grog-tempered plainwares from the later periods are identified as varieties of Baytown Plain (Phillips 1970). It is worth noting that all of the lower valley grog-tempered plainwares are difficult to distinguish out of context. This is particularly true of the Early and Middle Woodland periods. In the analyses of mixed Tchefuncte-Marksville components, neither Ford and Quimby (1945), Toth (1974, 1977), nor Shenkel (1980) was able to separate Tchefuncte Plain from Marksville Plain (Baytown Plain *var. Marksville*).

To this undistinguished ceramic fabric, the Tchefuncte applied a large variety of decorations, including simple and rocker-stamped designs made with several kinds of implements ranging from simple straight bars to denticulated combs. Geometric incised patterns were

made with both deep, narrow and wide, shallow lines. Other techniques included drag-and-jab incising, punctuating with several different tools and fingernails, pinching the clay between the thumb and
forefinger, impressing with an "S" wrapped cord, and check-stamping
with a bold, carved paddle. The majority of the decorated wares contain only one of the design techniques arranged in complicated zoned
and paneled motifs.

In addition to the plastic surface modifications, Ford and Quimby
also reported a red-filmed variant of the plainware. They noted a thin
film of red paint adhering to a few sherds and traces of red ochre in
surface cracks and coil fractures of a few others.

This array of decorative techniques was divided into a series of
broad, basically descriptive types, within which there was a wide
degree of potential variation. Tchefuncte Incised included all of the
material with incised lines only. This material exhibited a technique in
which the incising tool was "wiggled" across the surface of the vessel
to produce a jagged line. All of the rocker-stamped and dentate-
rocker-stamped material was named Tchefuncte Stamped, though it
was noted that the "wiggled incised" intergraded with narrow rocker
stamping, so that separation was sometimes difficult. Drag-and-jab
decorations were called Lake Borgne Incised, and decorations made
with the finger and fingernails were called Tammany Pinched. Tool
punctations set off in zones of incised lines were called Orleans
Punctated.

A minority constituent of the original assemblage was a sandy-
tempered ware, quite distinct from the temperless Tchefuncte material. This sandy ware falls into two series. The finer of the two was
identified as O'Neal Plain, with two associated decorated types, Alexander Incised and Alexander Pinched. The coarser of the two was
named Mandeville Plain with its associated types, Mandeville Stamped
and Chinchuba Brushed.

Starting in 1968, these broad types were subdivided into innumerable varieties with the implicit assumption that, by some process of
inductive enlightenment, a truer picture of the cultural-historical relationships of the Tchefuncte culture would be forthcoming. (For example, see Gibson 1968, 1974c, 1976a, 1976b; Phillips 1970; Rivet
1973; Shenkel and Holley 1975; Shenkel 1974, 1976; Weinstein and
Rivet 1978.) Since the original intent of the ceramic typology was to
clarify chronology, most of this recent work has been directed toward
that goal. It was hoped that chronological phases could be established
by seriation of the ceramic varieties obtained from different Tche-

functe components. In point of fact, the only declarative assertion along these lines was the interpretation of the Beau Mire site as a late Tchefuncte component (Weinstein and Rivet 1978). As will be shown, differences in the relative proportions of the several types in different components are more likely to be the result of differences of site function, vessel size, and sociogeographic groupings than of chronological variation.

The Oak Island sample contains all of the Tchefuncte types and many of the varieties that have been recently defined. One of the initial problems in the analysis of this sample was to decide what should be done with the sandy-tempered material. As noted, Ford and Quimby elected to divide it into two plainware series, Alexander and Mandeville, with their associated decorated types. More recently, Weinstein and Rivet (1978), following Phillips (1970), incorporated the sandy plainwares as a variety of Tchefuncte Plain, classifying the decorated sandy materials as varieties of the several decorated types. The implicit assumption was that the sandy-tempered material is the result of ecological factors and not cultural ones (i.e., the ceramacist obtained a sandy batch of clay and made what otherwise would be good standard Tchefuncte-style pots).

Both of these propositions were questioned. On review of the literature, it was noted that three variables were used in describing the plainwares: texture (ranging from fine to coarse), color (from dark gray to orange), and quality of cross section (well compacted to laminated). In the Oak Island sample, all of these variables are present and, further, they are independent. They exist in all possible combinations. Rather than have two, three, six, or no possible sand-tempered plainware variants, all of this material was lumped into a single series category or type. To determine whether this ware formed the basic plainware of the ceramic series independent of the typical Tchefuncte, the decorations, rim modes, and vessel shapes were also compared. The explicit assumption was that, if all of the other modes were identical, the presence of sand in the small percentage of the material would justify its inclusion in the overall Tchefuncte ceramic set. If, however, these modes were found to be different, the sand-tempered series should stand as an independent entity.

The latter alternative seems to be the case. In the Oak Island sample, and from what could be assessed from published pictures and the examination of three collections from other sites in the Pontchartrain basin, the sand-tempered material is, invariably, distinct from the standard Tchefuncte. Decorative ideas found on one ware were not

Table 2.1. Relative proportions of plain to decorated ceramics

Type	Basal Big Oak Island		Middle Big Oak Island		Upper Big Oak Island		Little Oak Island	
	N	%	N	%	N	%	N	%
Tchefuncte Plain	1,809	76.8	4,475	95.6	700	96.2	23,709	74.1
Tchefuncte Decorated	541	23.0	127	2.7	27	3.7	7,610	23.8
Mandeville Plain	3	0.1	70	1.5	0	0.0	613	1.9
Mandeville Decorated	2	0.1	10	0.2	1	0.1	73	0.2
Total	2,355	100.0	4,682	100.0	728	100.0	32,005	100.0

found on the other. The proportions of rim modes and treatments and the proportions of vessel sizes and shapes were distinct. Until such time as there is better understanding of the relationship of this sand-tempered series to other similar wares in the Southeast, such as Alexander, it shall be referred to as Mandeville.

Of the three pure Tchefuncte components represented at the Oak Islands, the midden matrix strongly suggests that there are functional differences, the basal stratum of Big Oak and Little Oak both being earth middens while the middle stratum of Big Oak is a shell midden contemporary with the neighboring Little Oak earth midden. Table 2.1 is a gross breakdown of the ceramics into decorated and undecorated by series. As the component matrices are dissimilar, so too are the relative proportions of decorated to undecorated ceramics. In the earth midden components, the percentage of decorated sherds is about 23 percent. In the Tchefuncte shell midden stratum, the percentage is only 2.7 percent. In the upper stratum of Big Oak, the mixed Tchefuncte-Marksville shell component, the percentage is only 3.7 percent.

Ceramic differences between the earth midden and the shell midden components are also notable in vessel morphologies and sizes. The rim sherds of the Tchefuncte series suggest that the vessels fall into three basic shapes: unrestricted simple bowls or cylindrical beakers, restricted globular pots, and restricted independent vessels having a slightly constricted orifice and a flaring rim. The measurable rims were arbitrarily divided into three size categories based on projected orifice diameter. A small vessel was less than 10 centimeters, medium vessels ranged between 10 and 21 centimeters, and large vessels were greater than 21 centimeters in diameter.

Table 2.2 is a compilation of the measurable rims of the Tchefuncte series from each of the components. In all cases, the simple unrestricted rim form is in the majority. The most complicated vessel form, the restricted independent, enjoys its greatest frequency in the earliest of the components, the earth midden at basal Big Oak, where it constitutes 30.4 percent of the sample. In the later components, its frequency drops to between 8 and 12 percent, a decline balanced by increases in both other forms.

Of greater significance is the distribution of sizes between the two classes of component. The earth midden components contain 61 and 71 percent large vessels; the shell midden components have about 60 percent medium and small vessels. It follows that the activities undertaken on the earth middens required more and larger vessels, presumably for cooking and storage. Further, since more of the earth midden vessels were decorated, they may have been considered more permanent fixtures in a habitation context. On the other hand, the smaller, predominately plain vessels found in the shell midden contexts would have had a more strictly utilitarian character, being used for transport of goods back to the earth midden village site.

Ceramic chronology has always been an important concern, and the gross compilation of ceramic distributions in table 2.1 may contain a

Table 2.2. Tchefuncte vessel morphology, combined plain and decorated

	Un-restricted		Restricted		Restricted independent		Total	
	N	%	N	%	N	%	N	%
Basal Big Oak Island								
Small	8	2.5	2	0.6	5	1.5	15	4.6
Medium	57	17.5	12	3.7	40	12.3	109	33.5
Large	113	34.8	34	10.5	54	16.6	201	61.9
Total	178	54.8	48	14.8	99	30.4	325	100.0
Middle Big Oak Island								
Small	24	6.2	17	4.4	7	1.8	48	12.4
Medium	142	36.8	36	9.4	16	4.1	194	50.3
Large	107	27.7	26	6.8	11	2.8	144	37.3
Total	273	70.7	79	20.6	34	8.7	386	100.0
Upper Big Oak Island								
Small	6	14.6	—	—	1	2.4	7	17.0
Medium	8	19.5	5	12.2	4	9.8	17	41.5
Large	14	34.2	3	7.3	—	—	17	41.5
Total	28	68.3	8	19.5	5	12.2	41	100.0
Little Oak Island								
Small	5	0.54	24	2.58	3	0.32	32	3.44
Medium	102	10.98	94	10.12	41	4.41	237	25.51
Large	468	50.38	129	13.89	63	6.78	660	71.05
Total	575	61.90	247	26.59	107	11.51	929	100.00

possible chronological indicator, at least for the Tchefuncte of the Pontchartrain basin. The sandy tempered Mandeville is almost non-existent in both the early and late components; in the contemporary assemblages from the middle Big Oak shell midden and the Little Oak village, Mandeville accounts for 1.7 and 2.1 percent, respectively. In the other components, the actual number of Mandeville sherds is so low that they could well be accidental inclusions. These percentages seem to indicate that Mandeville makes its strongest appearance between 300 B.C. and 200 B.C. and that it virtually disappears by the onset of Marksville.

A nontypological attribute that may have chronological significance and also be a further justification for the separation of the Tchefuncte from the Mandeville series is rim notching. Less than 0.1 percent of the rims from basal Big Oak are notched, increasing in frequency to 5.5 percent of the decorated rims and 5.7 percent of the plain rims by the middle Big Oak and Little Oak period. Only one of the 31 Mandeville rims was notched, and all of the Mandeville rims were simple and rounded, showing none of the variations of thickening, tapering, and flattening that are so characteristic of the Tchefuncte wares.

Another nontypological attribute that was thought to have potential chronological significance is the form of podal supports. Tchefuncte is characterized by a number of kinds of bases, the most frequent being tetrapods formed as either rectangular slabs or wedges or in a conical teat shape. Other minority forms include annular, flattened and slightly squared, and annular notched or multipodal. All of these forms are present in the earliest level of Big Oak, with the slabs most frequent at 58.2 percent, followed by teats at 34.3 percent. This same proportion is mirrored at the later Little Oak village, with slabs at 65.9 percent and teats at 33.3 percent. On the other hand, at middle Big Oak, the proportions are more even, with teats slightly outnumbering slabs at 47.6 to 41.3 percent. These podal support proportions correlate roughly with the proportions noted in the distribution of vessel sizes. The slab-shaped foot predominates on large vessels, which are in the majority in village locations. Small and medium vessels more frequently have the teat-shaped foot, and these forms are the most common at the special fishing station. These proportions hold for the Mandeville series. The majority of Mandeville vessels are medium and small, while the majority of Mandeville podal supports are of the teat variety.

Ceramic typology is the traditional means by which most cultural-historical relationships are established. As was noted in table 2.1, the majority of the sample from both sites is plainware. Table 2.3 is a compilation of the entire collection based on Shenkel (1980) as derived from the previously cited sources and following, where possible, the principles of taxonomic priority. It is readily apparent that the vast majority of each type consists of a single or, at most, two similar varieties. The other varieties represent a tiny, idiosyncratic minority. It was therefore decided to compare the decorated content of the several components utilizing a slightly modified version of the original types as defined by Ford and Quimby.

Since basal Big Oak and Little Oak were most similar in terms of site morphology and in relative proportions of plain to decorated ceramics, they were isolated for comparison. Table 2.4 shows a striking similarity in the percentages of the major types. Stamped varieties account for about 65 percent of the sample. Incised varieties account for about 30 percent of the sample. Lake Borgne Incised, the most carefully executed of the types in both samples, decreases from 3.1 to 2.5 percent, which is probably not particularly significant. Orleans Punctate, another well-executed ware, stays at 0.5 percent or less. One of the Orleans sherds from the basal Big Oak component is among the most elaborate of all the sherds in the entire collection from both sites. It consists of a bilobed arrow motif incised with fine lines and filled with pointed tool punctations. The arrow is placed in a plain panel that is bounded by meticulously spaced panels of drag-and-jab incising. Between the two samples, only Tammany Punctate shows any marked change, increasing from a single sherd representing 0.2 percent in basal Big Oak to 176 sherds or 2.2 percent from Little Oak. Weinstein and Rivet have suggested that Tammany Punctate is a late Tchefuncte marker (Weinstein and Rivet 1978:50–62), and their interpretation seems confirmed by these data. However, the single sherd of this type from basal Big Oak is a *var. Brittany*, which is supposed to be a late variety exclusively.

Though the middle component of the Big Oak site contains only 2.7 percent decorated sherds, the typological breakdown is rather unexpected in light of the results derived from the other components. The proportions of the majority types are almost exactly reversed: 24.7 percent are Tchefuncte Stamped and 63.3 percent are Tchefuncte Incised. This reversal in proportion was found to be a correlate of the similar differential noted in vessel size. Small and medium vessels were incised more frequently while stamping is more characteristic of larger vessels. Stamping and incising are taken to be a general utility decoration; they account for 88 percent to 96 percent of the Oak Island decorated ceramic sample.

Table 2.3. Oak Island ceramic distribution

Type	Basal Big Oak Island	Middle Big Oak Island	Upper Big Oak Island	Little Oak Island
Tchefuncte Plain	1,809	4,475	700	23,707
Tchefuncte Stamped				
var. unspecified	0	0	0	45
var. Tchefuncte	114	10	0	2,328
var. Gentilly	32	0	0	636
Tchefuncte Dentate Stamped				
var. unspecified	0	0	0	3
var. Vermilion	199	25	0	1,814
var. Orleans	12	0	0	442
Tchefuncte Incised				
var. unspecified	0	0	0	3
var. Tchefuncte	51	72	3	1,335
var. Marksville	14	0	0	65
var. Belle Helene	2	3	0	50
var. Sanders	2	0	0	9
var. Big Oak	35	2	0	262
Lake Borgne Incised				
var. unspecified	0	0	0	6
var. Lake Borgne	16	0	0	123
var. Cross Bayou	1	0	0	69
Orleans Punctate				
var. unspecified	0	0	1	0
var. Orleans	2	8	2	40
var. St. Clair	0	0	0	3
Tammany Punctate				
var. unspecified	0	0	0	2
var. Tammany	0	0	0	107
var. Brittany	1	0	0	0
var. Duckroost	0	0	0	27
var. Dutchtown	0	0	0	3
var. LaSalle	0	0	0	29
Jaketown Simple Stamped				
var. Sorrento	0	0	0	8
Tchefuncte Cord Impressed				
var. Tchefuncte	60	3	0	201
Tchefuncte Bold Check Stamped				
(cf. Deptford)	0	4	0	0
Mandeville Plain	3	70	0	613
Mandeville Incised				
var. Green Point	2	9	0	29
var. Ponchitolawa	0	0	0	7
Mandeville Stamped				
var. Mandeville	0	0	0	13
Chinchuba Brushed				
var. Chinchuba	0	0	0	1
Mandeville Punctate				
var. Bayou Castine	0	0	0	18
var. Chappepeela	0	0	0	1
var. LaSalle	0	1	1	2
Marksville Incised				
var. Marksville	0	0	10	0

(*continued*)

Table 2.3—*continued*

Type	Basal Big Oak Island	Middle Big Oak Island	Upper Big Oak Island	Little Oak Island
Mabin Stamped				
var. Mabin	0	0	2	1
var. Crooks	0	0	9	1
Mississippi Plain				
var. Yazoo	0	0	0	5
Barton Incised				
var. Arcola	0	0	0	2
Total	2,355	4,682	728	32,010

Table 2.4. Comparison of basal Big Oak and Little Oak islands

Type	Basal Big Oak Island		Little Oak Island	
	N	%	N	%
Tchefuncte Stamped	357	66.0	5,268	65.7
Tchefuncte Incised	164	30.3	2,337	29.1
Lake Borgne Incised	17	3.1	198	2.5
Orleans Punctate	2	0.4	43	0.5
Tammany Punctate	1	0.2	176	2.2
Other	0	0.0	2	0.1
Total	541	100.0	8,024	100.1

Chipped stone

Unlike the ceramic typology, the classification system used by Ford and Quimby in the original Tchefuncte report to describe the "projectile point" proportion of the lithic assemblage is not in current usage, even in a modified form. This system was developed by Willey and used to describe the points from the Marksville period Crook's site (Ford and Willey 1945). The Willey system is a codification of morphological attributes. The initial division is by haft shape, either simple or barbed. This shape is determined by the angle formed by the shoulder of the point with the longitudinal axis. The second division is based on blade shapes, of which there are four: ovate triangular or "leaf"-shaped, large triangular, small triangular, and "fir-tree-shaped," or having concave edges without flaring shoulders. These gross classifications are then subdivided further by the use of upper and lower case letters to specify consistent and specific differences in a particular set, such as size, thickness, and chipping techniques.

This system was abandoned with the publication of the Greenhouse report (Ford 1951) in favor of the system of named projectile point types then being developed in Texas. While Willey's coded system was developed to distinguish local variation through time and across space, the Texas type system was adopted to enable broad comparisons between Texas and Louisiana. It was felt that the local variations were better demonstrated in the ceramics. It is an interesting fact that, where broad geographical comparisons are drawn using the material from Louisiana, we look to the north and east for ceramic analogies, while we look to Texas for the relationships of the lithics.

A few Louisiana types have been defined. As might be expected, many of the Texas types that have been identified in Louisiana do not fit exactly into the Texas molds. For example, Ford found it necessary to divide the Texas Gary point into three variations, long, typical, and short. Naturally, those types defined in Louisiana have a better fit with Louisiana material. In keeping with the use of named types, the projectile point industry of the Oak Island excavations was initially classified using the standard references but with the admission that many of the identifications were stretching the point, especially with those that were Texas types.

The basal Big Oak projectile point sample consisted of only two specimens. This low number may be due to the difficulty of excavation in the water-logged muck and the small area of the basal component that was exposed. Both of these points have a general similarity to the Macon type (Ford and Webb 1956:54).

The upper Marksville–Tchefuncte component of the Big Oak site also produced a small sample of nine points. Three of these would be classed as Pontchartrains (Gagliano 1964:62) and another as a Macon. Three of the points might be considered of the Ellis type (Suhm, Krieger, and Jelks 1954:420) but are smaller and more finely made than is usual for that type. The last two points are unidentified barbed types with short, contrasting stems and "fir-tree" shaped.

The contemporaneous occupations of the midden of Big Oak and Little Oak provide the largest and most varied of the projectile point samples. In the Big Oak sample of 23 points, 19 would be classified as Pontchartrain or Kents, the difference being the presence of ripple flaking on the Pontchartrains. On several of these particular points, one edge was rippled and the other was not. Of the remaining four points, one would be a Delhi (Ford and Webb 1956:58–60), two would be Gary (Suhm, Krieger, and Jelks 1954:430), and the last a Macon. The Little Oak industry is far more diverse and much larger. Of 75 points, about half would be either Kents or Pontchartrains and the remaining half would be divided fairly evenly among the types mentioned, plus a few others. Several were unidentifiable according to established types.

At this superficial level of analysis, one thing was very clear. Even though we were not happy with the identifications of the points, the differences between the middle Big Oak and the Little Oak components were confirmed by the projectile point data. Big Oak had a major proportion of a few heavy dart point types while type frequencies at Little Oak were far more evenly distributed.

On further inspection, it was determined that there was more variation in the Oak Island lithic industry than the typological analysis indicated. The entire collection was submitted to a morphological-functional analysis by James Morehead. In this analysis, it was recognized that many of the objects called projectile points were multiple function tools as were many of the other nonpoint-looking objects. The so-called points were reidentified according to the method by which they were produced. The Willey system of coded characteristics was adopted as a primary descriptive device where applicable. The entire analysis is far too lengthy to reproduce here but can be found in Shenkel (1980).

The Little Oak lithic industry contained worked bifacial thinning flakes, worked primary flakes, blades, flakes, and bifaces. Chipping techniques include primary, secondary fine, lamellar and sublamellar, and scaling. Edges produced include scraper, knife, point, denticulate, serrated, and notched. Burin facets and retouch to form perforators are common. Of the hafted bifaces, 44 indicated modification beyond that of a simple projectile point. Ten had serrated edges; seven have one edge serrated and the other steeply retouched to form a side scraper. Three were double-side scrapers; one was a side scraper with a denticulated opposing edge. Eight of the pieces were denticulated or notched. One complex piece was pointed: one edge was denticulate, and the other was a scraper with distal perforator and a lateral microperforator. Two of the pieces had burin facets. Almost all of the pieces were well worn.

The middle Big Oak period hafted biface tools are less varied in the multiple modification category. Of the 21 whole specimens, eight have serrated edges on both sides and three are denticulated on both edges. Two of the specimens are double-side scrapers, and the remainder combine two edge types.

The strategies by which the initial biface reduction was undertaken may have some chronological significance. The upper and middle Big

Oak and the Little Oak samples were reduced by opposed platform bilateral chipping. Both of the points from the basal component from Big Oak were reduced by opposed platform longitudinal chipping. Stems of the Tchefuncte pieces were typically produced by both unifacial reduction of the lower lateral edges with retouch as necessary to finish the stem.

There were evidently two methods of hafting the Tchefuncte bifaces. Many of the specimens from the two largest samples have unthinned bases with cortex remaining, appropriate to hafting in a hollow socket. Others in the sample have thinned bases more appropriate to hafting in a split shaft. The hafting procedure did not correlate in any way with the other attributes of the pieces (stem formation, blade shape, or edge modification).

Other chipped lithics in the combined industries include both unifacial and bifacial pieces worked into picks, burins, notches, denticulates, and scaled pieces.

Ground-stone tools and other lithics

The ground-stone tool category from the Oak Islands is neither large nor particularly diagnostic. The largest sample was obtained from Little Oak and included a crude boatstone, three bar weights, two hammerstones, four hammer-like objects, three broken bifacial celt or ax blades, and three plummets. The basal Big Oak assemblage contained only one plummet preform and two other pieces of stone that had been abraded. The middle Big Oak occupation yielded four hammerstones, three plummets, a bar weight, and several ground stones of unknown function. The upper Big Oak component held three ground-stone pieces of unknown function.

In addition to the identifiable objects, there were a number of objects of tabular sandstone and opaline phytolith that may have been used as abraders or smoothers. At both Little Oak and the middle of Big Oak, unmodified quartz crystals were recovered (one large one from Big Oak and three small ones from Little Oak).

Lithic raw materials

Within the immediate vicinity of the Oak Islands, there is no source of stone out of which the various objects could have been manufactured. Most of the lithic material is available in the streams flowing into the north of Lake Pontchartrain, a distance of 30–40 kilometers. A few of the pieces had to have come from farther afield (the quartz crystals and several pieces of orthoquartz). The presence of these exotic stones might be an indication of long-distance trade. However, Gibson has suggested (Shenkel 1974) that their presence could be the result of scavenging of Poverty Point sites. This possibility was strengthened when it was noted that several of the Oak Island bifaces had differential weathering on overlapping flake scars, suggesting that the manufacturing steps could have been separated by several hundred years. It seems likely that the Tchefuncte were collecting from Poverty Point sites and Archaic sites as well when they went to the north of the lake to obtain their stone.

Miscellaneous artifacts

The bone tool industry of the Oak Islands is identical to that described by Ford and Quimby (1945) for the Tchefuncte as a whole. It contains socketed bone points, polished bone splinter points, harpoon heads, atlatl hooks, fishhooks, flakers, split bone awls, antler points, and perforated teeth. These objects are pretty simple and utilitarian. None is decorated, and only the perforated canine teeth seem to have had a decorative purpose.

One class of artifact is striking in its distribution. Twenty gouges made from the outer whorl of *Busycon* and a heavy celt made from the inner whorl of a *Strombus* were recovered from the middle component of Big Oak, and another gouge was recovered from upper Big Oak. These artifacts were not found in either of the earth midden contexts, basal Big Oak, or Little Oak. This lack contrasts interestingly with the ground celts that were recovered from Little Oak. It might be suggested that the shell gouges had something to do with the activities occurring on the shell middens that were not being performed on the earthen middens. The source of the shells to make these tools was probably an exposed relic barrier beach located about 3 kilometers to the west of Big Oak.

Other objects of interest include tubular clay pipes, of which three were decorated with incised lines and punctuations. One of these was also red filmed. All of the pipes were made of the sandy Mandeville paste.

A few Poverty Point objects were recovered from the Oak Island contexts. The middle component of Big Oak Island has two small objects of the biconical type. The Little Oak sample includes the nine identifiable objects with many fragments. Those that were identified include biconical, biconical grooved, melon, and spheroidal forms. No Poverty Point objects were recovered from either the basal level or the upper level of Big Oak.

Faunal remains

From each of the Oak Island components, there were recovered thousands of animal bones. The shell midden components of Big Oak has, in addition, a calculated 2,937 m³ of culturally deposited *Rangia cuneata* shells. The bones from several of the excavation units from both sites were analyzed in depth to produce information about minimum numbers of individuals and inferred meat weights obtained from the several species. The meat weight of the clams represented by the midden shell was calculated by comparing living specimens with the archaeologically recovered shell obtained from column matrix samples. In all, 43 species of vertebrates and five species of mollusca were represented. The major mammals recovered include, in decreasing order of numerical importance, white-tailed deer, muskrat, raccoon, and opossum. Other mammals, including bobcat, cougar, brown bear, dog, mink, squirrel, skunk, beaver, and cottontail, were represented by only one or two individuals.

Reptiles were represented by alligator and a variety of small turtles. A large number of fishes of both fresh- and saltwater species was noted. By far, the most abundant of these fishes was the freshwater drum fish. Fewer in number were several types of catfish, bow fin, buffalo fish, gar, saltwater drums and sheepshead, sea catfish, and shark. Birds represented an insignificant number of individuals, consisting of a few duck species, a spoonbill, an owl, and an eagle.

It has been demonstrated that the contemporary components of the Big Oak shell midden and the Little Oak earth midden are different in many ways (ceramic content, lithic assemblage, shell gouges, and stone axes, in addition to the presence or absence of shell debris). These differences suggested from the onset of the investigations that these two components were functionally different aspects of the same adaptation, the Big Oak shell midden being the remains of a special hunting, fishing, and shellfish processing station and the Little Oak earth midden a more generalized village. The basal component of Big Oak would be an earlier village, given the similarity of the matrix and the ceramic content.

This hypothesis of differential function was dramatically confirmed with the analysis of the faunal remains. The largest vertebrate component from both sites in terms of numbers of individuals and calculated meat weights was the freshwater drum fish. Their presence in the Big Oak shell midden was based on the identification of heavy, bony mouth parts known as pharyngeal grinding mills. None of these

Table 2.5. Combined meat weights, Big Oak and Little Oak islands,
late Tchefuncte period

Animals	Meat weight (kg)	%
Mammals		
deer	27,377.78	7.92
other	14,458.33	4.20
subtotal	41,836.11	12.12
Reptiles		
alligator	7,444.44	2.16
other	607.77	0.19
subtotal	8,052.21	2.35
Fish		
freshwater drum	138,500.00	40.03
other	28,149.99	8.15
subtotal	166,649.99	48.18
Birds		
all	342.22	0.01
Mollusks		
Rangia	129,161.00	37.34
Total	346,041.53	100.00

bones was found in the Little Oak assemblage, but there were large quantities of internural and dorsal spines of that species. In other words, there were fish heads on Big Oak Island mixed with the shells, and there were fish bones on Little Oak mixed with the other earth midden debris.

With the assumption that the contemporary components formed different aspects of a single occupational system, the meat weights for the various species were calculated and combined to reflect an approximation of the total meat consumed by the Tchefuncte people during that period, ca. 300–200 B.C. As can be seen from table 2.5, the freshwater drum fish was the most important constituent of the diet at 40 percent and the meat of the *Rangia* a close second at 37 percent. Deer were a distant third, providing only about 8 percent of the meat, less than the combined weights of the other fishes at slightly over 8 percent. Of the other mammals, muskrat and raccoon provided the bulk of the remains. Of the other taxa, only alligator, at slightly over 2 percent, is notable.

Cultural-historical relationships

The Tchefuncte culture is delineated in space and time primarily on the basis of its ceramic tradition. Most of its other characteristics are reflections of its adaptations and continuations of local Archaic and Poverty Point manifestations.

To find the origins of the Tchefuncte ceramic tradition, we must look beyond the geographical boundaries of the culture to the contemporary and antecedent cultures elsewhere in the Southeast. Though the Tchefuncte were the first peoples to make extensive use of ceramics in Louisiana, they were not the originators of their own tradition. Tchefuncte ceramics are a synthesis of a polythetic set of elements that had been developing for the previous two millennia, elements that coalesced at the end of the Poverty Point period. The broad range of attributes that characterize Tchefuncte is probably the result of the extensive trade carried on by the ancestral Poverty Point peoples. Material goods that appear in Poverty Point contexts, such as steatite, shell, trade ceramics, and exotic stones, often came from places where the local populations were well along in ceramic technology.

When the lower Mississippi valley peoples finally decided to adopt ceramics, they acquired an eclectic combination from many different neighboring traditions. The basic fabric of Tchefuncte pottery, the temperless or grog-tempered ware, may well be a local copy of the white, chalky St. Johns ware from Florida. Some sherds of St. Johns are known from Poverty Point contexts. Some of the design techniques found on Tchefuncte are known from the earliest ceramics from Stallings Island, which continue into the Toms Creek–Awendaw Complex. These elements include a variety of punctuations with tools and fingernails. The punctuations are placed randomly as well as in linear patterns that intergrade with drag-and-jab incisings as the individual punctuations become closer together. Also in the Stallings Island assemblage are incised and simple stamped techniques. Moreover, several varieties of Tammany Punctate, Lake Borgne Incised, Tchefuncte Incised, and Jaketown Simple Stamped are possibly eventual descendents of Stallings Island types. Certain incised and zoned incised motifs with punctuations occur on late Orange ceramics from Florida, and they continue to appear on St. Johns. The motifs and execution of these wares is similar to Orleans Punctate and Tchefuncte Incised. Rocker stampings and scallop shell impressing are found on the Alabama coast in Bayou La Batre in a period slightly earlier than the Louisiana contexts. Bayou La Batre also has podal supports of the slab and teat forms.

The ideas that were first expressed on the east coast may have come directly, as seems to be the case with the St. Johns material, or they may have been filtered through Wheeler in northern Mississippi and Alabama, or along the coast through Norwood and Bayou La Batre, or both.

A few of the Oak Island sherds were initially identified as "wiggled" incised, a fairly common variation of Tchefuncte Incised. On closer examination, it turns out that these patterns were produced by impressing a string or cord against the wet clay. Cord impressions are known from the contemporary Tchula culture from northern Louisiana and Mississippi as well as from Bayou La Batre.

Four sherds of a bold check stamp, similar to Deptford Bold Check Stamped, were found from the middle component of Big Oak. They appeared to be from the same vessel and were on a typical Tchefuncte paste. Deptford was contemporaneous at that time, and the presence of these sherds strongly suggests that, if not a Deptford pot, a Deptford paddle made its way to the Mississippi delta.

The relationships of the minority Mandeville series are not yet clear. There is probably a connection with the northern Mississippi and northern Alabama Alexander material, and the connection ultimately derived from a synthesis of sand tempering, which developed in West Florida or Georgia, and the resident northern Alabama Wheeler fiber-tempered complex. Bayou La Batre could also have been involved, as could early Tchefuncte. In Tchefuncte contexts, sand temper is most frequent in the later strata of the Pontchartrain sites. Since the Pearl River empties into the eastern Pontchartrain basin and has its headwaters in the heart of Alexander country, I suggest that future research will clarify the relationships showing that sand temper correlates with Pearl drainage and temperless corresponds with the drainage of the Mississippi.

The Tchefuncte peoples of the Oak Islands, as well as the other Tchefuncte sites on the shores of Lake Pontchartrain, abandoned these locations just as ceramic elements identifiable as Marksville were beginning to appear. The upper strata of many of these sites contain a light scatter of typical early Marksville ceramic types such as Crooks Stamped, Mabin Stamped, and Marksville Incised. Many of the standard Tchefuncte types disappear at this time, with only Tchefuncte Incised and Orleans Punctate present in any quantity. The sand-tempered Mandeville is also absent. The plain grog-tempered ware in these Marksville-Tchefuncte components is impossible to differentiate. Neither Ford and Quimby (1945) in the original Tchefuncte re-

port nor Toth (1974, 1977) in his analysis of Marksville components
was able to separate the plainwares found with both Tchefuncte and
Marksville decorated types.

In the original description of the Tchefuncte culture, Ford and
Quimby noted that Tchefuncte was the logical precursor of the succeeding Marksville. Since that time, the general opinion has been that
Marksville is some sort of lower Mississippi valley outlyer of the upper
valley Hopewell and not of lower valley origin. If Hopewell is considered a particular synthesis of certain elements combined in specific
ways, such may be the case. However, most of the separate design elements and many of the actual design motifs characteristic of both
Marksville and Hopewell are anticipated in the Tchefuncte: zone and
panel decorations, broad line incising, cross-hatching, simple and
dentate rocker stamping, and multiple designs on the same vessel. In
fact, all of these elements were widespread through much of the Southeast when the most complicated thing in the upper valley was an occasional vessel of Montgomery Incised.

Other Hopewell characteristics have precedence in the lower valley.
Raptorial birds are present in Poverty Point imagery. Lamellar blades,
delicate lapidary, clay figurines, and the extensive use of galena are all
found in Poverty Point contexts.

Another feature of Marksville generally considered to have a Hopewell inspiration is burial ceremonialism and the use of burial mounds.
Burial mounds have been ascribed to the Tchefuncte culture in the
Lafayette phase (Ford and Quimby 1945). This cultural feature has
been denied emphatically by Griffin (1979) on grounds of inconclu-
sive evidence. The Lafayette Mounds may well be much later structures that incorporated Tchefuncte midden material in their construction. Whether the Tchefuncte culture had burial mounds is
uncertain. Jon Gibson has been researching the Lafayette Tchefuncte
sites and assures me that at least five of the 12 Tchefuncte components that he has investigated have mounds, but confirmation must
await dates from definite structural contexts such as a crematory platform from within the mound.

That mounds are present in the Tchefuncte does not seem unreasonable. It is generally accepted that the preceding Poverty Point
peoples were extensively involved in earthwork and mound-building
activities; however, as in the case of the Tchefuncte Lafayette mounds,
solid contextual dates are also lacking for Poverty Point period
mounds. They could also, in fact, be later constructions incorporating
ancient midden fill.

A rather tenuous line of evidence suggests that mound building may even predate Poverty Point in Louisiana. Mounds and mound groups with Middle Archaic associations, dating to before 2000 B.C., have been noted at Banana Bayou, Amite River, Monte Sano, and the Hornsby site. Resolution of this question must await further research.

There are no probable Tchefuncte period mounds on the coast. All of the coastal Tchefuncte were living on small coastal midden sites. The aforementioned abandonment of the Pontchartrain Tchefuncte sites at about the point of transition to Marksville relates to a change in the environment; Lake Pontchartrain became fresh as the result of the continuing delta growth of the Mississippi River. The peoples, becoming increasingly "Marksville" in their ceramics, followed the brackish *Rangia* habitats to continue their particular brand of coastal adaptation.

Adaptation

The contribution of the Tchefuncte beyond the aspects of material culture lies primarily in the realm of developing a new adaptation. While most Poverty Point sites and most Tchefuncte phases are oriented toward the exploitation of terrace and river floodplain habitats, the Tchefuncte components of the Pontchartrain basin and at Week's Island were beginning to exploit the vast resources of the Mississippi River delta and the coastal plain. It is the thesis of this section that the specific adoptive patterns developed by the coastal Tchefuncte were highly specialized and were maintained by all of the subsequent populations in coastal Louisiana.

It is commonly held that coastal dwellers who rely on fish and shellfish are rather opportunistic generalists, eating anything they can catch, given the limits of their technology. Ford and Quimby certainly held this to be true of the Pontchartrain Tchefuncte.

At present, the coastal wetlands of Louisiana constitute about 25 percent of the total wetlands in the continental United States, and the annual seafood harvest ranges from 25 to 33 percent of the total for the United States. Modern commercial species include brown and white shrimp, blue crab, crawfish, menhaden, trout, redfish, and oyster. In addition, southern Louisiana has an alligator season with a sustainable yield of 15,000 to 30,000 animals a year. Another major coastal industry is fur trapping, with 80 percent of the commercial muskrats being taken from the marshes. The marshes of the coast are a major wintering ground for the Central Flyway migratory waterfowl. With this abundance of potential food resources, an interpretation of a generalized hunting and fishing economy would seem reasonable.

However, the quantitative data from the Oak Islands indicate that the majority of the animal foodstuffs were derived from two species, the freshwater drum and the *Rangia* clam. All of the species recovered would have been available from the immediate vicinity of the sites, whether near the shore of the lake or in the adjacent marshes, back swamps, and natural levees.

The key to this adaptation was the *Rangia* clam. All of the Pontchartrain Tchefuncte sites are located adjacent to what would have been ideal habitat for maximum *Rangia* productivity, near the mouth of freshwater streams flowing into the brackish lake. The *Rangia* are most prolific on muddy bottoms with occasional shocks of fresh- or saltwater to promote spawning. These shocks would be provided by spring floods from the streams and the intermittent storm surges coming from the Gulf of Mexico. Though the *Rangia* provided only 37 percent of the meat calculated for the Oak Island sites, their importance is greater in terms of site location and adaptive preference. The other major animal food constituent is the freshwater drum fish, and it is a *Rangia* predator. In other words, where there are *Rangia*, there are also freshwater drum. In an examination of the ecological relationships of the other fish species represented in the faunal sample, 82 percent of the minimum number of individuals present are known *Rangia* predators, and most of the remainder are potential *Rangia* predators. The bowfin and gar are both carnivores, preying upon other fishes. The fish community found in the archaeological contexts is that which would be expected from a *Rangia* bed near the mouth of a freshwater stream feeding into a brackish lake.

Byrd, in her analysis of the fauna at the Week's Island site, found comparable data, with *Rangia* and freshwater drumfish slightly less important and deer and bowfin slightly more important. It is significant that virtually every Louisiana aboriginal site on the coastal plain after Tchefuncte is associated with a *Rangia* midden. It is evident that the Tchefuncte developed the basic adaptation that characterizes the bulk of the remainder of Louisiana coastal prehistory. This basic economy underwent little or no change from its beginnings until historic contact. The primary locus of this adaptation was the *Rangia* clam bed. Associated with it were all of the other fish species habitually caught. Within the shifting environments associated with the evolving delta systems was a close succession of habitats, including brackish and fresh marsh, swamp, and levee forest. Although the Tchefuncte and their successors were primarily interested in the *Rangia* biome, the adjacent habitats were exploited to a limited degree.

It is reasonable to assume that these people also utilized plants for food, medicine, and manufacture. No macrofloral specimens were recovered from the Oak Islands, but Byrd had better luck at Week's. She listed 19 species: cypress, spearhead, greenbriar, hickory, walnut, willow, oak, hackberry, dock, smartweed, wild plum, grape, tupelo-gum, persimmon, storeax, haws, squash, gourd, and parsley. Within the brackish marsh to levee habitats, there are 88 species of plants that are known to have been used by the Indians in the ethnographic present. Many of these plants, especially those that may have provided starchy roots, occur in abundance immediately adjacent to the midden localities.

This specialized and specific adaptation to the habitats associated with the *Rangia* clam is the reason for the site occupation and abandonment seen for the remainder of Louisiana coastal prehistory. Since the coastal plain of Louisiana was constantly undergoing change due to the continually evolving Mississippi River delta, the locations of these optimal habitats were always shifting. The Indians, rather than adapt to a new environmental situation, simply packed up and moved to the next location in which the *Rangia* could be found.

Social organization

In all probability, the peoples of the Oak Island sites were organized as a patrilocal, exogamous band, which, in combination with other similar bands in the Pontchartrain basin, formed a linguistic or dialectic "tribe." Archaeologically, this "tribe" is represented by the Pontchartrain phase, and it is distinguishable from other, presumably contemporary, Tchefuncte site clusters or phases by differences in material culture distributions and adaptations.

The sizes of the village earth midden components, basal Big Oak and Little Oak, suggest a local population of 25 to 50 individuals. The distribution and content of the material culture point to an essentially egalitarian organization. There are no elaborate burials or concentrations of exotic trade goods or anything else to suggest differential wealth or social stratification. Nor is there anything that would suggest differential access to resources. The size of the population, its egalitarian content, and adaptive independence of the village units make the band level of organization the logical choice.

Band level organization is usually considered to occur in two varieties, the patrilineal band (Steward 1955), also called the patrilocal band (Service 1971), and the composite band (Steward 1955; Service 1971). The patrifocused band, be it lineal or local, is characterized by virilocality and band exogamy. Its nucleus is a group of related males, their wives from other bands, and unmarried daughters. It has a corporate nature, with resources owned or controlled by the local male group. The composite band, on the other hand, lacks explicit marriage rules and residential patterns and generally has a bilateral kinship system.

The patrifocused band exists where males play the dominant role in food procurement or specific territorial exploitation. The procurement team is a group of related males who maintain nominal control over their territory by occupation, which produces virilocality and de facto patrilineality.

Service argues that the patrilocal band is the natural form of organization at this level of cultural integration and that the composite band is the result of social disruption caused by contact with civilization (Service 1971:97). This view is not held universally. In a recent compilation of 101 hunting and gathering/fishing societies, only 19 were patrilineal and implicitly patrilocal, 13 were matrilineal, 8 were duolineal, and 61 were bilateral (Keesing 1975:134). The possibility of matrilineal bands is not considered by Service or Steward, but by analogous reasoning their existence must be accounted for by the dominance of females in the food procurement system. The duolineal and bilateral groups would be composite bands having mixed residence. Lee (1979) has argued that the composite band is more adaptive than an organization with strict rules of descent and residence for hunting and gathering groups in that it allows greater flexibility in situations where the constancy of the food resource may vary.

To determine the nature of band organization archaeologically, one must take into account the distribution of material culture and resource bases and then make assumptions about the nature of the organization that may be reflected in those distributions. For instance, one might expect patrilocality in a situation of nonrandom distribution of male-manufactured artifacts between sites or a uniform distribution of female-manufactured objects between sites. Both of these distributions would indicate males remaining in the same place while the females moved around as they married outside their natal band. Permanent male residency might also be expected if the resource base was locally circumscribed and male-exploited. Matrilocality expression of composite bands would be uniform distributions of artifact classes between sites and a variable productive resource base necessitating flexibility in residential patterns.

To determine the residence pattern of the Pontchartrain Tchefuncte, it is necessary to examine several factors. Historically, the Indians of the southeastern United States were matrilineal (Swanton 1946:654). Matrilocality with implied matrilineality is suggested for the Poverty Point culture, based on the nonrandom distribution of Poverty Point objects at the type site (Gibson 1974b:102). If Gibson is correct, matrifocus residence and descent developed in Louisiana before the Tchefuncte period and it was certainly modal afterward. It would not be unreasonable to assume that the Tchefuncte would be a part of a matrifocal continuum. If this were the case, we could expect to find a nonrandom distribution of female-related artifacts throughout the Pontchartrain basin where the females remained relatively sedentary and taught their daughters to produce in kind. The different sites within the basin would be expected to have a distinctly different signature in terms of female artifact types.

However, in the Pontchartrain basin, a number of features suggest that the patrilocal band is the better model. At least 20 sites are suspected of having Tchefuncte components. It is known that the original Tchefuncte site on the north side of the lake and the Little Oak Island site on the south side are contemporaneous. It is not unreasonable to assume that as many as ten villages may have been occupied at any given time. There were certainly enough viable clam beds on the lake's peripheries to support a population of this size without stress. Ten villages of a size comparable to the Tchefuncte site or to Little Oak Island would place the population for the entire basin between 250 and 500, the suggested maximum for the linguistic "tribe" (Service 1971:58).

Probable patrilocality is demonstrated by the distribution of ceramic types throughout the basin. If we assume that the women made the ceramics, as they did in the ethnographic present, and that they passed on to their daughters their skills and favorite designs, the uniform distribution of ceramic styles and types over several sites would be an indication of a uniform distribution of related females and would be the result of patrilocal band exogamy.

Table 2.6 is a compilation of the decorated ceramic distributions from three other Pontchartrain Tchefuncte components in the same typological categories used in table 2.4. As can be seen by comparing tables 2.4 and 2.6, Tchefuncte midden A and Little Oak Island are

Table 2.6. Decorated ceramics from other East Pontchartrain
Tchefuncte sites

Type	Little Woods		Tchefuncte A		Tchefuncte B	
	N	%	N	%	N	%
Tchefuncte Stamped	163	34.5	4,795	65.8	755	55.9
Tchefuncte Incised	265	56.0	2,112	29.0	422	31.2
Lake Borgne Incised	25	5.3	174	2.4	10	0.7
Tammany Punctate	0	0.0	53	0.7	88	6.5
Orleans Punctate	20	4.2	53	0.7	36	2.7
Other	0	0.0	103	1.4	40	3.0
Total	473	100.0	7,290	100.0	1,351	100.0

Table 2.7. Decorated ceramics from non-Pontchartrain
Tchefuncte components

Type	Russel Landing		Teche-Vermilion		Beau Mire		Poverty Point	
	N	%	N	%	N	%	N	%
Tchefuncte Stamped	127	35.9	97	39.0	127	6.0	31	24.4
Tchefuncte Incised	70	19.8	44	17.7	686	32.3	17	13.4
Tammany Punctate	97	27.4	65	26.1	749	35.3	62	48.8
Lake Borgne Incised	43	12.1	32	12.8	423	19.8	0	0.0
Orleans Punctate	12	3.4	10	4.0	104	4.9	0	0.0
Jaketown Simple Stamped	5	1.4	1	0.4	10	0.5	15	11.8
Other	0	0.0	0	0.0	25	1.2	2	1.6
Total	354	100.0	249	100.0	2,124	100.0	127	100.0

virtually identical. Tchefuncte midden B is within a few percentage points of the two. The Little Woods sites are actually quite comparable to the middle Big Oak component, and their small sample size might indicate that they also are fishing and work stations as opposed to full occupation villages. The close similarity of all of these components in terms of decorated ceramics is the strongest argument for the patrilocal exogamous band model.

Another argument in favor of that model is the uneven distribution of the primary resources around the basin. The clam beds that are the adaptive focus occur, as do the sites, at the mouths of the freshwater streams that feed into the lake. The middle component of Big Oak Island is the only site that has been identified as a special function initial seafood-processing station, and the nature of the material culture from that component appears overwhelmingly male-oriented. This male orientation suggests the possibility that a corporate group of related males owned the adjacent clam bed and that they formed the nucleus of a sedentary population.

Tables 2.4 and 2.6 probably represent Pontchartrain Tchefuncte components from the entire temporal range of the Tchefuncte period. It is known that at least Tchefuncte midden A and Little Oak Island are contemporary and that basal Big Oak is as much as 200 years earlier. Tchefuncte midden B and the Little Woods sites are undated and may fall anywhere within the period. The close correspondence in the percentages of the decorated ceramic types in all of these components suggests an extreme conservatism with little influence in terms of ceramics coming in from the outside until the end of the period, when Marksville motifs begin to be used.

The individuality of the Pontchartrain phase was tested by comparing the ceramic type distributions with other probable Tchefuncte period phases. Unfortunately, none of these other collections is dated radiometrically and, because of the uniformity through time of the Pontchartrain ceramics, it is doubted whether seriation is a valid chronological indicator. Therefore, until such time as dates are obtained, all of these components should be considered to be more or less contemporary and to reflect geographic rather than chronological variation.

As can be seen in table 2.7, the distributions of ceramic types from the other areas are distinct from the Pontchartrain phase sites as well as, for the most part, distinct from each other. In all of them, the ever-popular stamped and incised types of the Pontchartrain phase occur in much lower proportions, while the minority types in the Pontchartrain basin are correspondingly higher in frequency elsewhere. It is suggested that each of the components or component sets in table 2.7 represents an individual geographic phase of the Tchefuncte, each probably characterized much the same as the Pontchartrain phase by associated patrilocal bands forming linguistic "tribes," which, once formed, were relatively conservative for the whole Tchefuncte period.

3

Woodland Cultures of the Texas Coast

Lawrence E. Aten

Aten's research on the Texas coast in the decade since he was a co-organizer of the first conference on the archaeology of the Gulf coast has produced the synthesis provided in this chapter for an area of the coast for which few syntheses have been attempted. His concern here is with the Woodland ancestors of the small Texas coastal tribes such as the Karankawa, Bidai, and Akokisa, who were among the first southeastern Indians to be observed at length by Europeans in the first half of the sixteenth century. He begins with an overview of the Woodland cultural sequence of the area. In an admirable integration of archaeological and ethnohistoric data, he develops and brings to bear on the cultural-chronological framework a general model of sociopolitical and demographic change on the Texas coast from Early Woodland times to the historic period.

THE purpose here is to summarize my current views about the developmental history of Woodland cultures on the western Gulf coast frontier of the southeastern United States. This frontier is located on the coastal plain of the northern Gulf of Mexico (fig. 3.1). It extends from the Sabine River drainage on the Texas-Louisiana border westward to the Matagorda Bay area, and it is a region well known to stu-

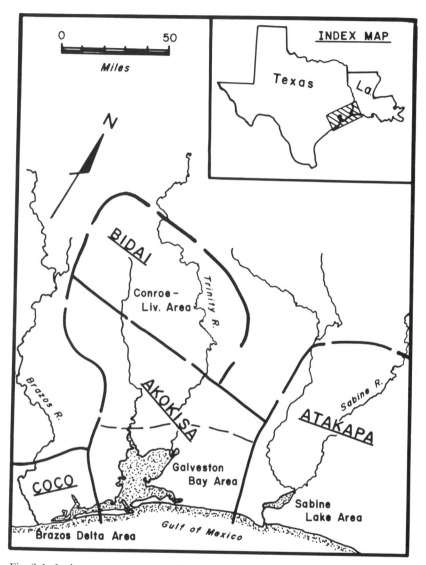

Fig. 3.1. Index map to upper Texas coast geography, archaeological areas, and ethnohistoric group territories.

dents of Cabeza de Vaca, LaSalle, Jean LaFitte, and Sam Houston. The environment of this region often strikes visitors as a monotonous repetition of flat prairies and marshes occasionally interrupted by small stands of hardwoods, sluggish streams wending to the Gulf, great estuaries, and long stretches of sandy beach. This description is true but superficial, for the coastal zone of the northern Gulf of Mexico is a diversified and dynamic environment which has taken on much of its present form and features concurrent with the duration of human occupation (Aten 1983a).

The upper Texas coast is a region of an extraordinarily high, if unevenly distributed, natural productivity. Soils, ranging from the predominant gumbo clays to the leached sands and silts of now-abandoned Pleistocene stream levees, were not suited to the prevailing modes of prehistoric agricultural technology. There were a few natural resources of the coastal zone known to have been coveted by societies in the interior (and vice versa), which served as driving forces behind archaeologically visible trading networks. The coast appears to have been largely a self-contained region for the resident ethnic groups, one which either was not exposed or was not particularly susceptible to dramatic change by political, technological, or ideological forces. However, much of the language, social organization, technology, design motifs, and ritual of this area appears to be similar to that of early southeastern Woodland cultures, even though the coastal Texas groups only occasionally interacted with theocratic chiefdoms such as the Caddo and Coles Creek.

Operational definitions of "Woodland" culture usually make reference to ceramics, incipient agriculture, expansion of regional exchange systems, and an elaboration of ritual frequently associated with conical burial mounds, reflecting increasing status differentiation. On the Texas coast, there are ceramics in common Woodland styles. And the Texas coastal cultures did share in use of other Woodland technological innovations, manifested incipient status differentiation in material culture and mortuary ritual, and may have had similar concepts of religion and magic. However, there was no horticulture, no regional exchange archaeologically visible on the scale seen at certain inner coastal plain ceremonial centers and mortuaries (Newell and Krieger 1949; Hall 1981), and no ranking or burial mounds. Moreover, woodlands are not found to any great extent. The term Woodland as used here is not intended literally to suggest cultures sharing Woodland adaptive patterns. Rather it loosely connotes activities by populations on a geographic as well as a cultural periphery of the southeastern Woodlands. A brief review of the somewhat more characteristic Woodland cultures of the interior of eastern Texas may be found in Shafer (1975).

The upper Texas coast Woodland cultures conventionally are differentiated from their Archaic period antecedents by the presence of pottery or arrow points, or both, in their technology. Indeed, it is not uncommon for the observation to be made that the technology of early ceramic/bow and arrow (i.e., "Woodland") cultures differs from the preceding Archaic cultures primarily in terms of these two artifact classes. This conclusion is probably premature about the culture as a whole; several major classes of data, some of them only newly accessible, have yet to be incorporated into the region's archaeological models. For example, analysis currently is under way on extensive subsistence data from both prepottery and pottery sites. These data include shell midden refuse washed through small mesh screen, producing archaeological faunas qualitatively different from those yielded by hand-picked or coarse-screened refuse. Also, techniques for determining season of site occupation are becoming generally available and open important new lines of evidence about both social and environmental interaction.

A particularly important new line of evidence for understanding even the relatively recent archaeology of the northern Gulf coast concerns analysis and reconstruction of ancient geography and climate. Although most archaeologists assume that late Quaternary environmental changes affected the nature and disposition of early archaeological sites along this coast, these changes have been analyzed only in broad outline. A key to describing the Archaic antecedents of the Texas coastal Woodland cultures is to know that the environments of most fixed locations on the land, whether now submerged or not, changed significantly throughout the late Quaternary. Earlier and later cultures alike were affected by this coastal evolution, although the most radical reshaping of the coast's geography and the major reorganization of its climate and biotic environments were experienced by the Archaic cultures. What still can be observed of Archaic archaeology on the *present* coast must be a severely truncated and highly selected segment of this record. An extended discussion and reconstruction of these early environments is included in Aten (1983a).

Despite these problems with preservation of the archaeological record, and despite certain definitional inconsistencies associated with Archaic and Woodland, the main point seems to be that the three most recent stages of cultural development of the eastern United States—Paleo-Indian, Archaic, and Late Prehistoric/Woodland—are coeval roughly with the three most recent phases of the region's geologic history: the period from the final phases of the Wisconsin glaciation to the thermal optimum; the period of the thermal optimum and its waning; and the onset and progression of essentially modern climatic and geographic conditions. Elsewhere I have used these units as the definitions of Early, Middle, and Late Holocene (Aten 1983a; also see Williams and Stoltman 1965:699 for a similar approach).

The Archaic period on the Texas coast spanned the time of major post–Pleistocene environmental changes, which required important shifts in adaptation. Evaluation of the prehistoric and environmental setting suggests that the Middle Archaic population on the upper coast must have consisted of a few relatively isolated bands that adapted to restricted habitats within an overall regional climate that was distinctly more arid than it has been in recent times. Beginning about 4,000 years ago, with the advent of humid environments on the upper coast, this population began to expand. This period of significant environmental evolution and consequent major changes in economic adaptations seems to have ended by approximately 3,000 years ago, more or less coincident with the culture-chronological period labeled on projectile point criteria as the Late Archaic. The subsequent thousand or so years probably was a time of numerous small-scale adjustments in population size, annual round scheduling, technology, and so on as the resident groups settled in to the essentially modern environments of the Late Holocene.

The populations of the Late Archaic appear to have been larger than those of previous periods and to have been on a trajectory of increase that extended unaffected into the Late Prehistoric–Woodland (Aten 1979:466–70). However, after pottery appeared in the upper Texas coast material culture, a host of modifications and innovations of one sort or another occurred over a period of several centuries, culminating in important cultural and systemic changes. Therefore, the onset of the Woodland on the upper Texas coast also is a period of enhanced visibility in the archaeological record. My goal here is to describe an evolutionary model characterizing the development of coastal Texas Woodland cultures by considering, in a historical framework, selected elements of technology, social structure, population, and information flow. Unless otherwise cited, all data discussed here are taken from Aten (1979, 1983a).

Historical framework

Ceramic assemblages are the principal chronological tool applied to Late Prehistoric–Woodland archaeology in this region and are supplemented by radiocarbon dating. Ceramics appeared about A.D. 100 and evolved through at least 18 indigenous types and descriptive categories which are currently recognized. The ceramic typological framework for the upper Texas coast is based, in order of priority, on attributes of temper, paste characteristics, and design. This framework employs the type-variety approach as described by Phillips (1970) and yields a classification sufficiently robust to remain relatively unaffected by within-class and within-technique (i.e., between archaeologists) variation. Classification decisions are based on the physical and distributional properties of ceramics with the result that there are (1) a minimum of subjective judgments in assigning specimens to a category, (2) criteria of regional significance to facilitate broad correlations, and (3) a sufficient number of categories to allow the approximate dating (supported by radiocarbon dating) of archaeological components.

A precision of within 200 years generally has been achieved for the Galveston Bay area, and it will not be difficult to achieve this precision elsewhere on the upper Texas coast once modest supplementary stratigraphic test data are obtained. The system of classification now used on the upper coast is described in table 3.1. The terminology applied to upper Texas coast ceramics in the table has gone through a complex evolution over the past 30 years; the interested reader may find a discussion of the history of this classification in Aten (1979:285–308).

Using both stratigraphic testing and surface collections from numerous sites on the upper coast, seriations of ceramic assemblages have been prepared for four principal sections of the region: the Sabine Lake area, the Galveston Bay area, the Conroe-Livingston area, and the Brazos Delta–West Bay area. These seriations are partitioned into ceramic assemblage periods based on unique combinations of types, varieties, and attributes. With these, however, it is possible to map the temporal and spatial distribution of elements of technology, subsistence, settlement, and ritual.

The best developed ceramic seriation for any area of the upper coast is that prepared for the Galveston Bay area (fig. 3.2) in the center of the region. The data used to prepare this seriation consist almost entirely of excavated material. A sequence of 64 radiocarbon dates associated with many of the seriated units confirms that this seriation also is ordered chronologically. The time range for each of the ceramic chronological periods in the Galveston Bay area is given in figure 3.3

East of Galveston Bay is the Sabine Lake area for which the historical framework remains one of the less well known. An initial formula-

Table 3.1. Galveston Bay area ceramic taxonomy (classes for rare or
unique specimens not included)

Untempered ceramics	
Clay–silt paste	
Plain	Tchefuncte Plain, *var. unspec.*
Rocker stamped	Tchefuncte Stamped, *var. unspec.*
Sandy paste	
[No red clay wash]	
Plain (homogeneous paste)	Goose Creek Plain, *var. unspec.*
Plain (thick, contorted paste)	Mandeville Plain, *var. unspec.*
Plain (paste intermediate between previous two categories)	Goose Creek Plain, *var. Anahuac*
Incised	Goose Creek Incised, *var. unspec.*
Rocker stamped	Goose Creek Stamped, *var. unspec.*
[Red clay wash]	
Plain and incised	Goose Creek Red Filmed or Goose Creek Red Filmed Incised, *var. unspec.*
Tempered ceramics	
Sand temper	
Plain	O'Neal Plain, *var. Conway*
Grog temper	
Plain (sandy texture)	Baytown Plain, *var. San Jacinto*
Plain (fine texture)	Baytown Plain, *var. Phoenix Lake*
Incised (sandy texture)	San Jacinto Incised, *var. Jamison*
Incised (fine texture)	San Jacinto Incised, *var. Spindletop*
Bone temper	
Plain and incised	Descriptive categories only
Shell "temper" (apparently fortuitous inclusions)	
Plain and incised	Descriptive categories only

tion prepared in the late 1960s (Aten and Bollich 1969) has not been
substantially modified. Because of the relatively frequent occurrence
of lower Mississippi valley ceramics in this area, the major temporal
periods in the Sabine Lake local chronology are being identified by
cross-dating to corresponding periods in the lower Mississippi valley
chronology (Phillips 1970). The earliest ceramic periods in both areas
appear to be approximately contemporaneous and consist of substantial quantities of Tchefuncte ceramics. Of particular interest in the
Sabine is the early appearance of grog-tempered varieties of Baytown
Plain along with Marksville Stamped, in contrast to the Galveston Bay
area 80 miles to the west, where grog-tempered ceramics do not appear until several hundred years later. With the principal exception
of a few Tchefuncte period ceramic types, most southern Louisiana
ceramics are not found on the Gulf coast west of the Sabine lake area.

Much more limited cultural-historical data are available for the

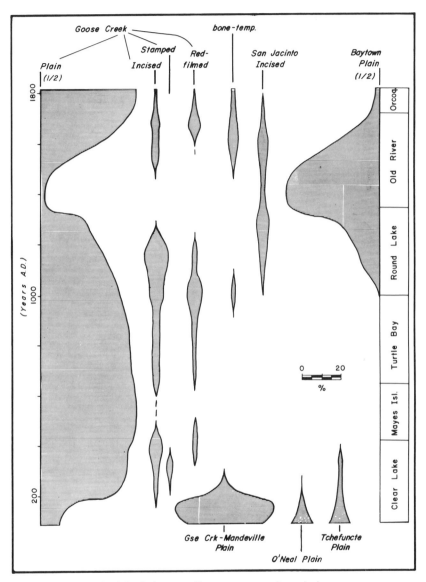

Fig. 3.2. Galveston Bay area ceramic seriation.

CHRONOLOGICAL PERIODS			PERIOD LIMITS [†]	
ETHNOHISTORIC	ARCHEOLOGICAL		ESTIMATED INITIAL DATE	ESTIMATED TERMINAL DATE
Late Historic	Historic/ Woodland	[Unrecog- nized]	A.D. 1810	A.D. 1840?
Early Historic		Orcoquisac	A.D. 1725?	A.D. 1810
Protohistoric	Late Prehistoric/Woodland	Old River	A.D. 1528	A.D. 1725?
			A.D. 1350	A.D. 1528
		Round Lake	A.D. 1000	A.D. 1350
		Turtle Bay	A.D. 650	A.D. 1000
		Mayes Island	A.D. 425	A.D. 650
		Clear Lake	A.D. 100	A.D. 425
	Late Archaic		$\pm$ 1000 B.C.	A.D. 100
	Middle Archaic		$\pm$ 3000 B.C.	1000 B.C.

[†] Limits refer to sidereal years which are estimated to nearest 25 years (Suess 1970: Plate I).

Fig. 3.3. Culture-chronological period intervals for the Galveston Bay area.

Brazos Delta–West Bay and Conroe-Livingston areas. What are available, however, are consistent with the general sequences developed for the Galveston Bay area, with the distinct difference that the diversity of ceramics is much reduced. In fact, practically all ceramic taxa are absent except Goose Creek Plain, Baytown Plain, bone-tempered plain, and occasional rare specimens of Goose Creek Incised and San Jacinto Incised. The greater proximity of the Conroe-Livingston area to the Caddo area of northeast Texas can be seen in a greater proportion of bone-tempered plainwares and Caddoan ceramic types, which are nearly absent on the coast.

Technology

The technology of native groups living on the upper Texas coast was unspecialized. It was oriented to locally occurring materials and facilitated a broad spectrum of resource extraction through hunting, fishing, and food collecting. It is clear that the ceramic technology consisted of a variety of common Woodland jar and bowl forms, although these have not been studied diachronically to determine their functional history. Of particular interest in the time-space distributions of nonceramic tools is the disappearance of dart points on the coast by about A.D. 400 and the introduction of arrow points around A.D. 500–600; the transition between the two is spanned by socketed bone points. Coincident with the appearance of arrow points is the use of alligator gastroliths as supplementary lithic tool source material. Major expansion in the occurrence and use of arrow points occurs from the late Round Lake period through the Old River period (ca. A.D. 1300–1700).

There are distinct suggestions of congruences in the distribution of artifacts and the group territories defined on the basis of ethnohistoric records. There was an apparently continuous evolution of ceramic assemblages in each of the four archaeologial areas, corresponding spatially to an ethnohistoric group territory (fig. 3.1). In addition, blunt socketed bone points, Tchefuncte ceramics, a large number of indigenous ceramic types, and almost exclusive occurrence of incised ceramics are characteristics of sites in the Atakapa and Akokisa territories. On the other hand, oyster shell knives and a proportionately large component of bone tempering in the ceramics is characteristic of sites in the Karankawa territory, whereas sites in the Bidai territory alone contain significant proportions of Caddoan ceramics. Lithic reduction techniques also are distinctly patterned, all of which suggests a continuity between ethnohistoric territories and the archaeological record at least back to the time at which ceramics first appeared on the upper Texas coast—about 1,900 years ago.

Social structure

Early European visitors described four principal ethnic groups inhabiting the upper Texas coast. From east to west, these were the western or Lake Charles Atakapa, the Akokisa (with "upper" or cold season and "lower" or warm season subterritories), the Bidai immediately above the Akokisa, and the Coco (fig. 3.1). The first three groups were Atakapan speakers, the latter the easternmost Karankawan-speaking tribe. Ethnohistoric documentation indicates that the Karankawa groups, the Akokisa, and probably the Bidai had an annual pattern of population aggregation into villages in the cold season and dispersal into band-sized (or smaller) groups during the warm season. The size of the cold-season village aggregates is not clear, but there are indications that they numbered from 100 to 400 individuals. The tribal organization was one in which periodically during the year sets of bands were aggregated into villages under a headman. It is at this level of the village that the strongest indications of group identity and highest levels of authority can be seen.

Although it seems certain that there were mechanisms available for linking together or marshaling groups of villages within a tribe for some purpose—warfare in particular—these apparently were ephemeral aggregations, possibly functioning under an authority figure (such as a war chief) who transcended the village headman. Nevertheless, it is a fact that the Spanish failed in their attempt in 1778 to create a Bidai-Akokisa confederacy and that there was a continuing focus upon village headmen by Spanish and French colonial officials seeking to gain influence with various native groups. These facts reinforce our perception that the greatest political integration among the protohistoric and historic period Woodland cultures of the upper Texas coast was at the level of the village headman who presided, perhaps only seasonally, over an aggregate of bands ranging up to possibly 400 individuals. In the early historic period, four or five villages with a combined population of 1,500 to 2,000 constituted the Akokisa, three villages comprised the Bidai, and there probably were two western Atakapa villages in Texas. There is no information on how many Coco villages there may have been.

Archaeologically, this macro-organizational concept is not so much confirmed as it is not contradicted. Many of its important features have never been tested. At the present time, archaeological and ethnohistoric data for the upper coast have led to the identification of at least 18 statuses within the social organizations of the area, among them headman; war chief; shaman; skilled craftsmen (and women) of various kinds, such as flint knappers, weavers, and shell bead manufacturers; "east" and "west" burial sodality members; two dance sodalities, which may have been identical with the burial sodalities; slaves; berdaches; and so on. Several of these statuses evident in ethnohistoric documents are recognized in archaeological mortuary data (Aten et al. 1976).

Most archaeological test excavations thus far have occurred in localities that are now predicted to have been occupied during warm seasons when populations were dispersed into small groups. Seasonality estimates performed on *Rangia cuneata* shells from shell middens (Aten 1972, 1981) all confirm the predicted warm-season use of the region. Testing directed at intrasite analysis has demonstrated that some sites were occupied briefly by a small number of persons (Aten 1983b). Testing methodologies, however, are not adequate to document the size of larger residential groups, even though the duration of stay can be determined. In other words, in larger shell middens on the coast, it is possible to excavate a series of habitation units, but it is not yet possible to determine which ones were contemporaneous, thereby representing a relatively large group, and which ones were discrete habitation episodes.

Population reconstruction

The question of population size of native Indian groups on the Texas coast has been addressed previously (Mooney 1928; Swanton 1952) for the historic period. However, these studies essentially viewed the historic period statically in spatial dimensions and did not account for the dynamic temporal dimension. To reexamine the element of population size, all historical notations of population size for the ethnic groups inhabiting the upper coast were enumerated in chronological order. Those entries that were redundant, obviously in error for one or another reason, or could not be correlated with the four identified ethnic groups were eliminated.

Through this means, eighteenth- and nineteenth-century population size curves were compiled for the Atakapa, Bidai, Akokisa, and Karankawa. Because the data available on population size for any one group are limited, it was assumed that similar curves resulting for several ethnic groups would constitute a degree of verification. In fact, the four sets of population data suggest more or less similar population histories among the ethnic groups inhabiting the upper coast. This information is consolidated into a model curve embodying the essential features of the region's population history (fig. 3.4).

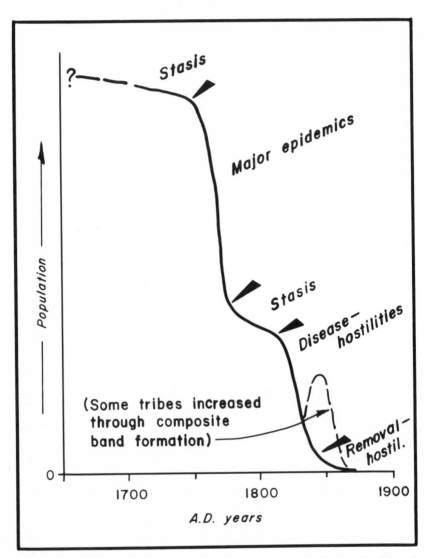

Fig. 3.4. Model of upper Texas coast population trends during the historic period.

This general model describes a period of apparent relative stability or slow decline in the early eighteenth century, followed by a major, in some cases almost instantaneous, drop-off in the third quarter of that century, followed either by another stasis or at least by a much reduced rate of decline into the early part of the nineteenth century. This reduction is followed by another sharp drop in the first quarter of the nineteenth century, with some groups becoming extinct and others showing a slight and short-lived period of population recovery, then going into extinction, usually about the middle of the century.

There are two principal features to this model: a "stair-step" form in which population size descends to extinction and frequently, on the last step, a slight rise or recovery. This latter feature is due to the consolidation of local groups of different tribes into composite bands. This stepwise decline has been shown to result primarily from epidemic disease. Reinforcing the devastating effect of epidemic disease were several other conditions such as chronic disease, psychological depression, and possibly even the consequences of strongly enforced incest rules.

It is not clear whether the maximum recorded size of these groups in the early to mid-eighteenth century was the zenith of their population trajectory. A review of epidemic disease in the vicinity of the upper coast indicated that there were definitely some minor outbreaks associated with earlier European incursions into the area. There was also opportunity for major, unrecorded population reduction prior to the eighteenth century, although there is no known indication of such in any oral tradition recorded by Spanish or French officials, clerics, or adventurers who reached the area. As will be seen, there is a consistency among several classes of information (social organization, recorded population sizes, demographic modeling according to certain incest rule assumptions) that gives some assurance that the group population sizes descibed here for the early eighteenth century are at or reasonably close to the historical population zenith (table 3.2).

Information exchange and mortuary ritual

One of the major vehicles for information transmission through a social structure is its ritual. Archaeologically, the most visible class of ritual on the upper coast is burial practices performed to connect the social group's existential propositions with its sacred propositions. Put somewhat less obtusely, it connects a group of individuals and the space and resources they perceive as their own with the realm of super-

Table 3.2. Ethnic group population sizes and densities

Territorial group	Area[a] (miles²) (± A.D.1700)	Estimated population zenith (per mile²)	Population density[b]
Atakapa (western)	[?]	1,333–2,000	[?]
Karankawa (all tribes)	5,500	4,000–6,000	1.09
Akokisa	–	1,333–2,000[c]	–
Lower (littoral) territory	1,800		1.11
Upper (interior) territory	2,800		0.71
Bidai	3,500	800–1,200	0.34

a. Rounded off to nearest 100 square miles.
b. When a population size range is given, densities were calculated for the larger population estimate.
c. Population was seasonally transhumant between littoral and interior territories.

natural entities, several of which are identified in ethnohistoric documents. Mortuary ritual was a means by which survivors transmitted important messages about social order to other members of their own group, to adjacent groups, and to the ever-present supernatural entities. It was a means of enhancing, or at least legitimizing, their power or rights vis-à-vis those of neighboring populations. Most important for our purposes, it is a form of information transmission that is archaeologically visible.

A distinctive body of mortuary ritual first becomes evident on the upper coast not long after Woodland ceramics appear, and this ritual seems to have become increasingly complex with the passage of time. The data upon which the current view is based are derived almost entirely from sites that probably were established by the Akokisa or their antecedents; the modest data from the areas of the Bidai, Coco, and the Atakapa seem consistent with this Akokisa sequence and are assumed to have been generally similar.

Prior to the Clear Lake period (± A.D. 100), no evidence of corpse disposal of any kind is known. Since a large quantity of preceramic midden refuse has been excavated, it seems fair to conclude that a different situation prevailed for disposal of the dead during the Archaic than was the case later. By way of explanation, there are four likely possibilities. (1) An individual's role and status relationships prior to Woodland times were not generally refined to the point that distinctive mortuary ritual symbolism was required to terminate the relationship or to facilitate the deceased's passage. (2) The requirements of mortuary symbolism were met in ways that lacked any archaeological visibility. (3) There was not a need for a band to signify association

with habitation locales, reflecting either an absence or a minimal occurrence of contact with adjacent social groups and competition with
neighbors for a territory or its resources. (4) Archaeologists have been
unlucky at discovering interments or other mortuary evidence of pre–
Woodland provenience.

While the last possibility seems unlikely, the other three each may
have contributed in some measure to the absence of an archaeological
mortuary record prior to A.D. 100. In any event, the appearance of
mortuary ritual in upper coast prehistory is one concomitant of the
Woodland cultures in this area. Four types of mortuary locality are
known at present to occur: cemeteries, isolated body interments, cremations, and bodies abandoned on the ground surface. The first instances of mortuary ritual appear in the Clear Lake period (A.D.
100–425), and their frequency is very low. By the end of the Turtle
Bay period (ca. A.D. 1000), the incidence of visible corpse disposal apparently increased to more or less the maximum level it was to attain
in the archaeological record (Aten et al. 1976).

The earliest mortuary evidence, dating to the Clear Lake period,
consists of a few isolated body interments, and these were all placed in
an unusual sitting or upright flexed position. Mortuary ritual involved
only adults and proportionately more males. No status differentiation
is evident, and all corpses were placed with heads facing to the east.
During the succeeding Mayes Island period (A.D. 425–650), there was
an increasing frequency of isolated burials, all flexed but now placed
in a horizontal position. Although most burials were pointing east,
some had heads placed to the west.

From the Turtle Bay period (ca. A.D. 650) to the protohistoric
(A.D. 1528–1725?), the incidence of burials increases, isolated interments remain frequent, and cemeteries appear. Initially the cemeteries appear to have had no internal organization, but by the time of
the protohistoric at least one cemetery had attained it. Nearly all burials were flexed; one burial known from this time was cremated. The
direction of orientation of the head gradually shifts over time from
predominantly east-pointing to nearly all west-pointing. By the end of
this evolution in the protohistoric, females were represented as frequently as in a normal living population, and infants and subadults
were often present.

Because skeletal parts of infants occasionally have been found in
Clear Lake period midden refuse, infanticide is thought to have been
practiced at that time. This, plus the presence of infants in later cemeteries, presumably indicates some changes in population control,

group energy budgets, and criteria for being accorded mortuary ritual. Another significant feature of upper coast mortuary practices was
the absence of any evidence of violent death, although such evidence
is found frequently inland and to the west, especially along the Brazos
and Colorado river valleys (Aten et al. 1976; Hall 1981). Finally, the
shift in body orientation from east- to west-pointing may reflect structural and conceptual evolution in the ritual system by differentiating
two burial sodalities.

Increasing differentiation of social personae is evident over time in
the mortuary ritual. This change must reflect growing heterogeneity
and structure in the social group. There is also a growing association
of mortuary ritual with localities of past habitation, and most evidence
suggests rather strongly that burial of the dead occurred in habitation
localities no longer used for that purpose. This evidence applies to
both isolated interments and cemeteries. This situation is consistent
with an assumption of a developing native conceptualization of space
and its differentiation into various sacred and secular use categories
including a category of the group's territory and its contained resources of food, other materials, and geographic characteristics.

A developmental model

So far in this overview, I have described a chronological framework
for the upper coast, outlined some of the macro-organizational features through which the populations grouped themselves, observed
historical dynamics pertaining to the size and density of social groups,
and examined mortuary ritual as a means of gaining ideas about the
basic currents of social development that occurred during the period
of Woodland cultural history on the western Gulf frontier. Now the
problem of constructing a first-approximation developmental model
can be approached.

Taken all together, the most historical and archaeological information is available for the Akokisa territory centering on Galveston Bay
(cf. fig. 3.1). Consequently, I will focus on this group and its territory
as the basis for suggesting a general model for the evolution of Woodland cultures in the region. Construction of the Akokisa model begins
with plotting the historic period population reconstruction just described. Because of the likelihood of very small population size during the Middle Holocene, we may posit a trend that declines, as one
goes back through prehistory, to a very small number around 4,000

years ago. The first problem is to suggest how these two extremes may be linked.

Ethnohistoric and archaeological data together establish that the Akokisa populations were dispersed in small groups, band-sized or less, during the warm seasons and were aggregated into villages during cold seasons. By the advent of the historic period, there appear to have been five of these cold season villages with maximum populations reaching about 400. The minimum functional size of these villages may be indicated by the population size at which composite bands evidently were formed, about 200 persons. Although this number was derived empirically from ethnohistoric records, an interesting theoretical confirmation of its validity can be derived from a consideration of incest rules.

In the Atakapa language, a dialect of which was spoken by the Akokisa, aunts and female cousins are merged terminologically as "sisters." There is a prohibition among the Atakapa against marriage with sisters, which implies a prohibition also on marriage with first and possibly second cousins. It has been shown that in order for groups below about 150 persons in size to maintain a stable population level, a variety of fertility techniques are needed to avoid the demographic cost of an incest prohibition (Hammel, McDaniel, and Wachter 1979). If incest rules were strongly enforced, there would be an important incentive not to let group size fall below about 150 persons.

Consequently, the estimated minimum village size of about 200 persons may have a functional basis. Populations below roughly 200 individuals could not function as an exogamous unit, and group size above approximately 450 could not be handled by the social structure. These constraints necessitated a fissioning process in which a group sufficiently large to function independently as a village budded off. This process is hypothesized to have been the manner in which Akokisa social organization was replicated. In figure 3.5, this history of village formation by budding is outlined in such a way that the interval between the Middle Holocene and the historic period can plausibly be bridged. The frequency of budding is hypothetical entirely, but the remainder of the model has a substantial factual basis.

As expansion of the population took place (the average increase was less than 3 persons per generation), the social processes of boundary formation (or formalization) appear. As population increased, the relationships among population size, technology, and available resources must have been adjusted. For example, burial data indicate

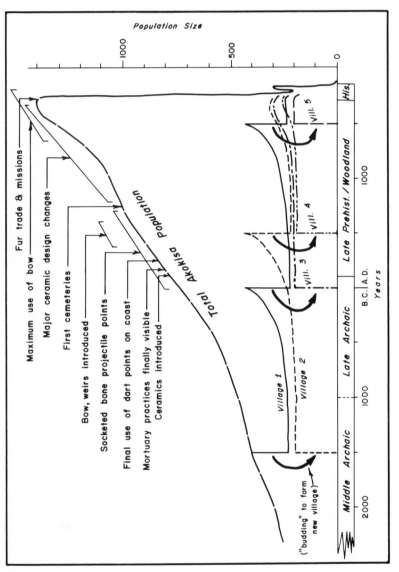

Fig. 3.5. Developmental model for the Akokisa.

that a decline in birth rate may have been an essential adaptive mechanism late in the prehistory of the Akokisa territory (Aten et al. 1976). Figure 3.5 also includes the time of occurrence of the major technological and cultural features discussed earlier. On this basis the Akokisa model can be partitioned into at least five components extending from prior to the Woodland cultures, A.D. 100–800, A.D. 800–1700, A.D. 1700–1770, and A.D. 1770 to extinction.

In the Late Archaic period, prior to about A.D. 100, no major innovations have been recognized. The period A.D. 100–800 contains major changes in technology and mortuary practices that imply significant changes in subsistence, cognition, and possibly social organization. It is in this period that artifact distributions first form recognizable sets paralleling the organization of historic period tribal territories. This period is the earliest time from which the boundaries can be suggested as they are known to have existed later. It is also in this period that important energy-harnessing technology enters the Akokisa system (e.g., the initial use of ceramic containers, the initial use of the bow and arrow as a replacement for the dart, and the likely appearance of tidal fish weirs). Use of the bow and the fish weir probably marks an important shift in subsistence emphasis from exclusively larger animals to a wider range of species and smaller individual body sizes. This adaptation of the subsistence technology to a more specialized mode may signify either growing competition for resources, increased length of stay at a given location, reduction in procurement range about a given location, shift in division of labor, change in absolute availability of other food sources (as, for example, occurred with the bison), or several of these causes acting in concert.

The period A.D. 100–800 is also marked by the first visible mortuary practices and by the first cemeteries. Although the content of mortuary ritual probably served spiritual purposes, cemetery location in or near habitation sites may constitute a symbol of entitlement to the resources of an area by villages or by their subordinate bands. Because this period is also the time during which the number of villages may have doubled, it is difficult not to see the growing formalization of ritual as another evolving cultural element for social order needed in a period when the subdivision and exploitation of space and of contained resources by the area's inhabitants were becoming more highly organized.

The third period in the model, roughly A.D. 800–1700, is characterized archaeologically by innovation in ceramic design styles. Late in this time range, during the Old River period, the use of the bow and arrow increased significantly. Although this change may reflect an altered hunting pattern (by this time the bison apparently had returned to the southern ranges; see Dillehay 1974), it may be that increased use of the bow reflected the inception of the fur trade during the Orcoquisac–early historic period.

The fourth period in the Akokisa model is approximately the first seven decades of the eighteenth century, during which the fur trade and the mission system, as well as the major effects of epidemic and chronic diseases, began to disrupt seriously the native cultural and social system.

Although not marked by archaeological data as clearly as the earlier periods, a fifth and final segment of this history is recognizable in the latter part of the eighteenth century and the early part of the nineteenth, when the Akokisa tribe became extinct. Because of the brief period of time involved, archaeological research cannot explore this period effectively without significant assistance from ethnohistoric sources.

Effects of environmental changes are difficult to assess during the period encompassed by the Akokisa model. The broad shift from arid Altithermal conditions to the seasonally moist conditions of the present day is obvious. Finer grained changes undoubtedly occurred, however. For this reason, the sequence of bison herd appearances on the southern ranges, including the Gulf coastal plain (Dillehay 1974), is included in figure 3.5. Although bison, even when present, formed a modest portion of coastal subsistence, they were an indicator for other less obvious conditions of change in moisture and temperature. In this light, significant increases in population, major reorientation of the technology, and probably important changes in the relationships among groups, both within and between tribal areas, are all attributable to the period in which bison were at first declining in numbers and then were absent entirely. Bison, per se, probably figure very slightly in this interpretation; the environmental modifications to which bison were responding, however, must also have had a significant impact upon upper Texas coast cultural patterns. Identification of these modifications must be the subject of future research.

The two developmental phases of upper Texas coast Woodland cultures are A.D. 100–900 and A.D. 1700–1770. The earlier period was extended and incorporated systemic changes: a major rise in energy demand resulting from population increases; adoption of a technology that permitted focusing the acquisition of food and other materials on previously inaccessible quantitative and qualitative segments of the area's biotic resources; increase in organizational and demographic complexity; and control of access to limited biotic resources by definition of boundaries.

The later developmental period probably was different qualitatively from the earlier period in several respects. For one thing, its duration was so brief that major changes must have been evident within the span of a single generation. For another, as new cultural elements appeared (such as linkage with the European economic system through the fur trade and missions), destruction of the native cultures also was proceeding through the media of severe population losses to diseases, rapid cognitive disruption, and possibly depletion of subsistence resources as a consequence of the removal of fur-bearing animals. The major impact of these changes may have been to shift the bulk of transactions away from generalized and balanced reciprocity and toward negative reciprocity as a result of the creation of composite bands, diminution of involvement of close kinsmen in day-to-day activities, increase in commercial relations with Europeans, and the onset of hostilities with Anglo settlers (particularly for the Karankawa tribes).

There are, in this model, strong hints that by the time the Old River period had been reached, significant evolutionary changes soon would be in the offing. Population was rising at an increasing rate even though average family size had declined. The level of intertribal raiding probably would have increased, and possibly a higher level of political integration might have developed within the tribe. In the absence of these consequences, major technological efficiencies would have been necessary. In any event, it seems highly probable that the "Early Woodland" character of the Texas coastal Woodland cultures was nearing a major transformation at the time the European invasion brought the native American history of the region to a close.

4

Late Prehistory in Coastal Louisiana: The Coles Creek Period

Ian W. Brown

Throughout much of the northern Gulf coast, the Late Woodland period is regarded as one of significant cultural change. In many parts of the Southeast, Late Woodland sets the stage for the Mississippian "climax" that followed. The first widespread construction of temple mounds and an intensification of agricultural pursuits have long been thought to characterize the Late Woodland in the interior alluvial valleys. On some parts of the coast, recent work has also revealed greater continuities between Late Woodland and Mississippian ceramic traditions than were once recognized (see chapters by Brose and Davis in this volume).

In coastal Louisiana and the lower Mississippi valley, Late Woodland is represented by the Coles Creek period, an interval that is usually believed to have been a time of major population growth, especially in the coastal zone. Although scores of Late Woodland sites have been discovered and collected on the Louisiana coast, there was no reported large-scale excavation of any coastal Coles Creek site prior to 1970. Ian Brown provides a synthesis of current knowledge of coastal Coles Creek chronology and subsistence, based on his own field research and that of a small group of other archaeologists, and considers some of the possible relationships among coastal groups in Louisiana and those of other Gulf coastal areas during the Late Woodland.

THE Coles Creek concept has a long heritage in lower Mississippi valley archaeology, used to define both a culture and a period. I have adopted the period definition here, since most of the discussion will revolve around a specific interval of time. The initial formulation of the Coles Creek period was based largely on ceramics. The distinctiveness of the Coles Creek ceramic complex was first recognized by Henry B. Collins (1932:16, Pl. 14) as a result of his work at the Deasonville site (21P1) in Yazoo County, Mississippi, but James A. Ford (1935, 1936:172–218) was the first to define the complex in detail. The Greenhouse site (28H2), a major mound complex in Avoyelles Parish, Louisiana, still remains the principal site upon which the Coles Creek definition is based (Belmont 1967; Ford 1951). Our understanding of this period has expanded in recent years from work in the Tensas and Yazoo basins (Brain 1969; Phillips 1970; Williams and Brain n.d.; Williams, Kean, and Toth 1966).

Coles Creek culture, characterized by its many small ceremonial centers (with platform mounds) surrounded by villages of varying sizes, developed between the mouth of the Red River in Louisiana and the southern portion of the Yazoo Basin in Mississippi in the late first millennium A.D. But Coles Creek influences also filtered into other areas, including the Louisiana delta. As a result, contemporary cultural developments in this area have been subsumed under the Coles Creek period (Kniffen 1936; McIntire 1958; Phillips 1970:920–22; Neuman 1977:16–17). Although the delta received strong stimulation from the north at this time, in both material culture and mound construction, important influences from coastal cultures to the east were also affecting delta populations. I will summarize our present knowledge of Coles Creek lifeways in the Louisiana delta, including data on settlement, subsistence, and material culture, focusing in particular on the Petite Anse region of west-central Louisiana, the area with which I am most familiar.

The Petite Anse region (fig. 4.1) includes portions of St. Mary, Iberia, and Vermilion parishes. It consists of five salt domes, the adjacent prairie terrace, the marshes, and the easternmost portion of the chenier plain. The Lower Mississippi Survey (LMS) of the Peabody Museum, Harvard University, conducted site survey and excavations in this region in 1978 and 1979 (Brown 1978a, b, 1979a–c, 1980a, b,

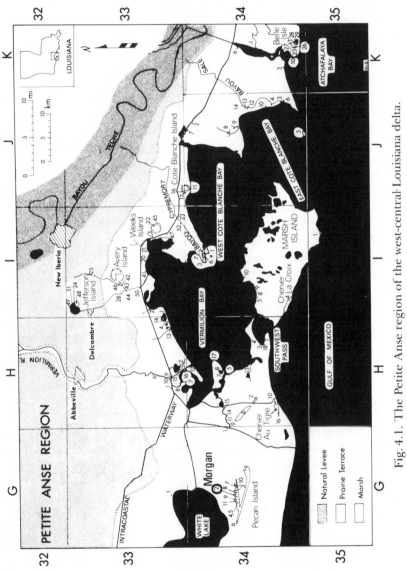

Fig. 4.1. The Petite Anse region of the west-central Louisiana delta.

1980–81, 1981, n.d.; Brown and Lambert-Brown 1978a–g; 1979; Brown, Fuller, and Lambert-Brown 1979). Although the region obviously represents only a microcosm of Coles Creek culture on the Louisiana coast, certain similarities in settlement, subsistence, and material culture were shared with contemporary peoples to the west and east.

Archaeological background

Coles Creek on the coast is currently dated between A.D. 700 and A.D. 1000. When Phillips' volume (1970) on the archaeology of the Lower Yazoo Basin came out, there was only one Coles Creek phase defined for the entire coast. It was called Bayou Cutler in honor of Kniffen's pottery complex (1936) of the same name. Phillips realized the phase needed subdividing, but he was unable to do so on the basis of the current literature. His definition of the Bayou Cutler phase was based solely on second-hand pottery counts resulting from McIntire's delta survey (1958), a limitation that Phillips (1970:920–22) freely admitted.

In the last ten years, our understanding of Coles Creek culture history in the delta has been refined markedly (fig. 4.2), largely due to archaeological work conducted by Coastal Environments, Inc. of Baton Rouge. The industry of Richard Weinstein, Sherwood Gagliano, Eileen Burden, Diane Wiseman, Kathleen Brooks, and Jack Bonnin in refining Coles Creek chronology has resulted in a lasting contribution to coastal prehistory. Their work at the Mulatto Bayou site (32R15) in St. Bernard Parish (Wiseman, Weinstein, and McCloskey 1979), the Gibson site (34M5) in St. Mary Parish (Weinstein et al. 1978), and the Strohe site (16JD10) in Jefferson Davis Parish (Bonnin and Weinstein 1975, 1978) has laid the stratigraphic foundations for the Coles Creek phases in the eastern and western portions of the delta. The establishment of phases has profited significantly from Jon Gibson's work (1976a, b, 1978) along Bayou Teche, the Vermilion River, the Mermentau River, and in the Lower Achafalaya Basin; Robert Neuman's work (1976, 1977) at Weeks Island (33I3); and James Springer's investigations (1973, 1974, 1976, 1979, 1980) at the Bruly St. Martin (16IV6) and Pierre Clement (16CM47) sites.

The original Bayou Cutler phase has now been divided into six phases (Weinstein, Burden, and Gagliano 1977; Weinstein et al. 1978; Wiseman, Weinstein, and McClosky, 1979). The new Bayou Cutler phase currently pertains only to the first half of the Coles Creek pe-

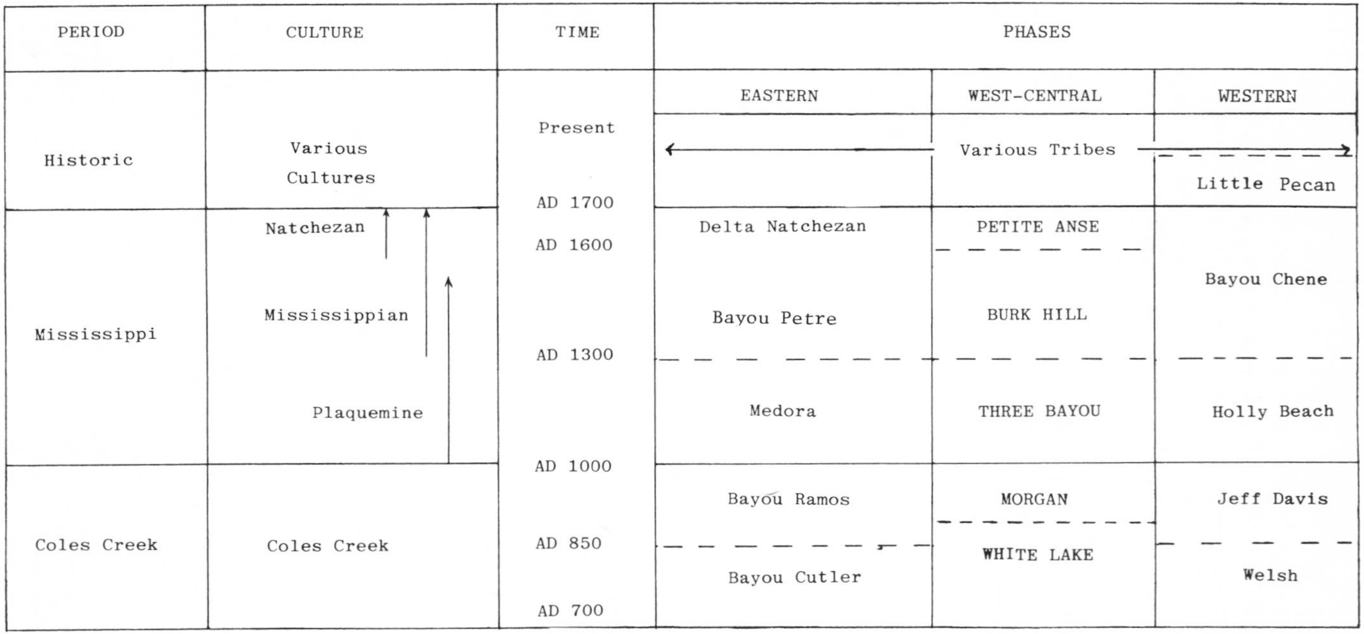

PERIOD	CULTURE	TIME	PHASES		
			EASTERN	WEST-CENTRAL	WESTERN
Historic	Various Cultures	Present		Various Tribes	Little Pecan
	Natchezan	AD 1700	Delta Natchezan	PETITE ANSE	
Mississippi	Mississippian	AD 1600	Bayou Petre	BURK HILL	Bayou Chene
	Plaquemine	AD 1300	Medora	THREE BAYOU	Holly Beach
		AD 1000	Bayou Ramos	MORGAN	Jeff Davis
Coles Creek	Coles Creek	AD 850	Bayou Cutler	WHITE LAKE	Welsh
		AD 700			

Fig. 4.2. Late prehistoric chronological sequence of the Louisiana delta (adapted from Weinstein et al. 1979: fig. 5-1).

riod in the eastern region. It is temporally equivalent to the Aden phase in the Lower Yazoo Basin. Typical ceramics of the Bayou Cutler phase are Baytown Plain, *var. Percy Creek* (often with the Bartholemew rim mode; see Brown 1980–81); Beldeau Incised, *var. Treadway* (Wiseman, Weinstein, and McCloskey 1979); Coles Creek Incised, *vars. Coles Creek* and *Campbellsville*; Mazique Incised, *var. Mazique*; Evansville Punctated, *var. Rhinehart*; French Fork Incised, *vars. Lafayette* (Gibson 1976a:34) and *Larkin*; and of course the primary decorated pottery Pontchartrain Check Stamped, *var. Pontchartrain*. (Type/ variety descriptions are in Phillips 1970, unless otherwise stated.) The Bayou Ramos phase, a rather tenuous Late Coles Creek phase equivalent temporally to the Kings Crossing phase in the Yazoo Basin, is characterized by Coles Creek Incised, *var. Mott*; Mazique Incised, *var. Kings Point*; Beldeau Incised, *var. Beldeau*; Avoyelles Punctated, *var. Avoyelles*; and Pontchartrain Check Stamped, *var. Tiger Island* (Weinstein et al. 1978). The *Pontchartrain* variety supposedly has less representation in the Bayou Ramos phase whereas French Fork Incised ceramics occur in both the Bayou Cutler and Bayou Ramos phases (Wiseman, Weinstein, and McCloskey 1979).

In the western portion of the delta, the Welsh phase is temporally equivalent to the Bayou Cutler phase. Ceramics typical of this phase are Pontchartrain Check Stamped, *vars. Pontchartrain* and *Tiger Island*; French Fork Incised, *vars. Brashear* (Weinstein et al. 1978) and *Lafayette*; Coles Creek Incised, *var. Coles Creek*; and an unclassified complicated stamped type. The later Jeff Davis phase includes Coles Creek Incised, *var. Mott*; Evansville Punctated, *var. Rhinehart*; and Baytown Plain pottery with tapered rims and fire-clouded surfaces (Weinstein et al. 1979).

The west-central delta sequence is based on the LMS investigations in the Petite Anse region. Material similarities with assemblages from sites at the mouth of the Red River suggest that the White Lake and Morgan phases are equivalent to the Middle and Late Coles Creek period, respectively (John Belmont, pers. comm.), A.D. 700–900 for White Lake and A.D. 900–1000 for Morgan. These estimates are supported by seven radiocarbon dates run by Teledyne Isotopes on charcoal samples from the Morgan site (34G2) mound 1 and midden excavations (all dates are uncorrected). Three are from definite White Lake contexts: 1190 ± 125 B.P. or A.D. 760 (I-11,997), 980 ± 120 B.P. or A.D. 970 (I-11,998), and 1210 ± 140 B.P. or A.D. 740 (I-11,999). Three others are from probable White Lake contexts: 1130 ± 75 B.P. or A.D. 820 (I-11,987), 1210 ± 75 B.P. or A.D. 740 (I-11,988), and 1055

± 150 B.P. or A.D. 895 (I-11,995). One from a Morgan phase context is 775 ± 125 B.P. or A.D. 1175 (I-11,986). The White Lake phase dates are consistent with the estimated range of A.D. 700–900, but the single Morgan phase date is slightly later than expected.

Settlement Patterns

Excavations at major mound centers, such as the Greenhouse (28H2), Winterville (19L1), and Lake George (21N1) sites, have contributed much in the way of understanding Coles Creek settlement elsewhere in the Mississippi Valley, but our knowledge of Coles Creek settlement patterns in the delta is minimal, largely because our scope of investigations has primarily been confined to test pits. Test pits are necessary for establishing chronological controls (e.g., Phillips, Ford, and Griffin 1951), but the Coles Creek peoples in the delta annoyingly did not confine their houses to the space of a 2-meter square. Small mounds, of pyramidal or truncated conical shape, were constructed by Coles Creek peoples, but mound sites were not the most usual type of settlement along the coast.

Surface survey has revealed a dense utilization of the delta during Coles Creek times. In the Petite Anse region alone, we have recorded 45 Coles Creek components, compared to 22 Marksville, 5 Troyville, and 30 Early Plaquemine (fig. 4.3). Some of these sites were small camps or hamlets situated on salt domes; typical examples are the Hayes Pond Ridge (33I8) and Middle Gate Bottom (33I33) sites on Avery Island (Brown 1980a; Brown and Lambert-Brown 1978g). Similar small sites have been found on cheniers (stranded beach ridges) in the western portion of the region. The Morgan site (34G2), situated on the Pecan Island chenier, is the only Coles Creek mound complex recorded in the Petite Anse region (Brown 1980b, 1980–81). Veazey (34G4, 5), another site on Pecan Island, is primarily known for its Marksville mounds (Collins 1927b, 1941), but an overlay of Coles Creek artifacts also exists at this site (Brown n.d.; Brown, Fuller, and Lambert-Brown 1979).

Other Coles Creek sites are located along bayous adjacent to salt domes. The Weeks Island site (33I3) is situated in this ecologically attractive location (Neuman 1976, 1977; Brown, Fuller, and Lambert-Brown 1979; Brown n.d.). But most Coles Creek sites exist in the marsh itself, located along the banks of shallow sloughs. The abundant brackish water *Rangia cuneata* clams, so apparent at low tide, are ample evidence of the attractiveness of such locations. In fact, most of the middens in the Petite Anse region are composed of clam shells, oysters being extremely rare. These small midden deposits are occasionally clustered around small, rather picturesque lagoons, as at the South of Onion Lake site (33H2) (Brown, Fuller, and Lambert-Brown, 1979; Brown n.d.).

Many shell middens are now stranded in the marsh, the bayous that once ran by them either having dried up or been diverted. Small trees, primarily hackberry, hercules club, and water locust, usually mark the location of these shell middens. Many Coles Creek sites in the region are buried under marsh muck and are known only through the industry of the dredge. Other middens are now totally surrounded by water, the result of shoreline currents eating away the marsh. Many sites are mere remnants of what they once were. A number of the Coles Creek components in the Petite Anse region are secondary beach deposits, sad testimony of the natural destruction that is occurring constantly.

Unfortunately we have little data on the types of structures the Coles Creek people lived in while occupying these shell middens, but some sort of protection against the elements is assumed. Curious phenomena detected at a number of sites are circular depressions averaging about 3 or 4 meters in diameter (fig. 4.4). We originally thought little of these features, attributing them to uprooted trees or pothunters. But some of the depressions are too large to have resulted from the scraggly growth of vegetation existing on the middens (fig. 4.5), and the thought of pothunters wading through miles of marsh to dig up a ton of shell for a reward of a few pieces of clay and bone did not make sense. Richard Beavers (1978:54) noted similar depressions in shell middens along the Sabine River on the Louisiana-Texas border. His suggestion that these were semisubterranean houses was tested in our own excavations at the Onion Lake site (33H3; Brown n.d.). A trench cut through the middle of the depression illustrated in figure 4.5 failed to reveal structural remains, but the layering clearly demonstrated that the excavation of the depression occurred in prehistoric times. Whether these features represent houses, however, remains unknown.

Subsistence patterns

Clearly the Coles Creek peoples of the Petite Anse region, and of the delta as a whole, were a marsh-adapted culture. Brian Duhe (1979) has used the expression "marsh-estuary efficiency" to describe the

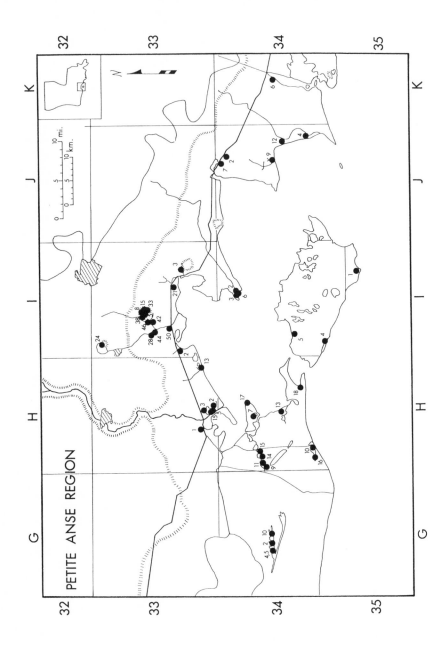

PETITE ANSE REGION

33H1	Intracoastal City (16VM33)
33H2	South of Onion Lake (16VM18)
33H3	Onion Lake (16VM17)
33H5	Onion Bayou 1 (16VM19)
33H13	Caldwell Camp (16VM105)
33H15	Onion Bayou 2 (16VM107)
33I2	Bayou Hebert (16VM26)
33I3	Weeks Island (16IB16)
33I5	Salt Mine Valley (16IB23)
33I8	Hayes Pond Ridge (16IB26)
33I15	Morningside (16IB113)
33I21	GIWW (16IB111)
33I24	Lake Peigneur (16IB100)
33I28	Bayou Carlin (16IB112)
33I33	Middle Gate Bottom (16IB137)
33I38	Bradford (16IB142)
33I42	Yellow Hills (Y16IBD)
33I44	Bottlewash (Y16IBC)
33I46	Shellbank (Y16IBA)
33I50	Fleur-de-Lis (Y16IBB)
34G2	Morgan (16VM9)
34G4, 5	Veazey (16VM7, 8)
34GI0	Copell (16VM102)
34H7	North Lake (16VM22)
34H9	Louisiana Fur Company Canal (16VM12)
34H10	Chenier au Tigre (16VM15)
34H11	Belle Isle Bayou (16VM11)
34H13	Hell Hole (16VM3)
34H14	Lege (16VM114)
34H15	Audubon (16VM115)
34H16	McIlhenny Camp (16VM116)
34H17	Redfish Point (16VM117)
34H18	Deadman Island (16VM118)
34I2	Oyster Bayou (16IB14)
34I3	Bayou Cypremort (16SMY7)
34I4	Chenier la Croix (16IB51)
34I5	Bayou Chene (16IB21)
34J2	Bayou Bartholemew (16SMY42)
34J4	Burns (16SMY6)
34J7	Mud Lake (16SMY152)
34J9	Jackson Bayou (16SMY154)
34J12	Salevee (16SMY157)
34K6	Possum Point (16SMY31)
35I1	Mound Point (16IB14)

Fig. 4.3. Coles Creek components in the Petite Anse region.

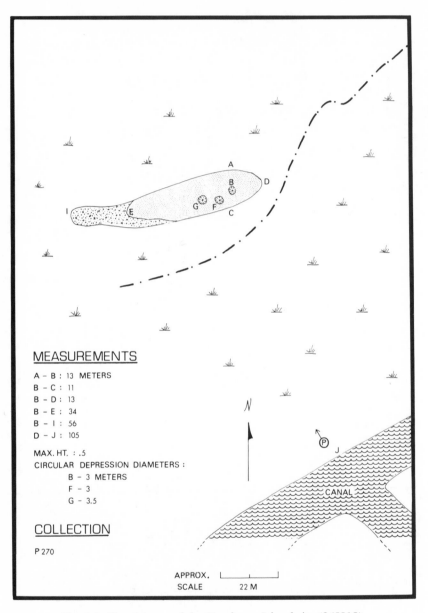

MEASUREMENTS

A – B : 13 METERS
B – C : 11
B – D : 13
B – E : 34
B – I : 56
D – J : 105

MAX. HT. : .5
CIRCULAR DEPRESSION DIAMETERS :
        B – 3 METERS
        F – 3
        G – 3.5

COLLECTION

P 270

APPROX.
SCALE   22 M

Fig. 4.4. Sketch map of the Deadman Island site (34H18).

principal adaptation of Troyville–Coles Creek peoples along the coast. Although clams were indeed an integral part of the Coles Creek diet, they were responsible for only a small portion of the overall subsistence (Byrd 1976a). And yet these shell middens are scattered throughout the delta. As there are relatively few places in the marsh

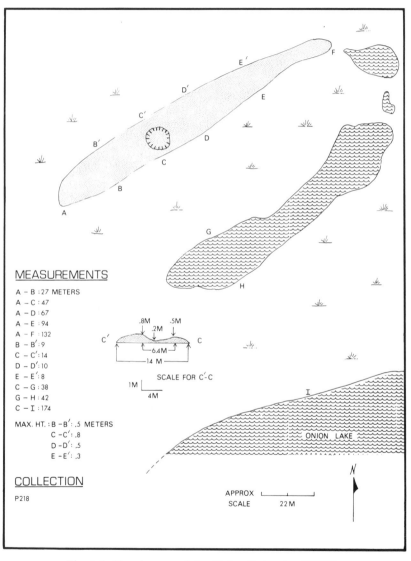

MEASUREMENTS

A – B : 27 METERS
A – C : 47
A – D : 67
A – E : 94
A – F : 132
B – B′ : 9
C – C′ : 14
D – D′ : 10
E – E′ : 8
C – G : 38
G – H : 42
C – I : 174

MAX. HT. : B – B′ : .5 METERS
C – C′ : .8
D – D′ : .5
E – E′ : .3

COLLECTION

P218

Fig. 4.5. Sketch map of the Onion Lake site (33H3).

itself that are dry enough for occupation, it is possible that Coles Creek peoples consumed shellfish primarily for the shell byproduct. One significant aspect of clam consumption is that the shells did provide a base for settlement in the marsh.

On the basis of excavations at Bruly St. Martin (16IV6), a Troyville–Coles Creek site located in Iberville Parish just west of New Orleans, James Springer (1980) revealed that fish were an extremely important part of the Coles Creek diet, much more than mammals at this site. Large fish, such as catfish and gar, were particularly common at that site. The most numerous mammals were deer, followed by bear, then by equal amounts of muskrat and raccoon. Reptiles formed only a minor part of the diet; birds were somewhat better represented, coots and ducks the most common, followed by geese and cormorants.

In the western delta we have some subsistence information from the Pierre Clement site (16CM47) on Little Chenier Ridge. Springer (1979) assigned a date of fourteenth century A.D. to this site on the basis of two radiocarbon dates, but it is clear from the material culture that the site is multicomponent. The Coles Creek period is well represented, and some of the bones were undoubtedly deposited by Coles Creek peoples. Mammals had a much stronger representation at Pierre Clement than at Bruly St. Martin. Muskrat, white-tailed deer, and raccoon were particularly strong, with weasel and otter also in evidence. Fish included gar, bowfin, sucker, and freshwater drum, and turtle and bird bones were also recovered.

In the west-central portion of the delta, much of our knowledge concerning Coles Creek subsistence comes from Weeks Island (3313) in Iberia Parish. Robin Futch's analysis (1979) of the faunal remains at this site revealed fish to be most common, both in terms of the number of elements and the minimum number of individuals. Typical fish were bowfin, gar, freshwater catfish, buffalo fish, and bass. A number of marine species were also found. As at Bruly St. Martin, mammals were second to fish at Weeks Island but did form the most important class of food in terms of biomass. Primary mammals during Coles Creek–Troyville times at this site were deer, muskrat, and raccoon; secondary mammals included opossum, swamp rabbit; eastern cottontail, and bobcat. Unlike Bruly St. Martin, reptiles were much more important in the diet of Coles Creek peoples at Weeks Island; the variety of turtles consumed included box turtles, pondsliders, mud turtles, common snapping turtles, and alligator snapping turtles. Birds eaten included Canada geese, snow geese, white-fronted geese, and wild turkeys.

The Morgan site (34G2) on Pecan Island in Vermilion Parish also has contributed information concerning Coles Creek subsistence preferences. Two test pits were excavated at this site, one in a deep midden deposit (P862) and another in slope wash from Mound 1 (P863) (fig. 4.6). The faunal assemblage from these pits was analyzed by Elizabeth S. Wing of the Florida State Museum and two of her assistants (Arthur Schneider and Sylvia Scudder), the data being reworked into final form by myself (Brown n.d.). Similar to both Pierre Clement and Weeks Island, principal mammalian species at Morgan were muskrat, deer, and raccoon. These three animals probably form the nucleus of Coles Creek diet in the Louisiana Delta, but it should be pointed out that they were undoubtedly also valued for their pelts. The most common reptiles were mud turtles and snapping turtles (both common and alligator), and the bowfin was the usual species of fishes encountered. Mammals of secondary importance included opossum, rabbit, gray wolf, river otter, mink, and bobcat. Secondary reptile species consisted of alligator, box turtle, painted turtle, Florida softshell, and green turtle. Secondary fishes included gar, alligator gar, sea catfish, gafftopsail catfish, white catfish, bass, black drum, red drum, and striped mullet. Birds were rare at Morgan, but included both migratory and year-round residents: pied-billed grebe, great egret, Canada goose, mottled duck, pochard, and American coot. A striking disconformity in the distribution of the faunal remains occurred at Morgan. Whereas turtles and fish were most common in the midden, mammals were more frequently found in the deposits washing down from the top of Mound 1. The differences may be a reflection of status. The individuals who occupied the mounds seem to have received higher proportions of deer and muskrat meat than the persons who resided in the flats between the mounds. Fish and turtle meat perhaps were considered low-class foods.

Material culture

For Coles Creek populations on the coast, material culture means primarily pottery. Bone and stone artifacts occasionally turn up on Coles Creek sites, but they are rare. The study of the pottery manufactured and decorated by these peoples provides the clearest evidence for long-range relations with peoples to the north and with other coastal populations to the east and west. The data presented here are from the Petite Anse region, a significant portion of the information coming from the test excavations at Morgan (fig. 4.6). The midden test

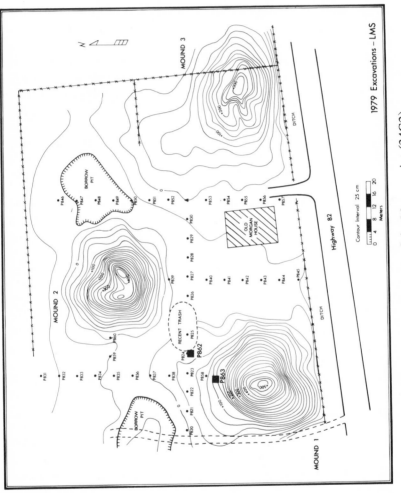

Fig. 4.6. Contour map of the Morgan site (34G2).

produced White Lake and Morgan phase materials (fig. 4.2), the latter being confined primarily to the top 20 centimeters. The mound test provided evidence only for the Morgan phase (Brown 1980b, 1980–81). I want to emphasize that the division between the two phases is an archaeological construct; there are no abrupt changes. The differences are largely in the form of varying percentages in the ceramic varieties and in changing rim mode treatments. Overall, the occupation of the site was continuous. The division of the sequence into phases primarily provides a means for refining chronological control. I also stress that the White Lake and Morgan phases are largely based upon two test pits and may not be indicative of changes experienced over the entire site, much less, for that matter, in the region as a whole. I believe that they are so indicative, but obviously more stratigraphic excavations are needed.

What follows is a survey of some of the principal decorated ceramics used during the White Lake and Morgan phases in the Petite Anse region. These objects are still undergoing analysis, so some conclusions here are subject to revision. First, I must point out the rarity of a number of important Coles Creek markers; Chevalier Stamped, *var. Chevalier* and Evansville Punctated, *var. Rhinehart* are virtually absent in the Petite Anse region, yet these ceramics are common in Cole Creek assemblages elsewhere in the delta and in other portions of the lower Mississippi valley. The classic varieties of Coles Creek Incised, *var. Coles Creek* and *Mott*, are also rare in the Petite Anse region during the Coles Creek period. What we do get during Coles Creek is something reminiscent of Coles Creek Incised, *var. Stoner*, a single overhanging line occurring far below the lip of the vessel. But unlike *Stoner*, the ware of the sherds is thin and polished, equivalent to Baytown Plain, *var. Vicksburg*. I call this pottery Coles Creek Incised, *var. Pecan* (fig. 4.7a).

Even more common is a variety of Coles Creek Incised bearing pointed or overhanging incisions with punctations placed randomly or in even rows between the lines. Some of these vessels occasionally bear a white slip or paint. At the Mulatto Bayou site (32R15) this type of decoration is classified as Coles Creek Incised, *var. Athanasio* (Wiseman et al. 1979). Identical material at the Greenhouse site (28H2) has been referred to as Coles Creek Incised, *var. Curtis* (John Belmont, pers. comm.; Ford 1951:74, pl. 16L, R). *Athanasio* also includes sherds bearing punctations within the incisions themselves, but Belmont (pers. comm.) has classified such material at Greenhouse (Ford 1951: pl. 16P–Q) as a separate variety (*Dozier*) of the Coles Creek

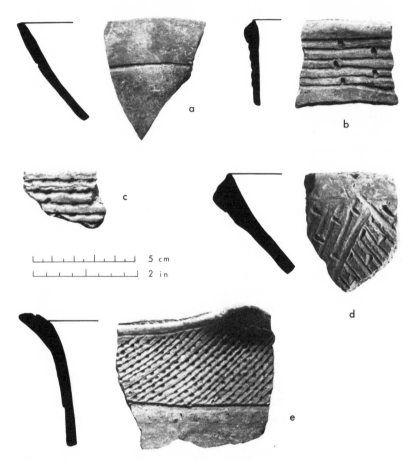

Fig. 4.7. Coles Creek period ceramics from the Petite Anse region. Coles Creek Incised: (a) *var. Pecan*; (b) *var. Athanasio*; (c) *var. Dozier*. Mazique Incised: (d) *var. Back Ridge*; (e) *var. Sweet Bay*. Provenience, Morgan (34G2): (a) P862F; (b) P862C1; (c) P862E2; (d) P862F3; (e) P862F1.

type. Both variations are common at the Morgan site. As the Mulatto Bayou site report has published precedence, I am using the *Athanasio* variety to account for sherds bearing punctations between the lines (fig. 4.7b) and the *Dozier* variety for punctations within the lines (fig. 4.7c).

Coles Creek Incised, *vars. Athanasio* and *Dozier* bear close parallels with the Florida type St. Petersburg Incised. This Late Weeden Island ceramic type is identical to the above varieties in everything but paste.

This type occurs in small numbers over the entire Florida Gulf coast, but it is fairly common around Tampa Bay on the eastern fringe of the Weeden Island region (Willey 1949:442, pls. 32g–h, 33j–k, 46f).

The same motifs carry over to the Mazique Incised type in the Petite Anse region, where the parallel lines are incised at an angle to the lip of the vessel rather than being parallel. Mazique Incised, *var. Back Ridge* bears punctations between the lines (fig. 4.7d); *var. Sweet Bay* has punctations within the incisions (fig. 4.7e). Quite a bit of care was taken in the making of Coles Creek Incised, *var. Dozier* and Mazique Incised, *var. Sweet Bay* vessels.

Another type that occurs with some frequency in the Petite Anse region is Larto Red, but this is not the *Larto* variety of Troyville times. The red slip occurs on a very thin ware equivalent to Baytown Plain, *var. Vicksburg*. Black paint occasionally accompanies the red. Larto Red, *var. Vaughn* occurs in good Coles Creek context at Morgan (fig. 4.8a). A contemporary type is Pasco Red of Central Florida and the central Gulf coast (Willey 1949:447, pl. 54A, d). Particularly well represented at the Morgan site on the Coles Creek time level is French Fork Incised, *var. Lafayette* (Gibson 1976a:34), including a variation of it which lacks the linear punctated borders (fig. 4.8b). *Var. Brashear* (Weinstein et al. 1978), however, is rare.

Complicated stamped pottery, widespread throughout the delta but generally in small amounts (Duhe 1979; Neuman 1981), is a common form of decoration at the Morgan site during the Coles Creek period. It has also turned up at a number of other sites in the Petite Anse region. I call this type Gainesville Complicated Stamped, following Jenkins' (1979) classification of complicated stamping on grog-tempered ware. Although this type is defined on the basis of investigations on the Central Tombigbee River of Mississippi and Alabama, it seems that the distribution of the type continues all along the coast. Jenkins set up *var. Gainesville* to account for sherds bearing a design of concentric circles (the bulls-eye motif). Thus far I have only established one variety of the type for west-central Louisiana, *var. Wauchope*), named in honor of Robert Wauchope, the first recorder of complicated stamped pottery in the delta (Wauchope 1947). A lot of variation in design exists in the Petite Anse region, but I have refrained from breaking the type down into additional varieties until space and time distinctions can be demonstrated.

As mentioned, the design typical of *var. Gainesville* on the Central Tombigbee River is a curvilinear treatment of concentric circles. The bulls-eye motif is also common in the Petite Anse region (fig. 4.8c),

Fig. 4.8. Coles Creek period ceramics from the Petite Anse region. Larto Red: (a) *var. Vaughn*. French Fork Incised: (b) *var. Lafayette*. Gainesville Complicated Stamped: c–g, *var. Wauchope*. Provenience, Morgan (34G2): (a) P862F2; (b) P862F3; (c) P862D; (d) P862B; (e) P862C1; (f) P862E3; (g) P863A.

but thus far I have not separated it from the other designs. In the Gainesville Reservoir the bulls-eye motif on grog-tempered ware dates to the Late Miller II subphase (A.D. 550–700), considerably earlier than *var. Wauchope*. As both Jenkins (1979) and Neuman (1981) have pointed out, this motif shares similarities with the type Swift Creek Complicated Stamped of Georgia, Florida, and Alabama. This type occasionally has a series of check-filled rays emerging from the circles (Jennings and Fairbanks 1939), a motif that has also been observed at Morgan (fig. 4.8d). However, the overall Swift Creek design is usually intricate, the bulls-eye motif forming only one small portion of the total design (Kelly 1938:27–29; Jennings and Fairbanks 1939; Willey 1949:378–83; Wimberly 1960:119–21, fig. 49A–C; Wauchope 1966: 54–57, figs. 208, 209a–z).

The bulls-eye motif is more characteristic of the southeastern types Savannah Stamped (Wauchope 1948: pl. XIXA, 1966:77–79, fig. 226), Pickwick Complicated Stamped (Haag 1939; DeJarnette and Wimberly 1941:97, fig. 72), and Lamar Stamped (Wauchope 1966: fig. 229), but these are formal relations reflecting no genetic connections. In overall design, there are close parallels with a late variant of Swift Creek Complicated Stamped found in northwestern Florida. Willey (1949: 429–31, 435, pls. 34, 35a–f) dated this variety to Weeden Island I times and described it as being a breakdown of the more elaborate earlier Swift Creek designs. The curvilinear treatment in the Petite Anse region, equivalent temporally to Weeden Island II (using Willey's terminology), represents a further breakdown.

An even closer relative, in both design and temporal positioning, is Tampa Complicated Stamped. This type, which has the bulls-eye as a principal motif, is common in the Tampa Bay–Manatee regions in Late Weeden Island times (Willey 1949:436–37, pl. 35g–j). Another contemporary type in the same region, also characterized by the bulls-eye motif, is Little Manatee Complicated Stamped (Willey 1949:444). The Tampa Bay–Manatee regions are on the eastern fringe of Weeden Island–related cultures, while the Louisiana delta is on the western fringe. As noted, the Tampa Bay–Manatee regions also share material parallels with Coles Creek Incised, *vars. Athanasio* and *Dozier*. Why these close similarities exist is a topic that merits some concern. If and when Gainesville Complicated Stamped is broken down further in the delta, the bulls-eye motif should be retained as the *Wauchope* variety.

Also characteristic of Gainesville Complicated Stamped, *var. Wauchope* is the nested rectangles motif (fig. 4.8e). Similar motifs occur on

Crooked River Complicated Stamped (late variety), which dates to Early Weeden Island times in northwestern Florida (Willey 1949: 435–36), and on Etowah Stamped (Wauchope 1948: pl. XVIIIB, row 2; 1966:64–69, fig. 217) and Lamar Stamped (Wauchope 1948: pl. XIXC; 1966:79–82, fig. 228a–g) in northern Georgia. As mentioned, Lamar Stamped also occasionally incorporates the bulls-eye as a decorative motif. St. Andrews Complicated Stamped (late variety), an Early Weeden Island ceramic of northwestern Florida, has the nested rectangle as its most common motif (Willey 1949:436), but an even closer relative temporally is Sun City Complicated Stamped. Found in the Tampa Bay–Manatee regions in Late Weeden Island times, Sun City Complicated Stamped represents a very late continuation of the nested rectangle motif along the eastern fringe of Weeden Island (Willey 1948: pl. XXd; 1949:437, pl. 36d–e). As noted, the bulls-eye motif also continues late in the Tampa Bay–Manatee regions.

A nice blend of check stamping and complicated stamping occurs in the Petite Anse region, a combination of nested triangles and square checks being the usual pattern (fig. 4.8f). Such combinations of check and complicated stamping are rare in the Southeast, but the practice has been reported from northern and southwestern Georgia and northern Florida (Duhe 1979). Willey's Florida-type New River Complicated Stamped (1949:386, fig. 29, pl. 21a–e) uses check stamping as a background decoration for curvilinear designs. Willey dated the type to the Santa Rosa–Swift Creek period, but more recent work by Milanich (1974:26, pl. 5n–o; Milanich and Fairbanks 1980:120, fig. 21c) has positioned it between A.D. 655 and A.D. 860, well within a Late Weeden Island context. It occurs as a rare type in the Upper Apalachicola Valley associated with the typical rectangular impressions of Wakulla Check Stamped, with a diamond-shaped check variant of Wakulla, and also with a linear check-stamped variant of this same type (Milanich 1974:26). As will be discussed, all of these variants are also characteristic of Pontchartrain Check Stamped pottery in the Petite Anse region during the Coles Creek period.

The material most closely related to the check and complicated stamping of the Petite Anse region may be Old Bay Complicated Stamped. This type, common in the Tampa Bay–Manatee regions in the Late Weeden Island period, is characterized by spirals, dots-in-circles, ovals, etc., against a background of small checks (Willey 1948: pl. XXe, 1949:437, pls. 35k, 36b–c). Once again we have close parallels, formally and temporally, between complicated stamped treatments in the eastern and western frontiers of Weeden Island cultural influences. It is hard to believe that this complex of motifs evolved independently, and yet an explanation for such close similarities in two areas separated by about 1,000 miles of coast does not immediately come to mind.

A final design characteristic of Gainesville Complicated Stamped, *var. Wauchope* in the Petite Anse region is the "Zipper" motif (fig. 4.8g), consisting of a linear stamped arrangement of small opposing triangular depressions. To my knowledge this motif has not appeared anywhere in the Southeast outside of this portion of the Louisiana delta.

Check-stamped pottery, in the form of Pontchartrain Check Stamped, is the most typical decorated ceramic of the Coles Creek period in the delta. A total of 5,173 Pontchartrain Check Stamped sherds from 45 sites in the Petite Anse region were analyzed and all but about 100 classified as to variety. The old and new varieties in this region are described in some detail elsewhere (Brown 1981), so I will present only a brief description of their characteristics.

The classic variety, *var. Pontchartrain*, consists of a waffle grid pattern of square or rectangular checks with all lands separating the checks having essentially the same width (fig. 4.9a). Contrary to Duhe (1979), I have refrained from dividing Pontchartrain on the basis of check size, changes in which have been found to be continuous and cyclical. Pontchartrain sherds on the whole tended to have a smaller mean size during the Morgan phase than during the earlier White Lake phase, but by the Three Bayou phase of Early Plaquemine times the size of the checks once again increased. To divide this continuous cycle into varieties does not make sense, especially when the full range of sizes existed at any one time. Therefore, I have taken the liberty of throwing Duhe's *var. Vacherie*, consisting of bold checks, and *Des Allemands*, consisting of small checks, back into the established *Pontchartrain* variety.

Another Pontchartrain Check Stamped variety found in the Petite Anse region is *var. Crawford Point* (fig. 4.9b). It consists of a grid pattern of impressed diamonds with all lands separating the checks having essentially the same width. The variety differs from Duhe's (1979) Troyville-related *var. Shellhill* in that the *Shellhill* depressed diamonds alternate with raised solid diamonds, whereas *Crawford Point's* depressed diamonds are separated by thin lands. The use of diamond-shaped impressions on check-stamped pottery has a long history in the Southeast; it is found in association with types ranging from Deptford Bold Check Stamped (Caldwell and Waring 1939) at the early

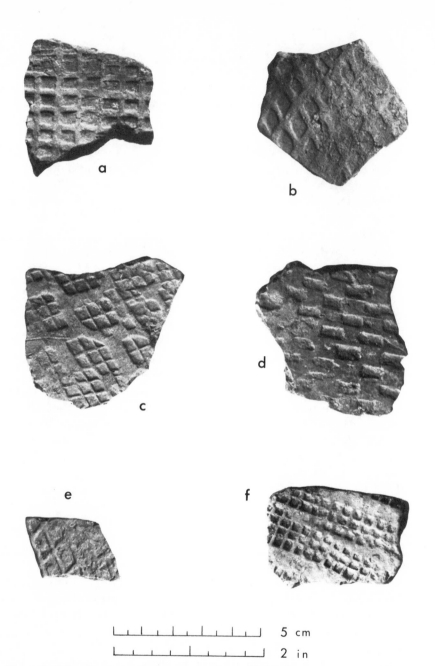

Fig. 4.9. Coles Creek period ceramics from the Petite Anse region. Pontchartrain Check Stamped: (a) *var. Pontchartrain*; (b) *var. Crawford Point*;
(c) *var. Fire Island*; (d) *var. Lambert Ridge*; (e) *var. Tabiscania*; (f) *var. Tiger Island*. Provenience, Morgan (34G2): (a) P862E3; (b) P862F1; (c) P862E1;
(d) P862D; (e) P862G2; (f) P863B.

end of the ceramic sequence to Ocmulgee Check Stamped (Fairbanks 1956) and Leon Check Stamped (Willey 1949:491–92) in historic times. The diamond impression clearly is not a good indicator of long-distance contacts, but it should be restated that a diamond-shaped variant of Wakulla Check Stamped existed in northwestern Florida contemporary with *Crawford Point* in the delta (Milanich 1974:26). *Crawford Point* reached its peak of popularity during the White Lake phase, but it continued to be made throughout the following Morgan phase.

Another variety of Pontchartrain Check Stamped represented commonly at Morgan is *var. Fire Island* (fig. 4.9c). It is characterized by a complex design of large diamond-shaped impressions containing a set of smaller checks of diamond or rhomboidal shape. This variety fits firmly within the White Lake phase of the Coles Creek period. Nothing like it, to my knowledge, has ever been found in the Southeast.

Lambert Ridge, another Pontchartrain Check Stamped variety, also has a strong representation at the Morgan site (fig. 4.9d). It consists of a checkerboard design of squares, rectangles, or oblong-shaped impressions. This variety occurs in both the White Lake and Morgan phases, but the design is rare overall in southeastern check-stamped pottery.

Another Pontchartrain Check Stamped variety, *Tabiscania*, was originally defined by Duhe (1979) as a Troyville marker. It has a grid pattern of squares, rectangles, or diamonds, each check containing a raised dot. The diamond-shaped check is most common at Morgan (fig. 4.9e), but the variety itself is rare. Raised dots within checks have also been noted on the type Deptford Geometric Stamped at the mouth of the Savannah River (Milanich and Fairbanks 1980:83) and on Leon Check Stamped in northwestern Florida (Milanich and Fairbanks 1980: fig. 42d).

The final check-stamped variety is *Tiger Island* (Weinstein et al. 1978; Duhe 1979). This variety is a form of linear check stamping, a series of check rows with narrow lands separated from other series by wide lands (fig. 4.9f). The wooden paddle was carved with anywhere from one to seven rows of checks, with two rows the norm in the Petite Anse region. The technique of linear check stamping has a long history in the Southeast, beginning with the type Deptford Linear Check Stamped (Caldwell and Waring 1939; Willey 1949:354–356, fig. 21, pl. 12) and its close cousins Booger Bottom Linear Check Stamped (Caldwell, Thompson, and Caldwell 1952:325, fig. 101; Wauchope 1966:48–52) and McLeod Linear Check Stamped (Wimberly 1953a, 1960:130–32, fig. 60B, D, F). A variant of linear check stamping occurs with Wakulla Check Stamped in southern Alabama (Wimberly 1960:177, fig. 63C), with Wakulla in northwestern Florida (Milanich 1974:26–27, pl. 5a–h; Milanich and Fairbanks 1980:129), with St. Johns Check Stamped in eastern Florida (Ferguson 1951:28), and with Glades Check Stamped in southern Florida (Ferguson 1951:30, pl. 3BB). The last three types mentioned above are roughly contemporary with Pontchartrain Check Stamped, *var. Pontchartrain* on the Louisiana Gulf coast. I tend to agree with Milanich (1974:27) that wherever check-stamped pottery occurs in abundance, some instances of simple stamping and linear check stamping also appear. The presence of such techniques is not necessarily evidence for an Early Woodland dateline. In the Petite Anse region the *Tiger Island* variety reached its peak of popularity during the White Lake phase but continued to be made with some strength during the Morgan phase.

Of the six varieties of Pontchartrain Check Stamped defined for the Petite Anse region, three varieties have thus far been recorded only for the Morgan site: *Fire Island, Lambert Ridge,* and *Tabiscania.* The other three varieties, especially *Pontchartrain,* are well distributed in the region (Brown 1981). Although *Pontchartrain, Tiger Island,* and *Crawford Point* were all made throughout the Coles Creek period, only *Pontchartrain* maintained its strength during Late Coles Creek times, continuing as a major ceramic during the Early Plaquemine Three Bayou phase. *Crawford Point* and *Tiger Island* peaked during the White Lake phase, and the *Fire Island* variety seems to be confined just to the earlier half of the period. Overall, it appears as if there was much more variation in Pontchartrain Check Stamped during the White Lake phase than in the Morgan phase.

In addition to creating new varieties of Pontchartrain Check Stamped, I have set up a number of rim modes on the basis of the Petite Anse investigations (Brown 1981). It was felt that a rim mode analysis would complement the type-variety approach in dealing with this assemblage and would perhaps be even more sensitive than varieties in determining space and time dimensions. Basically, the modes depicted in figure 4.10 are descriptive, what Rouse (1972:56–57) called intrinsic modes. They primarily reveal which attributes of a class of features are alike. These modes crosscut varieties. Some of the modes to be discussed fall into the realm of extrinsic modes as they shed light on the way in which features were made or used (Rouse 1972:56–57). The principal Pontchartrain rim modes in the Petite Anse region not only are numbered but are given a name. The others

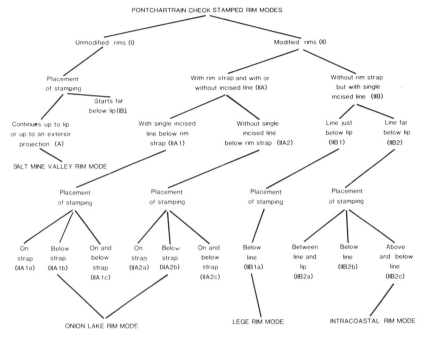

Fig. 4.10. Dendritic graph of Pontchartrain Check Stamped rim modes.

are presented because they may turn out to be significant modes in other portions of the delta.

One of the most common modes in the region is the Salt Mine Valley rim mode (fig. 4.11a), an unmodified rim with stamping continuing either right up to the lip of the vessel or up to an exterior projection. This mode is common in the White Lake and Morgan phases of the Coles Creek period and in the Early Plaquemine Three Bayou phase.

The Onion Lake rim mode, also extremely common, is characterized by an exterior rim strap, either with or without an incised line beneath the strap (fig. 4.11b–c). Stamping occurs below the strap. The Onion Lake rim mode is common during both the White Lake and the Morgan phases.

Somewhat less common but still well represented in the Petite Anse region is the Lege rim mode (fig. 4.11d). This rim has a single incised line located close to the lip, with stamping occurring below the line. This mode occurs in the Morgan phase and possibly in the White Lake phase.

Fig. 4.11. Pontchartrain Check Stamped rim modes in the Petite Anse region, *var. Pontchartrain*: (a) Salt Mine Valley rim mode; (b, c) Onion Lake rim mode; (d) Lege rim mode; (e) Intracoastal rim mode; (f) IIA2c rim mode. Provenience: Morgan (34G2): (a, e) P863A; (b) P862E3; (c) P862B; (f) P862G1; Onion Lake (33H3): (d) P878D1.

The fourth most numerous rim mode associated with Pontchartrain Check Stamped vessels is called the Intracoastal rim mode (Fig. 4.11e). It consists of a rim bearing an incised line located far below the lip, with stamping both above and below the line. As with the Lege rim mode, the Intracoastal mode definitely occurs during the Morgan phase and possibly during the White Lake phase.

The rim mode depicted in figure 4.11f has thus far only been given a number (IIA2c), as it is not as common as the other modes described. It probably should be named, though, because I think it will be found in considerable numbers east of the Petite Anse region. It is characterized by a rim strap, usually flattened, with stamping both on and below the strap. It has been found in large quantites on Wakulla Check Stamped in southern Alabama.

The rim modes associated with the established *Pontchartrain* variety at Morgan were analyzed with regard to provenience and function. It was assumed that flared jars, incurved jars, and beakers reflect the functions of cooking and storing food, bowls and plates reflect serving food. The analysis, which is discussed in detail elsewhere (Brown 1981), can be summarized as follows. The midden is characterized primarily by *Pontchartrain* vessels bearing the Salt Mine Valley and Onion Lake rim modes. Although cooking, storing, and serving functions are well represented in the midden, there is an emphasis on cooking-storing activities. The mound is also most strongly represented by the Salt Mine Valley rim mode, but the Onion Lake mode is scarce. Also occurring with some frequency, compared to the midden, are the Lege and Intracoastal rim modes. As in the midden, cooking, storing, and serving activities are well represented in the mound sample, but in this case there is a heavier representation of the serving function. I interpret the cultural significance of the different distributions to be that cooking and storing activities primarily occurred apart from the mounds and that serving activities were more common on the mounds. This interpretation is not surprising; one would expect the persons who occupied the mounds at Morgan to have been more accustomed to receiving than preparing food. As mentioned, those living on top of the mounds apparently were also more accustomed to eating mammal meat from these same serving vessels.

The rim mode analysis has refined the developmental history of Pontchartrain Check Stamped in the Petite Anse region and, through a consideration of function, has also contributed to our understanding of Coles Creek social behavior. Perhaps even more than varieties, vessel form and rim modes can highlight long-range cultural relationships. For example, it has long been known that three major check stamped types on the Gulf and south Atlantic coasts are generally contemporaneous in the interval between A.D. 700 and A.D. 1000. The broadly distributed St. Johns Check Stamped in eastern Florida, Wakulla Check Stamped in northwestern Florida and southern Alabama, and Pontchartrain Check Stamped in the Louisiana delta are the most clear-cut reflections of extensive coastal contacts in the St. Johns IIA, the Late Weeden Island, and the Coles Creek periods. No one, to my knowledge, has approached the comparison of these ceramics beyond the type level (e.g., Ford 1952), yet strong similarities in vessel form and rim modes exist along the extensive span of the Gulf coast. For example, the bowls and slightly flaring jars of Wakulla Check Stamped in southern Alabama (Wimberly 1960: fig. 62) reveal similarities with Pontchartrain not only in terms of vessel shape; the continuation of stamping up to the lip is equivalent to our Salt Mine Valley rim mode. Similarly, the Onion Lake and Lege rim modes are commonly seen on Wakulla Check Stamped in southern Alabama (Wimberly 1960: fig. 61). In Florida, the Onion Lake rim mode is called the "Weeden Island" rim (Milanich 1980:13). Most typical of Wakulla Check Stamped in Alabama is stamping on and below flattened rim straps (Wimberly 1960: fig. 63A–B). This rim mode occurs in the Petite Anse region (fig. 4.11f), but it is not found as frequently as the named modes. As mentioned, I suspect that it occurs more commonly in areas east of the Petite Anse region. This same rim mode is character-istic of Wakulla Check Stamped in Florida (Willey 1949: pl. 39a). The Onion Lake rim mode also occurs in northwestern Florida, as do the Intracoastal, the Lege, and the Salt Mine Valley rim modes (Willey 1949: pl. 39b, 40a, b, d–g). Clearly some important long-range cul-ture contacts are being reflected by the similarities in Pontchartrain Check Stamped rim modes over an extensive portion of the Gulf coast.

Summary

It should be evident that the Coles Creek period in the Louisiana delta represents one small part of a complex network of coastal and interior interaction. My discussion has largely revolved around con-nections with peoples to the east, but it should be noted that northern influences along the Louisiana coast were strong also. The appear-ance of the platform mound tradition in the delta and its associated ceremonial connotations is undoubtedly the result of stimuli from Coles Creek populations in the Tensas Basin–Red River Mouth re-gions to the north. But with regard to the standard utilitarian wares employed by delta Coles Creek peoples, connections are as strong, if not stronger, to the east. These relations are particularly evident for check-stamped pottery, especially rim modes, but there are close par-allels in complicated stamped pottery. Curiously, designs most similar to those associated with complicated stamping in the Petite Anse re-gion occur over 1,000 miles away in the Tampa Bay–Manatee regions of Florida. These regions are on the eastern fringe of an extensive zone of interaction dominated by Weeden Island–related cultures, whereas the chenier plain of Louisiana is on the western fringe. Why such decorative similarities should exist on the frontiers of the Late Weeden Island interaction network is at present unexplainable.

In addition to Coles Creek in the Louisiana delta, Weeden Island–related cultures had a strong impact on eastern Florida. Milanich and Fairbanks (1980:157–66) argue that the sudden appearance and rapid dominance of check stamping in the St. Johns region of eastern Florida was the result of strong influences emanating out of Weeden Island to the west. They see Weeden Island II influences occurring mainly in the realm of subsistence, primarily in regard to new ideas concerning maize horticulture. I have argued elsewhere (Brown 1979b; Brown, Fuller, and Lambert-Brown 1979) that horticulture probably did not constitute a significant portion of coastal subsistence systems until the Early Plaquemine Three Bayou phase in the Petite Anse region, but it is possible that maize horticulture was attaining some importance as early as the Coles Creek period in the delta. It is also possible that the material similarities between the regions are a reflection of contacts in other realms of life such as ceremonialism, but it should be reemphasized that the check-stamped pottery has utilitarian, not ceremonial significance.

At this time we do not know why the extensive similarities over the Gulf coast occur. Detailed descriptions and distributional studies of the various pottery decorations, vessel shapes, and rim modes are needed to resolve this cultural-historical problem. To shed light on evolving adaptive systems, so that we understand the lifeways of the people making the contacts, we also need more studies on the changing forms of subsistence and settlement patterns in the respective regions. Much has been done in the last decade to improve our knowledge of the Coles Creek period in the Louisiana delta and its relations to cultural developments to the east, but much still remains to be done.

Note

Many people contributed to the research upon which this paper is based. I particularly would like to thank Walter S. McIlhenny and John S. McIlhenny for their continued support of the Petite Anse Project. Financial aid was also received from the State of Louisiana (Historic Preservation Grant-In-Aid Award), the International Salt Company, and Avery Island, Inc. The Thaw Fellowship, awarded me by the Peabody Museum of Archaeology and Ethnology, Harvard University, provided additional support while the paper was being written. Other individuals who contributed directly to the success of the project are Edward M. Simmons, Lanier Simmons, Stephen Williams, Kathleen M. Byrd, Nancy Lambert-Brown, Richard S. Fuller, and many others too numerous to list. Edmund McIlhenny, Jr., and Paul S. McIlhenny generously offered the use of their hunting camp while excavations were being conducted on Pecan Island, and International Salt Company donated space for lab facilities for the duration of the project. Robert Neuman graciously permitted the examination of the Louisiana State University collections at various stages of the research. As always, Jeffrey P. Brain and John S. Belmont are my critics and conscience.

5

The Mississippi Gulf Coast

Dale Greenwell

If Gulf coast archaeologists agree on one point without hesitation, it is that Mississippi represents the major gap in published archaeological data. Much of the speculation about the causes of prehistoric cultural similarities between the lower Mississippi valley and Florida could be either strengthened or laid to rest if more were known about the Woodland and Mississippian prehistory of coastal Mississippi. Moreover, the Mississippi Gulf coast is an interesting area in its own right, differing environmentally from the massive delta-estuarine systems that dominate adjacent coastal Alabama and southeastern Louisiana.

Dale Greenwell makes an important contribution to an otherwise small literature. Although this volume is concerned primarily with the Woodland and Mississippian, Greenwell has included brief discussions of Paleo-Indian and Archaic materials because of the paucity of other published data from those periods on the Mississippi coast. For the Woodland and Mississippian, Greenwell summarizes a large corpus of mostly unpublished and often intriguing data, and he points, by example, to a potentially vibrant future for the study of prehistoric cultural change in coastal Mississippi.

THE Mississippi Gulf coast (fig. 5.1) (hereafter identified as the coast) has become, since 1970, an area of increasing archaeological interest

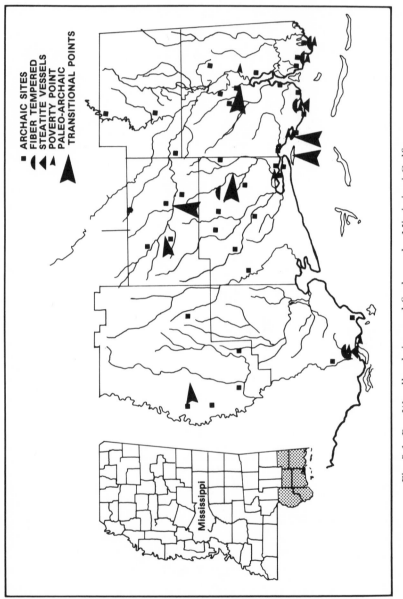

Fig. 5.1. Pre-Woodland sites and finds on the Mississippi Gulf coast.

and research. Earliest archaeological investigations by Clarence B. Moore in 1902 (Moore 1905b) and Calvin S. Brown in 1916 (Brown 1962) were little more than cursory surveys, consisting of brief visits to known mounds and middens, with no scientific procedures involved.

The first major site project was the excavation of the cemetery and middens at the Taneksanya site (22Ja504) in Jackson County in 1968. It was followed by accelerated archaeological activity on the coast. Richard Marshall of Mississippi State University conducted short summer field sessions at the Claiborne site (22HN501) and the International Paper Company site in Moss Point for several years prior to 1973. In 1968, I began to gather data on general subsistence-settlement patterns and to establish a workable ceramic classification for the Mississippi coast. Since 1970, the South Mississippi Archaeological Research Group (SMARG) and archaeology students from the University of Southern Mississippi, under my direction, have engaged in major excavations of eight sites and limited fieldwork on 13. More than 200 sites were sampled along the coast and more than 150 off the coast. The data collected have allowed the construction of a ceramic space-time distribution model for southeastern Mississippi and have provided information on house patterns, socioeconomic patterns, and artifact changes and distributions through time.

This chapter provides an overview of current knowledge of coastal Mississippi prehistory. Since so little in the way of site reports has been published, the discussion centers around a series of representative sites of the major prehistoric cultural periods. Attention is focused primarily upon the Woodland and Mississippian periods, which have been the principal research focus on the coast.

Paleo-Indian period

Although some private collections from southeastern Mississippi may contain a number of Paleo-Indian points, I have seen only two Clovis-like fluted points and one Dalton point. One of the fluted points is from a creek bottom in Jackson County, the other from a shelf overlooking a creek in Marion County (fig. 5.2, A), both of which should date to ca. 10,000 B.C. The Dalton point (fig. 5.2, D) was recovered from the Claiborne area in Hancock County on the Pleistocene terrace overlooking the Pearl River delta (Jerry Carver collection).

A common point found throughout Mississippi and believed to be from the transitional period (Paleo-Archaic 8000–6000 B.C.) is as yet

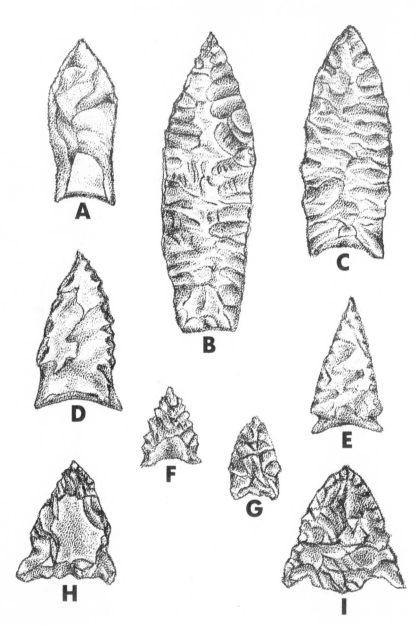

Fig. 5.2. Paleo and Archaic points from the Mississippi Gulf coast: (A) Clovis; (B) Angostura; (C) Searcy (?); (D) Dalton; (E) Cache River; (F) San Patrice (variant?); (G) unspecified; (H) Early-Middle Archaic; (I) Middle Archaic.

unnamed and has not been recovered from any dated context. It is produced from a thin flake, usually of flint or fine chert, pressure-flaked, trianguloid with serrated convexed siding, small side notching, concave ground base, and 4–6 centimeters in length (fig. 5.2, F and G). Five of these points have been found at one small site, Deer Island (22Hr501), off the Biloxi peninsula; no other artifacts were present. The five points were on the level of a fire lens within a shell midden on an eroding beachfront. Others have been collected throughout southeastern Mississippi. Deer Island is an oyster shell midden and does not contain other dietary remains.

Archaic

After the commencement of the Archaic period, the riverine-ridge environment gradually became an estuarine-ridge environment. The pursuit of forest fauna probably declined with the collecting of the ever-increasing varieties of edible plants, nuts, and berries.

Along the Mississippi coast, Archaic people were probably organized in small, nomadic groups; no midden remains of the preceramic periods on the coast suggest large population units. No Archaic house patterns, cemeteries, or long-term collecting stations have yet been identified, except for the limited information collected at the Powers site (22Ja588). It may be assumed that many Archaic middens rest below sea level, since we find shell middens of the succeeding Woodland period as much as 6 or 7 feet below sea level several miles offshore.

The large stemmed and corner-notched projectile points of the Early Archaic period are common in southeastern Mississippi. Riverine and lacustrine terraces retain most of the Archaic sites, which are characterized by reddened fire areas, cracked, fired stones, and debitage. Usually, there is a resource for pebbles nearby, and lithic workshop activity is abundant. Lithic stations are not found on the coast proper, because there are no such resources within 20 miles of the Gulf. The types of projectile points are numerous and include virtually the full range of southeastern and southwestern types (Bell 1958, 1960; Perino 1968, 1971).

Lithic materials include cherts, jasper, quartzite (especially "sugar-stone"), and flints from as far away as Arkansas, Tennessee, North Alabama, and Georgia, as well as native stone. Broad points with straight stems made from Dover chert have been found in every county of the coast area. Broad points of "sugar-stone" and smoky quartz have been found in the western area of the coast. No debitage has been recovered from Archaic sites along the coast, suggesting that point manufacture occurred elsewhere. Excavations on the Pearl River in Hancock County failed to produce retouched flakes, preforms, or debitage.

Preform caches have been found on the Wolf River and on Palmer Creek, both about 20 miles north of the coast. Lithic resources improve in quality, quantity, and size farther north, with suitable cobbles for knapping available approximately 60 miles inland. On inland river terraces, work stations provide vast quantities of debitage and discarded preforms and blanks.

The Powers site (22Ja588) in Jackson County, 20 miles up the Pascagoula River valley from the coast, is the best known Archaic site in the southeastern Mississippi area. Excavations in 1973 and 1978–79 produced sufficient data to reconstruct much of the activity there; the site is a good example of a small group of Archaic people revisiting a riverside camp over a number of years.

Carbonized scuppernong (*Bullis*), acorns, and hickory nuts (Lionel Eleuterius, pers. comm.) reflect late summer or early fall visits. Any faunal remains have disappeared. Postmolds suggest wind shelters or possibly small pole huts covered with light materials. Some hearths contain quantities of clay daubs of amorphous shapes, probably used to parch nuts or other foods. Hammerstones, a nut stone, honing stone, gravers, perforators, micro blades, and spear points were collected along with dart points. Several fire pits, each containing several dozen fire-hardened clay daubs, were filled with ash; those pits also produced nutshells and seeds.

Lithic artifacts include one point reminiscent of a Scottsbluff, but most points are of the Stanley type. The site has numerous occupation lenses, with the material described above being the lowest; that stratum is about 80 centimeters below the surface in an aeolian bluff formation of late Pleistocene–early Holocene age (Ervin Otvos, pers. comm.).

Late Archaic sites are usually found along estuarine shorelines that have been destroyed by erosion; the original midden matrix is usually disturbed, destroying the original context of the artifacts. Large blades and points similar to Lange (Bell 1958:figs. B, C, D, pl. 18) and Ledbetter (Bell 1958:pl. 33, figs. A–F) appear, along with other varieties common to the late Archaic period in the southeastern United States.

Bar weights, bola or net weights, drills, side and end scrapers, perforators, large flake blades, and amorphous clay cooking (?) balls begin to appear on the same sites. Many of the artifacts identified by

Turnbaugh (1978) in a number of maritime environments are present on the Mississippi coast. Stemmed lithic scrapers are absent, but shells probably served equally well. I am confident there are many intact sites along the coast awaiting discovery. Numerous sites located more than 40 miles from the coast have been identified and surface collected but not yet excavated.

Poverty Point

Jon Gibson (1973, 1974a, b) and Clarence Webb (1968, 1970, 1977) have described Poverty Point materials collected from three sites along the Mississippi Gulf coast (Greenwood Island, Apple Street, and Claiborne).

In 1969 and 1979, I directed excavations at Claiborne. The 1969 work was carried out to the north of the ravine (location of the major midden deposits), where at a depth of 15 centimeters below the surface a postmold pattern was discovered. Bulldozer activity had removed the plow zone of perhaps 10–15 centimeters. Three hut rings were ultimately unearthed, each facing a common center southward (fig. 5.3). The huts were constructed of cane poles and were probably covered with thatch or palmetto. They averaged 4.7 meters in diameter. Each appeared to have an entryway before the door, like the igloos of the Arctic region.

In one hut small fire pits were found on each side of the door, inside, both filled with ash. They may have been smoke pits to prevent flying-insect entry. Each pit contained one amorphous clay ball, similar to a simple type found with the more elaborate forms in the Poverty Point middens.

Before the excavation could be expanded in search of other huts (we had hoped to find a circle formation), the site was vandalized and destroyed. An attempt was made to salvage what remained, but before we succeeded, and without our knowing it, the site was covered by stacks of pulpwood.

Approximately 20 feet to the rear of the middle hut, three clay ovens were exposed by the land-clearing operations. I never saw them; they were discovered and extracted by Jerry Carver of Bay St. Louis (a local nonprofessional archaeologist). He described them as being about "two feet deep, eighteen inches wide, cylindrical in shape, with clay walls about four inches thick." In each, he recovered ash, charcoal particles, and several amorphous clay "cooking balls." Other people recovered several steatite vessels, inverted and stacked and of a coni-

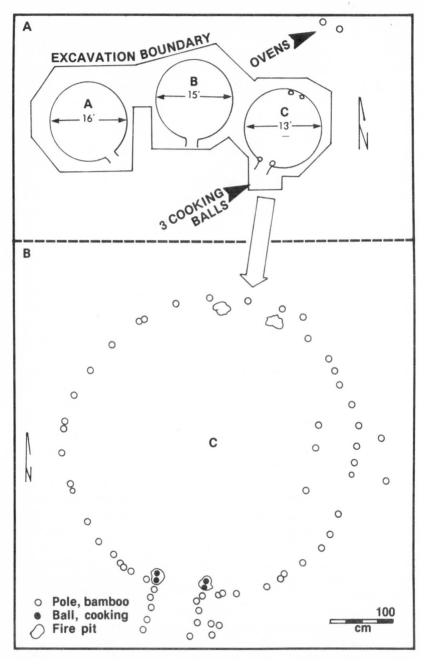

Fig. 5.3. House patterns at the Claiborne site: *above*, relative locations of the three exposed house rings; *below*, details of house ring "C."

cal shape, about 50 meters north of the huts (Charles Satchfield, pers. comm.).

The huts produced no ceramic data or midden. Flint, jasper and chert microdrills and gravers were found outside the huts. The floors were not discolored and suggested short-term occupancy. The area has produced, at approximately the same level, large broad quartz and chert Archaic points, such as the Ledbetter (Bell 1960:pl. 33, A, F).

The 1979 excavations yielded a smaller hut, about 2.7 meters in diameter, also made of poles, located on the south perimeter of the Claiborne site. Several lithic retouch flakes were recovered but no artifacts or ceramic data.

These huts were apparently of the earliest Poverty Point occupation of the terrace. Their nature suggests nonpermanent housing, consistent with a seminomadic Archaic pattern. A large variety of Paleo-Indian-Archaic transition and Archaic points have been recovered here. Strata above these produced typical Poverty Point material, especially the varied styles of "cooking balls," steatite and fiber-tempered sherds, plummets, gorgets, atlatl weights, effigies, and bone and stone tools and points. These are all consistent with the data from the Poverty Point site (Gibson 1974c; Webb 1968; Gagliano and Saucier 1963). One cruciform atlatl weight (?) of smoky quartz was recovered from Claiborne by Owen Heitzman of Bay St. Louis.

Gibson (1974c) mentions the Motley point as a possible warrior status point and suggests that a warrior class may have been maintained at Poverty Point. The paucity of Motley points at Claiborne (only one is known), as well as at other sites along the coast where Poverty Point cultural data are found, may support his theory. Pontchartrain, Edwards, and Gary points appear and seem to replace the large broad points.

The Jaketown perforators are not as common here as at other Poverty Point sites in the lower Mississippi valley. However, flint drill "bits" 1–5 centimeters long are numerous. The majority are 1–2 centimeters in length and are trifacial or quadrofacial. Even on the smallest tools, both ends of the bit are used, suggesting hafting. Associated with drills are microblades, microgravers, and what appear to be microwedges.

Although the Poverty Point culture appears in other sites across the Gulf coast and even into West Florida (Hunter 1975), the inventory is limited. The best samples are found in Jackson County at two major sites and in Harrison and Hancock counties. Greenwood Island (22Ja516), the easternmost site in Mississippi with a Poverty Point

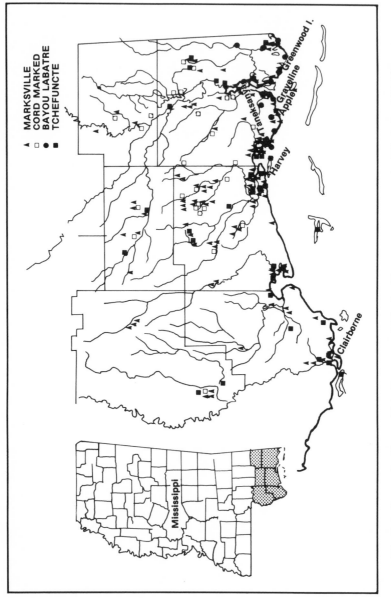

Fig. 5.4. Bayou La Batre, Tchefuncte, and Marksville components on the Mississippi Gulf coast.

component, is primarily of the Bayou La Batre–Tchefuncte period. The Poverty Point data (characteristic of that period) consist of hundreds of biconical clay objects. At Apple Street (22Ja530), the biconical clay ball is in association with melon-shaped, grooved-pierced, and spheroid clay balls. No cylinder forms appear except at Claiborne. Effigy fragments appear, but they could be independent of Poverty Point.

Tchefuncte–Bayou La Batre period

The Bayou La Batre culture may extend back to ca. 1200 B.C. (Reed Stowe, pers. comm.); at least one scholar disagrees, however, placing the beginning between 500 and 1000 B.C. (Shenkel 1980). On the Mississippi Gulf coast, sites containing Bayou La Batre ceramics invariably produce Tchefuncte ceramic varieties, and usually Deptford and Alexander as well.

The introduction of fiber-tempered pottery from the east appears to be contemporary with the earliest Bayou La Batre components in Jackson County, whereas Tchefuncte traits, moving into Hancock County from the west, appear to arrive after fiber-tempered ware was introduced, in the declining years of the Poverty Point period Claiborne site. No Tchefuncte sherds have been identified, to my knowledge, from Claiborne. Which fiber-tempered ware arrived first is certainly unknown at this time, but the fact remains that Bayou La Batre grit-tempered ware is associated with the well-finished fiber-tempered ware previously discussed, which appears to be related to the Orange ceramic series of Florida.

The Woodland cultural tradition seems to have its earliest representation, if ceramics is to be the principal criterion, in Jackson County at Greenwood Island (22Ja516) (fig. 5.4). The ceramic assemblage is predominantly Bayou La Batre, with Dunlop and Deptford types present. The Tchefuncte culture of southern Louisiana makes up a small percentage of the total sherd collection and is represented by Tchefuncte, Lake Borgne, and Mandeville Stamped types. Most of the decorated sherds are stamped with Deptford motifs (linear, simple, and check stamping).

Bayou La Batre ceramics (Wimberly 1960; Ford 1969) diminish significantly toward the west as Jackson County terminates; they all but disappear farther west. An occasional sherd may be found as far west

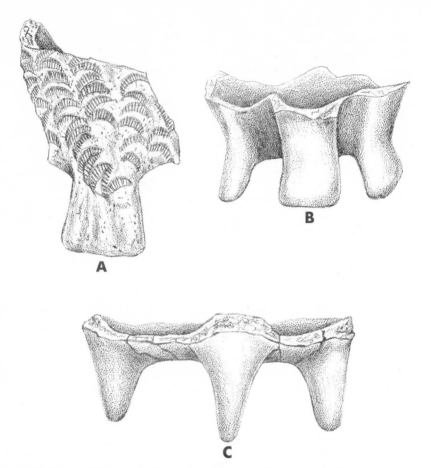

Fig. 5.5. Tchefuncte period ceramics from the Mississippi Gulf coast: (A) Apple Shell Impressed; (B, C) Tchefuncte Plain, *var. Apple.*

as the Pearl River, but components containing the ceramic assemblage terminate before Biloxi Bay is reached.

The Tchefuncte ceramic complex, typical of the Lake Pontchartrain area (Shenkel 1980), is well represented across the Mississippi coast. Tchefuncte sherds (stamped, dentate-stamped, and incised) and Mandeville sherds (stamped, incised, and punctated) are found as far east as the Pascagoula Bay area, while Orleans Punctate, Tammany Punctate, Lake Borgne Incised, and O'Neal varieties seem to terminate near Graveline Lake (Apple Street Site, 22Ja530). Crooks Stamped and a shell rocker stamping, not unlike the later type Santa Rosa (fig. 5.5A) (Ford and Quimby 1945; Shenkel 1980), are found as far east as Taneksanya (22Ja517); beyond that site to the east a second type, also similar to Santa Rosa, appears.

The best information on this period comes from two sites that were partially excavated in recent years: Apple Street and Taneksanya. Apple Street is unusual in several ways. Like most Tchefuncte period sites (Ford and Quimby 1945; Shenkel 1980), it is situated in a marsh-estuarine environment, but the midden is more than 100 meters from the marsh. It is lunate in shape and is located to the "rear" of the settlement (away from the marsh). Below the midden, composed mainly of *Rangia cuneata* shells, house patterns were uncovered; postmolds were also found between the midden and the marsh. The geomorphology in the estuary adjacent to the site has changed since occupation, and it may be that the site originally bordered a shallow bayou or the Graveline Lake itself, filled considerably in recent centuries by alluvium.

Poverty Point objects are numerous in nonshell portions of the site. In several areas of the site, caches of "cooking balls" have been found in the occupation stratum, approximately one-third meter below the surface. A peculiar vessel form is present at Apple Street: long pods and wedges, often 5 and 6 in number, on round pot bottoms (fig. 5.5A–C). The range of the pod length is about 3–5 centimeters; the wedge forms are within the same length range, with distal-end widths of 3–7 centimeters. Although the vessel forms are typical of the Bayou La Batre and Tchefuncte phases (Willey 1960; Phillips 1970; Stoltman 1978; Ford 1969), the dimensions are unusual. No other Mississippi coast site has produced clay vessels with such prodigious podal supports.

The majority of the vessels are large pots, medium- to well-fired, coarse sand-tempered, yellow, tan, and buff in color. There are also clay-tempered and very fine sand-tempered wares of the same forms. Although some of the designs and tempering suggest "Alexander" ware (Phillips 1970), the vessel forms are unique and should perhaps be identified as "Apple." Apple Street vessels have produced a number of designs that are reminiscent of Mayan ceramics of the Yucatan Peninsula (fig. 5.6A–B).

The Taneksanya site, approximately 6 miles west of Apple, is a later Tchefuncte site and may date from the end of the Tchefuncte period

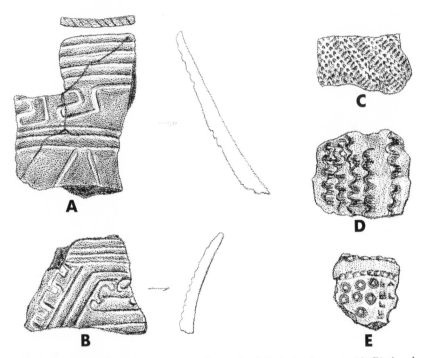

Fig. 5.6. Early Woodland ceramics from the Mississippi coast: (A, B) Apple Incised, *var. Blades*; (C) Tchefuncte Dentate Stamped, *var. Orleans*; (D) Bayou La Batre Scalloped Impressed; (E) Tammany Punctate var. unspecified.

in this area. Ceramics are generally well fired and clay tempered with smooth surface finishing, almost identical to the succeeding Marksville ceramics. Designs are more carefully applied than in any other Tchefuncte–Bayou La Batre site collections of the coast, and the upper site levels include early Marksville sherds.

Again, Deptford pottery (Wimberly 1960) is present in large quantities, and Tchefuncte, Mandeville, Tammany, and Crooks designs are also well represented. Vessels are tall and taper at the bottom, and some have small tetrapodal bases, with both pods and wedges present; a few bases are flat discs or squares, typical of the Big Oak and Little Oak Islands near New Orleans (Ford and Quimby 1945; Shenkel 1980).

Several complicated stamped designs on sand-tempered ware are present in the pottery assemblage. They are like Swift Creek stamps but are not identical to any motifs published from the Swift Creek region; consequently they have been tentatively identified as Tanek-sanya Complicated Stamped (fig. 5.7D).

The Taneksanya site is located on a small peninsula. Approximately 4 feet above the center of the site, and not buried by shell midden, is a burial area. It is currently elevated about 20–30 centimeters and was apparently at least another 20–30 centimeters higher before vehicular traffic packed and eroded it. It was evidently originally a small burial mound.

In 1968 most of the cemetery was unearthed. Twenty-one skeletons, all adults and approximately equal numbers of males and females, were found. The burials were flexed or bundled. There was no evidence of cremations or pit burials. Burials were essentially in three levels, with the lowest interments 57 centimeters below the present

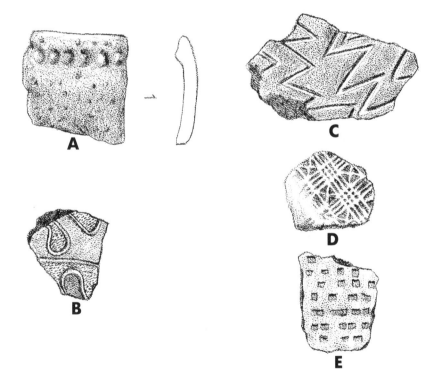

Fig. 5.7. Lake Woodland ceramics from the Mississippi coast: (A) Tchefuncte Plain, *var. Sky Lake*; (B) Apple Dentate; (C) Taneksanya Incised; (D) Taneksanya Complicated Stamped; (E) Bayou La Batre Stamped.

surface. None of the burials extended below the original topsoil, suggesting that each body was laid on the surface, probably after some clearing preparations, and then covered with earth. This burial exercise was probably repeated with each individual. Burials did not include grave goods typical of the Burial Mound I period, although one female had a shell pendant around her neck and another had a grooved, pierced, keg-shaped clay object, reminiscent of Poverty Point.

Another Tchefuncte–Bayou La Batre cemetery was unearthed on Greenwood Island in Jackson County. It was much like that at Taneksanya in elevation and proximity to a bayou. Rangia and oyster shell middens surrounded and covered much of the cemetery. In the 1960s the adjacent bayou was dredged for a ship channel; immediate erosion of the site exposed and then destroyed numerous burials. Collectors destroyed the remaining burials, but not before six could be unearthed and studied. Their deteriorated conditions did not allow removal. Three adults, a male and two females, were buried in flexed positions, head-to-head in a pinwheel fashion. The other three, also a male and two female adults, were flexed. Collectors had made craters in the cemetery, leaving thousands of human bone fragments scattered among their spoil. It is estimated that at least two dozen skeletons were destroyed.

Another Tchefuncte burial area, a small mound 20 miles north of the coast in Harrison County, was excavated by a local landowner who had unearthed it years ago. He described the burials and showed me the ceramic fragments recovered from the tumulus. Ceramics were Alexander and Tchefuncte types. The mound was described as a small elevated area, about 2 feet high and perhaps 15 feet in diameter at the base. There were five burials, in a pinwheel fashion, apparently head to head, and all flexed. The cemetery was located approximately 75 yards from a small creek.

The Bayou La Batre–Tchefuncte people, like the Deptford people of Georgia and Florida, were well adjusted to the marsh-estuarine environment but moved inland at certain times to collect foods and raw materials. Deer bones in middens along the coast do not include skull parts or vertebrae. It is possible that the deer were processed at kill sites and hunting camps and that only quarters with long bones and several other parts were brought to the estuarine sites.

Bone awls, needles, gauges, harpoons, points, and fishhooks are common at sites during this period. Mabin and Gary points of jasper, flint, and chert are numerous. Shell tools were apparently used for dressing skins and for woodwork and other special purposes, because lithic scrapers, cleavers, choppers, adzes, microtools, and celts are essentially absent on the coast. Stone drills are present but not common. However, on inland Tchefuncte sites (Bayou La Batre ceramics have not yet been identified on riverine sites in southeastern Mississippi) along streams and ridges, the stone tool kits include scrapers, choppers, and knives, along with spear and dart points. Lithic workshops are also found in these sites, along with hearths and sherds. These may represent hunting stations or seasonal collection camps or both.

Several submerged sites of Hancock County in the Gulf (oyster reefs today) have produced Tchefuncte, Marksville, and even Middle Mississippi wares. These are frequently picked up during oyster dredging (Jerry Carver and Don Demetz, pers. comm.). Evidently some sites have been inundated as a result of subsidence.

Many Tchefuncte–Bayou La Batre sites along the coast are currently being investigated. Portions of house patterns have been recovered at two sites, and one complete hut pattern at another (22Ha534). The house at the latter, the Harvey Site in Biloxi (fig. 5.8), was approximately 8 feet in diameter, with walls formed by poles placed upright in sandy soil about 18 inches apart; it was probably covered with thatch, mats, or hides. Pole diameters are 4–6 centimeters. Portions of other structures suggest oval or round huts up to 16 feet in diameter and made of poles covered with a light material. Hearths, as well as small deposits of kitchen midden, are found on the floors.

During this period, ceremonialism was developing in the Deptford cultural period to the east, in Florida and Georgia (Sears 1956; Milanich and Fairbanks 1980), but there is little evidence of it in coastal Mississippi. The only objects that may reflect religious paraphernalia are clay elbow and flat pipes and an occasional fragment of human effigy.

Marksville–Santa Rosa period

The earliest Marksville sites recognized on the coast are in the Pearl River delta area of Hancock County. These usually overlay Tchefuncte shell middens and include plain ware and early Marksville incised pottery types. Curvilinear incising replaces the preceding Tchefuncte rectilinear motifs (Shenkel 1980). The Swift Creek complex is barely represented on the Mississippi coast. Only four Swift Creek

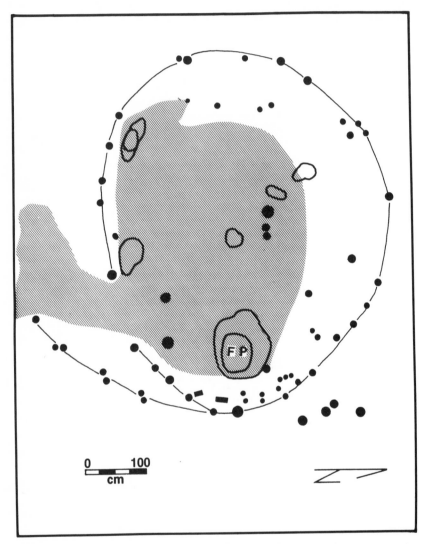

Fig. 5.8. Tchefuncte–Bayou La Batre house pattern at the Harvey site (22Ha534); note the windbreak for prevailing southeast winds.

Complicated Stamped sherds have been found, each at a separate site. All four locations are on an apparent single route across Jackson County (fig. 5.9).

Like their predecessors, and probably like their ancestors, the Marksville people continued to focus upon a marsh-estuarine food base

(Shenkel 1980). Ubiquitous in the middens are remains of *Rangia cuneata* and white-tailed deer (Cook 1976; Stoltman 1978). Marksville is associated with many small sites inland in the coastal plain riverine and lacustrine systems.

Marksville sites are numerous in the freshwater stream (ridge-ravine) environments. Hardwood stands apparently were utilized often for hunting and gathering. Lithic workshops are small and discarded tools and weapons few. Gary and Mabin projectile points are common. Inland more than 20 miles, stream bottoms contain small pebbles suitable for knapping. The amount of debitage suggests a minimum of lithic manufacturing; during this period, lithic artifacts practically disappear from artifact assemblages. On the coast, only an occasional point is recovered from extensive Marksville period middens and village sites.

Bone awls, harpoons, and gouges are common, and cannon bone handles and fishhooks (cut from the deer astralagus bone) continue to be used. Tools normally used in producing baskets, drilling wood, cutting antler and bone all but disappear. The cannon and ulna bones of deer remain sources of tool material, and incising occurs on them. Shells may be the graving tools. By late Marksville–Santa Rosa times the ulna tool has disappeared, along with the bone hook, and only the cannon bone seems to remain, probably as a tool handle.

Net-impressed pottery leaves an excellent record of net materials. Today's nets have the same appearance and suggest that a needle and thimble were used by the Woodland people in net-making. The twine is very small and the meshes uniform.

Shells and cane may have replaced stone and some bone artifacts. Milling and nut stones are also absent. Again, grinding and pounding were probably performed with nonlithic instruments, such as the wooden mortar and pestle that were common in the historic period (Swanton 1946).

The large village sites of the Issaquena–Santa Rosa culture are the first of this size to appear after Poverty Point times. They are best represented on the coast by the Harvey (22Ha534) and Graveline (22Ja502) sites. Harvey was extensively investigated by SMARG and USM students, under my direction (1972–75), and the same groups excavated portions of the Graveline.

The Harvey site produced a true Marksville ceramic assemblage, with occupation extending into the Troyville period. More than 20,000 sherds were recovered from the village midden. Most of the Marksville varieties, Santa Rosa series (especially Alligator Bayou, Basin Bayou,

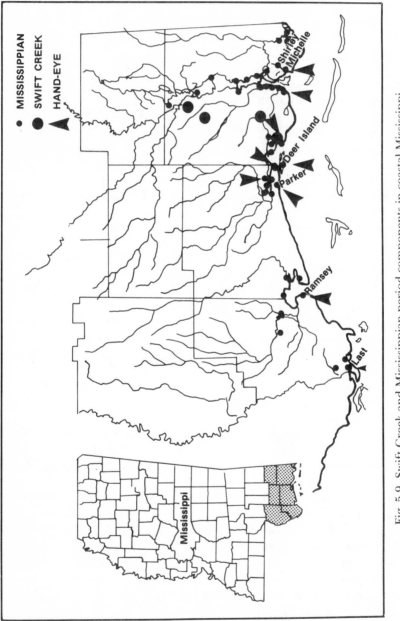

Fig. 5.9. Swift Creek and Mississippian period components in coastal Mississippi.

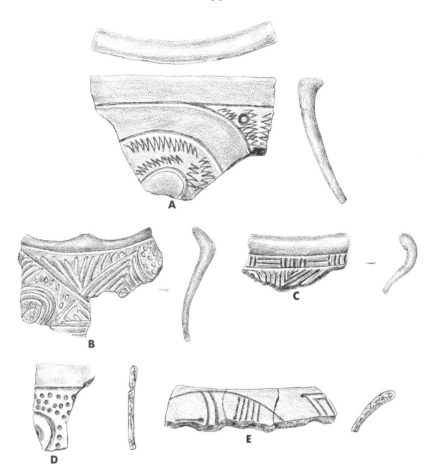

Fig. 5.10. Middle Woodland ceramics from the Mississippi coast: (A) Marksville Incised, *var. Troyville*; (B) Graveline Incised (similar to Marksville Incised, *var. Spanish Fort*); (C) Harvey Incised (similar to Marksville Incised, *var. Yokena*); (D) Churupa Punctate; (E) Weeden Island Incised.

and early Weeden Island), and several new varieties dubbed Harvey Incised make up the bulk of the ceramic assemblage (fig. 5.10). Perhaps more than 90 percent of the sherds are well-fired clay-tempered wares, and about one-third are decorated.

Data collected suggest that the earliest occupation was by a relatively large band (compared to population units before them) who resided on a freshwater stream terrace. Over the years, the settlement expanded eastward, leaving behind kitchen and shell middens on top of the older occupation areas. Below the Marksville component there was a small Tchefuncte camp, already mentioned.

The first Marksville attempt at settlement (radiocarbon dated to ca. 2000 B.P.) was destroyed soon after construction, apparently by a hurricane. In every area of the excavation (19 excavation units in an acre), there is a sudden deposit of white marine sands approximately 15–20 centimeters thick. Below the sands are postmolds forming house patterns with almost no discoloration in the sand. These structures had wall posts 10–15 centimeters in diameter placed in the soil upright at intervals of less than a meter. No clay daub was found, so it is assumed that light materials were used for wall and roof coverings. Bone tools of types used in weaving are present and may represent mat weaving. Mats may have been used for wall covering. This practice may have been continued into the historic period; it was observed among the Acolapissa on the Pearl River in 1700 (Rowland and Sanders 1932). Portions of the house patterns indicate structures about 5–7 meters in diameter. Both round and oval plans are suggested, and straight-walled structures may have been constructed as well.

In the next level, after the storm, large round and rectangular structures were erected. House patterns often overlap, indicating frequent rebuilding rather than congestive occupancy. Sizes range from 2.7 to 5.6 meters in diameter for the round houses, and about 4.5 by 7 meters for the one complete rectangular structure. Wall supports are of the same size and spacing as in the prestorm level.

The round houses have no center posts, suggesting a light, domed roof. Fire and trash pits are scattered throughout the floors. Clean floor areas along the walls mark the sleeping areas, while entranceways are mottled as if well traveled. At least one house had a windbreak at the entrance.

The upper level of occupation at the site is from the Troyville period. House patterns remain unchanged, except for one possibly octagonal structure containing burials. About half of the house pattern remains, encircling two burial pits. The posts were smaller than those used before, with diameters of less than 8 centimeters. One burial pit contained two adult skeletons, tightly bundled and disarticulated, with skulls carefully placed at the northeast end of the skeletal collections.

The other burial pit contained a jumble of bones, with skulls of nine individuals, including male and female adults, adolescents, and infants. About half of the original skeletal elements of those individuals are present. Burials were not disturbed after interment, suggesting that elements were missing when deposition of the bones took place.

One adolescent skull was burned, and one adult radius was cut along the shaft before or shortly after death. This burial pit is not typical of a Woodland burial. Both burials were in shallow pits within the structure's floors.

The Graveline site demonstrates the continuum of Marksville–Santa Rosa into Issaquena–Weeden Island. Marksville–Santa Rosa ceramics are found in the lower occupation level, while Mound A at the site was constructed in the Issaquena–Weeden Island Ib or II period. This truncated platform mound, extensively investigated, was constructed over the village midden left by the Marksville and, later, Issaquena peoples. The mound was apparently constructed within the Issaquena period. No ceramics later than this period have been recovered anywhere in the area (over 30 acres), which at one time included at least 13 mounds (8 remain).

During mound construction the work stopped at least three times, allowing humus to cover the mound, before a white sand platform was installed on its top. The platform was at least 6 by 6 meters square when the mound was about 1.5 meters high. Postmolds suggest that a small structure of poles was erected on the platform. The posts were 5–8 centimeters in diameter, about a meter apart. Later, another 0.5 meter of soil was added. Perhaps a second structure was erected on top, but traces of it have disappeared with erosion.

In the Marksville occupation zone, below and adjacent to the mound and below the midden lens, double post patterns are very common. They are reminiscent of the Adena culture of Ohio but do not have the characteristic outward slant (Willey 1960; Jennings 1974). This peculiar pattern also appears on the Rudloff site, four miles to the north. During the Issaquena occupation, the posts suggest house patterns typical of those at Harvey.

Ceramics from Graveline include beakers, jars, bowls, and dishes. A new vessel form appears for the first time: a shallow but broad "spittoon," well fired and finished with a yellow-tan wash. The ceramic series established at the Harvey and Graveline sites is found along the coast, extending into the riverine-lacustrine areas of the insular coastal strand.

The Weeden Island culture, found to the east, is poorly represented in coastal Mississippi. Weeden Island pedestaled effigy vessels, like those from Kolomoki (Sears 1956), are absent, as are pottery caches in mounds. However, the red painted (slipped) and red-on-buff restricted-mouth bowls found in early Weeden Island mounds to the east are present. Clarence B. Moore tested seven of the Graveline

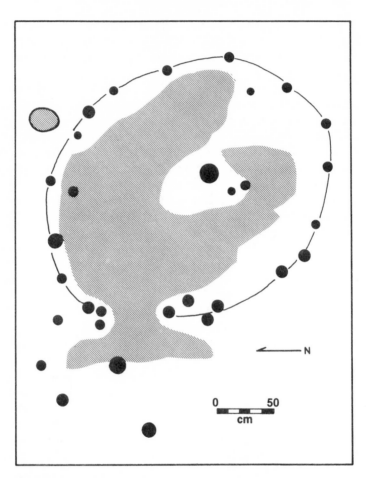

Fig. 5.11. House pattern from the Marksville–Santa Rosa occupation below the "Deer Island phase" on Deer Island.

mounds around 1902, searching for burials and pottery caches, and
reported none (Moore 1905d; Brown 1926).

One other house pattern from the Marksville period was uncovered
on Deer Island. It contained Santa Rosa–like stamped sherds on the
interior floor. The structure was 2.8 meters in diameter and round
(fig. 5.11) like the others from this period. The same general house
type—a pole-thatch- or mat-covered hut—was apparently introduced
during the early Poverty Point period (or before) and remained the
principal house type until historic times.

Transitional-Mississippi period

At present, data are limited for the Late Woodland period, primarily because chronologies for the Marksville to Mississippi period have not been confirmed. Several dates from Deer Island are within this transitional period (ca. A.D. 700), but questions remain about ceramic series within that period.

The Late Woodland period is represented by the Coles Creek culture along the western coast and by sites with a number of ceramic types in the east. The latter include Wakulla Check Stamped, West Florida and Mulberry Creek Cord Marked, and other Weeden Island types. The culture of the lower Mississippi valley meets those of the Alabama-Georgia-Florida region in coastal Mississippi.

During this period, the riverine middens (collecting stations?) show a change in meat sources, as evidenced by faunal remains. Large turtles and alligators of all sizes become the principal meat sources, supplemented (apparently) by gar, drum, and deer, as well as by the usual estuarine fauna of the other periods.

Deer Island (22Hr500) has given us our best data for the Mississippi tradition on the coast. (It is more proper, in my opinion, to refer to the late coastal cultural periods as associated with a Mississippian rather than a Gulf tradition because of the strong influences from beyond the coastal regions.) Deer Island contains the largest Mississippian village site on the coast. It extends, presently, about 700 feet along the longitudinal axis of the island and spans its width, now about 250 feet. Artifacts constantly washed ashore suggest that the site was much larger than it presently is; indeed, 70 feet of the outer face disappeared in a hurricane in 1969.

During the Late Woodland period, some Weeden Island ceramics were still present. Later ceramic styles of the Mobile Bay area were also common. The majority of Mississippian period ceramics appear to be from the Pensacola, Fort Walton, Pinellas, Safety Harbor, Moundville, and Bottle Creek series with small differences. Plaquemine and Natchezan ceramics are also present.

Traits of the Early and Middle Mississippian periods are seen in mounds and ceramics on the coast. Few traits beyond those have been identified after extensive research at four Late Woodland–Mississippian sites (Deer Island, Michelle, Parker, and Last). The only complete house pattern yet unearthed is a Coles Creek period hut at the Tillis site in Biloxi (fig. 5.12). Otherwise, only small sections of house patterns and ramadas are known (Michelle and Deer Island).

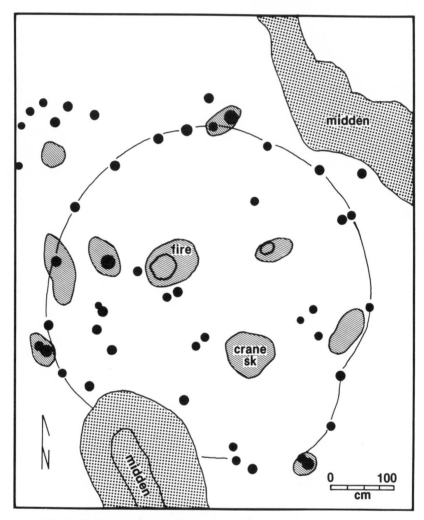

Fig. 5.12. House pattern from the Coles Creek period, Tillis site.

During the Weeden Island II (Willey 1949) or III–IV periods (Brose, this volume), villages developed inland in an ecotone between coastal scrub and marsh-estuaries and hardwoods of the coastal strand (Milanich and Fairbanks 1980). Swanton (1946) stated that farming became extensive in the rich soils beyond the coast; however, some farming mixed with fishing must have occurred on the coast itself.

No large quantities of Southern Cult materials and certainly no major temple mounds have been discovered. The cult assemblage on coastal sites is limited when compared to interior towns of the Mississippian period elsewhere in the Southeast. Since the Mobile Bay area has many more Southern Cult traits than this coast, and since westward into southeastern Louisiana there are even fewer, it seems that our nearest major "cult center" was east or north, probably Bottle Creek or even Moundville (Alabama).

Coastal ceramics are similar to Mississippian series present throughout much of the Southeast at this time. Collared vessels, loop and strap handles, and incising and punctated designs are all present, but Bear Point types are absent. Many vessels from the lower Mississippi valley eastward into Georgia and Florida are similar to those from the Mississippi coast.

For years, many of the multilinear incised sherds found at transitional period sites on the coast were classified as "Coles Creek," and no doubt the Coles Creek ceramic tradition influenced the area during the continuum to Mississippi from Woodland. But closer examination and vessel reconstruction show few sherds that are truly Coles Creek. This tradition does exist on the coast but is restricted to the area around and west of the Biloxi. Instead, D'Olive varieties are dominant.

A Deer Island ceramic series has been tentatively established as an analytical device to begin to understand the local Mississippian ceramics. Moundville-like pottery is present in significant percentages, but the tempering on the coast is usually heavy crushed clam and oyster shell. The large casuellas and jars are typically Mississippian in style, but the incised and punctated designs, although similar to West Florida and the lower Mississippi valley wares, differ somewhat (fig. 5.13). The Bottle Creek ceramic series is well represented.

Moundville Engraved and Incised designs (fig. 5.13), especially on polished ware, are common, including the hand and eye motif. However, only several sherds show a typical hand and eye motif (Pensacola Incised) (Wimberly 1960). One is a pipe bowl (Mary Anderson Picard's collection) from Point Aux Chennes on Biloxi Bay (fig. 5.13C). Another cult motif found on one burnished sherd is a series of crosses in circles around the waist of a restricted bowl; it was recovered from Deer Island.

The Deer Island shell mound, excavated by SMARG and USM under my direction in 1973–75, produced some other unusual data. Besides those vessel designs named, Mississippian ceramic traits included animal effigy appliqués typical of the Mississippian tradition elsewhere: cat, owl, bird, duck, deer, dog, frog, and human (Sears 1956; Willey 1960; Ford 1969; Jennings 1974).

Dale Greenwell

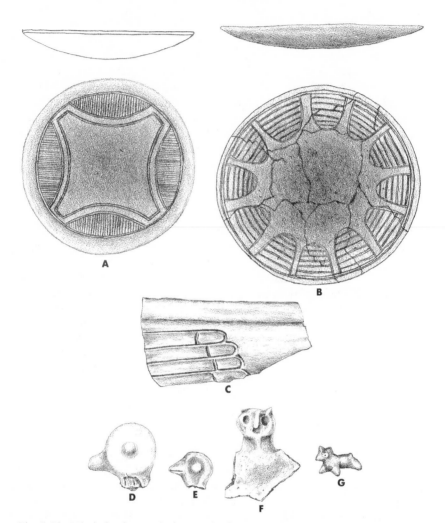

Fig. 5.13. Mississippian period ceramics from the Mississippi coast: (A) D'Olive Incised, *var. Maryawn*; (B) D'Olive Incised, *var. Deer Island*; (C) Pensacola Incised; (D–F) effigy head adornos; (G) clay dog effigy.

The owl is the most common on vessel bodies but seems to have been replaced by the duck and bird profiles (fig. 5.13D–F) on rims (Sears 1974). Human heads, full face with sloping foreheads but with narrow profiles, appear on rims of bowls. The Deer Island ceramic assemblage is fully represented at the Michelle Mound (22Ja578) to the east and at the Last site (22HA511) to the west.

Approximately 3–5 percent of the shell mound was excavated on Deer Island, and six skeletons were recovered. Two were practically pulverized by foot traffic over the years and could not be studied very well. Two others (adult males) were bundle burials. Neither had mandibles, nor were any lower teeth present. Three yards away, the skeletons of an adult female and small child were recovered. The female was in a flexed position, head west, face north, with the child cradled in her lap. On her upper chest was a worked perforated right horizontal ramus (jawbone) of a subadult, with all the teeth present.

Bundle burials in shell middens have been found in Mississippian sites in marsh and estuarine locations in Hancock, Harrison, and Jackson counties, i.e., across the coast. Only two mounds (Michelle and Deer Island) and one village (Shirley) have produced articulated burials. (Shirley also has produced Weeden Island–like materials; see fig. 5.14.) Every major Mississippian period midden contains bundle burials.

Several possible small temple mounds, Ramsey mound (Bay St. Louis) and the Michelle mound, have not been sufficiently tested. Test pits in the latter produced postmolds of a structure wall.

Population stress is reflected in the late Mississippian middens on the coast. In periods past, suitable mature *Rangia* were collected, but late period middens contain a large percentage of very small clams and even smaller oysters and periwinkle snails. All sizes of drum, catfish, mullet, gar, and sheephead are abundant throughout the middens, but analysis of the middens shows that deer and other mammals were no longer common food sources. Alligator, shark, muskrat, and rodents are present but usually in small numbers. Only at Deer Island is the oyster common.

Hurricanes would probably discourage large and permanent villages on the coast, and riverine seasonal floods would discourage alluvial plain (deltaic) settlements in this otherwise sedentary period (Turnbaugh 1978). Therefore, it is probable that the larger portions of the population avoided permanent settlement on the coast proper, at least after the Woodland period (ca. A.D. 700).

Farming communities and even fortified towns were found on the Pascagoula River, away from the Gulf, by the early white explorers (Greenwell 1968). The historic Indian settlements nearest to the Gulf were the Biloxi, more than 15 miles north of the Gulf on the Pascagoula River, and the Acolipissa, about four miles from the Gulf on the Pearl River. There were no coastal settlements of any kind between those two rivers or along the coast anywhere during the early historic period. Several contact period sites have been examined and have

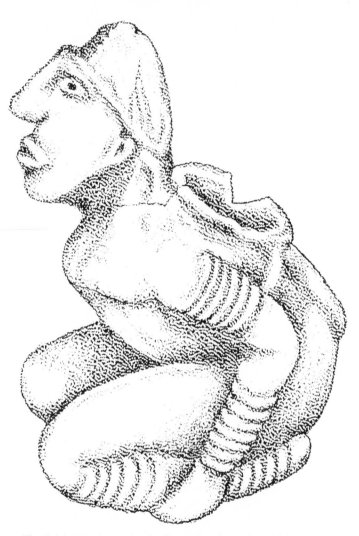

Fig. 5.14. Weeden Island effigy pipe from the Shirley site.

yielded aboriginal artifacts in association with trade beads, pipes, ceramics, glassware, and gun flints.

Historical narratives of the nineteenth century refer to numerous middens along the rivers, bayous, and bays. Those that were accessible to vehicles (including wagons and boats) were sources of shell, which was processed into lime to use in cement. Early roads and streets were paved with middens. These same narratives tell of the sherds and artifacts found on the shell-paved roads. Today innumerable ab-original middens lie buried beneath the seawalls and highways of the Mississippi coast. Only 400 or so sites are known, and research con-tinues on these coastal sites in southeastern Mississippi to gather more data regarding the aboriginal people who occupied that region in the past.

Note

The author is grateful to the following individuals for providing the information, assistance, or access to collections that contributed to the preparation of this article: Ted Brown, Blades Buster, Jerry Carver, Don Demetz, Larry Galle, Owen Heitzman, Robert Jones III, Mary Stebley Pitcard, Charles Satchedield, Ray Wallace, Jack Wright, Ervin Otvos, J. Richard Shenkel, Reed Stowe, Jean Heartfield, and espe-cially Joyce Richie, Mellie Shofner, Jim Keeney, George Barlow, Bill Turner, Powers Dunnaway, Jim Tribble, and Anthony Galle.

6

Archaeology of the Louisiana Coastal Zone, 1970

to the Present

Robert W. Neuman

Although almost 50 years have passed since the first major archaeological research was undertaken in coastal Louisiana, relatively little is known today about prehistoric demography and subsistence in the area. Shenkel's and Brown's chapters reflect some recent efforts to fill this gap. Robert Neuman, a longtime champion of the importance of coastal archaeology, rounds out the picture of recent work on physical anthropology and subsistence for each major prehistoric cultural period on the Louisiana coast.

IN my logbook for 24 September 1968, I describe a field trip on which Ned and Lanier Simmons guided me. In the morning we left Avery Island, Louisiana, in their Lafitte skiff, which was carrying an aluminum canoe and food and drinks, and boated over to examine the Morton Shell mound at Weeks Island. We also went to the western environs of Vermilion Bay and along bayous and canals where we stopped and surface-collected and photographed six other shell middens. After returning to their home on Avery Island, Ned and Lanier beguiled me with facts and lore about the Louisiana coastal zone. By the time I arrived back in Baton Rouge, I had been indoctrinated with the realization that the Louisiana coastal zone was a bountiful region in many aspects and that its archaeological potential was no exception. And for the next three years (with grants from the Morton Salt Company, the National Science Foundation, and assistance from the Louisiana Research Foundation of Avery Island) I expended most of my time excavating the Morton Shell mound (Neuman 1972) and inspecting other sites throughout the Louisiana coastal zone.

In 1971 I was contracted by the National Park Service to prepare an archaeological assessment of the Louisiana coastal zone, including inland areas along streams and lakes affected by tidal fluctuations. During the summer of 1972 several students and I (assisted by the Louisiana Wildlife and Fisheries Commission, the staff at the Sabine National Wildlife Refuge, and future members of what was to become the Louisiana Archaeological Society) inspected 65 selected sites in Cameron, Calcasieu, Jefferson Davis, Plaquemines, and St. Bernard parishes. The final report was accepted in 1973 and published in 1977. This 43-page booklet (Neuman 1977) summarizes the history of archaeological endeavors in the region, pointing out the tremendous devastation of archaeological resources that has occurred since the early nineteenth century and the dearth of attention paid to this region by professional archaeologists prior to the 1970s. The assessment also contains a list of all then-recorded sites in the Louisiana coastal zone, accompanied by descriptive data on the nature of each site (oyster or rangia midden or mound), site dimensions, artifacts (which with few exceptions meant surface collections), and the culture period or periods assigned. (I would be remiss if I did not acknowledge the fact that almost all of these data were gathered by geologists and geographers from Louisiana State University who were using archaeology to unravel problems dealing with the ever-changing Louisiana coastal zone: Richard J. Russell, Fred B. Kniffen, William G. McIntire, Sherwood M. Gagliano, and Roger T. Saucier.)

In summarizing the information in the assessment, I was surprised by the large number of recorded sites in the region, a total of 466 (fig. 6.1). Although the general cultural sequence for the prehistoric era was documented, it was also noted that "research relative to man's utilization of the available resources, his settlement forms or burial patterns have barely emerged. It may be said that the archaeological literature is almost devoid of a systematic, quantified study and report of man's exploitation of the natural resources in the Louisiana coastal region" (Neuman 1977:31). An exception is Ford and Quimby's 1945

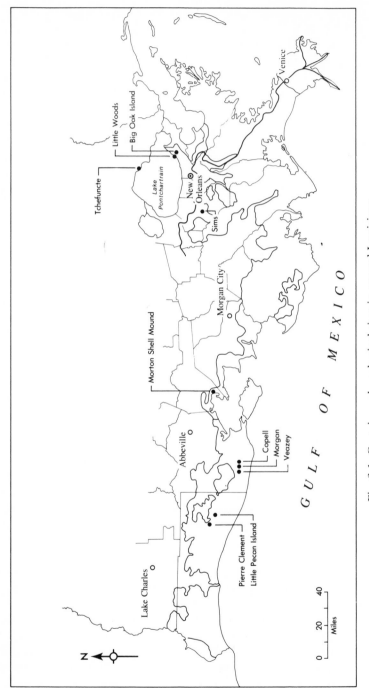

Fig. 6.1. Certain archaeological sites in coastal Louisiana.

memoir on the Tchefuncte site along the north shore of Lake Pontchartrain. Since Ford and Quimby first wrote their report, there have been advances in our knowledge of archaeology, including physical anthropology, burial patterns, and subsistence. There follow reviews of some of the old and new data.

The earliest archaeological deposits on which we have pertinent data have been assigned to the Tchefuncte culture, which began about 500 B.C. Human skeletal remains have been found at the Tchefuncte site (Snow 1945) in St. Tammany Parish, the Little Woods sites (Czajkowski 1934), the Big Oak Island site in Orleans Parish (Ford and Quimby 1945; Shenkel 1974), and the Copell site, Vermilion Parish (Collins 1927b, 1941; Hrdlička 1940). Together these remains contain about 30 primary burials and no less than 52 secondary burials. Generally the postcranial elements were fragmented and in a poor state of preservation. With one exception, the primary burials were found in flexed positions; one individual was buried in a prone position. It appears that all of the primary burials were adults. Burial orientation data are difficult to derive, but at the Little Woods sites, at least, it is reported that six human skeletons were 4 feet apart and parallel to each other. Unless the Copell site individuals were primary burials, which is not stated clearly by Collins, primary burials of the Tchefuncte culture in Louisiana are not characteristically associated with funerary artifacts. There is one exception, a primary burial from the Little Woods midden associated with two quartz crystals. If the Copell burials were primary, they were associated with an unquantified number of shell, bone, and stone artifacts and red and yellow pigments.

Tchefuncte secondary burials consist of bundle burials or scattered postcranial elements and isolated skulls. There seem to be no grave goods associations, but once again the situation of the Copell site is uncertain. Nor are there any burial pits for either primary or secondary Tchefuncte burials. Skeletal remains or bodies were simply placed on a midden surface and covered with shells. It seems apparent that the primary and secondary burial patterns were contemporary.

Most of the physical anthropological data are drawn from craniometric studies by Collins, Hrdlička, and Snow. All of their data are derived from adult skeletal elements of both sexes. The skeletal collections are representative of a homogeneous population; however, there is a noticeable sexual dimorphism, males being mesocranic and females quite brachiocranic. Facial lengths were large, and females have the broadest nasal dimension. Based on limited data from some of the burials, Snow estimated that male stature was about 5.5 feet. Almost all of the bones examined by Snow exhibited pathologies; dental caries were rare but abcesses common.

Prior to the 1970s, most of our subsistence data for the Tchefuncte culture came from Ford and Quimby (1945), who listed the animals represented at the type site and noted that deer bones were the most common. Except for the ocelot, the species listed are what one would expect for the north shore of Lake Pontchartrain. Both oyster and rangia shells were present. Unfortunately none of the faunal data were quantified, nor were the bird bones identified to species.

The first modern zooarchaeological analysis of Louisiana material was done for a master's thesis at Louisiana State University by Kathleen M. Byrd (1974). She analyzed the excavated Tchefuncte remains from the Morton Shell mound in Iberia Parish and found that, in terms of edible meat, the deer was the most important source of animal protein, followed by the alligator, raccoon, goose, crane, turtle, gar, bowfin, catfish, and sunfish. Numerically, ducks were poorly represented. From the botanical remains from the same component, Byrd identified the edible species as hickory, acorn, plum, grape, persimmon, squash, and bottle gourd. Radiocarbon dates ranging from 325 B.C. to A.D. 295 indicate that these are the earliest examples of squash from anywhere along the Gulf coast.

Of course, when dealing with coastal sites in Louisiana, we cannot ignore the molluscan remains of the *Rangia cuneata*. Strangely enough, Byrd (1976a) found that its dietary importance may be more illusory than real. A person would have to eat almost 26,000 *Rangia cuneata* to equal about 50 pounds of deer meat. Furthermore, *Rangia cuneata* is not very nutritional; it is low in protein, fats, carbohydrates, and calories. Why was rangia exploited? Byrd suggests that an answer lies in the fact that it was numerous and easily procured and that it comprised a reliable supply of food.

Another interesting aspect of Tchefuncte subsistence is that crustaceans are not represented. They are not reported from any prehistoric Indian sites in coastal Louisiana and are a most rare commodity in all sites along the entire northern Gulf coast. This absence is not a case of poor preservation. Abstinence is almost incomprehensible for present-day Louisianians, but, conversely, the prehistoric Indian population would have looked askance at our misappropriation of the *Rangia cuneata*. Perhaps the answer lies in the fact that the Indians did not know of Tabasco pepper sauce.

The archaeological culture following Tchefuncte was Marksville. Almost nothing relevant to Marksville physical anthropology or burial patterns has ever been published. Pertinent information is limited to a brief statement by Henry Collins that burial mounds at the Veazey site in Vermilion Parish "yield fragmentary bones, including some skulls with slight frontal flattening and long bones showing lesions apparently produced by syphilis" (Collins 1941:146). The burials (whether primary or secondary is not stated) were associated with pottery, bone, shell, stone, and copper artifacts, and red and yellow pigments. Marksville on the coast remains little studied *and* little represented in the archaeological record.

Following Marksville, the Troyville–Coles Creek culture is represented, at least in pottery surface collections, at far more sites in the Louisiana coastal zone than any other cultures. Information on physical anthropology and burial patterns comes from the Pierre Clement (Springer 1973) and Little Pecan Island sites (Wauchope 1947) in Cameron Parish, the Morgan site (Collins 1927b) in Vermilion Parish, and the Morton Shell mound (Neuman 1972) in Iberia Parish.

Pierre Clement, excavated and reported by James W. Springer, then of Yale University, is a shell midden resting upon a chenier. It contained three human skeletons. Burial 1 was in an extended supine position. Burials 2 and 3, a short distance away, were in shallow pits, in similar positions; they were side by side, parallel to each other but oriented in opposite directions. None of these burials was associated with funerary objects. Not far away on another chenier at the Little Pecan Island site, reported by Robert Wauchope, then of Tulane University, six human burials that had been placed in shallow pits were exposed. All six were in flexed positions, but one was in a "more upright position" (Wauchope 1947:186), and behind it was an infant skeleton. Presumably, all of the flexed burials were adults. There were no funerary offerings.

While excavating at the Morton Shell mound in 1970, I exposed a cemetery area roughly 40 feet in diameter. Its base consisted of a culturally deposited layer of fine grey silt, sometimes as much as 2 feet thick. Over this grey floor was a 4-foot deposit of rangia shells containing no less than 275 human individuals. Although there were several primary flexed burials and occasional finds of articulated torsos and limbs, most burials were bundles of one or more individuals or loosely scattered human bones. The Morton Shell mound people also had a ritual of breaking the limb bones of the secondary interments, a rite found elsewhere in Louisiana and other states. None of the interments were associated with funerary objects.

With one exception, all the physical anthropological data for the

Troyville–Coles Creek culture in the Louisiana coastal zone come from the Morton Shell mound cemetery. I am indebted to Louise M. Robbins of the University of North Carolina, Greensboro, who examined, analyzed, and wrote a detailed report on the human skeletal material excavated from the Morton Shell mound (Robbins 1976). Her analysis is summarized here. The skeletal elements represent the remains of 7 fetuses, 14 infants, 25 children, 28 adolescents, 83 females and 105 male adults, and 13 other adults of undetermined sex. Once again, conspicuous sexual dimorphism was apparent. Male long bones and particularly their brow ridges were massive, and zygomatic bones, maxillae, and lower teeth were significantly larger than those of the female adults. Males were also markedly taller than females, averaging more than 5.5 feet.

Osteological anomalies include perforated olecranon fossae on the distal humeri of adult females. Other common anomalies include taurodent dentition leading to the fusion of teeth roots and single and multiple ear exotoses or bony outgrowths; the latter were also quite common on other bones of the skeleton. An adult femur was found to have been drilled through the medullary cavity, and an adult frontal bone contained a number of drilled holes that exhibited different stages of healing prior to the death of the individual.

Robbins remarked that a pathological infection pervaded most of the population, young and old. In the more severe cases it affected most of the bones of the body and the skull. She diagnosed this disease as yaws and noted that it probably led to the death of the most infected individuals. Certainly it would have lowered immunological defenses, and a person with open, running, and stenchful sores would probably have been (at the very least) restricted in social activities.

I find it intriguing that Robbins found a small percentage of the skeletal material that was noticeably dissimilar from the phenotype range of the majority of the population. These "strangers" were smaller and more gracile and lacked the characteristic sexual dimorphism. Nevertheless, when they were buried, they were accorded the same rituals as the majority of the Morton Shell mound population.

Finally there is the remark by Henry Collins (1927b) about an unstated number of skulls and other bones from the Morgan mounds which he investigated in 1926. He said that the skulls exhibited pronounced frontal-occipital flattening and that the long bones showed evidence of syphilis.

Troyville–Coles Creek subsistence information is derived from the

Morton Shell mound and the Pierre Clement sites. Robin S. Futch, for her master's thesis at Louisiana State University, conducted a zoo-archaeological analysis of the remains from the Troyville–Coles Creek deposits at the Morton Shell mound (Futch 1979). As one might expect, she found the same range of species reported by Byrd (1974). Other percentages also followed the same pattern: fish, 38 percent; mammals, 33 percent; reptiles, 22 percent; and amphibians and birds in very small percentages. Most of the fish are from brackish- or fresh-water environments. Several marine species were identified—shark, mullet, drum, and flounder—but they are poorly represented and are known to visit freshwater habitats. Parenthetically, I know of little substantive evidence of the prehistoric exploitation of marine resources in Louisiana, except, of course, the oyster. It seems that the freshwater and estuarine environments in the study area provided for the Indians' dietary needs.

From the shallow midden at Pierre Clement, Springer (1973) reported deer, muskrat, raccoon, otter, and weasel, with deer and muskrat predominating. Fish species consist of gar, bowfin, suckers, and freshwater drum, with gar and drum predominating. Turtles and one unidentified bird are also reported. The midden was composed of oyster and rangia shells intermixed.

Succeeding Coles Creek in the coastal region is the Plaquemine culture. I am unaware of any data published or in manuscript form that is pertinent here. Consequently, I will move on to the Mississippian period culture(s) for which pertinent data are also lacking. Only from the Mississippian component at the Sims site in St. Charles Parish is there information on burial patterns. Dave D. Davis of Tulane University excavated at this site, and I am indebted to him for the following information. In the village midden, about 1 foot below the ground surface and closely spaced, were the remains of five individuals. Three adults were represented by an extended burial, a flexed burial, and an isolated skull, respectively; the fourth and fifth burials consisted of flexed burials of an adolescent and an infant. There were no funerary artifacts associated with the burials.

In reference to subsistence data from the Sims site, Davis reported that, in contrast to most of the known sites in the area, freshwater *Unio* shell predominated in the mound and village middens he excavated. Other sites in the area are characterized by brackish-water rangia and saltwater oyster shells. From his field observations, Davis noted that deer, raccoon, and muskrat bones predominate, and there seems to have been less attention directed toward the taking of the swamp rabbit, drum, bowfin, gar, and catfish.

It appears that since the beginning of the 1970s some inroads have been made toward learning about the physical anthropology, burial patterns, and subsistence economics of the prehistoric Indians of coastal Louisiana. A few comprehensive, basic studies have been completed, and these have added significantly to knowledge of the Tchefuncte and Troyville–Coles Creek cultures. But pertinent data for most of the prehistoric cultures are still notable only for their absence. One way to remedy this situation would be intensive excavations at carefully selected sites characterized by good preservation of biotic remains. Luckily, such sites are not rare in the Louisiana coastal zone.

7

Mississippian Period Cultures
in Northwestern Florida

David S. Brose

Largely as a result of Gordon Willey's monograph of 1949, north-western Florida is probably the area of the U.S. Gulf coast best known to most North American archaeologists. Following the publication of Willey's substantial synthesis, flesh was added to his framework by such archaeologists as Ripley Bullen, William Lazarus, William Sears, and Hale Smith. The pace of work quickened in the late 1960s and in the 1970s, and understanding of prehistory in northwestern Florida is preparing for a new synthesis.

David Brose takes a major step toward such a synthesis for the later prehistoric periods in this chapter. Although he focuses upon Fort Walton, he pays considerable attention to Weeden Island phases and their developmental relationships with the early Mississippian in the Florida Panhandle. He also provides an updated perspective on Mississippian period ceramic similarities among Fort Walton, Pensacola to the west, and Safety Harbor to the south, and he suggests a new approach to interpreting ceramic variability in northwestern Florida that ties ceramic variation to differences in subsistence-settlement systems and polities during the late prehistory of the area.

PREVIOUS investigations reveal that the Fort Walton archaeological complex has displayed significant differences in its temporal and geographic extent and its inclusive cultural materials. Varying perspectives have led to definitions of Fort Walton as a regional expression of a particular sociopolitical stage; as a diagnostic ceramic assemblage, or series of ceramic phases; as a distinctive local settlement-subsistence system; or as a specific temporal period within one or more vaguely described geographic areas. Each of these interpretations yielded different and occasionally conflicting descriptions of Fort Walton and of the origins and processes of change through time (Fairbanks 1952, 1965b, 1971b; Ford, 1952, 1969; Caldwell 1958; Griffin 1967; Bullen 1971; Goggin et al. 1971; Brose 1974; Brose and Percy 1978; Jenkins 1978; Gibson 1980).

Recent investigations have provided chronological refinement of ceramic sequences and data on sociocultural integration, cultural geography, economic adaptations, and external relationships, which all suggest that, prior to understanding processes, the data must be reorganized (Brose 1980b; Knight 1980a; Milanich and Fairbanks 1980; Scarry 1980a, b, 1983), and regional phases must be distinguished to describe adequately late prehistoric and early historic cultures in northwestern Florida itself.

Between A.D. 950 and A.D. 1150 the region is represented by different cultural-ecological adaptations along the Gulf coast and at interior riparian zones. Both the coast and the interior are relatively diffuse in their economic adaptation and are cross-cut by a number of locally based (but nonexclusive) settlement-subsistence systems. They represent derivatives of three regionally autochthonous ceramic traditions (Incised-Punctated Gulf, South Appalachian Stamped, and a minor Middle-Eastern Cord-marked), all of which show areal overlap in this phase. During this period of ameliorated hemispheric climate, distinctive Mississippian ceramics (representing a tradition *later* associated with distinctive socioceremonial manifestations and a structured settlement-subsistence system) appear somewhat simultaneously at a number of loci throughout the region, introduced by as yet indeterminate processes (cf. Caldwell 1958; Griffin 1961; Bullen 1968).

From A.D. 1150 to A.D. 1350 the prehistoric cultures (and the atmospheric climatic pattern) of the region develop a dichotomy between coastal zones and interior riparian or lacustrine zones or both. In the coastal zones, conservative complexes retain their diffuse economies, although several geographically differing settlement-subsistence systems exist. In these zones the local Gulf ceramic tradition does not undergo appreciable change, despite the proximity of diffuse and diffused Mississippian models. The cultures of interior riparian and lacustrine zones during this period undergo differential rates and types of change, resulting in what appear to be similar (and interacting), moderately focused economic adaptations, accompanied (to various degrees) by aspects of a socioceremonial structure similar to the earlier proximal Mississippian patterns. Nevertheless, geographically distinct differences in settlement and subsistence patterns persist, as do residua of local ceramic traditions. Interior zones may be characterized by the variable acceptance (or adaptation or adoption) of some Mississippian ceramic attributes, modes, and techniques, phenomena accompanied by the southeastward expansion of stylistic aspects of the Middle-Eastern tradition (DeJarnette 1952, 1976; Jenkins 1979).

From A.D. 1350 to A.D. 1500 it seems appropriate to infer (by drawing heavily upon the earliest historic accounts) that there were both relatively loosely structured *and* highly structured Mississippian societies in northwestern Florida (although their interrelationships are uncertain). This inference reflects the enduring distinction betwen coastal and interior zones during a period which began with mild climate but rapidly shifted after A.D. 1450 into a pattern of long cold winters and short drier summers. Throughout the period the subsistence patterns of the coastal zone represent an economic adaptation which remains balanced at best, in structure reminiscent of earlier Weeden Island ceremonial-domestic site distributions (Biedma, in Smith 1968; Bryson and Murray 1977).

The ceramic tradition along the Gulf coast during this phase is dichotomized, with the eastern and southeastern areas predominantly represented by Gulf tradition attributes and techniques (although some Mississippian vessel modes occur) while the ceramics of the west coast are predominantly Mississippian in attribute and technique (although both Mississippian and Gulf tradition modes occur as do occasional reflections [or refractions or reinterpretations] of older Gulf tradition ceramic attributes in certain motifs). The interior riparian lacustrine zones show a clear shift to a still uncertain number of economically focused, hierarchically structured (Mississippian-like) settlement-subsistence systems, many of which display the archaeologically appropriate sociotechnic appurtenances. The ceramic assemblages of the interior zone show a combination of Mississippian modes, South Appalachian ceramic tradition techniques, and both a wide variety of Mississippian and a select number of Middle-Eastern tradition attributes along with a number of transliterated Gulf tradition ceramic motifs, present in specific sites and portions of the area (Holmes 1903; Brannon 1909; Griffin 1949a; Willey 1949; Bullen 1950, 1958; Fairbanks 1956; Caldwell 1962; Wauchope 1966; Gardner 1969; Smith 1978).

The phase A.D. 1500–1700, a time of massive cultural and climatic deterioration, is characterized by inadvertent (and deliberate) European-induced aboriginal population displacement and disappearance throughout North America. In the interior zones of this region there appears to be an early abandonment of many noncentral towns (and, based on the *Entrada* accounts, even of some major population centers). This displacement is followed by inevitable population decline and a European political mandate for aboriginal population resettlement ("Rural Pacification") and then by further gradual (although occasionally catastrophic) aboriginal population decline. The coastal zone, more frequented by Europeans, shows an accelerating rate of population decline, alleviated only by the insufficiently slower decline into cultural oblivion of the resettled mixed ethnic groups at trade and mission centers. In both zones this demographic picture is accompanied (or caused?) by the wretched climate and an erratic but irreversible trend toward aboriginal economic clientism within European colonial systems (Hawkins 1848; Swanton 1939; Smith 1948, 1951; Willey 1949; Boyd, Smith, and Griffin 1951; Boyd 1958; Wauchope 1966; Biedma, in Smith 1968; Crosby 1972; Larson 1980; Tesar 1980).

Prior to the early-eighteenth-century disappearance of autochthonous northwestern Florida populations, the coastal zone reflects the short-lived triumph of Mississippian ceramic technology, attributes, and modes, whose increasing southeasterly expansion was probably stopped in North Florida only by destruction of the aboriginal cultures. In interior northwestern Florida, this latest phase is represented by an initial shift to assemblages characterized by Mississippian ceramic modes, and by a few South Appalachian Ceramic tradition attributes. Neither ceramic execution nor technique are "typically Mississippian." This phase ends indistinctly in the smoke and confusion of the colonial wars of 1703–15. When the historic, acculturated, aboriginal populations of northwestern Florida are next seen, they have abandoned the coastal zone save for economically specialized seasonal use, have been concentrated in a small number of interior riparian sites, convenient to European political and economic needs, and display a material technology equally derived from south-central

Georgia and from north-central England (Pierce 1825; Swanton 1911, 1922, 1928a, b, 1939, 1946; Priestley 1928; Spellman 1948; Boyd, Smith, and Griffin 1951; Smith 1951, 1957; McMichael and Kellar 1960; Chase 1962, 1968; Sears 1962a, b, 1968, 1977; Broyles 1963; Cottier 1968; Penman 1976; Brose and Percy 1978; Jenkins 1978; Milanich and Fairbanks 1980; Walthall 1980; Schnell n.d.).

Mississippian in northwestern Florida, rather than being homogeneous, thus represents societies varying in time and space as well as in structure and content, in response to the political, economic, and atmospheric changes in the southeastern United States from the tenth through the nineteenth centuries of our era. I will attempt here to establish "boundary conditions" (both in time and space, and in diagnostic content) whereby some significant concatenations may be recognized. Finally, a speculative model will be presented in which the processes of Mississippian origins and development in northwestern Florida are integrated with these data.

Regional environments

It may be relevant to reiterate first that, while from the Ohio Valley/ Great Lakes perspective the entire Southeast appears homogeneous, there are in fact significant environmental differences across this area which are reflected by the settlement, subsistence, and socioceremonial patterns of the late Weeden Island societies (cf. Willey 1945, 1949; Goggin 1947; Sears 1954, 1958, 1961, 1977; Trickey 1958; Kelly 1960, n.d.; Wimberly 1960; Fairbanks 1964; Brose and Percy 1974b; Percy and Brose 1974; DeJarnette et al. 1975a–b; Steinen 1977; Brose 1979; White 1981).

Coastal marshes from Tampa Bay north and west to the Ochlockonee River vary from a few hundred meters to five kilometers wide (Sellards 1912). Low-lying and wet, generally with less than a meter of relief, their vegetation consists of grasses, rushes, and sedges. Seaward are sand beach ridges, generally under 30 meters wide, with crests about 50 centimeters above the marsh, supporting live oak, *Ilex vomitoria*, and *Sabal palmetto*. Extending from the ridges to shallow mud flats (at extreme low tides exposed for up to a kilometer), these beaches are interrupted by inlets connected with meandering tidal creek channels and subject to frequent tidal inundation. In the marshes, remnant flatwoods islands standing about a meter above the surrounding marsh support *Pinus elliottii*, *Sabal palmetto*, *Ilex vomitoria*, *Serenoa repens*, and *Baccharis halimifolia* (Harper 1914; Shelford 1963;

Delcourt 1978). Only the barrier beaches and occasional flatwoods islands are suitable for habitation (cf. Fairbanks 1964, 1965b; Percy 1971; Larson 1980).

West of the Ochlockonee, coastal marshes are absent and flatwoods abut the barrier beaches, which are wider. From Santa Rosa Sound west, beaches are over 50 meters wide and have higher barrier ridges than in the eastern Panhandle. In that zone, a series of offshore islands parallel the coastline with a mixed vegetation of tidal and freshwater marsh, scrub oak, and pine. Large, infrequent trees represent those species on the beach ridges. Most larger islands are about 3 kilometers seaward, and the many small submerged Pleistocene rivermounts bays, sounds, and lagoons are very shallow. Estuarine conditions prevail, and a variety of emergent vegetation is easily obtainable (Pierce 1825; Sellards and Gunter 1918; Stockdale and Bryenton 1978).

Poorly drained due to minimal relief and the shallow natural hardpan, flatwoods extend inland, generally rising from about 1 meter in elevation to nearly 60 meters at the Cody Scarp. Forests consist of longleaf pine, with local communities of slash pine and pond pine and a dense understory of palmetto and wire grass interspersed with forbs, shrubs, and vines (Harper 1914:248–53, 291–313; Shelford 1963:76; Clewell 1971). Swamps, in the shallow depressions two to three meters lower than surrounding flatwoods, support cypress, pond, or bay vegetation, while the streams seasonally flow across low swampy zones behind the low river levees. Dense vegetation and seasonally wet ground make the flatwoods relatively inhospitable except for narrow riverbank levees and scattered, low "xeric" hammocks, characterized by oaks, cabbage palmetto, and pine, along with dense undergrowth.

In the interior, the Northern Highlands represent high land masses separated by stream valleys (Puri and Vernon 1964:10–11). The dissected uplands are characterized by rolling hills with strong relief and few sizable level areas, except along large streams (Hubbell et al. 1956: 5–8, 15–23; Hendry and Yon 1958:10–11; Delcourt and Delcourt 1977; Brose and Percy 1978). In the Panhandle, higher land is from 50 to 100 meters above sea level, generally lower to the east, with some elevations of 150 meters in southwestern Georgia.

Southern upland vegetation is an open longleaf pine–scrub oak–wire grass forest association, with sandy areas of sand pine and scrub oak. Northern upland forests are mixed hardwood and pine. Cypress, slash pine, and black gum occur at ponds in low areas throughout the uplands, although less frequently than in the flatwoods. Dense bottom-land hardwood gallery forests with growths of cane and creeper char-acterize large bottomlands, especially along the Apalachicola River, where the upland floodplain is over 2 kilometers wide.

The northern extension in southern Georgia, the Tifton Upland, is bounded by the escarpment of high, steep bluffs which form the southern border of the Flint valley and are continuous with the high Torreya bluffs east of the Apalachicola River, where relief of up to 80 meters occurs. West of the Chattahoochee River, the uplands extend into southern Alabama as part of the Southern Pine Hills (ibid.).

The Marianna Lowlands, a zone of flat stream valleys cut into low, gently rolling hills is formed partly on older terrace formations (Cooke 1939:18–19; Hendry and Yon 1958:11–12), peneplained by a sequence of stream erosion and solution of underlying limestone deposits (Hendry and Yon 1958:17–20). Open forests of longleaf pine prevail, although sinks in northeast Jackson County are fringed with hardwoods, which also border streams as large as the Chipola River (Harper 1914:193–208). These Marianna Lowlands are part of the larger Dougherty Lowland zone extending into Alabama and Georgia along the lower Chattahoochee and Flint rivers (Komarek 1962; Mitchell 1963).

Modern climate across the region is relatively uniform, with some-what more moderate temperatures and precipitation along the coast. The mean January temperature is 54°F; the mean July temperature is 82°F. In the summer months, temperatures regularly top 90°; in win-ter, subfreezing temperatures are not uncommon (Butson 1962; Wood and Fernald 1974:58–59). The mean annual frost-free period for the northern portion of the region is 240–70 days, for southern areas 270–300 days. Freezing temperatures at present are common from mid-November through early March (Wood and Fernald 1974:62–63; cited in Percy 1976) and may be longer and more severe in the river valleys of the north.

Rainfall increases slightly from south to north and from east to west across the area. In the east, mean annual rainfall is 52 inches; from Choctawhatchee Bay west, it exceeds 60 inches, reaching a high of 64 inches in central and southern Okaloosa and Walton counties (Butson 1962:60). The rainy season is July to September, when there is nearly a fifty-fifty chance that some rain will fall on any given day, and a sec-ond high point occurs in early spring. October and November are the driest months.

The sandy soils of western Florida are generally slightly to moderately acidic and rather poor for agriculture, except under modern management (Florida Division of State Planning 1974). Neutral to slightly basic loamy soils favorable for primitive agriculture do occur as levee deposits or as tributary springhead sediments at irregular areas along the larger streams. The Tallahassee Red Hills, a flat rolling portion of the southern uplands, is an important area of sand loam soil in northeastern Leon County. Harper (1914:278–79) noted that "This region was cultivated by the Indians long before the white man came, and until the last few decades it was the leading agricultural section of the State in proportion to its size. . . . Even yet, after three-quarters of a century of cultivation by whites and negroes, most of the farmers do not consider it necessary to use commercial fertilizer."

Fauna in the area include white-tailed deer, panther, bobcat, black bear, the Florida wolf, and a few smaller carnivores. The gray squirrel, fox squirrel, cottontail rabbit, marsh rabbit, and opossum are also common (Sherman 1952; Harlow 1959; Golley 1962; Lemon 1967; Mutch 1970; Percy 1974). Modern bison were documented by Percy (1974) from the mid-sixteenth century to the early eighteenth, but only one bison faunal element has been reported from a prehistoric site. Percy (1974) noted that several species of birds were reported for the Panhandle (cf. Stevenson 1960), the most important of which, from the standpoint of aboriginal use, included wild turkey, bobwhite quail, mourning dove, ducks, and geese. The coastal marshes are important wintering grounds for migratory waterfowl (Chamberlain 1960; Linduska 1964). Oysters, clams, conchs, and many other species of shellfish, as well as fish, occur in abundance in coastal marine waters. Fish and a variety of mollusks are also plentiful in inland streams (Jordan et al. 1930; Clench and Turner 1958). Reptiles are all too common everywhere (Carr and Giwa 1955). In general, as Percy notes (Brose and Percy 1978), the Highlands have greater potential for agriculture and hunting and the coast for fishing and shellfishing.

As Larson (1980) and Smith (1978) have pointed out, the greatest variety of resources and the densest concentrations thereof are to be found along the major rivers cutting through this region. These characteristic dendritic drainage patterns can be divided into a series of north-south exotic drainage systems that flow to the Gulf. The principal basins are (from west to east) the Perdido, Escambia, Blackwater, Yellow, Choctawhatchee, Apalachicola, Ochlockonee, and Aucilla (Kenner et al. 1967, 1969). These are geomorphologically isolated, and communication from one to another is difficult. Scattered throughout the Panhandle are internal drainage basins centered on Karst lakes and ponds (cf. Brose and Percy 1978). The principal lakes are Miccosukee, Jackson, and Iamona, although hundreds of smaller Karst lakes exist, especially in the eastern parts of the northern uplands region.

Weeden Island

In 1974 George Percy and I presented two papers concerned with the concept of Weeden Island in the Panhandle region of Florida and the lower Flint and Chattahoochee river valleys in Georgia and Alabama (Brose and Percy 1974a; Percy and Brose 1974). After a review of previous studies, we developed a ceramic phase sequence based upon available data from sites throughout western Florida, southwestern Georgia, and southern Alabama (although few such data were dated). We first suggested a refinement of the ceramic subdivisions of Weeden Island that discarded Willey's Weeden Island I/II. Here I note that as far west as Panama City, early Weeden Island is accompanied by Early and Late phases of Swift Creek, as defined by Phelps (1966a, 1969, n.d.). Ceramically the two phases are poorly distinguished by varieties of rim treatment or stamp motif within types of Swift Creek Complicated Stamped. Phelps had proposed these phases to take the place of Willey's Santa Rosa–Swift Creek period, since Santa Rosa ceramics are absent from middens in this part of the Panhandle. Farther west (in the area of Escambia and Pensacola bays) Santa Rosa types are present in the middens, and Santa Rosa–Swift Creek still may be a viable concept (cf. Willey 1945, 1949). Percy and I stated that "Weeden Island 1 was characterized by a few Weeden Island series incised and punctated types (Carrabelle Incised, Carrabelle Punctated, Keith Incised, and Weeden Island Incised) and a dominance of late variety Swift Creek Complicated Stamped in middens. In Weeden Island 2, a much greater variety of Weeden Island pottery types is present, excluding only specialized mortuary classes such as effigies and cut-out vessels, which seldom occur in middens. In Weeden Island 3, Wakulla Check Stamped appears, and there is a slight decline in the importance of complicated stamped. In Weeden Island 4, complicated stamping disappears. In Weeden Island 5, there is a dominance of check stamping in middens, a very limited representation of incising and punctating, and a minor occurrence of corn-cob marked pottery"

(Percy and Brose 1974:14–15). Plain ceramics are common through-out all phases.

We also noted that this sequence of ceramic phases would be per-haps inadequate to describe in detail ceramic trends in the peninsular Gulf coast areas of Florida (where, at least in mounds of the Tampa Bay area, complicated stamped ceramics appear far less important). Allowing for some degree of regional variation, our sequence charac-terized extant ceramic trends for purposes of studying change in other aspects of Weeden Island culture. We emphasized that problems of burial mound ceramic chronology might be somewhat distinct as Sears (1973) noted. Currently available radiocarbon dates from northwest-ern Florida indicate a range for Weeden Island 1–5 of A.D. 150 to A.D. 900 or 1000.

Early Weeden Island settlement in the Apalachicola-Chattahoochee-Flint area is marked by nucleated communities, which are few in num-ber. Because of a paucity of excavation, little is known about village life during this part of the Weeden Island period. During late Weeden Island 5, the number of sites increases in the Mariannas Lowlands, as well as along the Apalachicola and the lower Flint and Chattahoochee and in the hills to the east of the Apalachicola (Brose and Percy 1978).

The archaeological work performed in the intervening six years has accumulated only data that support this model of regional Wee-den Island settlement-subsistence changes (cf. Chase 1968, 1978; Jones 1971; Percy 1972a, b, 1976; Jones and Penman 1973; F. Schnell 1973, 1975a, b, 1978, 1980; Tesar 1973; Bullen 1974; Toth 1974; De-Jarnette [ed.] 1975; Kelly and Smith 1975; Smith 1975, 1977; Jenkins 1976; Nance 1976; Percy and Jones 1976; Walthall and Jenkins 1976; Jeter 1977; Steinen 1977; Wing 1977; Bense 1978; Caldwell and Smith 1978; Brose 1979, 1980a; Knudsen 1979; Kohler 1978; Schnell, Knight, and Schnell 1979; Gibson 1980; Milanich and Fairbanks 1980; Walthall 1980; Scarry 1983).

These efforts have also resulted in the compilation of a series of radio-metric absolute dates for many of the Weeden Island 1–5 compo-nents. In general, these suggest that Weeden Island 1–2 (what Willey in 1949 called Weeden Island 1 sites, as well as many which he consid-ered mixed Santa Rosa–Swift Creek and Weeden Island sites) date to the period A.D. 150–450 (cf. Brose 1979; Milanich and Fairbanks 1980). What Willey considered mixed Weeden Island I/II, now Wee-den Island 3, dates to the period A.D. 400–600. Weeden Island 4 dates to A.D. 600–800. The most critical period for this thesis, Weeden Is-land 5 (Willey's late Weeden Island II, in 1949, and Caldwell's Wakulla of 1955), has been dated by seven determinations to an average of A.D. 850 at the Sycamore site in the upper Apalachicola valley (Milanich 1974; Milanich and Fairbanks 1980); to A.D. 1000 ± 140 at the Lynn's Fishpond site on the Middle Chattahoochee in Barbour County, Alabama (Scarry 1983); and to A.D. 824 ± 85 at the Nichols site on the Wakulla County Gulf coast (Daugherty et al. 1971).

The Weeden Island period displayed a shift in the mortuary reflections of social status differentiation from those earlier "attenuated Hopewellian" patterns. In later Weeden Island 2 mounds there is an increase in secondary and primary bundle burials as well as "semi-autonomous" artifact caches, especially whole pots, unassociated with specific burials, fewer of which are found in internal structures such as crypts, stone or log, tombs or submounds. By Weeden Island 3 most mounds yield a few large ceramic sherd deposits or pavements. By Weeden Island 4 (A.D. 600–800) individual grave lots have disappeared as have premound and intramound structures and nearly all exotic items. Small mounds without burials were shown to be far more common, as were mounds with large mortuary populations and status-free reinterments in earlier mound groups. Regional differences were strongly marked between areas east and west of St. Andrews Bay (cf. Lazarus 1960).

Weeden Island 5 showed a major shift in two directions. The West Florida coastal region was marked by a continuation of previous mortuary trajectories, with a small number of widely spaced large mortuary zones, unassociated with any occupation areas and characterized by either numerous small mounds or cemeteries within which every member of the population appears to be represented, each accompanied by one or two killed ceramic vessels (Schoolcraft 1849; Fewkes 1924; Lewis 1931). The terminal Weeden Island mortuary activities of interior regions (still poorly known) are Weeden Island II/Fort Walton mounds associated with villages, such as Chipola cutoff, where a large number of scattered bundle burials with no grave goods occurs together with a smaller number of primary burials associated with several killed ceramic vessels (often quite distinctive, and occasionally exotic, types). We argued that the small number of such sites known was due to the rapidity with which such a pattern was replaced by the Mississippian pattern with segregated secondary temple mound and primary village cemetery interment, and we suggested that many of the large Fort Walton mounds were likely to have such a Weeden Island 5 core (Brose and Percy 1974a:14–21).

Without question, we then viewed (as I still do view) such shifts in

mortuary status differentiation as the highly correlated socioceremonial reflections of the regionally changing settlement-subsistence
patterns. In each region (the western Gulf coast, the interior, and the
central Gulf coast), no break appears in the proposed sequences from
a rather uniform Weeden Island 1 to the strongly differentiated final
Weeden Island 5 or to the equally regionalized early Fort Walton–
Safety Harbor societies after A.D. 1000.

Beyond this level of argument, too little grounded perhaps in the
minutiae of material culture with which archaeologists are most com-
fortable, it is possible to demonstrate in the very details of artifact
technology and style a similar continuum with regional variations
from Woodland to Mississippian societies.

Fort Walton ceramics

Mallory McCane-O'Conner (1979) has compared the repertoire of
design motifs and the characteristic decorative elements of Weeden
Island and Fort Walton ceramics from Florida. She related the Weeden
Island pedestal cutout effigy zoomorphic jars directly to the zoomorphic Fort Walton–modeled effigy bottles and bowls, noting not only a
similarity in species representation but a strong similarity in conven-
tionalization of anatomical features. A similar relationship in styliza-
tion was recognized for the conventionalized snake motif. McCane-
O'Conner stressed the similarity between Weeden Island and Fort
Walton of such nonzoomorphic design elements as the arch, swastika,
scroll, teardrop, circle, cross-within-circle, triangle-and-oval, and concentric circle, as well as the representation of less common anatomical
features such as eye and hand. She noted that Weeden Island design
motifs, decorative elements, and vessel forms were better integrated
than were later Fort Walton ceramics, and she concluded by suggesting that "Although there is some carryover from the Weeden Island to
the Fort Walton period style, the aesthetic orientation appears to be
quite different." McCane-O'Conner related these differences to less
individualistic Fort Walton societies (McCane-O'Conner 1979:11),
with greater social peer pressure (and lower standards of craftsman-
ship) in ceramic manufacture.

In a companion paper, Malinda Stafford performed an attribute
analysis of Weeden Island ceramic design attributes. She not only
demonstrated that the northwest Florida coast and inland northern
Florida were more similar in this respect than either was to the central

Gulf coast area (Stafford 1979:13–21), but her reconstructed sequences of ceramic design as well as the frequencies and "field locations" of analytical elements appear strikingly similar to those recently developed for Mississippian sites in Alabama (Ford 1952, 1969; Hardin-Friedrich 1970, 1979, 1980; Scarry 1979a, 1983; Steponaitis 1980a, b).

These continuities in ceramic decoration are even more impressive when we realize that McCane-O'Conner and Stafford were dealing with poorly provenienced pottery which spanned at least twelve centuries, from Weeden Island 1–2 to protohistoric Fort Walton–Safety Harbor. We should thus expect that the latest Weeden Island sites and the earliest Fort Walton–Safety Harbor sites would display the closest similarities in ceramic design. The satisfaction of these expectations would require analysis not only of demonstrably late Weeden Island ceramic assemblages but of early Fort Walton–Safety Harbor assemblages as well. This analysis can not be adequately done, since outside of the Apalachicola Valley few such sites are documented, but there are three lines of inference which may allow us to approach a solution to the problem.

First, as I noted in 1979, various northern Florida Weeden Island sites have yielded ceramics similar to Sears's (1953) "Mercier Mississippian" (cf. Moore 1901:469 (fig. 68); 1902:135 (fig. 8), 140–46, 158 (figs. 27, 28, 42), 280 (fig. 246); 1907:452, 456). Also, Moore (1918:551 [fig. 26] and 552 [fig. 28]) reported materials from Weeden Island burial mounds on the upper Choctawhatchee River with decorations and vessel shapes of Mississippian character (free red and white painting, zoned red painting, gourd effigies, and Mississippian-shaped bottles). From the Weeden Island 3 mound at Samson's Landing, dated to ca. A.D. 600 (Percy 1976), Moore (1903:489–91) obtained Mississippian-shaped vessels in association with numerous complicated stamped and check-stamped pots. Similar associations of Mississippian modes with stamped pottery occur at the mound below Hare's Landing.

Sears (1954) believes that several Tampa Bay area mounds reflect a sociopolitical pattern similar to the Natchez (and similar to that reconstructed by Sears for Kolomoki). But, as I concluded in 1979, the original reports on these sites (Moore 1903; Fewkes 1924; Bullen 1950; 1952) indicate that they are no more "Mississippianized" than many other Weeden Island mounds on the coast to the northwest.

As an example, I here illustrate (figs. 7.1–7.3) some of the ceramics

Fig. 7.1. Weeden Island ceramics from Cedar Key mound, from Smithsonian Institution cat. 8262-3, 8269 (neg. no. 80-15800), courtesy Smithsonian Institution.

Fig. 7.2. Weeden Island ceramics from Cedar Key mound, from Smithsonian Institution cat. 8261, 8264-8 (neg. no. 80-15799), courtesy Smithsonian Institution.

recovered by H. Clark in 1869 from a Weeden Island 3 mound on Cedar Key and presented to the Smithsonian Institution in 1880. Notched flanged rim bowls, pseudo-cazuela bowls, rim lugs and adornos, and incised design reminiscent (or "preminiscent") of Cool Branch Incised and Mound Place Incised are all present.

A relatively high frequency of carinated-shoulder bowls, beakers, and short-necked bottles has always been characteristic not only of Safety Harbor–Englewood, but of the central coast Weeden Island (cf. Willey 1949; Sears 1977). Indeed, George Luer's recent investigations at the Aqui Esta mound near Punta Gorda on the south side of

Fig. 7.3. Weeden Island ceramics from Cedar Key mound, from Smithsonian Institution cat. 8260 (neg. no. 80-15798), courtesy Smithsonian Institution.

Charlotte Harbor have yielded a Safety Harbor ceramic assemblage showing considerable decorative continuity with the local Weeden Island incised ceramic repertoire and containing several incised vessels that are quite similar to the Andrews and Nunnally Incised ceremonial pottery found in the middle Chattahoochee (Schnell, Knight, and Schnell 1979; Luer and Almy 1980b). Two radiocarbon dates thus far received for the Aqui Esta mound fall in the tenth and early eleventh centuries A.D. As in the Pensacola area on the northwest coast, the few Safety Harbor sites that have yielded historic materials are best considered *terminus ante quem* dates for this complex which appears to span at least four centuries; they show many of the same shifts in ceramic decoration that occur in the Chattahoochee-Apalachicola valley between A.D. 1050 and A.D. 1500 (cf. Willey 1949; Milanich and Fairbanks 1980; Scarry 1983). I also point out in this context that, just as on the northwest coast, Willey (Willey and Woodbury 1942; Willey 1949) gradually lost control of these very real Weeden Island –Mississippian transitional assemblages by accepting a priori a model of abrupt population displacement and rejecting as "mixed" all components with both Weeden Island II and Fort Walton or Weeden Island II and Safety Harbor ceramics. When investigations are restricted to the extremes of *any* continuum, transitions cannot be recognized and disjunctions must be expected whether or not they are real (cf. Krieger, 1945, 1951; Brose and Percy 1974b, 1978; Percy and Brose 1974; Brose 1975; Scarry 1983).

There has also been a furious discussion of Fort Walton origins and relationships that involves the Fort Walton–Moundville ceramic relationships and the place of the Pensacola "series" therein (Willey 1949; Caldwell 1955; Sears 1967, 1977; Steponaitis 1976, 1980b; Jenkins 1978; Knight 1979, 1980b; Schnell, Knight, and Schnell 1979; Schnell 1980). Scarry (1983) has carefully reviewed the relevant ceramics and their contexts, and his statement is worth quoting:

> In light of our increased control over the Moundville data, those indications of connections between the Fort Walton cultures and the Moundville system take on new meaning . . . [nonetheless] . . . there is surprisingly little hard evidence of exchange between Moundville and Fort Walton. Steponaitis noted the surprising lack of Fort Walton vessels from Moundville itself (1978). I have examined five possible Fort Walton vessels in the Moundville assemblage. . . . while the vessels did resemble late varieties of Point Washington Incised and [Andrews] Incised, they were obviously not from either the Marianna Lowlands, the Upper Apalachicola Valley, or the Tallahassee Red Hills. . . . these vessels, assuming they are Fort Walton, represent a late period in the Fort Walton sequence and thus have little bearing on the question of origins. . . . I feel confident in stating that they should represent late, probably Moundville II/III burials.

Scarry also noted the presence of a middle Fort Walton phase *Lake Jackson* (his Apalachicola) *Plain* vessel and handle from the Moundville I occupation at the Bessemer site (A.D. 1050 ± 85: DeJarnette and Wimberly 1941). He argues that the Mississippi Plain, Moundville Incised, and Cool Branch Incised ceramics, which in local paste are a major part of Middle Fort Walton phases in the Apalachicola valley and from the early levels at Rood's Landing, occur in both Moundville I *and* West Jefferson phase contexts in Alabama. Thus they do not indicate that Roods–Early Fort Walton must equate with late Moundville. Scarry noted that Steponaitis's Carthage Incised, *var. Moon Lake*,

which occurs from Moundville I to Moundville III, closely relates to
Columbia Incised and Marsh Island Incised from the Roods and Fort
Walton phases *after* A.D. 1150–1250 and, further, that the Moundville
I Hemphill Engraved, *var.* Elliot's Creek, equates with what he has
called Yon Engraved, *var. Yon*, which occurs in the middle to late Apalachicola valley Fort Walton phases *after* A.D. 1150. Scarry (1983) concluded his discussion of specific ceramic analysis by postulating that
(1) Moundville I and the Cayson phase of Fort Walton in the Apalachicola valley are coeval (each dating to about A.D. 1100–1200); (2) the
two represent the first ranked societies in their areas; (3) Moundville
III is coeval with early Yon phase Fort Walton (A.D. 1375–1550);
(4) early Fort Walton dates to sometime before A.D. 1100; however,
(5) ranked societies in both the Fort Walton and Moundville sequences
probably do not appear until after A.D. 1100.

It may also be of interest to turn to the Pensacola series ceramics
which characterize the Florida northwest coast. In spite of Knight's
(1980a) contention, excavated and surface materials from the Bottle
Creek site at top of the Mobile delta contain no more specifically "Pensacola" pottery (*sensu strictu*) than do the collections from Moundville
itself (cf. Steponaitis 1978, 1980a, b): Mississippi Plain ceramics predominate at both. The Bear Point mound to a large extent was free of
Mississippi Plain ceramics but, in addition to the Pensacola Engraved
vessels, contained an unknown amount (and in unknowable context)
of sand- and grit-tempered check-stamped ceramics, as well as several
grit-tempered Lake Jackson and Fort Walton Incised bowls (Moore
1901:423 ff.). Several of those ceramics in the Smithsonian collection
that were excavated by Walker (1885) are illustrated in fig. 7.4. The
Fort Walton mound itself did not yield Pensacola ceramics "almost
to the exclusion of anything else" (Knight 1980a:22). Even after all
"Weeden Island" ceramics were post hoc separated and even ignoring the ratio of over 4,000 Fort Walton plain sand-tempered body
sherds to only 850 shell-tempered sherds recovered by Fairbanks
(1965a:257–58), the reconstructable vessel ratios (from Moore 1901;
Willey 1949; and Fairbanks 1965a) were 13 Fort Walton (sand- and
grit-tempered) vessels to nine Pensacola (shell-tempered) vessels. Indeed, while recent excavations into the Fort Walton mound have
failed to reach the undisturbed early construction stages, they have
recovered five restorable Fort Walton vessels and four Pensacola series vessels from unsecure context. It appears that most of the Pensacola series ceramics reported initially were associated with burials
intrusive into all but the final mound stage (Lazarus and Fonaro

Fig. 7.4. Fort Walton–Pensacola ceramics from Bear Point and Live Oak Plantation, from Smithsonian Institution cat. 58195 (neg. no. 80-15801), courtesy Smithsonian Institution.

1975). The brief review of ceramics from sites in the Choctawhatchee Bay region by Lazarus and Hawkins (1976) shows an average of 26 percent shell-tempered vessels and 74 percent sand- and grit-tempered vessels per site (a Fort Walton to Pensacola ratio of 3 to 1). Indeed, it still appears to me (as it did in 1978) that the most "pure" Pensacola sites and cemeteries around the bay reported by Moore (1901, 1902, 1918) and Lazarus (Adams and Lazarus 1960; Lazarus 1961, 1964a, b, 1971; Lazarus, Lazarus, and Sharon 1967) are just those sites that are in some part latest. They thus have little bearing on any discussion of what "early Pensacola" will look like or date to. I would suggest that the "break" between Moundville and Fort Walton lies east of Mobile Bay and that the "tension zone" was the area around Bon Secour Bay, where Moore (1905b:280–96) claimed to have recovered not only shell-tempered, check-stamped, and incised ceramics with effigy heads and loop handles but also incised shell-

Fig. 7.5. Shell-tempered black burnished bottle from Sternberg's excavation of a mound on the Florida coast south of Fort Myers, from Smithsonian Institution cat. 314018 (neg. no. 80-15796), courtesy Smithsonian Institution.

tempered and grit-tempered inverted "urn burial" cazuela bowls associated with Pensacola Engraved bowls.

I thus retain my preconceptions that Pensacola (*sensu strictu* and not simply Mississippian ceramics) is relatively late even in the northwesternmost Florida coastal regions and that east of Mobile Point there is still no reason to reject the hypotheses that Pensacola represents a veneer on an earlier Fort Walton regional complex. To quote Scarry (1983:125, In. 1) once more:

> It is highly likely that many of the confusing aspects of coastal Fort Walton chronology will be cleared up when Coblenz's study of Pensacola ceramic development is completed. Coblenz (personal communication) has indicated that data from Mobile Bay suggest strongly that Pensacola cultures were in existence long before European contact. Further, he has indicated that the Pensacola sequence is in many respects similar to that which I have developed for the Fort Walton cultures. Specifically, he notes the existence, ca. A.D. 1100, of Pensacola ceramic complexes which resemble in numerous traits, modes, types, and varieties, the ceramic complexes of Fort Walton III which also date to ca. A.D. 1100.

Indeed, there is a suggestion in the Smithsonian collections from the work of Sternberg (1876) that late Pensacola ceramics extend southeast in Florida to Collier County (figs. 7.5–7.7).

Fort Walton phases

Largely based on the work directed by Percy and Brose, but also utilizing data from previous research in the Apalachicola Valley and related areas, Scarry (1979a) identified six phases for the late Weeden Island and Fort Walton periods: Wakulla, Chattahoochee Landing, Bristol, Cayson, Sneads, and Yon.

The Wakulla phase (the best known) has been widely recognized as a temporal and regional variant of Willey's Weeden Island II culture (cf. Hurt 1947; Bullen 1950; Kelly 1960; Milanich 1974; Percy and Brose 1974; Sears 1977). Sites are common in the Upper Apalachicola and Lower Chattahoochee valleys as well as on the coast, and several have been investigated in detail. The present definition of the phase is largely based on data acquired by Milanich at the Sycamore site, 8Gd13, and Percy at the Torreya site, 8Li8 (Milanich 1974; Percy

Fig. 7.6. Shell-tempered black burnished incised (Pensacola?) jar with simple curved lug appliqués, from Sternberg's excavation of a mound on the Florida coast south of Fort Myers, from Smithsonian Institution cat. 314020 (neg. no. 80-15795), courtesy Smithsonian Institution.

5 CM.

2 IN.

Fig. 7.7. Shell-tempered black unburnished incised (Pensacola?) jar with complex curved appliqué lugs, from Sternberg's excavation of a mound on the Florida coast south of Fort Myers, from Smithsonian Institution cat. 314019 (neg. no. 80-15795), courtesy Smithsonian Institution.

1971, 1972c). As defined by Scarry (1979a), the Wakulla phase (equated to Percy and Brose's Weeden Island 5) is marked by high frequencies of Wakulla Check Stamped. At Sycamore, Wakulla Check Stamped formed 47.6 percent of the total assemblage and 81.5 percent of the decorated wares (Milanich 1974:16, table 4). At Torreya, it comprised 66.3 percent of the total assemblage and 97.7 percent of the decorated pottery (Percy 1976: table 9). Percy and Brose (1974:6) noted that Wakulla phase assemblages included "very limited representation of Weeden Island types featuring incising and punctating, and a minor occurrence of corn-cob marked pottery." At Sycamore, Cob-marked formed 4.6 percent of the assemblage (7.9 percent of decorated pottery) (Milanich 1974:16). Plain Wakulla phase ceramics are divisible based on surface treatment. Smooth plain accounted for 52.5 percent of the Sycamore plain wares.

Radiocarbon dates for the Wakulla phase cluster in the ninth century A.D., suggesting a time span for the Wakulla phase between A.D. 800 and A.D. 900. This Wakulla phase, as defined in Apalachicola valley ceramics, corresponds to the period during which the entire Southeast was marked by relatively mild climate, with lesser but still adequate summer precipitation and relatively long, warm summers. Winters, however, appear to have grown considerably cooler and drier than the modern "normal" (1930–60) throughout the period from about A.D. 750 through A.D. 1000 (Gunn et al. n.d.; Mitchell 1963; Lamb 1966; Bryson and Baerreis 1968; Watts 1971, 1980; Denten and Karlen 1973; Sanchez and Kutzbach 1974; Wendland and Bryson 1974; Baerreis, Bryson, and Kutzbach 1976; Bernabo and Webb 1977; Bryson and Murray 1977; Delcourt and Delcourt 1977, 1978a, b; King and Allen 1977; Delcourt 1978).

These data correspond remarkably with the hypothesis (Percy and Brose 1974; Brose and Percy 1978) that culturally this period was a rather unstable time. The cause that we initially suggested was a basic change in subsistence patterns, involving significantly greater dependence on agriculture. Agriculture, including both corn and squash, is first documented in the northwestern Florida area during this late Weeden Island–Early Fort Walton period (Milanich 1974). It appears to have been practiced on a small scale, suggesting small garden patches owned by individual small families, which had contributed relatively little to subsistence through early Weeden Island. We believe that agriculture increased gradually in importance and was responsible for the small but cumulative population increases reflected at least in the river valley areas and along the Gulf coast (Brose and

Percy 1978). After several years of intensive survey efforts (Tesar 1979, 1980), there is still little evidence for any Wakulla phase occupation of the interior region. Our initial hypothesis—competition for limited agricultural land (Percy and Brose 1974; Brose and Percy 1974a, 1978; Brose 1975)—has been evaluated in light of ethnographically derived models of southeastern warfare and was criticized by Gibson (1980) with some effect. Given the regional climatic changes documented for this period, it still looks good to me (cf. Brooks 1971).

The Chattahoochee Landing phase, based on data from Chattahoochee Landing, Curlee, and Cayson, differs from the Wakulla phase principally in its initial relationships to Mississippian elsewhere in the Southeast, according to Scarry (1983). It is certainly ephemeral as far as I can see (cf. White 1981).

Chattahoochee phase assemblages are still marked by high check-stamped frequencies, now reduced to 20–30 percent of the total and 55–80 percent of the decorated pottery. Bullen (1958:351) noted that the check-stamped sherds from Chattahoochee Landing are "similar to those from the Fort Walton zone of site J-5 but differ from those found at sites J-18 and Ja-62 and in the Deptford zone at site J-5. Those from G-4 were made of a less sandy paste and have the smooth, frequently black interior surfaces lacking at sites J-8 and Ja-62. They do not have a Weeden Island type of rim. There is less difference, however, in the character of the stampings themselves." Unfortunately, Bullen's distinctions are not sufficient to distinguish Wakulla phase and Chattahoochee Landing phase components. In the ceramic assemblages of the Chattahoochee Landing phase, Fort Walton ceramic types first appear. Wakulla Check Stamped and Northwest Florida Cob marked and Cord marked ceramics continue in reduced frequencies. Lake Jackson Plain, Cool Branch Incised, Point Washington Incised, and Marsh Island Incised occur in low frequencies at the lower levels of Cayson and Curlee and in Bullen's tests at Chattahoochee Landing itself. In this phase, known components include large mound-village complexes on the Apalachicola levee. At Chattahoochee Landing this component is approximately 20–25 acres in extent, although, in contrast to Scarry (1979a, 1983), White (1981) still notes the presence of numerous scattered small sites at this time.

Radiocarbon determinations of A.D. 950 ± 130, A.D. 970 ± 105, and A.D. 1010 ± 130 have been obtained for the Chattahoochee Landing phase component represented in the early plaza and wall trench levels at the Cayson site (cf. Brose et al. 1976; Brose and Percy 1978). The reconstructions of local climate for the Chattahoochee Landing—

Bristol phases of A.D. 950–1100 appear to indicate a temperature generally warmer than modern normal, but the increasing dryness and mildness of winters from about A.D. 1000 to about A.D. 1150 may have lessened winter precipitation in the interior, along the Torreya upland–Cody escarpment, while it extended (especially along the Gulf coast) the frost-free growing period (Baerreis and Bryson 1965; Bryson and Wendland 1967; Bryson and Baerreis 1968; Baerreis, Bryson, and Kutzbach 1976; cf. Griffin 1961; Watts 1969; Whitehead 1972; Dean and Robinson 1976; Wright 1976; Gunn and Mahula 1977; Delcourt 1978; Delcourt and Delcourt 1978b).

The Bristol phase at the Yon site differs from those of the Chattahoochee Landing phase in that while Wakulla Check Stamped, Cobmarked, and Cord-marked ceramics continue as elements, they do not dominate. The most common decorated wares are Point Washington Incised (incised lines parallel to the rim of the simple bowls), Marsh Island Incised, Fort Walton Incised, and an undefined engraved ware. Most sherds, tempered with somewhat micaceous fine sand, possess smoothed, black exteriors and interiors; vessel forms include open bowls, standard jars, flaring rim bowls, carinated bowls, and a few bottles and beakers (Brose et al. 1976; Scarry 1979a, 1983).

Four radiocarbon determinations for the components at the Yon site average A.D. 1000. The Bristol phase assemblage resembles some of the ceramics recovered from the middle Chattahoochee valley at Cemochechobee (Schnell, Knight, and Schnell 1979). However, some of the excised pottery resembles early ceramics at Moundville I (cf. Steponaitis 1978), as do those at Roods (Caldwell 1955; Chase 1959, 1963).

The Cayson phase (at the Cayson, Curlee, and Gulf Power Scholz Parking Lot sites) forms the major occupation at the type site, and at Curlee and Cayson it stratigraphically overlies the Chattahoochee Landing phase. It firmly represents a major Mississippian development. Ceramics are marked by Lake Jackson Plain, Pensacola Plain, Lake Jackson Incised, Fort Walton Incised, and Cool Branch Incised. Marsh Island Incised, Point Washington Incised, Wakulla Check Stamped, and Northwest Florida Cob-marked appear but in lesser frequencies (cf. Brose 1974; Brose et al. 1976; Brose and Wilkie 1980; White 1980, 1981).

Five radiocarbon samples from a Cayson phase occupation at the type site and one from Curlee date A.D. 1010–1180 (Brose et al. 1976; White 1981). Cayson phase components, unlike those of the previous phases, are diverse in size, ranging from the large ceremonial center at Cayson (ca. 13 hectares) to the small hunting camp at the Power Plant site (1,500 m²) (Brose et al. 1976; Brose and Percy 1978; Brose and Wilkie 1980). From most major sites, recovered ethnobotanical and pollen samples document the full agricultural commitment of these Mississippian societies (Watts 1969; Brose et al. 1976; Clouse 1978; Delcourt and Delcourt 1978a; Brose 1980b; White 1980), and support the reconstructions of major climatic changes occurring throughout the Cayson and Sneads Fort Walton phases, changes that offer considerable insight into the cultural behavior of the period. From approximately A.D. 1100 to A.D. 1230, summer precipitation appears to have gradually decreased to modern norms throughout the lower Southeast (Lamb 1966; Craig 1969; Gunn et al. n.d.). However, the period from A.D. 1200 to about A.D. 1280 appears to have represented a dramatic and rather sudden shift to a summer weather pattern of considerable dryness, nearly duplicating the weather pattern of July 1931; this aridity appears to have lasted until about A.D. 1350–80. During that 100–150-year period, most of the region shows a 25–75 percent decrease in summer precipitation patterns. However, the Three River area of Florida, Georgia, and Alabama shows a slight (up to 25 percent) increase in summer precipitation (Baerreis and Bryson 1965; Lamb 1966; Bryson and Wendland 1967; Denten and Karlen 1973; LaMarche 1974; Sanchez and Kutzbach 1974; Wendland and Bryson 1974; Baerreis, Bryson, and Kutzbach 1976; Bryson and Murray 1977; Delcourt and Delcourt 1977, 1978a; Gunn and Mahula 1977).

During this same period, A.D. 1150–1250, there was what is interpreted as a clear winter warming trend, with markedly longer growing seasons and with but locally heavier winter precipitation. After A.D. 1250 winters apparently grew slightly drier and colder so that, in this region of the Southeast, the pattern by A.D. 1350 was similar to the normal modern for fall through spring (Griffin 1960, 1961; Bryson and Baerreis 1968; Watts 1969, 1980; Baerreis, Bryson and Kutzbach 1976; Bryson and Murray 1977; Gunn et al. n.d.). It is during this period that the first good evidence of what Tesar called Early Apalachee Fort Walton first appears in the Red Hills area around Tallahassee (Anonymous 1974; Tesar 1979, 1980; Scarry 1983:85–91). There are also numerous aspects of the late Cayson phase ceramic assemblage that are similar to those from the undated contexts at the Fort Walton mound (Fairbanks 1960, 1965a) as well as at some Alabama River phase sites (Cottier 1968; Sheldon 1974; Nance 1976) at the Abercrombie (Fairbanks 1955) and Seaborn mound sites (Neuman 1961), at the Cool Branch site (Huscher 1971) dated to A.D. 1276 ± 105, in Alabama, and at the Lake Jackson site, where Jones (1982) dated the basal stage of Mound 3 to A.D. 1227 ± 85). The expansive nature of these clearly Mississippian cultures (in economy, socioceremonial organization, and ceramics) parallels (but need not result from) the geographically widespread expansion of coeval Mississippian societies throughout the country (Griffin 1967; Smith [ed.] 1978).

During this phase of Fort Walton in the Santa Rosa Sound, the Choctawhatchee, and the St. Andrews Bay areas, there was a trend to larger sites with less dispersal of the population. The Fort Walton mound seems to have been the nucleating center for all of Choctawhatchee Bay, at least until very late Fort Walton; then, along with Pensacola ceramics, a number of separate community areas, each marked by a cemetery or a burial mound and a large number of tightly clustered middens, seemed to become important (cf. Tesar 1973; Bense 1978). Lazarus (1971) suggested that Fort Walton villages of the Choctawhatchee Bay area consisted of individual small family house areas, interspersed with artificially prepared midden ridges used as garden plots. So far, this pattern has not been noted for Weeden Island (nor has it actually been proved for Fort Walton of this date) (Brose and Percy 1978). Following Bullen (1949) and Gardner (1966, 1969, 1971), Scarry (1983) saw this as the period in which the interior region of the Marianna lowlands yielded the first evidence of a regional Fort Walton complex. Tesar (1980) and Payne (1980) have speculated that the distinctive spatial arrangements characteristic of the Tallahassee (Lake Jackson) Early Apalachee may have originated at this time (cf. Griffin 1950:99–112; Fryman 1971). Indeed, the miscellaneous ceramics that accompanied John Rogan's 1883 report to the Smithsonian BAE Mound Exploration Program suggest that occupation of the Letchworth, or Lake Miccosukee, mound group (8Je337) was also begun at this time, as were, apparently, several small Fort Walton sites reported by Phelps around Ochlocknee Bay (Phelps 1966b). Whether this Fort Walton expansion was due to an improved semitheocratic bureaucracy (Scarry 1980b) or to climatic opportunism (Griffin 1960, 1961), not only did it occur by A.D. 1300 but it established the regional variants in Fort Walton (if not in Safety Harbor as well) that remained relatively intact until Spanish contact.

The Sneads phase, which follows Cayson in the Upper Apalachicola, continues many ceramic concepts from the earlier phase; while Lake Jackson Plain, Lake Jackson Incised, and Fort Walton Incised dominate the assemblages, Wakulla Check Stamped and Pensacola Plain gradually disappear. At the Cayson site, Pensacola (Mississippi) Plain forms 20.9 percent of the plain ware in the lowest levels, with grit-tempered comprising 46.9 percent and sand-tempered 25.2 percent. In the upper levels at Cayson, shell tempering is found in 7.7 percent of the plainware, grit tempering is found in 75.8 percent, and sand tempering in 14.0 percent. This trend, which Scarry suggested began as the replacement of sand tempering in the Bristol phase, continues into the Yon phase. A similar trend in temper was observed at the Singer-Moye site in Stewart County, Georgia, a Rood's phase site (Knight 1979). However ephemeral or geographically restricted to the Upper Apalachicola it is, Sneads phase components have been identified at J-2, J-5, Coe's landing, Curlee, Yon, and North Flat Creek. One radiocarbon date for the Sneads phase occupation at the J-5 site was A.D. 1300 ± 250 (Bullen 1958), and the ceramics of Scarry's Sneads phase equate with Bullen's Fort Walton 3 (Bullen 1958). Similar Rood phase ceramic assemblages from the Cemochechobee site on the Chattahoochee appear to relate to the period during which Nashville Negative-Painted effigies were acquired (after A.D. 1250).

The Yon phase, the latest clear ceramic phase in the Apalachicola Valley, is seen by Scarry (1983) in the uppermost levels of the Yon site midden and represents a change in ceramic ware characteristics and in type frequencies. Yon phase ceramics contain heavy grit tempering and lack the smoothed, frequently black surfaces continuing the trend Scarry saw earlier in the Cayson phase, when Lake Jackson Plain and Lake Jackson Incised appear as grit-tempered varieties. Other types, however, such as Fort Walton Incised, continued to appear on both grit- and sand-tempered pastes.

The Yon phase is characterized by grit-tempered complicated stamped and incised-punctated types, which differ slightly from the ceramics of the later Leon-Jefferson period in Leon County. Standard jars are the common vessel form, and the most frequent motifs are bulls-eyes and bulls-eyes with dotted crosses. Rims, frequently pinched or marked with cane impressions, closely resemble Lamar Complicated Stamped in the Middle Chattahoochee (Brannon 1909; Fairbanks 1956; Chase 1962; Broyles 1963; Huscher 1971; Penman 1976).

Some grit-tempered Fort Walton Incised or Incised-punctated sherds show rims that are notched. Other incised sherds are related to Lamar Bold Incised (Willey 1949:493). Finally, a check-stamped ware similar to Leon or Mercier Check Stamped with rhomboidal checks occurs. Scarry suggested a correlation between the Yon phase ceramics and the Bull Creek materials in the Middle Chattahoochee (Sears 1956, 1967; McMichael and Kellar 1960; Scarry 1979a, b, 1983). Radiocarbon dates obtained from the type site for the Yon phase were A.D. 1310 ± 105, and A.D. 1420 ± 120. An A.D. 1400 date was obtained by Bullen for the Yon phase in the upper levels of site J-15, and the date of A.D. 1470 ± 70 from upper levels at Lake Jackson Md 3 (Jones 1982) appears to relate to a similar ceramic phase, which indeed has been characteristic of the Lake Jackson site itself.

Climate and Mississippian culture variation in northwestern Florida

The climatic reconstructions for the earlier parts of the Yon phase suggest that between A.D. 1350 and A.D. 1450, there was little change from the pattern of warm, wet winters and cool, dry summers of the previous century (Lamb 1966; Bryson and Murray 1977). There appears to have been a major local amelioration of the general region summer aridity by about A.D. 1400 (Bryson and Baerreis 1968) so that over the Three River portions of northwestern Florida there would have been quite wet summers, showing little direct effect on the "dustbowl" period of A.D. 1250–1350 farther west. Mild, slightly variable, nearly modern winter weather appears to have continued in this region from A.D. 1350 up to about A.D. 1450, after which a massive and very rapid shift occurred to long, dry, very cold winters characteristic of the sixteenth century (Griffin 1961; Sanchez and Kutzbach 1974; Baerreis, Bryson and Kutzbach 1976; Bryson and Murray 1977).

There does not appear to be any significant change in the geographical distribution or economic adaptation of the differing regional Fort Walton complexes in most of northwestern Florida, although the period is marked by the introduction of Southern Cult ideography (Waring and Holder 1945; Waring 1968), suggesting to me a breakdown in mundane economic-political social regulation. It is likely that the strong Mississippian ceremonial patterns, developed first in the Apalachicola and then found in the Tallahassee interior region, had become fully established along the Florida Gulf coastal regions by the end of this phase. This appears to represent the time at which the initial introduction of Moundville II–III ceramic technology, and some ceramic vessel modes, occurred in the Alabama River (Cottier 1968; Peebles 1970, 1971; Sheldon 1974; Steponaitis 1978, 1980b); at sites in the middle Chattahoochee (Scarry 1979a, b, 1983;

Schnell, Knight, and Schnell 1979; F. Schnell 1980; G. Schnell 1980; Knight 1980b; White 1980, 1981) and along the West Florida Gulf coast (Tesar 1973; Lazarus and Hawkins 1976; Brose and Percy 1978; Knudsen 1979; Scarry 1979b, 1983).

This period is certainly the earliest to which the Pensacola Engraved ceramics can be assigned at Moundville (Steponaitis 1980a), again suggesting that they did not float downstream. Along the eastern coastal region there appeared to be a shift of emphasis, with no clear documentation for major Fort Walton ceremonial centers west of the Grady site mounds at the mouth of the Apalachicola River (V. J. Knight, pers. comm.). Payne (1980) has suggested that Percy and Brose (1974) may not have oversimplified the situation: "In Fort Walton, shellfishing is important at coastal, but not inland, sites. Thus, tentatively, it appears that coastal Fort Walton groups were not as strongly committed to agriculture. . . . There is no evidence that coastal Fort Walton sites are seasonal stations of inland agricultural communities." Nonetheless, as I later noted (Brose and Percy 1978), there is still no clear evidence to relate these small eastern coastal Late Apalachee or Yon phase Fort Walton sites to the larger Fort Walton political centers to the north (cf. Payne 1980; Tesar 1980). Perhaps the low frequency and erratic distribution of the shell-tempered Pensacola ceramics along the eastern coast (Sears 1962a, b, 1977; Phelps 1969; Brose and Percy 1978) are due to the seasonally limited nature of Fort Walton economic activities in this region after A.D. 1350. The area was certainly thinly occupied during the Spanish Entrada and Mission periods (Priestley 1928; Swanton 1935, 1939; Smith 1948, 1957; Fairbanks 1952, 1964; Milanich and Fairbanks 1980).

These expansive Mississippian characteristics are also evident in the Fort Walton interior regions. There, in the Tallahassee Red Hills and the lower Chattahoochee-Flint river valleys below the fall line, Lamar and Lamar-influenced ceramic technology and design elements (but few vessel modes) appear on late Sneads and Yon phase sites (Caldwell 1955; Chase 1962; Broyles 1963; Schnell 1970, 1975b; Caldwell and Smith 1978; Scarry 1979a, b; White 1980, 1981; Belovich et al. 1982). There appears to be a considerable intermixture of more traditional Fort Walton design motifs, with Lamar stamping, or of Lamar-like rim appliqués on Lake Jackson Plain jars, seen especially in the upper disturbed levels of the Yon and Curlee sites in the Apalachicola River valley (White 1981; Scarry 1983). While difficult to document, due to the disturbed nature of the deposits thus far known, it is my impression that we could easily seriate (post hoc) the transition in that

region from Late Fort Walton to Leon-Jefferson ceramics. It should
be pointed out that this situation does not occur in the Marianna Lowland interior (cf. Gardner 1969, 1971; Scarry 1983), where limestone-
tempered late Fort Walton is the latest (although limited) aboriginal
manifestation. Nor does the transition appear clear in the Tallahassee
interior region, where Lake Jackson (Sneeds-Yon) Fort Walton assemblages with only a minor admixture of Lamar ceramic elements appear to date to the final occupation of the Lake Jackson site (A.D.
1530 ± 85 for the final Md. 3 stage), or in the hierarchically related
small mounds (Velda for example) or farmsteads (Jones and Penman
1973; Tesar 1979, 1980; Payne 1980; Scarry 1980a, b, 1983; Jones
1982). Nonetheless, the density of population and the emphasis of
Fort Walton political and ceremonial activities have clearly left the major river valleys after A.D. 1500. They appear centralized in the Tallahassee region, but there may also have been another center at Fort
Walton, far more closely related (in ceramic styles at least) to the Mississippian populations to the west. Also at this time the Safety Harbor
complexes on the west coast south of the Suwannee River were fully
developed. We know virtually nothing about the late prehistoric complexes of the coastal bend area, other than the occasional presence of
both Safety Harbor and Pensacola materials at Cedar Key.

It is probably significant that the phases from late Yon into Leon-
Jefferson, that is, from A.D. 1500 to about A.D. 1650, which Smith
(1948) called Mission Apalachee (Hispanicized Fort Walton), correspond so neatly with "the Little Ice Age," a period of much moisture
and cold, very long winters (with average conditions approximating
the notorious 1976–77 winter). It is possible that even in Florida,
frost-free seasons may have been so shortened and irregular during
this climatic episode that the agricultural commitment of the Tallahassee Red Hills (Lake Jackson) Fort Walton societies became disad-
vantageous (cf. Griffin 1961; Baerreis and Bryson 1965; Sanchez and
Kutzbach 1974; Bryson and Murray 1977). While summer precipitation and temperatures along the Gulf coast seem to have been somewhat more stable and apparently rather warm and wet, late spring
and early fall frosts would have placed a premium on those limited
areas of well-drained and sheltered arable soils. That scarcity may be
of some value in explaining the hostile aboriginal cultural and economic interactions of the period—patterns of rapid cultural destruction under the impacts of competing Spanish, French, and English
militaristic imperialism and the documented introduction of new and
virulent epidemics (Crosby 1972; Ubelaker 1974). Certainly, study of

the aboriginal cultures of the Fort Walton region after A.D. 1700 will tell us less about Mississippian cultures on the Gulf coast than about colonial European politics in Carolina and Quebec.

Note

Beyond indicating my continuing respect for the herculean work of Gordon R. Willey, I should state that, for good or ill, this paper could not have been written without the efforts of many archaeologists who have worked in this region of the Southeast. My sometime students John Scarry, Nancy White, and Duncan Wilkie not only physically recovered many of these data but, with Russell Weisman, have offered thoughtful and critical evaluations (only some of which I have accepted). My professional colleagues have shared with me their data and ideas, among them Judy Bense, Ian Brown, Dave Davis, David DeJarnette, Roy Dickens, James Griffin, John Griffin, Ned Jenkins, B. Calvin Jones, Bennie Keel, Jim Knight, Yulee Lazarus, Jerald Milanich, Jerry Nielsen, George Percy, Frank and Gail Schnell, Vincas Steponaitis, Louis Tesar, John Walthall, and Stephen Williams. I offer them sincere thanks and more sincere apologies for any misinterpretations I may have made. I thank the Harvard Peabody Museum's Lower Mississippi Survey and the Smithsonian Institution for my participation in the January 1980 B.A.E. Mound Exploration Conference, at which time I was able to inspect many of their early collections, and for their willing photographic assistance.

Perhaps my greatest unacknowledged debt is to William Sears, who has passed over most of this ground before. With Olympian hindsight I have argued against many of Sears's published complexes and proposed sequences and sociocultural interpretations of the archaeological data he has ably gathered. Yet, behind these details, his goal has been the demonstration that this region can be critical to understanding the prehistory of the entire Southeast.

All in all, however, I would rather Moore had stayed in Philadelphia.

8

Late Prehistoric Adaptation in the
Mobile Bay Region

Vernon J. Knight, Jr.

Mobile Bay is the mouth of the second largest river delta on the U.S. Gulf coast. It is tied, through the Mobile-Alabama-Tombigbee river system, to the enormous Mississippian center at Moundville; at various times in prehistory, Mobile Bay cultures were also in direct or indirect contact with the lower Mississippi valley, southern and central Georgia, and northwestern Florida. At the time of European contact, the bay was the home of the Tomeh and Mobile Indians. Knight argues that these "tribes" are historic representatives of late prehistoric groups that were responsible for the Pensacola complex, a ceramic tradition that stretched from northwestern Florida through the Mississippi River delta. Within the Pensacola complex, local subsistence and settlement patterns were highly variable. Those of the Mobile Bay region were adapted to the exigencies of deltaic horticulture and seasonal hunting and gathering, with seasonal movements adjusted to periods of flooding of the Mobile delta. Knight elaborates upon this assessment through an integrated consideration of archaeological and ethnohistoric data from the Mobile Bay area.

MODERN approaches to prehistoric coastal adaptations have rightly tended to emphasize the uniqueness of livelihoods gained partially

198

from the oceans (Yesner 1980), in contrast to the various potentials of inland existence. By drawing the lines of investigation in this manner, it becomes possible to isolate general coastal economic types, which facilitates broad-scale evolutionary comparisons. But when we begin to examine the Gulf coast north of Mexico as a unit—say at the time of initial European contact—we find anything but uniformity. Instead we find a thorough mixture of social and economic phenomena, from the stratified but nonhorticultural Calusa on the Florida coast to the partially horticultural chiefdoms of the northern Gulf to the egalitarian hunter-gatherers of the Texas coast. Trying to account for these differences is a matter of specifying the conditions for smaller segments of the coast that might have favored certain sets of adaptive strategies over others.

The importance of horticulture in places along the northern Gulf coast in late prehistoric times has become a debated but important issue. The increase in calorie production that the introduction of horticulture brought may be related to apparent differences in demography and settlement along the coast. Focusing on the Mobile Bay region of the Alabama coast, I will take the position that traditional littoral adaptive strategies were significantly modified in late prehistoric times to integrate cultivation as an important component of the local economy. An ethnohistorical assessment of indigenous Mobile-Tomeh economic patterns of the early eighteenth century reveals a distinctive mode of delta horticulture successfully merged within a scheduled subsistence cycle of hunting, fishing, and gathering. This pattern yields important clues concerning how the earlier Pensacola period chiefdoms of the Mobile Bay region must have been materially provisioned.

The Pensacola complex

The late prehistoric period in the Mobile Bay region is marked by a variant of the Pensacola ceramic complex. Pensacola ceramics were first informally described and illustrated in the archaeological literature by Dr. Andrew Bigelow of the Wesleyan Institute of Newark. Bigelow (1853:190–91) discussed some of the major characteristics of the ceramics—shell tempering, incising, and polishing—and he illustrated typical sherds. Many years later, in 1899, a collection of whole Pensacola-style vessels from a sand mound at Bear Point, Alabama, was obtained for the U.S. National Museum by Francis H. Parsons of the U.S. Coast and Geodetic Survey. Clarence B. Moore also conducted a number of excavations in the Mobile Bay region during the

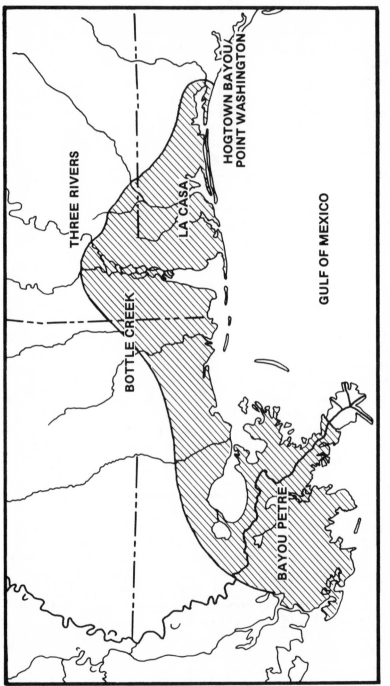

Fig. 8.1. Pensacola complex: distribution and variants.

years 1899–1905, obtaining quantities of Pensacola-style ceramics and publishing the results (Moore 1905a, b, c).

It was on the basis of Parson's and Moore's museum collections that the initial conception of a "Mobile-Pensacola ware" was offered by William Henry Holmes (1903:104–7). This concept was essentially the Pensacola complex as we recognize it today, with the addition of the closely related Alabama River ceramic series from central Alabama. Holmes called attention to the representational life-form elements in the ceramics, and he correctly identified stylistic relationships with the Mississippian ceramics elsewhere. The modern definition of the Pensacola complex derives from Gordon R. Willey's report on the Florida Gulf coast (1949:463–66), where it is lumped with the Fort Walton complex because of Willey's restricted sample. Current opinion favors a segregation of Fort Walton from Pensacola (Sears 1977:176–77), but the Pensacola ceramic types set up by Willey survive essentially intact and have been useful in recent work with minor modifications.

The distribution of Pensacola ceramics defines a broad ceramic style area which embraces several discrete manifestations from Louisiana to Florida rather than a tight, coherent unit of cultural-historical significance. The approximate distribution of the complex, with some of the identified regional and temporal variants, is shown on the accompanying map (fig. 8.1). These variants are not only ceramic; there are also indications of differences among settlement types, settlement patterns, relative time depths, and so forth. It seems clear that we are dealing here with a number of societies under the Pensacola rubric with potentially separate histories and that we cannot properly speak of Pensacola as a single prehistoric system.

Although several successive chronological refinements of the Mobile Bay sequence have been published (DeJarnette 1952; Trickey 1958; Wimberly 1960; Trickey and Holmes 1967, 1971), the late portion of the sequence remains undated and poorly understood. Preceding the appearance of the Pensacola complex in the area are two Weeden Island related phases, Tates Hammock and McLeod (Walthall 1980: 167–72). Tates Hammock site components are distributed along Mississippi Sound west of Mobile Bay into coastal Mississippi. They appear to represent the continuance of a littoral hunting and gathering mode of existence which can be traced back in place at least as far as the Bayou La Batre period, ca. 1000–500 B.C. Tates Hammock ceramics are to be equated with Wimberly's hyphenated construct "Weeden Island–Coles Creek." McLeod phase components, on the other hand, cluster on the lower Tombigbee River above the Mobile delta. Rather than a coastal phenomenon, McLeod is best considered a central-based riverine adaptation of the coastal plain. McLeod phase material culture is generally comparable to Wakulla material culture along the Apalachicola River in northwest Florida. The Tates Hammock and McLeod phases overlap in time, although McLeod is in a general sense slightly later. Based on ceramic cross-dating, it seems unlikely that either construct survives beyond A.D. 1000.

In addition to these two phases, there is some evidence of yet another complex, unnamed, which is characterized by a predominance of cord-marked ceramics and may locally overlie McLeod (Trickey and Holmes 1967:25). This evidence remains slim, and at present there is little basis for an assessment of the position or importance of this complex relative to the overall sequence.

A beginning date for the subsequent Pensacola complex is at present impossible to fix with any confidence. Some of the recognized components have yielded European trade materials and are very late; nevertheless there are several threads of evidence that suggest a surprisingly early appearance. These are, first, the consistent association at several sites of Pensacola ceramics with certain Plaquemine types of the lower Mississippi valley which are dated in the A.D. 1200–1350 range; second, the presence of stylistic attributes that are consistently early in Moundville ceramics to the north; third, the association of the salt pan type Langston Fabric Marked at a Pensacola salt production site on the lower Tombigbee River (Trickey 1958:394; decorated salt pan ware of this type appears to disappear prior to Late Mississippian times both in Alabama and in the Southeast generally). Following these admittedly slim leads, a useful estimate for the appearance of the complex in the Mobile Bay region may be set at ca. A.D. 1250. This estimate still leaves a considerable time gap from A.D. 1000 to A.D. 1250, with no good candidates to fill it other than those found by arbitrarily moving up the dates for McLeod or by pushing back those for Pensacola still further. At bottom, the whole matter of dating without dates is ticklish, unrewarding business.

At any rate, it is increasingly clear that Pensacola, at least in the Mobile Bay region, is not merely protohistoric. It has a relatively long and complex developmental history which will have to be sorted out before any firm pronouncements about changing adaptive strategies can be made.

At the late end of the sequence, the Pensacola complex apparently survives into the first half of the eighteenth century (table 8.1). For example, small amounts of shell-tempered sherds, probably Pensacola series, have been recovered in eighteenth-century contexts at Fort

Table 8.1. Illustrative ceramic frequencies from an early contact period site on Mobile Bay (1Bal96) (from DeJarnette, ed. 1975)

Type	N	%
Shell temper		
Plain		
Pensacola Plain, coarse var.	2,106	51.97
Discoidal	2	.05
Effigy fragment	1	.03
Pensacola Plain, fine var.	896	22.11
Discoidal	1	.03
Effigy fragment	2	.05
Incised		
Moundville Incised	34	.84
Pensacola Filmed Incised	10	.25
Pensacola Incised	162	4.00
Residual Incised	1	.03
Engraved		
Moundville Engraved	4	.10
Moundville Filmed Engraved	4	.10
D'Olive Engraved	16	.39
D'Olive Filmed Engraved	6	.15
Filmed		
Pensacola Black Filmed	38	.94
Punctated		
Residual punctated	10	.25
Total shell temper	3,293	81.29
Grit temper		
Plain		
Alachua Plain	437	10.79
Incised		
Ft. Walton Incised	3	.07
Stamped		
Leon Check Stamped	11	.27
Prairie Cord Marked	2	.05
North Fork Simple Stamped	13	.32
Pinched		
Lochloosa Punctated	1	.03
Total grit temper	467	11.53
Clay temper		
Plain		
Residual plain	244	6.02
Incised		
Residual incised	28	.69
Filmed		
Residual buff filmed	1	.03
Total clay temper	273	6.74
Sand temper		
Plain		
Residual plain	10	.25
Incised		
Residual incised	1	.03
Filmed		
Residual buff filmed	8	.20
Total sand temper	19	.48
Total	4,052	100.04

Condé on Mobile Bay (Harris 1969:57–58). This period witnessed the influx of a number of refugee groups into Mobile: remnants of Apalachee, Chatot, and Tawasa from North Florida and remnants of Taensa, Chitimacha, and Choctaw from the west. This influx is reflected in the archaeological remains; eighteenth-century aboriginal ceramics from the Mobile Bay region show much diversity and many styles, indicating contacts and movements over a wide area. Most of this evidence has not been systematically studied, but it is worthy of more attention.

Environmental considerations

Obviously much can be said about the environmental setting of the Pensacola sites in the Mobile Bay region, bearing on an understanding of late prehistoric adaptive strategies. Here we can only summarize some important features.

The Mobile-Tensaw river delta is formed a short distance below the confluence of two major river systems, the Tombigbee and the Alabama. The watershed drained by these two systems is second in size only to the Mississippi basin in the eastern United States. The delta is long and narrow, beginning approximately 40 miles above Mobile Bay and flowing southward through a series of distributaries, interconnecting streams, small bays, and swamps. Flanking the delta on either side are navigable rivers—the Tensaw on the east and the Mobile on the west. The numerous delta islands are annually flooded during predictable periods of high water in the months of February through April, the peak coming in March. The delta soils are consequently annually replenished by siltation.

These rivers drain into Mobile Bay, a submerged river valley 8 miles wide at the mouth of the rivers, extending south about 30 miles to the Gulf of Mexico, where the bay is some 25 miles wide. At the Gulf, Mobile Bay is protected by sand spits, forming a complex estuarine system marked by shallow beds of marsh clam (*Rangia cuneata*), a brackish water species, and oyster (*Crassostrea virginica*), both of which were intensively harvested by the prehistoric inhabitants.

The delta system transects the elevated, cuesta-like Citronelle formation of Pliocene and Pleistocene age (Cooke 1926:295–97; Boone 1974). This circumstance results in a series of flood-protected bluffs on both the eastern and western margins of the delta. During the historic period these bluffs were occupied in places by villages of resident aboriginal groups.

The vegetative pattern characteristic of the delta is the typical swamp or bottomland forest type. That of the hinterland beyond the delta to the east and west is largely longleaf-slash pine forest, the so-called pine barren, a fire subclimax (Crocker 1969:74) whose successional trend is toward a mixed hardwood forest climax (Quarterman and Keever 1962). Larson (1980:38–47, 51–54) has argued for the monotony of a pristine variant of this forest type on the coastal plain, stressing its singularly meager potential to support economically important fauna. While this assessment is credible in a relative sense, it is nevertheless important to recognize that the low productive potential of the longleaf-slash pine forest is locally mitigated by factors of soil, drainage, and slope. For example, Crocker (1963) states that one-fifth of the gross longleaf forest area of southern Alabama is occupied by fire-resistant branch bottoms, which support dense mixed hardwood communities. These "fire islands" provide food and cover for deer, turkey, and other wildlife. The potential of the longleaf forest to support exploitable sources of animal protein is a direct function of the local availability of mast. In short, the dynamics of vegetative succession in the longleaf area, together with variation in topography and drainage, suggest that mast production, hence animal protein production, may have been locally higher in portions of the area than that suggested by Larson's blanket characterization.

Relative access to high-mast-producing coastal plain forests (see Hedlund and Knight 1969) may lie behind differences in the success of the procurement of large game attributed to coastal aboriginal groups. For example, French observers impressionistically noted that such inhabitants of the Mississippi delta as the Chitimacha, Washa, and Opelousa were wanting in large game (Giraud 1974:73); on the other hand, the Mobile and Tomeh of the Mobile delta are reported to have harvested large game "in quantity" (Knight and Adams n.d.:7).

Types of sites investigated

With the exception of the historic sites of Fort Condé (Harris 1969), Fort Louis (Harris 1970), and Port Dauphin (Curren 1971:10), only two types of sites within a larger range of late sites in the region have been explored to any extent: the unique multiple mound center on Bottle Creek and a general class of seasonal estuarine fishing encampments. Missing from the current data base are delta farmsteads and permanent villages along the marginal bluffs, both of which are documented in the postcontact period.

The Bottle Creek site, a Pensacola mound center located in the middle of the Mobile-Tensaw delta, is easily the largest and most striking of the known late sites in the area. Bottle Creek is undoubtedly the site that the historic Mobile Indians revered as sacred, according to the French, and from which Bienville in 1700 recovered a number of clay figurines on a mound summit (Hamilton 1910:56; Higginbotham 1977:70n).

The best description of the site to date is also the earliest, written by Andrew Bigelow in 1853 for the *American Journal of Science*. According to Bigelow, the site lies upon a slightly elevated tract on the southwest bank of Bottle Creek, surrounded on the northern, western, and eastern sides by swamps. There are two large platform mounds: the larger is approximately 49 feet tall with a base 104 feet long and 46 feet wide; the other is lower but broader and has a terraced summit. On the latter Bigelow recovered quantities of typical Pensacola ceramics, and of these he gives a modest account. Adjacent to the platform mounds was a borrow pit. At the opposite end of the tract, about 1,200 feet from the larger mound, is a third, somewhat smaller mound from which Bigelow reports a burial accompanied by large, globular bluish glass beads, apparently from the description an eighteenth-century bead type. Lining the northern and western sides of the site are several more low mounds in a row, which together merge with a rectilinear embankment. Bigelow excavated in one of these mounds, uncovering a hearth. Along the southwest margin of the site he located an artifically excavated canal or moat (Bigelow 1853).

David L. DeJarnette of the Alabama Museum of Natural History briefly explored the site in 1932, excavating a 10-foot test trench in the plaza area at the foot of the largest mound, along with several smaller test pits. The recovered material was analyzed in the early 1960s by Nicholas H. Holmes, who reports an assemblage made up almost wholly of Pensacola ceramic types (Holmes 1963).

Another site class for which there is some information consists of seasonal estuarine fishing encampments. These conspicuous shell midden sites range in size from small lenses of shell only a few meters across, which typically line the bayous of the delta, to large shell middens several meters thick on the margins of Mississippi Sound. In the northern part of Mobile Bay the middens tend to consist of marsh clam (*Rangia cuneata*); those lining Mississippi Sound tend to consist of oyster (*Crassostrea virginica*) (Curren 1976: fig. 2). A number of these sites have been tested or excavated, and a significant proportion of them bear Pensacola components. Reported sites include the Dauphin Island "shell mounds" (1Mb72), which were briefly investigated by Moore (1905b:295), and the Strong's Bayou site (1Ba81), excavated during the depression era by the Alabama Museum of Natural History (DeJarnette, Anderson, and Wimberly 1941). Pensacola components at such shell midden sites typically overlie earlier Woodland components (see Wimberly 1960: tables 9–13, 17, 18), indicating some continuity in the exploitation of estuarine resources.

To date, the most thoroughly reported of the Pensacola shell midden sites are those that lie at the mouth of D'Olive Creek (1Ba196 and 1Ba251) on the northeast shore of Mobile bay. These sites were investigated during two field seasons, 1973–74, by the University of Alabama Museums under contract to the Alabama Highway Department (DeJarnette 1976). Both were linear middens consisting of compact zones of *Rangia* valves alternating with zones of sand, extending to an average depth of 60–80 centimeters.

Botanical remains were recovered from one of the D'Olive Creek sites (1Ba196), including hickory nuts, persimmon seeds, acorns, and mulberry seeds. DeLeon (1976:220) suggests that these indicate a June or July to late November occupation. Quantities of maize cobs found in small "smudge-pit"-like features represent the only direct evidence of cultigens so far identified in the region (fig. 8.2).

Based upon his zooarchaeological analysis of one excavation unit in site 1Ba196, Cailup B. Curren reconstructed the type of faunal procurement represented. He concluded that fish were the most important class of animals taken. Ten fish species were present, of which black drum (*Pogonias cromis* L.), gar (*Lepisosteus* sp.), and sheepshead (*Archosargus probatocephalus*) were most numerous. Less significant in the site economy were marsh clams, reptiles (11 species identified), mammals (6 species identified), and birds (2 species identified). Noting the kinds of fish represented and the lack of such artifacts as bone points, hooks, or net sinkers at the site, Curren (1978:49) suggests that the "core of the faunal procurement system . . . was probably some form of tidal trap," recalling that the Spaniard Bazares had seen a tidal trap on Mobile Bay in 1558. The tidal range at the site is presently about 1.5 feet, and Curren described two variations of tidal traps that would have been effective near the site. I suspect that this system is one of relatively great time depth in the region and that tidal trap technology is far and away the most efficient system among its competitors for extracting animal food from the estuarine environment.

The relative dietary contribution of *Rangia* clams at the D'Olive

Fig. 8.2. Maize cobs *in situ* at IBA196.

Creek sites, as calculated using the method advocated by Byrd (1976a), is very low. *Rangia* were probably gathered only as a supplementary resource in connection with operating the tidal trap, the traps being placed to take advantage of the dependence of black drum and sheeps-head on these molluscs for food. Perhaps generally along the Gulf coast large *Rangia* middens may flag former weir sites.

Sometimes included within treatments of Mobile Bay region ar-chaeology is a separate cluster of protohistoric mound, habitation, salt procurement, and burial sites which exists on the lower Tombigbee River above its juncture with the Alabama River. Sheldon (1974:190–97) has discussed five of the major protohistoric sites in this area, suggesting their affiliation with the "Burial Urn culture" of central Alabama. While data from these sites are minimal, their geographical situation on a meander belt of the Tombigbee River characterized by oxbow lakes suggests a rather different riverine adaptation from that represented by the Pensacola sites farther south. I consider these sites for all practical purposes outside the coastal orbit, and they will not be further treated here. It suffices to say that they are both culturally and ecologically distinguishable from the bulk of the coastal sites, while granting at the same time the ceramic relationships between Pensacola and the interior Alabama River and Wilcox series. The lower Tombigbee sites, it might be added, fall within the sphere of the historic Grand Tomeh, an aboriginal group numbering about 600 in 1700, whose main settlement was located near present-day McIntosh Landing (Higginbotham 1977:60n; see also Giardino, this volume). The Grand Tomeh were related to the Little Tomeh or Naniaba, who with the Mobile inhabited the head of the Mobile-Tensaw delta.

The question of coastal horticulture: conflicting views

It has often been assumed, for various reasons, that the Mississippian expressions along the Gulf coast were substantially horticultural (Willey 1949:539–40; see also discussion by Lazarus and Goggin 1971:52–53). Such a position is justifiably called into question. On the other hand, the existence of a relatively large Pensacola mound center on Bottle Creek in the Mobile Bay region suggests a certain degree of nucleation and sedentism, and maize has been found archaeologically at D'Olive Creek on Mobile Bay, a find that leads to significant research questions. Precisely how was maize horticulture integrated into the historically littoral orientations of pre–Pensacola life in the Mobile area? To what degree did regional Pensacola society move toward a horticultural strategy? Did the integration of horticulture into a coastal existence contribute anything toward a postulated increase in sedentism, nucleation of population, or the rise of ranked social organization during Pensacola times?

Representative of the more cautious assessments of the possibilities for Gulf coastal horticulture is the view of Lewis Larson. He contends (1980:216–18, 222), briefly, that horticulture was absent or played a negligible role among Gulf coast Mississippian societies west of the Apalachicola River (that is, west of the rather exceptional Apalachee). Entering into his judgment is a consideration of soil and climate, linked with an ethnohistorical interpretation. This point of view is related to a broader conviction that coastal adaptations during Mississippian times were, of necessity, qualitatively different from any of the major developments along the interior rivers of the Southeast (Larson 1980:229) necessitating different approaches. For Larson, coastal adaptations cannot be considered merely as extensions or attenuated versions of Mississippian cultures of the interior, due to obvious differences in resource utilization, and the "barrier" effect of the resource-poor longleaf-slash pine forest. This conclusion is, in principle, I believe, correct, although we need to examine more carefully his denial of the horticultural potential of the Gulf coast.

Where coastal horticulture did occur on the Atlantic coast, it took on a particular pattern, which Larson has gone to some trouble to reconstruct (1980:206–9, 218–19). Since he takes the case of the Orista and Guale as paradigmatic of the limitations of coastal horticulture, it is instructive to review the features of that case.

Orista and Guale horticulture was carried out by isolated families living in farmsteads near their fields. Arable soils were found only in thin, scattered parcels, and these were quickly depleted, requiring the farmsteads to relocate regularly in search of more productive soil. Fields were apparently fallowed after a few seasons and were brought back into civilization only much later. Maize was planted in early spring and harvested in early summer. The supply of horticultural products lasted only until late summer or early autumn, at which time the Indians resumed their hunting and gathering pursuits until the next spring.

This pattern of shifting cultivation necessitated by the depletion of isolated tracts of soil capable of tillage prevented any nucleation into permanent villages. Instead, the residences of chiefs seem to have served the purpose of a village, during annual aggregations such as harvest ceremonies. Larson considers the prehistoric Irene site on the Georgia coast, with its chief's house mound, council house, and mortuary, as typical of such coastal centers of periodic aggregation of a usually dispersed populace (Larson 1980:219; see also Caldwell and McCann 1941).

Larson's portrayal of coastal horticulture and settlement may be compared with Curren's reconstruction of late prehistoric subsistence in the Mobile Bay region. Unlike Larson, Curren assumes that horticulture played a major role in the annual economic cycle on the Gulf coast. Curren's model of scheduling is derived (and Larson would undoubtedly judge this an inappropriate choice) from the economic cycle of the interior Choctaw, as inferred from the well-known Lincecum myth (Lincecum 1904; Campbell 1959).

For Curren, the subsistence pursuits of the Mobile Bay region Indians would entail a scheduled population movement between "villages," at which some of the people would remain at all times of the year, and various hunting, gathering, and horticultural loci. By adjusting the Choctaw schedule to hydrographic charts describing monthly river levels in the Mobile-Tensaw delta, he is able to suggest optimum times for each phase of the cycle. The preparation and planting of fields would occur during a period of village residence immediately following the annual late spring runoff. Following planting, most of the summer would be devoted to gathering estuarine foodstuffs such as fish, turtles, and marsh clams by dispersed groups, while the river level remained low. Late summer would occasion a return to the villages for the harvest and storage of crops. As late fall and winter approached, the river level would begin to rise, limiting access to many delta resources. The population would again disperse, collecting oysters through the winter near the mouth of the bay, utilizing stored resources, and pursuing winter game (Curren 1976). Curren, then, differs from Larson mainly in crediting the inhabitants of late prehistoric coastal Alabama with permanent villages and with a relatively substantial and significant amount of horticulture.

Historic Mobile-Tomeh economy

My approach to these questions begins with a search for models of subsistence, settlement, and organization in the ethnohistorical record of the indigenous inhabitants of the Mobile-Tensaw delta, the Mobile and Little Tomeh. That record is a spotty one at best, the most informative accounts coming from the period of French exploration of the Gulf coast in the early years of the eighteenth century. By this time, too, these coastal groups had seen some amount of disruption from sporadic earlier European contacts, particularly from the English-inspired slave trade.

The Mobile and Little Tomeh of the early eighteenth century had a relatively vigorous society and an economy well suited to the delta environments of the Mobile Bay region. We may be assured that their economic strategies bear some relationship to those of their immediate prehistoric predecessors in that environment.

French documents of the period 1699–1710 make it abundantly clear that the Mobile Bay region was aboriginally among the most populous and horticulturally productive regions of the northern Gulf coast. In 1700, after the Indian population had undoubtedly been in decline for some time, the combined census of the Mobile and Little

Tomeh was estimated at 800 (a figure exluding the Grand Tomeh, residing just above the delta, and the Pensacola, who at that time resided in the lower part of the delta). Beginning with the hardships of the French colony at Biloxi in 1699, the French relied for survival on surplus Indian maize from the Mobile and Tomeh, and for the next decade the French periodically dispersed their ranks among them in times of scarcity (Sauvole, in Higginbotham 1969:46, 48; Higginbotham 1977:400). Levasseur's account of 1700 explicitly compares the Mobile and Little Tomeh with the Indians of the lower Mississippi valley with regard to subsistence, concluding that the former were a better source of emergency aid, being "very rich in maize, beans, and squash" (Knight and Adams n.d.:9). Indeed this was one of the primary reasons for moving the recently founded French colony from Biloxi to Mobile. The supply of surplus maize was generally stable and does not seem to have been limited to the immediate postharvest period. For example, Sauvole speaks of obtaining maize stored in the Indian villages during May of 1700, and he observes that the Spanish had done likewise six months earlier (in November 1699) (Rowland and Sanders 1929:9–10).

The crops raised by the Mobile were maize, beans, squash, and watermelons (Knight and Adams n.d.:18). In March 1702, when Bienville was sent to reconnoiter the Mobile-Tensaw delta islands, he reported seeing numerous abandoned "habitations," whose abandonment he attributed to warfare (Higginbotham 1977:70). Iberville's account of the same year and Levasseur's of two years earlier make it fairly clear that these "habitations" were in reality small, seasonal delta farmsteads (Iberville, quoted in Swanton 1922:161–62; Knight and Adams n.d.:7), "separated by families." These small family farmsteads, distributed throughout the delta on restricted parcels of arable land, were flooded during the January–April high water period (D'Artaguiette, in Rowland and Sanders 1929:63). Siltation from the annual flooding undoubtedly renewed the soil's fertility, decreasing or eliminating the need for fallowing.

These farmsteads were related to permanent, named villages flanking the delta along the bluffs on the eastern side, in areas safe from flooding. In 1700, there were five such villages belonging to the Mobile and a sixth belonging to the Little Tomeh. These villages were linked by roads east of the delta (DeBeauchamps, in Mereness 1916:262). At least one such village consisted of houses of chiefs (*ougas*) and sub-chiefs (*outactas*), a public square, a "temple" (McWilliams, ed. 1953: 63–64) (the temple may have once contained a "perpetual fire";

see Charlevoix 1977:154), and a number of additional rectangular houses. All five Mobilian villages seem to have been subject to a single paramount chief, while the Little Tomeh are said to have had two "Great Chiefs" (Knight and Adams n.d.:16).

Documentary sources of this period also serve to amend the picture of Mobilian hunting and gathering activities inferred from the faunal and botanical remains recovered at the D'Olive Creek sites. Levasseur mentions the accessibility of "peaches" (*Prunus* sp.), grapes, oaks, and chestnuts along the Mobile River. He also observes that, among the Mobile, hunting was performed by young and older males and that the principal animals taken were buffalo, deer, bear, and turkey (Knight and Adams n.d.:17, cf. also comments by D'Artaguette, in Rowland and Sanders 1929:52–53, 63).

In sum, the Mobile-Tomeh economic adaptation to the environment of coastal Alabama consisted of a pattern of delta horticulture, merged within a strategy of scheduled activities balanced among gathering, fishing, and hunting. Much like the Orista-Guale pattern on the Atlantic coast, Mobile-Tomeh horticulture relied on isolated farmsteads with small tracts of arable soil under cultivation. But unlike the Orista-Guale area, the delta soils probably did not require frequent fallowing. Productivity was relatively high, the principal threat being excessive flooding. Perhaps related to the stability offered by the year-round storage of horticultural products was the existence of small but permanent villages in areas safe from floodwaters, centering chiefly on residences.

I suspect that this pattern is basically similar to the economic orientation of late prehistoric Pensacola society in the Mobile Bay region. While survey data are inadequate to demonstrate an affinity between Pensacola settlement patterns and historic Mobile and Tomeh settlement, the Bottle Creek site suggests a delta village centering on the residence of a paramount chief. Such large prehistoric shell midden sites as Strong's Bayou and Dauphin Island on Mississippi Sound do not suggest a separate coastal orientation, but rather a pattern of seasonal dispersal and reaggregation.

Conclusion and comparisons

The question of the role of horticulture in the late prehistory of the Mobile Bay region will not be decided by environmental considerations alone nor fully by reference to eighteenth-century economic practices. My intention has not been to demonstrate precisely what kind of system was actually in place: we do not have the archaeological data to decide. Larson's portrayal of late prehistoric Gulf coastal economies may be generally sound, but it ignores French accounts of the horticultural productivity of the Mobile Bay region. Curren's discussion credits the economy with substantial horticulture but relies upon a questionable model of scheduling derived from the interior Choctaw. My position has been to let the Mobile and Little Tomeh speak for themselves, insofar as possible, concerning what late prehistoric existence on the Alabama coast must have been like. I postulate that changes in demography, settlement, and social organization that probably occur with the appearance of Pensacola systems in the area are bound up with the integration of specialized delta horticulture into a traditional estuary-oriented mixed economy. The introduction of delta horticulture would have provided a calorie subsidy balancing the protein production of estuarine fishing, allowing an increased overall production level and the possibility of greater permanent population. The high cost of maize-beans-squash horticulture is offset by its year-round storage potential compared to that of fish, resulting in a more stable supply of nutrients. On the other hand, its introduction would have been at the expense of former dietary diversity, since field preparation would have displaced seasonal collection of wild resources in the late spring.

In comparing Mobile Bay region systems with those of other areas of the Gulf coast, I suggest several distinguishing variables as among the most relevant: access to arable, renewed delta soils: access to nearby flood-protected areas suitable for permanent settlement; access to tidal bays with tidal ranges suitable for fish weir technology; access to shellfish beds; and degree of access to mast-bearing forest types. In areas to the east and west of Mobile Bay, for example the Florida coast near modern-day Pensacola or the Texas coast where aboriginal subsistence is so well described by Nuñez Cabeza de Vaca (Bandelier 1905:54–74), adaptive strategies would have been correspondingly different and more limited to estuarine resources.

The early historic inhabitants of Pensacola Bay, as attested by the Luna chronicles, did practice limited horticulture. But the lack of "subsidized" soils similar to those cultivated by the Mobile and Tomeh probably resulted in an adaptation for Pensacola Bay more similar to the Orista-Guale pattern of the Atlantic coast than to that of coastal Alabama. That is, horticulture must have focused on rapidly depleted, isolated parcels of soil, requiring frequent shifting of farmsteads and effectively preventing permanent village nucleation. In fact, the pattern of late single-mound centers situated among estuarine camps discussed by Brose and Percy (1978:102–3) as typical of the northwest Florida coast recalls that discussed by Larson for the Atlantic coast, namely, chiefly residences serving the purpose of villages for seasonal ceremonial aggregations.

On the other hand, the lower Apalachicola River region, at the head of the delta of that stream, is ethnohistorically described as another horticulturally productive area. Here a Mobile-like system may be applicable. The village of Aute, related to Apalachee, is reputed to have been in this location. Nuñez Cabeza de Vaca described Aute as "where the Indians had plenty of corn and also beans and melons, and that, being so near the sea, they obtained fish" (Bandelier 1905: 29–30). While the evidence is sketchy, the geographical similarity between the Mobile-Tensaw delta and the smaller delta of the Apalachicola River does seem to correlate with similar accounts of subsistence practices and of the importance of horticulture in the two regions. This suggests that the type of economic strategies developed in coastal Alabama may be of wider significance.

9

Protohistoric Cultural Interaction along the

Northern Gulf Coast

Dave D. Davis

For over three decades, archaeologists have noted ceramic similarities among northwestern Florida, Mobile Bay, and the Mississippi River delta during several Woodland and Mississippian periods. There has been considerable disagreement about the directions in which various stylistic traits moved, but little consideration has been given to the cultural processes that might have produced population interaction and the spread of styles along the coast. As shown in the chapter by Knight, the protohistoric period was one of the times when there were strong similarities in ceramic styles along much of the northern Gulf coast. In this chapter, Davis summarizes some of the similarities that are visible archaeologically, then, using early historic sources, suggests some of the kinds of population interaction that may have been prevalent on the northern Gulf coast during protohistoric times. The pattern that may best account for many of the broad similarities and the specific differences among northern coastal ceramic styles during this period is one of small, sociodemographically unstable groups that interacted frequently but erratically through a process of shifting political alliances.

216

ARCHAEOLOGISTS have speculated about long-distance contacts along the U.S. Gulf coast for well over 35 years. Most of this discussion has dealt with ceramic similarities between the lower Mississippi valley and northwestern Florida, and, to a lesser degree, the Mobile Bay area. Evidence of contact between the Mississippi valley and the other two areas has been cited for every major cultural period from Deptford and Tchefuncte to historic times. Despite frequent mention of similarities between Louisiana and coastal areas to the east, there has been little systematic effort to document them quantitatively, much less to consider the full range of cultural processes that might have produced such similarities.

One period for which we might hope to understand better the cultural causes of long-distance stylistic similarities along the Gulf coast is the terminal Mississippian, or what might loosely be termed the protohistoric—the sixteenth, seventeenth, and early eighteenth centuries, when aboriginal peoples of the coast were in the penumbra of history. These were years of significant demographic and cultural change for all southeastern societies, and their historic visage does not fully reflect their precontact culture patterns. Moreover, early historic reports about Gulf coast Indians are spotty in coverage and often incomplete or inaccurate in information. Nonetheless, written records add a dimension to our perspective on protohistoric societies that may be culled for clues about the nature of long-distance interaction and diffusion.

This chapter is concerned with the late prehistoric and protohistoric periods along the segment of the Gulf coast that lies between Choctawhatchee Bay and south-central Louisiana. The purpose is to consider what the available written records can tell us about the nature of protohistoric cultural interaction along the north-central Gulf coast. I am especially concerned here with the kinds of social contacts and movements of people that might have resulted in the movement of stylistic ideas and materials over relatively long distances.

Similarities in ceramic styles among some parts of the northern Gulf coast were fairly strong during the late prehistoric and protohistoric periods. However, the proper interpretation—the cultural "meaning"—of these similarities is difficult to grasp, for four reasons. First, the number of large controlled excavated samples is relatively small. Second, our chronological control leaves much to be desired. We have only a handful of absolute dates for late Woodland and, especially, Mississippian period sites on the coast from the Florida Panhandle through Louisiana, and there have been no detailed interareal comparisons in recent years. Third, the excavated and reported late prehistoric and protohistoric sites are distributed irregularly over the region, with little published data from the Mississippi coast and only two sizable Mississippian period assemblages from coastal Louisiana. Consequently, geographic distribution patterns cannot yet be delineated in any precise way. Finally, we have only a limited understanding of the relationships between different kinds of cultural interaction and different levels of similarity in ceramic styles. This limitation is not unique to southeastern archaeology but is endemic to the entire discipline of prehistory.

Efforts to account for long-distance stylistic similarities in the prehistoric lower Southeast have often used one of two explanations: trade and direct population intrusion. "Diffusion" has served as another catchall interpretation, but it has been an essentially negative explanation, employed when similarities between units compared were too great to invoke trade and too few to argue for actual population intrusion. Diffusion has thus been used primarily as a descriptive concept; it can only become an explanation when it can be related to some particular kind of social interaction that can cause an exchange of stylistic ideas.

In the case of the late prehistoric and protohistoric periods on the northern Gulf coast, we can identify from historic records several different sources for along-coast movement of ideas and goods. These sources are different kinds of population movements and patterns of social interaction, each of which should be manifested differently in the archaeological record. The archaeological data base itself, as has been noted, is spotty. Such data as exist exhibit along-coast stylistic similarities that cannot be comfortably explained by large-scale, long-distance population movements or by trade. The historically identifiable cultural interactions that seem best to fit the archaeological situation as we now understand it were produced by rather erratic, short-term population movements coupled with shifting alliances among adjacent relatively small tribal groups.

Archaeological evidence: long-distance stylistic similarities

Ceramics provide the primary archaeological evidence for long-distance contacts among coastal peoples. The strength of stylistic similarities between the lower Mississippi valley and the Florida Panhandle–Mobile Bay area varies from one cultural period to another, and, for all periods, archaeologists have disagreed about the direction of influence. Resemblances between the Early Woodland Tchefuncte culture (Ford and Quimby 1945; Shenkel, this volume) and the Bayou LaBatre complex (Wimberly 1953a, b) have been known for many years. For the Middle Woodland, Wimberly (1960) suggested that the south Alabama Porter phase (DeJarnette 1952) was strongly influenced by Marksville, although some have recently questioned this view (Walthall 1980: 155).

The greatest interest in long-distance contact has focused upon Baytown–Coles Creek ceramics in the lower Mississippi valley (Brown, this volume) and those of the Weeden Island periods in northwest Florida. These similarities have been documented and discussed from various perspectives by a number of researchers. John Goggin, one of the early investigators to stress the significance of along-coast contacts, regarded Weeden Island as the donor culture (Goggin 1949: 34–39), and Ford (1952: 280–81) shared this view. William Sears (1956) viewed the situation in the reverse, and Willey (1949: 562–68) argued that the coast was a two-way street, with the direction of influence changing over the period of time covered by Weeden Island and Swift Creek. Still others have noted the resemblances between Coles Creek and Weeden Island but have remained noncommittal about the direction of influence (e.g., Haag 1971: 24; Milanich and Fairbanks 1980: 131).

The few archaeological data that have been cited as evidence of long-distance coastal trade are from the Middle and Late Woodland periods. Sears (1962b) suggested that the small numbers of zoned rocker-stamped vessels that occur in early Swift Creek mounds in northwest Florida were traded into that area from the lower Mississippi valley. A similar argument might be made for zoned rocker-stamped vessels from Wimberly's Porter Marksville phase in the Mobile–lower Tombigbee area. A case might also be made for complicated stamped pottery that has been found in small quantities in Coles Creek assemblages from coastal Louisiana at such sites as Bruly St. Martin (Springer 1973, 1976), Bowie (Davis 1981), Morgan (Brown, this volume), Mulatto Bayou (Wiseman, Weinstein, and McCloskey 1979), and Sims (Davis 1981). Complicated stamping has no developmental antecedents in this area, and virtually all of its known occurrences are contemporaneous with Swift Creek and Weeden Island in Florida. Curiously, however, as Brown's data (this volume) indicate, complicated stamping seems to be more prominent in Coles Creek assemblages from south-central Louisiana than in those from the southeastern part of the state, the reverse of the pattern that would be expected if these ceramics were trade goods from northwest Florida.

In the case of the Mississippian periods, the dominant external forces affecting both areas have long been thought to have come from the north. Invasions by interior Mississippian groups have been posited for both northwest Florida (Willey 1949:569–70; Sears 1964) and the Mississippi River delta region (Sears 1964; Phillips 1970:19). Some years ago, Ford suggested that there might be a relationship between Bayou Goula Incised of the lower valley and Willey's (1949:463) Washington Point Incised (Ford 1952:353). More recently some other researchers have pointed to certain stylistic similarities between the Louisiana and Florida-Alabama coasts at Mississippian time levels (e.g., Springer 1973:171; Knight, this volume), and one has even suggested that Mississippian culture patterns arrived in the Mississippi River delta by way of the Florida Panhandle (Springer 1973:171).

Invasions or major population movements are often posited to explain what appear to be sudden breaks or changes in the archaeological record. In some cases, such explanations are supported by later research. In others, later work shows that the apparent breaks reflected not movements of people but gaps in archaeological research. To some extent, the latter seems to be true of the Gulf coast. Recent work in southern Louisiana (Davis 1981) and the Florida Panhandle (Brose, this volume) has shown greater continuity between Lake Woodland and Mississippian ceramics in both areas than was once supposed. In the Mobile Bay area, the Pensacola complex, which was once thought to be almost entirely protohistoric, now seems to extend back several hundred years before contact (Knight, this volume). This does not mean that important movements of peoples between the interior and the coast did not occur during late prehistory but rather that mass decimation or displacement of Gulf coast groups by Mississippian "invaders" is a less attractive idea than it used to be.

Just as we are beginning to see greater local stylistic continuity during late coastal prehistory, we are also beginning to see greater along-coast similarities than have been documented previously. Until recently, comparisons between the Mississippi River delta and areas to the east were severely constrained by an absence of large excavated samples from the former area. The Mississippian period Bayou Petre phase, which grew out of work by Kniffen in the delta over 40 years ago (Kniffen 1936), with more recent updating by Phillips (1970:951–53), has been defined from surface collections and extremely limited test excavations. Nonetheless, Kniffen's Bayou Petre phase

collections and those of McIntire (1958) do suggest eastern affiliations. For example, in several of the late prehistoric collections reported by McIntire from sites in St. Bernard, Plaquemine, and Lafourche parishes (all in deltaic Louisiana), specimens identified as
Pensacola Incised, Moundville Incised, and Fort Walton Incised together comprise over 60 percent of the decorated ceramics. It is of
some interest that a number of the same collections include noticeable
quantities of types, such as the Natchez variety of Leland Incised,
Australia Incised, and Harrison Bayou Incised, that are uncommon to
the east but are associated with Mississippian period ceramic assemblages farther north in the lower valley.

During the late 1970s, the first large stratigraphically controlled
samples of Mississippian period ceramics from the Louisiana coastal
zone were excavated during two separate projects. One of these was
part of a major program of excavations on Avery Island by a Harvard
University group working under the direction of Ian Brown (1978a, b,
1980a). This work documented a sixteenth- or early seventeenth-
century occupation of the island by Mississippian groups. On the basis
of strong ceramic similarities with the southern Yazoo basin, Brown
suggested that the Mississippian occupants of Avery Island were an
intrusive population whose presence was directly related to the production of salt.

The second project was undertaken by a Tulane University group,
working under my direction, farther east in the Mississippi River
delta. The focus of this work was the Sims site (16Sc2), a multicomponent Coles Creek and Mississippian site in St. Charles Parish,
Louisiana. Sims, which rests on a relict crevasse distributary system
about six miles south of the present-day main channel of the river, is
among the largest sites in deltaic Louisiana, extending for some 900
meters along the bayou's edge, with artifacts found on the surface
over an area of some 32 acres. Originally, the site's topography was
broken by five earth mounds. Three of these remain, the largest
110 feet long and 7 feet high.

To date, excavations have been concentrated in the midden areas
and have yielded assemblages dating to the late Coles Creek, early
Mississippian, and protohistoric periods. The Coles Creek and Mississippian ceramics have been discussed in relation to other late prehistoric assemblages from the delta in an earlier paper (Davis 1981). A
few aspects of the protohistoric assemblage have also been described
(Davis and Giardino 1980); a comprehensive analysis of that material
has been completed by Marco Giardino but has not yet been pub-

lished. A radiocarbon date of A.D. 1740 ± 65 and a thermoluminescence date of A.D. ~ 1810 were obtained from the protohistoric midden. The early Mississippian component provided a thermoluminescence determination of A.D. ~ 1088, while a TL analysis for the Coles Creek occupation yielded a date of A.D. ~ 812. Very few European goods were included in the protohistoric assemblage, which is not so surprising since the immediate area was not settled by whites until the 1830s.

Ceramics from the earliest component are typical late Coles Creek materials, dominated by check stamping and by straight-line incised motifs expressed in such types as Coles Creek Incised, Mazique Incised, and Beldeau Incised. Some of these, including Pontchartrain Check Stamped and Coles Creek Incised, carry over in small quantities into the early Mississippian period, although the two occupation periods are separated by a hiatus at this particular site. Yet the early Mississippian assemblage contains a variety of elements that are similar to the Pensacola complex from Mobile Bay and northwest Florida. This transitional interval from Late Woodland to more recognizably "pure" Mississippian ceramics is not yet well documented in the Mobile–Pensacola Bay areas. Thus, we can only say at present that early Mississippian period ceramics from the Sims site contain some features that are characteristic of later Pensacola ceramics to the east and some elements that tie it to the early Mississippian farther north in the valley, along with stylistic remnants from late Coles Creek times. The new elements include a considerable number of shell-tempered wares (averaging 21.8 percent of early Mississippian ceramics at Sims) and noticeable numbers of curvilinear-incised, shell-tempered sherds which I have previously classified as varieties of Leland Incised (Davis 1981), but which are in fact far more similar in execution, paste, and other features to Pensacola Incised as that type is defined farther east (e.g., Willey 1949:464; Trickey 1958). Yet, as was noted, ceramic similarities to areas farther north in the lower Mississippi valley are also quite strong.

Although there are some points of comparison at the early Mississippian level, it is in the protohistoric assemblage that we see the greatest similarities between the delta and the Pensacola "heartland." These are especially visible in the predominance of materials that we have been classifying as variations on Mound Place Incised, Leland Incised, and the Manly variety of Matthews Incised (Phillips 1970). These specimens bear strong similarities to Pensacola Incised and

Moundville Incised ceramics from Mobile Bay and the western coast of the Florida Panhandle.

Because there is as yet no other published excavated Mississippian period assemblage of significant size reported from this area of the Mississippi River delta, it would be premature to suggest a phase designation for the protohistoric Sims site assemblage. I do suggest that the term "Bayou Petre phase" might better be put aside until we have a larger number of stratigraphically controlled Mississippian samples from this area. However, it also seems to me that Knight's argument (this volume) that his Pensacola complex extends into the eastern Mississippi River delta (an idea suggested some years ago by Sears [1964]) receives considerable support from the Sims site and some additional support from other surface collections made by many individuals over the years (e.g., Kniffen 1936; McIntire 1958; Gagliano, Weinstein, and Burden 1975). I would also stress the importance of defining this Pensacola pattern and the known variability within it as precisely as possible at an early date, lest we find the archaeological literature once more filled with a good idea that causes unnecessary confusion in the future for want of rigorous definition.

To be sure, there are differences between the eastern delta and the Mobile-Pensacola area. The protohistoric assemblage from Sims, for example, has a lower frequency of shell tempering (23.3 percent) than is common to the east, and it seems to contain more straight-line incised pieces and punctated elements than assemblages from Alabama and Florida. These numbers are not surprising, but they serve to re-emphasize Knight's definition of Pensacola as a broad complex which connotes a number of historically important similarities but which also encompasses considerable local variation. In this sense, Pensacola might be regarded as a subareal tradition, following the definition of "tradition" by a Society for American Archaeology seminar in 1955 as "a socially transmitted . . . series of systematically related units which persists through time" (Haury et al. 1956: 39).

One fascinating aspect of the Pensacola complex is its very linear distribution. It seems to be confined as a complex largely to areas within 20 or 30 miles of the coast; within that band, most of the known sites are in deltaic and estuarine environments. Of course, there are specific types that also occur in the interior river valleys some distance from the coast, but along-coast stylistic coherence appears to be considerably stronger than that between the coast and interior. This geographic pattern has been discussed by other authors for the Mobile and Pensacola Bay areas (Sears 1977; Knight, this volume). The large number of surface collections reported by Kniffen (1936), McIntire (1958), Altschul (1978), and others indicate that Pensacola tradition ceramics in Louisiana are strongly represented only in St. Bernard, Plaquemine, Lafourche, St. Charles, and Terrebonne parishes—that is, in eastern and southern parts of the delta that are dominated by deltaic and related estuarine ecosystems.

The considerable stylistic similarities among collections from many protohistoric (and late prehistoric Mississippian) sites between Choctawhatchee Bay and south-central Louisiana are undeniable. The most widely shared features that set these collections apart from contemporaneous assemblages of the interior include prominence of coarse shell-tempered wares (Pensacola Plain, Mississippi Plain) with major decorative motifs that include the designs found on Pensacola Incised and Moundville Incised. Within these patterns there are also various locally distinctive ceramic traits, but the similarities are sufficient to suggest some continuing cultural interaction along the north-central Gulf coast during the late prehistoric and protohistoric periods.

Documentary evidence: sources of stylistic diffusion

From the start, the value of documentary evidence as a source for models of aboriginal cultural interaction is limited by the reliability of the early chroniclers. European assessments of aboriginal demography are often ambiguous, and some were undoubtedly inaccurate. Many of the seventeenth- and eighteenth-century descriptions of coastal population distributions and movements were not based upon systematic census efforts but were instead the results of brief visits to isolated points along the coast. Some records are, in fact, grounded only in hearsay. Moreover, we know that many of the early explorers were given to exaggeration when it suited their ends.

In addition to the effects of biases stemming from the situations of the observers, the picture is confused by the European presence itself, which dramatically altered precontact patterns through displacement and gradual decimation of native groups. These European-induced changes were well under way by 1670–1720, the period in which our most detailed sources on the northern Gulf coast were written.

Some of the most direct effects of colonization, such as military attacks upon specific groups, are relatively easy to identify and segregate for analytical purposes. However, the effects upon population distributions and interactions of such factors as the slave trade, missionization, and disease are more difficult to chart. The roles of chronic and epidemic disease are especially critical, since their effects were often in play well ahead of actual colonization in many areas. Such was the case along most of the north-central Gulf, where there was little significant European settlement prior to 1700. Yet Le Page DuPratz (1774:292) estimated that, by the second decade of the eighteenth century, the aboriginal population of the region had been reduced to one-third or less of its previous size. Catesby, writing in the mid-eighteenth century, noted the then-prevailing scholarly belief that North American Indian populations overall had declined to one-fourth or less of their precontact numbers (Catesby 1731–43, II:xv–xvi). Many twentieth-century authors believe that the decline between 1540 and 1700 was even more severe (e.g., Mooney 1928; Swanton 1946; Dobyns 1966; Milner 1980).

In the end, efforts to estimate the specific value of disease-related population decline are futile, since too many of the relevant variables cannot be reconstructed. This futility is evident in the fact that population estimates for the Southeast published in this century, based upon essentially identical data, vary by a factor of about ten. Even reconstructions by southeastern specialists working from relatively good sources for limited areas vary by factors of about four or five (e.g., Willey 1949; Milanich and Fairbanks 1980). We can document specific cases in which communities were decimated by smallpox, measles, or some other disease, but isolated cases may not reflect regional change.

In any event, the specific magnitude of population decimation is of less interest here than the fact that it was of large scale. Even recognizing this fact, it is impossible to assess accurately its effects upon patterns of interaction among coastal communities. Nevertheless, it is still possible to see through the veil of colonization some relative contrasts between the coast and the interior, as well as some kinds of intercommunity relationships that probably predate contact, and that are, in that sense, truly aboriginal patterns.

One generalization that is readily accepted by most researchers concerns the sizes and distributions of populations along the northern Gulf. Documentary sources give every reason to agree with Swanton's conclusion that coastal societies tended "toward small units which only sporadically gathered into larger bodies" (Swanton 1946:19). Population seems to have been concentrated near the deltas of rivers from Santa Rosa Island to the Pearl, and along Bayou Loufourche and old Mississippi River distributaries in southern Louisiana (be-

cause of flooding, the Mississippi itself around and below New Orleans was very sparsely inhabited). These patterns are evident in the
very earliest Spanish and French documents for the north-central
Gulf coast.

If individual settlements were small, so were sociopolitical units.
There is little historical evidence for any politically unified entity comprised of more than three villages on the northern Gulf coast, with
the possible exceptions of the Acolapissa (for whom six villages on the
lower Pearl were recorded by LaHarpe in 1699; also see Giardino, this
volume) and the Mobile and Tomeh (Knight, this volume).

The sociopolitical and demographic landscapes on the northern
Gulf coast were thus rather sparsely filled (in comparison with the
interior alluvial valleys) and highly fragmented. But the individual
tribes did not live in isolation from each other; interactions were frequent. What was the nature of these contacts, and what do they suggest about long-distance stylistic similarities within the coastal zone?
Historically visible processes that might have resulted in along-coast
movement of goods and design ideas fall into three broad categories:
trade and exchange; contacts by hunting and war parties; and population movement.

Trade was probably not a significant mode of cultural interaction
among Gulf coast groups in protohistoric times. The historic records
yield considerable negative evidence concerning coastwise exchange.
As Charles Hudson has noted, "the most important circuit of exchange was between the coast and the interior" (1976:316; see also
Swanton 1946:736–40). Salt, fish, seashells, cassina, and a few other
items were traded from the coastal area into the interior. There was
also some rather localized exchange among coastal groups, such as
the trade of flint for pottery that occurred between the Attakapa and
the Karankawa (Dyer 1917), but there is little overall evidence for
long-distance trade along the coast itself. This lack of evidence probably reflects the fact that there were few important commodities that
were needed in any coastal area that could be more readily obtained
from another coastal area than from the interior. For this reason, if
anything was traded over long distances along the coast, it is likely to
have been manufactured goods; it is just such items, in the form of
ceramics, for which there is some archaeological evidence of along-
coast trade.

Of course, direct trade is not the only source for the movement of
goods over long distances. Both trickle trade and itinerant traders,
such as those that we know operated in some of the interior river val-

leys during the early historic period (Swanton 1946:736–37), could have produced the same results. Distinguishing among these three kinds of trade is important, for each has different cultural implications. Direct long-distance trade implies long-distance contact between peoples; itinerant and trickle trade do not. Trickle trade requires short-distance contact between adjacent populations, while itinerant trade may occur among populations without any other significant contact.

Trickle trade and small-scale reciprocal exchange may well have gone unnoticed or unrecorded by early chroniclers. These processes could have resulted in the eventual transport of goods over long distances without any direct contact between the groups supplying the articles and those receiving them, but there is little positive evidence for any consistent or significant trickle trade or reciprocal exchange within the geographic area occupied by the Pensacola tradition. Altogether, both archaeological and historical data indicate that along-coast trade was slight, and it is difficult to imagine any reasonable mechanisms by which such trade could have produced or maintained the level of stylistic similarities that occurred during the late prehistoric and protohistoric periods.

Excursions by war and hunting parties were not infrequent in the early historic Southeast, including the coastal zone. Iberville's encounter with a hunting party of Bayou Goula at Biloxi in 1699 (Iberville, in French 1875) is a good example. Another is provided by the Alabama, whose self-defined hunting territory extended into what is now Louisiana. However, neither hunting parties nor warfare as it was practiced over most of the Southeast are likely *in themselves* to have been significant sources for the diffusion of ceramic styles within the coastal zone. Neither occurs under conditions that are conducive to much interchange of either stylistic ideas or products. Moreover, both were the province of males who, by all accounts, were not the makers of pottery. The main contribution of warfare to stylistic diffusion would probably have occurred through permanent capture of females. We have little historical information about female captives among Gulf coast groups, but in the Southeast as a whole they generally fared better than male captives. (Hudson 1976:254–55) and were often assimilated into the captors' communities. Unfortunately, the role of this process in stylistic diffusion cannot be accurately documented either archaeologically or historically. Beyond this, there is no reason to believe that either warfare or extended-range hunting was directly responsible for the spread of ceramic styles, although they may have created or reinforced frameworks for other kinds of contacts between groups.

Population intrusion is another major source for the long-distance movement of styles. In the northern Gulf coast area, at least three kinds of population movements can be detected, or at least hypothesized from documentary sources. The most strongly patterned were seasonal movements between the coast and interior, which are documented for the Attakapa (Post 1962) and for groups around Mobile Bay (Iberville, in French 1875:43) and which probably also occurred for some other coastal groups. Coast-interior seasonal rounds have also been documented or suggested for various areas of the northern Gulf coast during the Late Woodland and Mississippian (e.g., Altschul 1978; Aten 1979; Knight, this volume). However, localized population movements in seasonal rounds would probably have had little effect upon long-distance cultural interaction.

A second category of historically recognizable population movement was an essentially single-step intrusion covering a relatively long distance (i.e., in excess of 50 miles). Movements of this kind increased after 1702 with the disruption of the Spanish missions in Florida and with the establishment of the French posts at Biloxi, New Orleans, and Mobile. Serving as points of European trade and, in some cases, as islands of safety, the French posts exerted a certain centripetal force, especially upon smaller tribes. Movements of remnants of the Bayou Goula, Biloxi, Chawasha, Houma, and several other groups to the vicinity of newly founded New Orleans after 1718 illustrates the trade and defense value of proximity to European settlements (Penicaut, in Margry 1879–88:5). The French settlement at Mobile witnessed a similar pattern, drawing in some of the Apalachee, Biloxi, Chatot, Mobile, and Pascagoula, among others (Swanton 1946:73). Indeed, all of the early historic migrations of Gulf coast groups over such distances seem to have been due to the presence of Europeans. When such movements bring together substyles from widely separated areas, it may be possible to detect them archaeologically, as work by DeJarnette, Jenkins, Knight, and others at two sites on Mobile Bay has illustrated (DeJarnette 1976). Thus, coastal peoples moved about quite a lot in the early years of contact, but the movements that probably reflect aboriginal patterns cannot be characterized as long-distance intrusions.

However, these contact-related population shifts were superimposed upon a history of locational instability that probably predates European colonization. There is considerable reason to agree with

Quimby's (1957) conclusion that frequent but irregular tribal and community movement in parts of the coastal zone was grounded in precontact social factors. We know, for example, that such groups as the Acolapissa, Pascagoula, Quinipissa, Washa, and some of the Biloxi—the "wandering tribes," to use Iberville's words (Iberville, in French 1875:43)—often formed alliances among themselves or became temporary clients of interior groups such as the Choctaw or Chickasaw. Most such alliances seem to have been ephemeral and, although they were related clearly to intertribal conflict, historic documents are often vague about the specific factors that gave rise to such associations. In some cases, such as the alliance between the Bayou Goula and Mugalasha (Margry 1879–88: 4:169–72; Gravier, in Thwaites 1896–1901:65:157) or that between the Biloxi and Pascagoula (LaHarpe, in Margry 1879–88:5:243–306), two or more ethnically distinguishable groups were co-occupants for a time of a single settlement. Eventually, the alliances broke down, either because of strife or because one or both parties found other motivation to leave.

At the present time, we can only guess about the social factors that lay behind these erratic short-term, and usually short-distance, population movements. In the interior alluvial valleys, community movements caused by declining agricultural yields apparently were not uncommon. We do not know whether this factor was important along the coastal strand proper, where agriculture was considerably less significant. Coastwise movements and alliances may also have been stimulated by pressure from or conflict with larger agricultural groups of the interior. Alternatively, locational instability may have been due in part to some basic structural flaw in the sociopolitical organization of some coastal groups. In any case, the result was a great deal of irregular movement both by individual communities and entire "tribes" within the coastal zone that cannot be readily attributed to pressures of European contact.

I suspect that such erratic short-distance population movements and shifting alliances played important roles in maintaining the Pensacola tradition that is documented in the archaeological record. Rather than reflecting a single population expansion or significant direct interaction between small sociopolitical groups that were separated by considerable distances, the Pensacola complex may represent diffusion that resulted from a complex series of short-distance population movements coupled with ephemeral alliances, intermarriage, and some actual settlement co-occupation by adjacent coastal groups.

Reflections and conclusions

There were considerable ceramic similarities among northern Gulf coast societies from northwest Florida to Louisiana during several Woodland and Mississippian periods. Although the most widely cited stylistic parallels have been those between Weeden Island and Baytown–Coles Creek, it is beginning to appear that similarities during the Mississippian, especially during the late Mississippian, may have been greater.

It is possible, as many have suggested, that the huge center at Moundville had something to do with the "Mississippianization" of the entire northern coast from the Choctawhatchee to south-central Louisiana—that is, that these areas exhibit strong stylistic similarities in part because they shared a common cultural progenitor from the interior. This position must be regarded as one of several alternative hypotheses which can be confirmed or disconfirmed only with additional stratigraphically controlled data. No one would deny that there was contact of some type between Mississippian groups on the coast and those of the interior. However, "contact" and the spread of ceramic styles can occur in a variety of ways, and ceramic similarities may reflect a number of processes of social interaction other than population intrusion and direct trade.

Moreover, regardless of their origin, along-coast stylistic similarities were maintained well after the decline of Moundville as a major center. Historic documents provide some positive and negative evidence about the kinds of interactions that may have served to maintain such similarities along the northern Gulf coast, at least during the protohistoric period.

Single-step long-distance population movements undoubtedly did occur from time to time, but this process is insufficient to explain fully the archaeological data at hand. Direct long-distance trade and warfare also probably occurred along the coast during later prehistory, although the former seems to have been insignificant in the contact period, and neither seems to provide a mechanism for maintenance of the major stylistic similarities that existed between the Mobile–Pensacola Bay areas and deltaic Louisiana.

The archaeological data currently available suggest that the Pensacola complex might profitably be regarded as a subareal tradition, connoting a broadly shared style with numerous specific typological similarities but marked also by some stylistic and technological features that are distinctive to local areas within the tradition. This perspective is consonant with historic indications of a region marked by (1) a rather fragmented sociopolitical landscape made up of relatively small tribal groups and (2) irregular but frequent short-distance movement and short-term alliances that brought those groups into contact sufficiently often for broad stylistic homogeneity to be maintained but with sufficient continuity of local group identity for local area distinctions to persist.

This is a very large hypothesis to bring to bear upon a relatively small body of controlled archaeological data. On the other hand, archaeological research always proceeds from some interpretive perspective, even if it is only a hypothesis to be considered along with others. In considering long-distance stylistic similarities along the Gulf coast, we will benefit from recognizing the complexity of interactions that occur among societies and communities and from trying to gear our research methods to detect better the products of different kinds of social interactions.

Certainly, more archaeological data are needed before we can even describe adequately the specific patterns of long-distance similarity that marked the northern Gulf coast in late prehistoric and protohistoric times. However, productive analysis of those data will also require classification schemes that are capable of reflecting the significant similarities and differences that exist among later prehistoric ceramic assemblages from the northern Gulf coast. At present, two changes are needed, one practical, the other methodological. As a practical first step, some effort to systematize typological nomenclature for late prehistory on the northern Gulf coast is in order, with the minimal goal of eliminating redundancies among the lower Mississippi valley, central Alabama, and northwest Florida schemes, parts or all of which are currently used in the classification of coastal materials. Ultimately, a more comprehensive system developed specifically for the north-central coast would probably be of most value. For the purpose of testing hypotheses about cultural interaction within this area, we would be best served by a classification that allows stylistic attributes, which diffuse more readily, to be treated separately from more basic technological features.

10

Documentary Evidence for the Location of Historic Indian Villages in the Mississippi Delta

Marco J. Giardino

Some of the most anthropologically and historically intriguing questions about coastal aboriginal populations concern the earliest period of European colonization. During those years, Indian societies of the coast (as elsewhere in the Southeast) underwent massive demographic and social changes. The availability of European journals, letters, maps, and other documents makes it possible to chart the course of some of these changes, but some aspects of contact period aboriginal life were never recorded in any detail. Archaeological study of protohistoric Indian societies has the potential to complement the information from written sources. However, the conjoining of archaeological and historical data for the Gulf coast often presupposes an ability to relate specific archaeological sites to particular aboriginal groups. This is a difficult task in many parts of the Gulf coast, since early historic aboriginal communities were often highly mobile, and the record of their movements is often sketchy.

Giardino illustrates many of the difficulties that are encountered in identifying early historic village locations and presents some of the methods that can be used to make the most of the available historical information. His focus is the Mississippi River delta, but the problems and methods he considers are applicable to many areas of the Gulf coast.

THIS paper is concerned with the location and inhabitants of southeastern Louisiana Indian villages which are documented in French records written in the late seventeenth century and the early eighteenth. Through the integrated analysis of travel accounts, early maps, chronicles, census records, and letters, an attempt is made to provide a basis for archaeological excavations of sites dating from this significant period when Indian groups from the lowermost Mississippi River delta region adjusted to French colonization.

Initially, this type of analysis should result in a series of large-scale maps in which "the historical, as well as the prehistoric, village sites of our Indians will be recorded with a high degree of accuracy" (Swanton 1922:10). In addition to primarily historical understanding of documentary data, such research can stimulate more processual analysis aimed at the interpretation of the relationships between human behavior and material culture.

An important step toward the latter task is the identification of archaeological cultures with tribal or ethnic groups described in historic accounts. An appropriate method is the direct historical approach, which can initially be employed only on sites whose occupants have been specifically identified (Strong 1935; Wedel 1938; Hally 1971).

There is a need for resurrecting the direct historical approach in the lower Mississippi valley, both as a first step toward identifying the material culture of specific ethnic groups and as a response to the too-common practice of affirming the presence of a specific ethnic group by the recovery of a single ceramic type (Jennings 1941:179–80). Such correlations are usually based upon little more than untested assumptions and educated guesses. Commonly, uncertainty about which tribes made which ceramic type leads to questions about the specific association rather than about the premise sustaining it (Quimby 1957:161).

Prior to suggesting relationships between particular ceramic types and specific sociocultural groups, historically documented archaeological sites must be excavated to supplement the available ethnological and historical information. Data bearing on the occupants' material culture must be explicitly detailed and incorporated in hypotheses that can subsequently be tested and archaeologically validated (cf. Fairbanks 1971a:70).

The recognition of the material culture of a particular tribe or group requires the identification of the residences and communities of those social units (Hally 1971). After we understand the recent occupation of the lower Mississippi valley—especially the association between specific groups and specific ceramic complexes—we can take a large step toward understanding the prehistory of this area (Kniffen 1936:416).

The union of archaeological and ethnohistorical data promises more significant results than simply locating the village sites of historically documented Indian tribes. Historic evidence provides the archaeologist with an abundant reservoir of potentially testable hypotheses ranging from subsistence models to inquiries into human relationships and human social behavior; it erects frameworks that can be fleshed out by archaeology. Through archaeological recovery of the material culture of the American Indian we can reconstruct more complete images of Indian life as it was during the time of European exploration and colonization. With the aid of the direct historical method, artifacts, burial complexes, settlement distribution, and community plans can provide information about the prehistoric inhabitants of the region. There are other research questions: What was the nature and degree of Indian intergroup relations? What routes did their movements follow? What changes were occasioned by the European intrusion? And, most difficult, what comprised a "tribe" as documented by the French?

A particularly interesting issue revealed by ethnohistorical information, one crucial to the understanding of tribal organization and artifact variability, is toponymy. As will be shown, the names recorded by the French denoting tribal groups often may not have actually signified those social units. Some names have been shown to lack tribal specificity, and have more generic references (cf. Gatschet 1884; Swanton 1911, 1946). Other purportedly tribal names may have denoted geographical locations. Thus, the same group encountered in different locations by different contemporaneous explorers may have received dissimilar names. As will be further detailed, the latter case may account for the discrepancies between the names Mugulasha and Quinipissa, which evidently refer to the same tribe encountered in two disparate places. Some documented names may have referred to totemic clans or to selected social segments such as warriors or chiefs. Still other names may have resulted from erroneous transcriptions or dialectical variety.

No simple answer concerning the toponymy of native historical tribes will be forthcoming. However, the problem of group affiliation and material variability can be approached through the use of the community and its archaeological counterpart, the component, as the minimal social unit for analysis (Willey and Phillips 1958: 21–22; 45). As an operational unit, the community can be recognized ethnographically without necessitating, initially at least, an understanding of the structure and composition of such an entity. Archaeologically, the component, or artifactual assemblage, is usually the most readily recognized element of social significance. Components can be combined into larger units such as phases which are of paramount importance in establishing, defining, and explaining regional or synchronic relationships, and tribal movements in the immediate past (Griffin 1966:11). Similarly, communities can be aggregated into larger units such as tribes and societies, allowing the recognition of societal behavioral patterns indicative of ethnic behavior and ethnic boundaries (Deetz 1965; Hill 1968; Longacre 1968; Hodder 1978, 1979).

The results of this study include the identification of several localities that are most likely to furnish archaeological remains of the documented Indian villages. Future archaeological excavation of some of these sites may yield sufficient data to define the material culture of specific tribal groups, particularly if the sites are found to consist of single components.

Geological considerations

Relocating historically documented Indian villages on a modern map of southeastern Louisiana requires some geological reconstruction. Following an approximation of the river's physiography for the eighteenth century, the distances and localities covered by early French explorers were plotted from extant accounts, travelogues, chronicles, diaries and letters. When compared to the historical accounts, eighteenth-century maps provide some graphic correlations, but archaeological data were the least useful for this study.

The present course of the Mississippi River, from Baton Rouge to Head of Passes, is generally similar to that traveled by the French at the end of the seventeenth century and during the first decades of the eighteenth. Cutoffs and oxbow lake formation, which produce major changes in the length of the river, do not occur in the southernmost delta (McIntire 1958: 23). Some lateral migration of the river channel has occurred during the last three centuries, resulting from the continual erosion of cutbanks and aggradation of point bars (Fisk 1944;

Saucier 1974). Perfunctory inspection of both recent and French colonial maps illustrates the lack of significant modification in the Mississippi River course since the early 1700s. Consequently, when retracing the distances journeyed by French explorers along the Mississippi, little compensation for geomorphic changes is needed north of Head of Passes.

However, there is considerable historical and geological evidence indicating a general gulfward progradation of the Mississippi River mouth since the time the main flow of water occupied the present channel (during the Plaquemine subdelta, a complex which began forming ca. 1,000–1,100 years ago [Kolb and Van Lopick 1958; Frazier 1967]). Although few doubt that the Mississippi delta has been advancing rather rapidly (Russell 1936:39), there is significant disagreement, particularly among early sources, concerning the employment of different points of measurements along the many passes and jetties of the birdfoot delta.

For the accurate reconstruction of early travel routes, it is important to arrive at a reasonable estimate for the lengthening of the Mississippi River since LaSalle first reached its mouth in April 1682. Bienville (Louisiana Indian Miscellany 1937–38) provides an estimate of delta progradation of ca. 75 meters per year, or slightly less than 6 leagues. Similarly, DuPratz (1774:118) states that one century was sufficient to extend the land by 2 leagues, or by a rate of 18 miles per 300 years. (The French league is usually equated to 3 miles [Poisson, in Thwaites 1896–1901: 67:302–42; Butler 1934; Higginbotham 1969:28n.]) LaSalle apparently used the French post league, which equals 2.42 miles. The estimates reported by the French during their daily travels were often approximations. A 3 mile league, therefore, is sufficiently exact for this study.)

Several nineteenth century estimates specified a rate of delta advance into the Gulf of Mexico averaging 300 feet per year (DuBow 1847; Corthell 1880; see also Morgan 1977). More recent measurements of delta growth reflect the enormous amount of river management, including levee construction and channel modification, in the present century.

An approximate increase in river length of 6 leagues or 18 miles since the late seventeenth century is confirmed, in part, by historical and archaeological data. This information concerns the location of Fort La Boulaye, the first French settlement built on the lower Mississippi River, dating from 1700. The fort was a prominent landmark for early chroniclers and cartographers, long after its abandonment

in 1715 (see, for example, the Ross map of 1775). Early French accounts reveal that this fort was located on a ridge approximately 17 or
18 leagues from the Gulf (Iberville, in Margry 1879–88: 3: 393; Gravier 1700, in Thwaites 1896–1901: 65: 161; Cox 1905: 152n.; Butler
1934: 5). During the 1920s and late 1930s, structural and artifactual evidence probably representing the remains of the seventeenth-
century occupation of Fort La Boulaye was uncovered during the
dredging of the Gravolet Canal, north of Phoenix, Louisiana (Riis
1936). Following the Mississippi for 18 leagues from where the remnant of the fort was discovered allows us to approximately locate the
position of the river mouth during the period of initial French exploration of the Gulf coast. This reconstructed location is indicated as
A in figure 10.1, located approximately 6 leagues upriver from the
southernmost jetty of the southwest pass.

The apparent correlation between geological and historical evidence provides the criteria for the elimination of 6 leagues from modern area maps for purposes of this study. Additional confirmation of
this reconstruction is provided by early locational information for
New Orleans (Charlevoix 1923; Bienville and LeMoyne n.d.).

Locations of Indian villages

Several interesting results, some suspected by southeastern scholars,
became evident during the reconstruction of Indian village locations
from documentary sources. It soon became apparent, for instance,
that during the French period (1682–1763), the Louisiana Indians
commonly moved their habitations, frequently settling in villages previously occupied by other Indian groups. In addition, several examples of Indians settling in villages still inhabited by other groups are
found in the historic documents from this period.

Although the evidence for mergings and dislocations of tribes are
numerous, the social and political mechanisms underlying these movements are far from clear. Warfare was undoubtedly a major cause for
the unsettled pattern of village locations described in early documents. Most likely aggravated by French imperialism, Indian warfare
probably originated in pre-European times (Kroeber 1939: 148–220;
Quimby 1957: 165; Gibson 1974a). Ethnohistorical accounts of war
or the results of bellicosity are many. LaSalle and his men described
the widespread massacre of the Tangibaho tribe at the hands of the
Tchouchoumas in the spring of 1682 (Margry 1879–88: 1: 604–5,
4: 168). Similarly, Joutel details the arrival of a victorious Cenis war

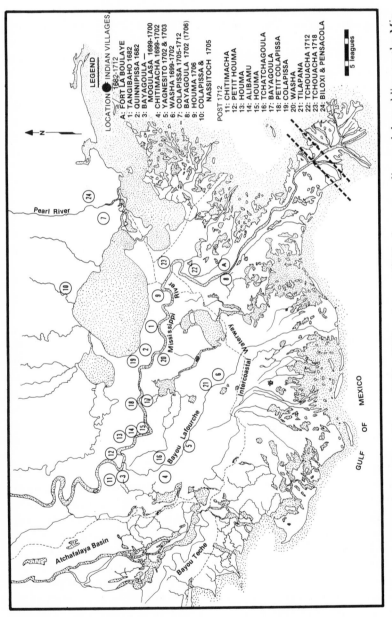

LEGEND

● INDIAN VILLAGES.

LOCATION

1682–1712

A: FORT LA BOULAYE
1: TANGIBAHO 1682
2: QUINNIPISSA 1682
3: BAYAGOULA –
   MOGULASA 1699–1700
4: CHITIMACHA 1699–1702
5: YAGNESITO 1702 & 1703
6: WASHA 1699–1702
7: COLAPISSA 1705–1712
8: BAYAGOULA 1702 (1706)
9: HOUMA 1706
10: COLAPISSA &
    NASSITOCH 1705

POST 1712

11: CHITIMACHA
12: PETIT HOUMA
13: HOUMA
14: ALIBAMU
15: HOUMA
16: TCHATCHAGOULA
17: BAYAGOULA
18: PETIT COLAPISSA
19: COLAPISSA
20: WASHA
21: TILAPANA
22: TCHOUACHA 1712
23: TCHOUACHA 1718
24: BILOXI & PENSACOLA

5 leagues

Fig. 10.1. Locations of Indian villages, 1682–1712 and post–1712; the upper diagonal dotted line on the Mississippi delta shows the extent in the late seventeenth century; lower line marks the extent ca. 1712.

party in May 1687, after they had killed or captured 48 of the enemies men and women (in French 1846: 160).

Other illustrations of native hostilities were noted among the Bayagoula and Mugulasha. (In this paper the term Bayagoula refers to the people, the terms Bayougoula and Bayou Goula refer to the French concession of M. Paris and the modern Louisiana town, respectively.) Iberville reports the scalping injuries sustained by the deputy chief of the Mugulasha during the Indian's captivity (in French 1875: 68). Also mentioned in French documents are attacks by the Bayagoula on the Mugulasha (Margry 1879–88: 5: 429), the Taensa on the Bayagoula (Penicaut, in McWilliams 1953: 64; LaHarpe 1971: 75; Bienville and LeMoyne n.d.), the Ouma on the Bayagoula to avenge the latter's incursion on Ouma hunting grounds (Iberville, in French 1875: 72; Sauvole, in Higginbotham 1969: 34), the Tunica on the Ouma after the former had escaped the attack of the Chickasaw (Claiborne 1880: 29; LaHarpe 1971: 100), and the Ouma on Tunica (Penicaut in McWilliams 1953: 161). All these events occurred within the first five years of French settlement on the Gulf of Mexico.

The missionary Gravier gives further evidence for warfare among neighboring tribes. During his voyage to the Gulf along the Mississippi River, Gravier describes the "defensive posture" of the Taensa and Ouma villages encountered during his descent of 1700 (Shea 1861; French 1875; Thwaites 1896–1901: 67). DuRu, the chaplain included in the Iberville expeditions of 1699 and 1700, mentions a defensive palisade surrounding the Bayagoula and Colapissa villages (Butler 1934: 65). The murder of St. Cosme by Chitimacha warriors occurred while these Indians were en route to make war on the Bayagoula (Penicaut, in McWilliams 1953: 71). In 1713, the Chickasaw, Natchez, and Yazoo ambushed the Techouacha and captured several members of this lower Mississippi valley tribe as slaves (Penicaut, in McWilliams 1953: 159). These numerous examples leave little doubt that raiding and warfare, often resulting in the enslavement and virtual elimination of entire "tribes," were common aspects of native intergroup social relationships. As such, they can be viewed as significant mechanisms for the frequent movements and mergings of Louisiana Indian peoples (Davis, this volume).

Closely akin to the results of warfare, and less understood, are the roles of intertribal alliances in determining the location of particular groups along the major river courses of the lower delta area. Documentary sources illustrate the ever-changing pattern of native alliances, often pitting former friends in bloody conflicts against each other. Stranger still is the apparently frequent occurrence of massacres veiled in the semblance of alliance or cohabitation. As mentioned, the Bayagoula ambushed the Mugulasha in 1700 despite their former alliance, their close linguistic ties, and their occupation of the same village (Margry 1879–88: 4: 159; DuRu, in Butler 1934). The enslavement of several Tchouacha people and the murder of their chief by a party of Chickasaw, Natchez, and Yazoo occurred during an avowed calumet ceremony (Penicaut, in McWilliams 1953: 159). The Tunica attack on the Ouma at the latter's village, where the former enjoyed refuge from Chickasaw belligerence, offers another example of intergroup relations directly influencing the frequency and direction of tribal movements (see the section on the Ouma below).

The maps and chronicles dating from the early decades of France's colonization of the lower Mississippi valley reveal the effects of these transitory alliances and of the warfare on the settlement pattern of historic Indian tribes. Relocation of native groups during the first half of the eighteenth century was a frequent occurrence. Just as common was the complete disappearance of documented groups from the historic record. Less readily recognizable in documentary sources, however, were the sociocultural causes underlying these examples of aboriginal behavior.

One possible explanation for placing Indian villages on the locations identified by French documents may have been the environment. South of Baton Rouge, there is little available land that is habitable without the construction of major structures for flood protection. The reoccupation of the same habitation site by different groups, contemporaneously or sequentially, may have been necessitated, in part, by the availability of habitable locations. The locating of French concessions (Cruzat 1940: 122) and of modern towns in southeastern Louisiana, seems to have been determined by the occurrence of ridges or other relatively high ground, at least until construction of protective levees enabled the draining and settlement of lower-lying areas.

The understanding of Indian culture and the native manner of locating settlements is complicated by the confusion regarding the names given by the French to the groups they encountered. As mentioned, it is often impossible to determine whether the appellations represent tribal units or subtribal elements such as moieties, lineages, or clans. The occasional inability of the French to relocate Indian groups mentioned in the accounts of earlier expeditions (e.g., La-Salle's) seems to illustrate a lack of French understanding of Indian toponymy. Expecting perhaps that each emically elicited title represented the exact rendering of tribal names, the French chroniclers assigned sobriquets with little comprehension of the social units these names described.

Several Indian "tribal" names assigned by the French apparently referred to lineage or moiety distinctions. Thus, Mugulasha, from the Muskhogean *Imukalasha*, meaning opposite phratry (Gatschet 1884: 112), appears on both the Mississippi River and Mobile Bay (Louisiana Indian Miscellany 1937–38), underscoring the generic nature of the term; similarly, the words Colapissa or Acolapissa, and possibly Quinipissa, translate from the Choctaw language as "men who see and hear" or "sentinels and spies" (Gatschet 1884:112). Commonly, these tribes were the first groups met by the Europeans when entering rivers or lakes in the Gulf region. Again, as in the appellation Mugulasha, these terms appear to signify generic rather than tribal categories.

Choctaw clans or *iksas* were an important unit of native social life. Often several clans were represented in a single village (Swanton 1931:77, 81). Conversely, the same clan may at times have been represented in more than one village. Although totemic clans have not been recognized conclusively in Choctaw culture, their occurrence in the southeast, among the Creek as well as among western and central Louisiana tribes, is well documented (Gatschet 1883:148, 1891:63; Swanton 1911:108, 349, 1931:79; Eggan 1937; Haas 1939).

The Muskhogean term "choucouacha" or "tchoucoucha," referring to the raccoon (Read 1928:456, 1931) or opossum (Margry 1879–88: 4:155), may have been the source of such "tribal" names as Tchouacha, Touchas, Taouachas and Ouacha. Whether these Muskhogean names for the Chitimachan groups just listed (Swanton 1917:47) refer to lineage groups or represent war emblems, as does Chochichoumas ("red crawfish") (Swanton 1911:29), cannot be clearly ascertained. The occurrence of the term "Tchouacha" on Mobile Bay (LeMaire n.d.) and between the Mississippi River and Bayou LaFourche again raises important questions as to the significance of these terms.

Another potential explanation of recorded names may be functional. Some towns, particularly those most strongly affiliated with the Choctaw, were designated "red" towns and were governed by warriors (Gatschet 1884:112; Swanton 1928b, 1928c). The term "Ouma" may have referred to one such community, as did the terms "Kawita" and "Alibamu" (Gatschet 1884:112). Although probably segments of larger tribal groups, the red towns may have been erroneously recorded as tribal units. The paucity of women encountered by the

French in certain Indian villages (Iberville, in French 1875) may also have characterized these kinds of specialized settlements.

One further complication concerning the naming of native groups by Europeans involves the employment of one Indian language to identify the villages of neighboring groups speaking different tongues. Thus Attakapa is a Muskhogean word meaning "man-eaters." The Chitimacha, whose name in Muskhogean may mean "those who have cooking vessels," called themselves *panteh pinunkansh*, meaning "men altogether red" (Gatschet 1884:45). The often sudden disappearance of Indian names from early records may not indicate extinction but rather a renaming of similar groups in different languages.

The various names assigned to the Indian by the French often confused tribal, locational, functional, and possibly parental designations. Although the toponymic confusion complicates the task of following the movements and destinies of Louisiana tribes, the documentary evidence currently available enables clear recognition of several native village locations. For example, in the case of the Bayagoula tribe, the historical sources consulted in the course of this study may provide significant indications leading to a reassessment of the results of the archaeological excavations of the Bayou Goula site (16IV11) conducted during the Works Progress Administration era (Quimby 1957).

Certainly one of the most important factors determining the frequency and destination of Indian movements was the European incursion of the seventeenth and eighteenth centuries. As dictated by the direct historical approach, an attempt is made here to subtract the European presence in an effort to identify more clearly native patterns of social behavior that subsequently can be applied to earlier periods for which documentary resources are scanty or absent. The direct historical approach may be the best method available for understanding the influence of the sixteenth-century Spanish *entradas* on the native populations of the southeastern United States.

Bayagoula, Mugulasha, and Quinipissa

There is considerable evidence of the virtual identity, or at least close similarity, of these three native groups. Whether it was the result of a true history of amalgamation or not, the Bayagoula, Mugulasha, and Quinipissa share similar settlement histories. After 1700, only the Bayagoula are recorded in French accounts.

A close relationship between the Quinipissa and the Colapissa is also likely (French 1875:225; Higginbotham 1969), and it is apparent from some historical documents that there was a close relationship and possibly equivalence of the Colapissa and Bayagoula tribes (Bienville and LeMoyne n.d. Margry 1879–88: 4: 429). These two groups were in the process of final amalgamation with the Oumas by 1739 (Claiborne 1880).

Even more documentary evidence exists attesting to the probable correspondence of the Quinipissa and Mugulasha. The French at Biloxi came to believe that the Quinipissa encountered in 1682 and 1685 by LaSalle and Tonti, respectively, were the same tribe called by them Mugulasha and thus revived the former name for both political and conceptual reasons (Iberville, in French 1846: 37; Margry 1879–88: 4: 171; Butler 1934: 19n.). Information received by Sauvole from the explorer Douay and from the Quinipissa-Mugulasha chief confirmed this correlation (Higginbotham 1969: 37).

Iberville in 1699 believed that the Mugulasha and Bayagoula were identical to the Quinipissa (Margry 1879–88: 4: 120, 190–91; Cox 1905: 25n.), while Sauvole believed that the Bayagoula were a different tribe from the Quinipissa (Higginbotham 1969: 37). Until toponymic studies provide more evidence concerning the referential meaning of the tribal names, the relationships among these three tribal groups must remain uncertain.

Two ethnohistorical lines of evidence illustrate the close relationship between Quinipissa and Mugulasha, if not their total identity. When Henry de Tonti descended the Mississippi to the Gulf in April 1685 searching for the LaSalle expedition, he deposited a letter for LaSalle with the Quinipissa tribe, located at that time in the area of present-day new Orleans (Claiborne 1880: 19). This missive (reproduced in French 1875: 30–40) was delivered to Sauvole by the Mugulasha chief in 1699 (Iberville, in French 1875: 100). Similarly, when Iberville first encountered the Mugulasha chief, the Indian was wearing a coat of blue serge given him by Tonti fifteen years earlier (Iberville, in French 1875: 71; Fortier 1904: 38). Although both items could have certainly been traded from the Quinipissa to the Mugulasha, the balance of the evidence indicates that these two native groups, described by different names, may have belonged to the same tribe.

The task of reconstructing Indian village locations recorded by French expeditions thus begins with the Quinipissa, with the expectation that the information presented for this group will shed considerable light on the location and movement of the Bayagoula and Mugulasha, neither of which is mentioned in LaSalle's or Tonti's memoirs. Further information concerning the Quinipissa is presented in the discussion of the Colapissa tribe.

The Quinipissa village recorded in 1682 by LaSalle was apparently located in the area of modern Good Hope and Destrehan (Margry 1879–88:1; Membre and Tonti, in Cox 1905). Tonti's estimate of 32 leagues from the Gulf of Mexico for the Quinipissa village was confirmed in January 1700 by Iberville and Sauvole (Higginbotham 1969: 31n.), who describe an abandoned Quinipissa village consisting of seven or eight cabins located west of present-day New Orleans at a portage from Lake Pontchartrain to the Mississippi (the Tigouillon portage) (LaHarpe 1971; see Swanton 1911 for a west-bank location of this village). An abandoned Colapissa settlement was owned by Sieur Lavigne when La Page Du Pratz lodged in the New Orleans area in 1722. DuPratz describes the settlement as being one league from New Orleans on Bayou Choupic (1774:18). It appears possible that the general area described by the accounts of the LaSalle expedition as the home of the Quinipissa tribe may have been occupied cyclically by Colapissa and Bayagoula parties until French concessions ended the Indian tenure on this portion of the Mississippi.

The Quinipissa name is rendered in several different but recognizable forms in early French maps. Minet (1685a, b) locates the Tinipissa on his map, as does Franquelin on his 1684 map (Thwaites 1896–1901:63: frontispiece). Neither map is sufficiently detailed to provide more than a relative position of native groups along the Mississippi toward the end of the seventeenth century.

The Tangibaho or Maheoula (Membre, in Cox 1905), located 2 leagues from the Quinipissa on the Mississippi River, had been almost decimated by the Tchochoumas in 1682. The Tangibaho were most likely a branch of the Colapissa, providing further evidence of this group's residence in the general area between Lake Pontchartrain and the Mississippi. (The Tangibaho will be discussed further in the next section.)

Until the Quinipissa name was resurrected by the French in 1699 (possibly as an attempt to legitimize the rediscovery of LaSalle's Colbert River (the Mississippi), no mention is made of this tribe. Douay's list of Indian tribes he encountered in 1685–90 does not include a reference to the Quinipissa. Again, the accounts of Iberville's first trip record the futile attempts to elicit information concerning the Quinipissa from the Bayagoula and Mugulasha (French 1875:70–71; Margry 1879–88:4:190–91, 5:119–21).

Congruent with these arguments of Mugulasha-Quinipissa identity, the location of the former tribes has been seen as a continuation of the settlement history of the Quinipissa. The Mugulasha were living in the same village with the Bayagoula when they were first encountered by the French (Iberville, in Margry 1879–88: 4: 190–91, 431; Sauvole, in Higginbotham 1969). The Indians described to Iberville their village location on the Mississippi River and provided him with routes of travel across Lake Pontchartrain to the Mississippi mouth (Sauvole, in Higginbotham 1969). It is quite apparent from the documents concerning the French interaction with the Bayagoula-Mugulasha group that these natives were well acquainted with the river, the area south of Baton Rouge, and the Gulf coast, at least as far as the lands of the Biloxi Indians. The location of Fort La Boulaye was selected for Iberville by a Bayagoula Indian (Margry 1879–88: 4: 371).

When the Iberville expedition finally reached the Bayagoula-Mugulasha village in March 1699, they described its location as 60 leagues from the Mississippi's mouth, 35 leagues below the Oumas (Margry 1879–88: 4: 119, 155; DuRu, in Butler 1934). This village, the first encountered by Iberville while ascending the river's course, must have been located in the area of present-day Donaldsonville (fig. 10.1; see also DuPratz 1774: 158; Margry 1879–88: 5: 393; Gravier, in Thwaites 1896–1901: 65: 163, 171). This site has been proposed as the most likely place for fortification by LaSalle (Margry 1879–88: 1:553). Absence of any mention of the Bayagoula village in the Donaldsonville area in April 1682 and the lack of a 1699 Quinipissa occupation in the area of New Orleans, where the tribe had been first seen by LaSalle, seem to indicate that large-scale, possibly cyclical, movements of people were commonplace along the river at the end of the seventeenth century. Evidence also exists identifying the area south of Baton Rouge and along portions of coastal Louisiana and Mississippi as the hunting grounds of the Bayagoula (Albrecht 1945: 7) and possibly the Colapissa and Quinipissa.

Cartographic evidence supporting the location of the 1699–1700 Bayagoula-Mugulasha village at Donaldsonville is presented by DeLisle's maps of 1702, 1703 (Cummings 1958: pl. 43), and 1718 (Paullin 1932: pl. 24), Moll's 1715 translation of the 1703 DeLisle map, Moll (1701), Gentil's map of ca. 1700 (Paullin 1932: pl. 22b), and LeMaire's map of 1716. The Ross map drafted in 1765 shows clearly the location of the ancient Bayagoula village near the site of Donaldsonville (1775). All these sources seem to imply that the excavated remains from site 16IV11, the Bayou Goula site, did not represent the Bayagoula village visited by Iberville and DuRu (cf. Brown 1976: 194). Quimby clearly accepted "the possibility that two different sites rather than a single site are involved in the [Bayagoula] history" (1957:102). He further contended that if, in fact, such was the case, 16IV11, the site excavated by Doran and Smith in 1940–41, represented the later occupation dating from after 1718 when the French concession of M. Paris occupied the site (Beers 1911; Quimby 1957).

There is clear evidence that the Bayagoula tribe lived around Donaldsonville in 1699. Iberville is most emphatic concerning the accuracy of his 60-league estimate from the Mississippi's mouth to the village in question (Margry 1879–88:4:119), stating that it was derived "de mon estimation et des deux pilotes que ay avec moy" (Margry 1879–88:4:181). Further, the Bayagoula and Mugulasha apparently did not erect mounds (Swanton 1932:588), although two platform mounds were found on site 16IV11 (Quimby 1957). These structures, however, appear to have been constructed in prehistoric times (Quimby 1957:117–18, 143) and may not have been in use when the French visited the Bayagoula.

Ascertaining the location of the 1699 Bayagoula-Mugulasha village is considerably more difficult when using north to south criteria (i.e., downriver). The principal difficulty centers on the identification of the "fork" of the Mississippi River, mentioned by Membre (Cox 1905: 143) and vainly sought by Iberville (Margry 1879–88:4:412). In some accounts this branch of the Mississippi appears to refer to Bayou Manchac, connecting the Bayagoula village to the Biloxi area through Lakes Maurepas and Pontchartrain. Other documents seem to designate Bayou Lafourche as the Mississippi's fork.

Since the branch of the river is commonly cited by travelers as a physiographic starting point for measuring daily travel distances, its location on modern maps is crucial in order to reconstruct downriver travels. Until this fork is more conclusively identified, much information relevant to locating the 1699 Bayagoula village must remain unused for the moment.

There exists some significant documentary evidence placing the Bayagoula-Mugulasha village at the present site of Bayou Goula, Louisiana. The most convincing evidence so far uncovered for this location is a map drafted by DeLisle in 1701, based on information gathered by the geologist LaSueur in 1700 (Shea 1861). It includes several sextant readings (denoted as "hateur observe") clearly placing the Bayagoula village in the area of 16IV11. The Mississippi River is reproduced with surprising accuracy on this map, which surely provides the most contradictory locational evidence to the proposition locating the 1699 Bayagoula-Mugulasha village in the area of Donaldsonville.

Closer examination of the LaSueur voyage is required, but the account of this significant expedition is only partially available (in La-Harpe 1971), as far as inquiries could determine.

Further information concerning the placement of the Bayagoula village in 1699 at Bayou Goula includes the Penicaut account (in Mc-Williams 1953:23n.) and the Charlevoix account (1923). LaHarpe (1971) places the M. Paris concession in the area of 16IV11, but the 1724 census of the Mississippi River colony locates this early French habitation 28 leagues north of New Orleans, or in the area of Donaldsonville (Cruzat 1940:122).

The name Bayougoula given to the Paris concession in 1718 adds considerable confusion to the issue of village location of the 1699 Bayagoula and Mugulasha. It is possible that the site visited by Iberville and described by DuRu as having been occupied by the Bayagoula for 600 years (Butler 1934:20) was located near Donaldsonville. Thus the naming of the Paris concession remains unclear. It would be easy to assume that the name derived from the tribe that most recently or most substantially occupied the area during the first decades of the eighteenth century. Little information is available for the period following the displacement of the Bayagoula by the Taensa in 1706, until their identification near the Ouma and Little Acolapissa around Vacherie ca. 1720. The Bayagoula briefly settled near Fort La Boulaye following the attack by the Taensa in 1706 (fig. 10.1).

It may be possible, then, that the Bayagoula, following a brief occupation near the fort, moved to the area of site 16IV11. It is more likely, however, that the Paris concession was given the name Bayougoula based on the general vicinity and familiarity of the French with this tribe. The area that includes Donaldsonville and 16IV11, as far north as Baton Rouge, is documented as Bayagoula hunting ground. Istraouma (modern-day Baton Rouge) separated the Ouma from the Bayagoula territories (Albrecht 1945).

More problem-oriented excavation of the 16IV11 site, complemented by additional ethnohistorical information, is needed in order to address explicitly the question of Bayagoula village identification and thus enable ascription of the material culture excavated at 16IV11 either to a particular tribe or to an episode of French settlement.

Similar approaches are sorely needed for the Donaldsonville area. Despite the final location of the 1699 Bayagoula-Mugulasha village, the area of Donaldsonville, from which Bayou Lafourche leaves the Mississippi River and flows toward the Gulf of Mexico, was an important nexus in native communication and interaction. It is likely that many tribes settled at or near this junction during late prehistoric times. The occupation of this area during the eighteenth century is discussed below.

Following the Bayagoula attack on the Mugulasha in 1700, the latter never reappear in the ethnohistoric record. The movements of the Bayagoula after 1718 are relatively easy to follow. After a brief stay near the fort (Penicaut, in McWilliams 1953), the Bayagoula are located at Wallace, Louisiana, near Vacherie and Edgard (De la Tour map of 1720, in Riis 1936: map 4; see also fig. 10.1). With the exception of the Bienville and LeMoyne manuscript (n.d.), which locates the Bayagoula in the area of LaPlace (otherwise denoted as the post-1718 site of the main Colapissa village), most early-eighteenth-century documents locate the Bayagoula near Vacherie after 1718 (DeCrenay map 1733, in Swanton 1922: pl. 5; D'Anville map 1752, in Riis 1936: map 6; DuPratz map 1757; Ross map 1775). Claiborne, quoting the 1739 journal of a French officer traveling to fight the Chickasaw, describes the Bayagoula in an advanced stage of merger with the Ouma and Colapissa near Vacherie (1880:66). Amalgamation and smallpox reduced the Bayagoula's population, and little information is available concerning them after the 1730s.

Finally, it may be important to note that in 1730, in response to widespread fear of Indian attacks generated by the Natchez uprising, Governor Perrier built several blockhouses and palisades at the principal French concessions, Tchoupitoulas, Cannées Brulées, New Orleans, Les Allemands, Pointe Coupee, and Bayougoula (Claiborne 1880:43). This episode of French construction may be represented, in part, by the excavated remains of the structures at 16IV11 (see also Brown 1976).

Ouma

When encountered by LaSalle and Tonti in 1682–85, the Ouma lived near the Red River, north of Baton Rouge. This group, or a closely related group, was responsible for the bloody attack on the Tangibaho village described by the French (Margry 1879–88: 1:556; Cox 1905). Described as the "bravest nation on the river" by Tonti (Cox 1905) the Ouma remained north of the Bayagoula until 1706 when an attack by the Tunica forced all or part of the Ouma to flee to the area of New Orleans, where they are depicted in the LeMaire map of 1716 (fig. 10.1).

When first encountered by Iberville in March 1699, the Ouma lived in a defended village of 70 to 140 cabins (French 1875: 84–85; Gravier, in Thwaites 1896–1901: 65: 147–49). They are recorded as attacking and capturing several Bayagoula in retaliation for invasion of their hunting grounds (French 1875; LaHarpe 1971: 33). Often noted as the enemies of the Colapissa and Bayagoula, they possibly continued the rivalry that produced the Tangibaho slaughter of 1682.

The aggression of the Ouma may have caused the movement of the Taensa from the Bayagoula village, which they had usurped in 1706, to the area of Luling, Louisiana, before 1713. Finally chased to Bayou Manchac, the Taensa resettled in Mobile Bay in 1715.

In 1709, the Ouma occupied the area between Donaldsonville and Union (Penicaut, in McWilliams 1953: 129–30; fig. 10.1). LaHarpe places them in 1718 in three villages between Burnside and Convent, 12 leagues north of the "Tinsas" concession. Other documentary evidence for the Ouma village locations in the area mentioned include the 1720 De la Tour map (in Riis 1936: map 4); the Charlevoix (1923) account of his 1722 trip; the D'Anville map of 1752 (in Riis 1936: map 6), which also includes the Petit Oumas in the area of Darrow; and the 1722 DuPratz visit to the Ouma village at Union, denoted as the oldest on the river (since 1718?) (DuPratz 1774). During the Poisson visit of 1727, the Ouma site referred to a French habitation owned by M. de Ascenis since 1721 (Thwaites 1896–1901: 67: 297; Mereness 1916: 34, 42; Maduell 1972: 28; see also fig. 10.1).

It is interesting to note the continued tripartite division of the Ouma into a "grand" village and two "petit" villages. On March 20, 1699, Iberville encountered three Ouma chiefs living in the same village near the Red River (French 1875: 84; Margry 1879–88: 4: 184). The late-eighteenth-century movement from the Mississippi area occurred in three waves reminiscent of the previous three-village organization (Curry 1979).

Between 1739 and 1758, the Ouma are described as being in the process of amalgamation with the Bayagoula and Acolapissa (Claiborne 1880), although three Ouma villages continue to appear in contemporary documents. Possibly, one of the three sites is the French habitation, one is Ouma headquarters at Burnside, and one village is denoted as the site of the Petit Ouma, at Darrow. With the exception of the arrival of the Alibamu at Union around 1765 or earlier (Ross 1775), the Ouma continue to occupy exclusively the area between Burnside and Darrow until 1766, when the majority of the remaining tribe moved south toward Terrebonne Parish (Swanton 1946: 140; Curry 1979).

Colapissa

The Colapissa are often equated with the Quinipissa (French 1875: 225; Gatschet 1884; Higginbotham 1969). The Colapissa interviewed by Sauvole had never heard of either LaSalle or Tonti (Higginbotham 1969: 25). The Tangibaho were described as belonging to one of the Colapissa villages, located, according to the Bayagoula, 50 leagues inland, near the headwaters of the Pearl River (Margry 1879–88: 5: 218). In 1705 or earlier, the Tangibaho were located along a bayou of the same name and along Pontchartrain (McWilliams 1953; fig. 10.1). Until 1718 the Colapissa villages were situated along the Pearl River, called by them Tulcascha (McWilliams 1953), at Bay St. Louis, or Kato-outon (Butler 1934), and in the area of Mandeville, where they occupied the same village with the Natchitoches from 1705 to ca. 1718 (fig. 10.1; McWilliams 1953).

After about 1718, the Colapissa were located in the area of LaPlace (fig. 10.1; De la Tour map of 1720 in Riis 1936; map 4; D'Anville map of 1752 in Riis 1936; map 6; Ross map 1775; Claiborne 1880; Charlevoix 1923; McWilliams 1953). Several post-1718 references to the Little or Petit Colapissa are available which locate them in the area of present-day Garyville, west of the Grand Colapissa village at LaPlace and opposite the settlement of the Bayagoula (fig. 10.1; De la Tour map of 1720 in Riis 1936: map 4; DuPratz 1758; Charlevoix 1923).

There is an interesting document (Bienville and LeMoyne n.d.) which refers to the Bayagoula tribe as living in the area of the Colapissa village at LaPlace. It seems to support the proposed identification of the Colapissa and Bayagoula as similar, or at least very closely related groups, in the eyes of the French. The close spacing of the Colapissa, Little Colapissa, and Bayagoula villages along the Mississippi River, as shown by post-1718 documents, is reminiscent of the distribution of the contemporary Ouma village farther up the river.

Ouacha

The Ouacha practiced a wandering life along the coastal areas of southeastern Louisiana. They were closely allied with the Tchouacha and Chitimacha with whom they shared many linguistic similarities (Swanton 1917, 1946: 204). Their territory included the area between the Mississippi River and Bayou Lafourche. Lake Salvador was at one time known as Ouacha Lake (De la Tour 1720 map, Riis 1936: map 4; D'Anville 1752 map in Riis 1936: map 6; Romans 1776 map; Darby

1816 map), while Bayou Lafourche was once named Riviere de Ouachas (Iberville, in Margry 1879–88: 4:165). The close affiliation between Ouacha and Chitimacha may be indicated by the naming of Bayou Lafourche as "Riviere des Chitimachas" (D'Anville 1752 map in Riis 1936: map 6; Romans 1776; LaHarpe 1971) in other sources. Similarly, Bayou Plaquemine, an important access into the western Louisiana basins like the Atchafalaya, was called at times both River of the Ouachas (Ottens and others 1730 map) and River of the Chitimacha (LaHarpe 1971).

In 1699, the Ouacha were living along Bayou Lafourche, in the area of Thibodeaux (fig. 10.1). They were first encountered by Iberville during his first ascent of the Mississippi in the area of Donaldsonville (Margry 1879–88: 4:154). The Ouacha were, in that instance, in the company of several Bayagoula. In 1700, Bienville descended the Lafourche course in order to visit the Ouacha at their village but received a belligerent welcome from them when he approached modern-day Labadieville and Supreme (Margry 1879–88: 4:432; Swanton 1911:298).

The DeLisle maps of 1702 and 1703 (1703 map in Cummings 1958: pl. 43) depict the Ouacha near the Houma-Raceland area. By 1703 the Ouacha were allies of the French and Ouma against the Chitimacha (LeMaire n.d.; McWilliams 1953). After this time, these Indians are of little consequence in the history of the area, often being referred to as petty tribes (Sibley 1806:6).

In 1715, the Ouacha were located in the area of Hahnville, Louisiana (fig. 10.1; Bienville and LeMoyne n.d.; Margry 1879–88: 5:557, McWilliams 1953). Between 1722 and 1738 they were living in the area of Les Allemands (DuPratz 1757; Claiborne 1880:66) and were merged with the Chitimacha soon after, most likely as the result of European pressure. One of Bushnell's informants among the Chitimacha may have been a Ouacha (1917:301).

Tchouacha

One of the earliest accounts involving the Tchouachas concerns the loss of their chief and several members to a combined Natchez-Yazoo-Chickasaw attack (Penicaut, in McWilliams 1953; Swanton 1911:193, 300). Bienville and LeMoyne (n.d.) place the Tchouachas in the Scarsdale–Belle Chase area, close to English Turn, on both sides of the Mississippi River (fig. 10.1). Contemporary maps (LeMaire 1716; DeLisle 1718, in Paullin 1932: pl. 24) place this group along the seacoast and

shores of Barataria Bay, probably referring to their general territory
(fig. 10.1).

In 1722, the Tchouacha settlements around English Turn were
found to have been abandoned (Charlevoix 1923), although apparently the tribe was still living close by, probably near modern-day
Bertrandville (De la Tour map of 1720 in Riis 1936: map 4; D'Anville
1752 map in Riis 1936: map 6). Several Tchouachas were living near
New Orleans when they were attacked by a group of Negroes armed
by Governor Perrier in 1730 (Dumont 1753). In 1739, the journal of
the French officer cited by Claiborne (1880: 65) described the Tchouachas at the German settlement of Les Allemands, near Taft or
Hahnville (fig. 10.1).

Documentary evidence provided by the Ross map, drafted in 1765
and published in 1775, shows the Bertrandville settlement abandoned.
The last evidence of Tchouacha habitation prior to their amalgamation with Chitimachan tribes places this small group in the area of
New Orleans in 1758 (Cruzat 1925: 594). During later colonial times
(1718–63), most Indian groups, particularly the small remnant tribes
like the Tchouacha and Ouacha, moved frequently around the New
Orleans area (Orleans, Jefferson, and Plaquemines parishes), often
hunting for the French settlers and generally trying to avoid the European expansion which by 1750 had reached both sides of the Mississippi River as far south as Phoenix, Louisiana (Vivier, in Thwaites
1896–1901: 69: 209–11).

Chitimacha

The most enduring of the tribes considered in this study, the Chitimacha, lasted into the twentieth century as an entity, due primarily to
their inaccessible location in south-central Louisiana (Gatschet 1883;
Swanton 1911, 1946). The earliest settlements and explorations of the
western range of the Chitimacha, around St. Mary and St. Martin
parishes, occurred as late as the 1780s and 1800s (Robin 1805; Landreth 1819; Cathcart 1945; Comeaux 1976; Gibson 1978).

The eastern Chitimacha group, probably represented in part by the
Tchouacha and Ouacha, suffered a major defeat at the hands of the
French as a punishment for their murdering of St. Cosme in 1703
(Bienville and LeMoyne n.d.; Penicaut, in McWilliams 1953). This
group continued to occupy the area between the Atchafalaya and the
Mississippi rivers until modern times (Gatschet 1883; Swanton 1911).
They are recorded in this region as early as 1702 by Delisle as Touti-

machas (fig. 10.1). This designation appears in DeLisle's 1718 map (Paullin 1932: pl. 24) and on the LeMaire 1716 map. The area of lakes between the Mississippi and Lafourche courses was called "Lacs des Chitimachas" in 1718, and the general region that includes Iberville, Assumption, St. James, Lafourche, and portions of St. Martin and Terrebonne parishes has long been considered Chitimacha territory (McWilliams 1953; LeMaire n.d.).

A Chitimacha settlement appears in the post-1718 records along the Mississippi River in the area of White Castle and Bayou Goula (fig. 10.1, McWilliams 1953; Bienville and LeMoyne n.d.). This location places the village in proximity to the Paris concession at Bayougoula where it continued at least until 1739 (D'Anville map of 1752, in Riis 1936; map 6; Claiborne 1880; Charlevois 1923). Ross (1775) continued to place the villages of the Chitimachas in the Bayou Goula vicinity up to 1765. As mentioned, in the early decades of the eighteenth century, particularly around 1730, Bayou Lafourche was known as "Riviere du Chitimachas," as was Bayou Plaquemines farther north.

The principal access to the west-central area of Louisiana, traditionally the territory of the Chitimacha, was through Bayou Plaquemines, also called at one time River of the Outimachas and Magenesito (Iberville, in Margry 1879–88: 4: 172). All indications are that the term Chitimacha referred to several tribes or communities, possibly including such groups as the Tchouacha, Ouacha, Yagnesito, and Tilapani (see next section). The ethnohistorical and archaeological information concerning these Chitimacha groups should be examined exhaustively for several reasons, including the geographical location of the Chitimacha between the apparently agricultural Muskhogean societies (including the Ouma, Acolapissa, and Bayagoula) and the primarily hunting, fishing, and gathering tribes of western Louisiana and coastal Texas. Further study may provide important information concerning acculturation and the significance of the Mississippi River as a barrier to east-west communication and diffusion. Documentary evidence of the military alliance of groups on one side of the Mississippi River against those groups living on the opposite shore can be found in the 1700 account by DuRu (Butler 1934).

Another important aspect of Chitimachan culture is the persistence of native stylistic motifs, particularly in basketry, into recent times. Since these stylistic elements were often employed on ceramics (Swanton 1911: 347–48, 353), Chitimachan ceramics dating from the sixteenth and seventeenth centuries may be relatively easier to recognize in the archaeological record. One possible example of Chitimachan motifs found on ceramics from protohistoric periods is the type Cracker Road Incised, found most commonly in the west-central regions of southern Louisiana (Ian Brown, personal communication). The design bears some apparent similarities to a motif called "alligator entrails," frequently found on recent examples of Chitimachan baskets (Swanton 1911:pl. 24b).

The large amount of ethnohistorical information collected and available for the Chitimacha should enable the formulation of more testable hypotheses than would be possible when dealing with other native groups from southeastern Louisiana. Also, the relative isolation of the Chitimacha heartland from European settlers until the nineteenth century may provide a greater chance for the archaeological identification of village sites once occupied by such groups.

Other "tribes"

Several other native groups are encountered in the French documentary sources dating from the period under investigation. Their appearance and their duration of settlement in the area are usually brief and discontinuous. Little ethnohistorical information exists concerning them; thus the task of tracing their movements and eventual fate is complicated.

Two groups briefly appearing in the written records of French colonial Louisiana are the Tilapani and Yagnesito. The former appear for a brief period in villages along Bayou Lafourche, near Thibodaux, possibly occupying sites previously settled by the Ouacha (see above). Two late maps (D'Anville 1752, in Riis: 1936:map 6; Ross 1775) mention the old, abandoned Tilapani villages in the Thibodaux area, but no further evidence concerning this Indian group could be located.

The Yagnesito (or Magenesito?) appear in local historic maps as early as 1702 (DeLisle) in the area of Labadieville (fig. 10.1). Another DeLisle map, published in 1703 (Cummings 1958:pl. 43), places the Yagnesito farther south along Bayou Lafourche where they apparently continue to live until about 1718 (see LaMaire 1716 map; DeLisle 1718 map, in Paullin 1932:pl. 24). This group was evidently a close neighbor of the Ouacha and possibly other Chitimachan groups during at least the first two decades of the eighteenth century. Their relationship to other Chitimachan groups and their general style of life is little known and will probably be recovered only through archaeological research.

In 1718, a group called the Tchatchagoula (DeLisle 1718, in Paullin 1932: pl. 24) is found north of the Tilapani, in or near a site previously occupied by a Toutimacha people in 1703 (DeLisle 1703, in Cummings 1958: pl. 43). Their date and history are the least known of local peoples, and there is little hope, at present, for learning more about this native group.

Little is known also concerning the Okelousa or Onquilouzas except that they were allies of the Ouacha (Swanton 1911:298) around 1699. They are found west and north of Pointe Coupée in 1722 (DuPratz 1774), peripheral to the study area.

The final group of relevance for this study is the Taensa Indians. They appeared south of Baton Rouge in 1706 when they displaced the Bayougoula (LaHarpe 1971). Ouma pressure forced these people from their pre-1713 settlements near Luling, often called the Tinsas Concession (LaHarpe 1971), to Mobile Bay through the Manchac region (McWilliams 1953). They may have returned to the Donaldsonville area around 1763–64 (Swanton 1946: 188).

Summary and conclusions

This documentary study demonstrates that in southeastern Louisiana there still exist several localities where there is good potential for finding and excavating the remains of historically documented Indian villages. For example, the area along the Mississippi River between Darrow and LaPlace appears to have been the focus for native occupation, particularly between 1710 and 1760. The groups or "tribes" occupying this area primarily were descended from the Muskhogean nations based farther east. The half century of occupation that should be represented archaeologically in this region of Louisiana is significant for understanding acculturation and culture change, and possibly for recovering the last preserved examples of Indian material culture containing evidences of pre-European Indian styles.

The area along the Mississippi River seems to have been a significant cultural boundary between agricultural, primarily Muskhogean-related groups and hunting, fishing and gathering peoples of various ethnic affiliations who pursued different, more mobile socioeconomic cycles (e.g., Attakapa, Karankawa).

West of the Mississippi River, in the area formerly considered the territory of the Chitimacha and associated groups, the potential for studying the material culture and social structure of native groups seems, at present, better than in eastern parts of Louisiana. Slower

European intrusion due to the highly inhospitable marshes and low prairies has resulted in the preservation of several Indian communities into this century. It has been possible, therefore, to recover and examine many examples of Chitimacha material culture, particularly baskets. Further, the slower industrial expansion in the central Louisiana region has preserved more archaeological sites. The study of documented Indian peoples and their local settlements may be profitably initiated west of the Mississippi River in the hope of formulating and testing cultural hypotheses that can later be applied to eastern Louisiana historic sites.

One possible strategy for the archaeological examination of the relationships between group membership or ethnic composition and variability in material culture has its source in studies of documented village locations. It may be possible to isolate components that are the archaeological remains of communities composed of relatively homogenous social units (e.g., the Tchouacha villages near English Turn). The measurement and definition of artifact variability at these sites should be compared to that from sites that are documented as the habitations of several recognizably different groups (e.g., the Colapissa-Natchitoches village near Mandeville, or possibly the elusive Bayagoula-Mugulasha village dating from the years 1699–1706). It may be possible to predict the amount of stylistic variability resulting from the activities conducted at a site by single or multiple ethnic groups.

The discussion of group membership and artifact variability raises the important question of defining and identifying the significant variability-producing social units. Whether it will be possible to distinguish among the assemblage deposited by a single lineage residing in a community compared to that resulting from a site's occupation by a multiple lineage unit compared to the deposits of a multi-"tribal" community is a question that must be explicitly formulated and tested. Data gathered from such locations as the Petit Ouma and Grand Ouma villages, or the Petit Colapissa and Main Colapissa settlements, may provide a valuable beginning toward identifying the social sources of specific artifact variability.

Archaeological literature contains several encouraging examples that tend to justify the kinds of archaeological projects recommended by the documentary analysis presented above. A number of sites identified in historic records as native villages have been located and, in part, excavated (Collins 1927a; Ford 1936; Griffin 1937; Jennings 1941; Setzler and Jennings 1941; Lewis 1943; Fewkes 1944; Caldwell

1948; Griffin and Bullen 1950; Goggin and Sturtevant 1964; Deetz 1965; Neitzel 1965; Brain 1977, 1979).

The potential for understanding the relationship between human behavior and artifact manufacture is particularly good in the southeastern United States, where, due possibly to the lesser degree of female acculturation to European life, the ceramic styles of the sixteenth-, and the seventeenth-, and possibly the eighteenth-century tribes have maintained native features for a long period of time, despite the European presence (Fairbanks 1958:53–55; Matson 1965:73; Hally 1971:57).

Ethnographic information provides some examples of group cohesiveness represented in material styles manufacture. Thus, Chocataw bands could be distinguished by their pouches (Swanton 1931:42). Common also were hieroglyphic-like designs on tablets and structures identifying particular groups and war emblems to enemies and neighbors (Swanton 1911, 1946; Hudson 1976). Scanty records concerning tribal methods of ceramic manufacture have been preserved. The Bayagoula were said to temper their pottery with shell (Butler 1934: 20), while, at least historically, this tempering material was never used by the Chitimacha (Bushnell 1917:305).

Once documented sites have been archaeologically excavated and the interpretations presented, the task of interpreting contemporary archaeological assemblages is made simpler. Surface collections and limited testing will often be sufficient to ascribe protohistoric and historic sites to particular cultural groups (Hally 1971:60). Further, the number of historic period aboriginal sites that are not recorded in ethnohistoric documents surely exceeds the recorded examples. Such Louisiana mound complexes as Gibson (16TR5), Sims (16SC20), and Dulac (16TR38) that have been found to contain historic period components can be investigated with the realistic hope of providing specific cultural association for the archaeological remains.

Finally, continued archival research and wide-ranging examination of museum collections, both in the United States and in Europe, may provide additional evidence of the material culture of specific groups. Just as early European explorers collected floral, faunal, and mineral specimens for their sponsors in Europe, so too they may have collected artifacts to illustrate the culture of specific native groups. Continued archaeological and ethnographic research, jointly pursued, promises to provide interesting and most important contributions to theoretical and historical studies of human behavior.

11

Prehistoric Development of Calusa Society in Southwest Florida: Excavations on Useppa Island

J. T. Milanich, J. Chapman, A. S. Cordell,
S. Hale, and R. A. Marrinan

From an archaeological point of view, perhaps the least known area of the U.S. Gulf coast is southwestern Florida—the part of the Florida coast between Charlotte Harbor and the Florida Keys. For years, it was widely believed that archaeological site densities in this area were low, and prior to 1970 little information about the archaeology of southwestern Florida was published. Yet this was part of the territory of the enigmatic Calusa, first encountered by Spanish explorers in the sixteenth century. The Calusa have long been regarded as an interesting case by cultural ecologists because the complexity of their social organization, the density of their populations, and the magnitude of their interaction with other groups seemed difficult to reconcile with their essentially hunting and gathering subsistence base.

In their research on the development of prehistoric Calusa subsistence, the authors are, literally and figuratively, breaking new ground. Working in an area where little detailed archaeological work has been done, the authors have integrated zooarchaeological and technological analyses of prehistoric Calusa sites on Useppa Island in an effort to test ethnohistoric models of Calusa subsistence with quantified archaeological data. In so doing, they have also illustrated an approach that should stimulate similar research in other areas of the Gulf coast.

DURING the sixteenth century the southwest Florida Gulf coast and the adjacent mainland from Charlotte Harbor southward at least to the northern portion of the Ten Thousand Islands was the region of the Calusa Indians. The Calusa, unlike most other Florida aborigines in the sixteenth century, did not cultivate plants for food. Maize and beans, both grown throughout much of the southeastern United States, were apparently not grown within the Calusa coastal region. Unlike most other nonagriculturalists throughout the world, however, the Calusa developed a complex sociopolitical system. Modern anthropological studies of the Calusa have focused on this uniqueness. We view our study as another step (albeit a small one) in the long-term investigation of the Calusa peoples, their prehistoric ancestors, and the development of their sociopolitical system. Such an investigation also promises to yield data regarding the relationships between human cultural systems and the natural systems of the coast region, a topic of interest to archaeologists working along the Gulf of Mexico.

Most of the information about aboriginal peoples in coastal southwest Florida comes from late-sixteenth-century letters (1566–70) written by Spanish Jesuit priests who were firsthand observers (Zubillaga 1946) and, to a lesser extent, from archaeological investigations. John Goggin and William Sturtevant (1964) have synthesized many of these data, along with other Spanish archival materials. Their article, "The Calusa: A Stratified Nonagricultural Society (with Notes on Sibling Marriage)," remains the most thorough overview of Calusa society. More recently, Father Clifford Lewis (1978) and J. T. Milanich and Charles Fairbanks (1980:241–50) have offered additional overviews of the Calusa, although both rely heavily on the earlier work of Goggin and Sturtevant.

Nearly all of the anthropologists investigating the Calusa agree that their relatively propitious marine environment provided the subsistence base for the development of this complex, nonagricultural society. For example, Goggin and Sturtevant conclude:

> Calusa subsistence was based on the abundant, relatively stabilized food supply provided by the rich inshore marine resources. The role filled by agriculture in other cultures of comparable type was here filled by intensive fishing. It is conceivable that the cooperative work patterns necessary for taking mullet by the net were related to other areas of Calusa interaction. (1964:207)

In an impressive master's thesis, Randolph Widmer (1978) has reviewed and synthesized much of the ecological data from southwest

Florida along with archaeological and ethnohistoric observations regarding the Calusa and their prehistoric ancestors (the latter represented by numerous archaeological sites along the coast). Widmer's model seeks to explain the nature of the cultural-ecological adaptation of the southwest Florida coastal aborigines. He reaches a conclusion similar to that of Goggin and Sturtevant, while making the point that the Calusa social-political system may have been the best kind for successfully adjusting to their environmental conditions:

> A tropical estuarine resource base, quite unlike an anadromous fish resource base . . . will certainly allow for the development of so-called "complex systems." In point of fact, it almost necessitates the development of centralization and ranking to provide the degree of coordination and efficiency to adequately cope with population pressure, not only stimulated by sedentism but also by the extremely high "carrying capacity" which allows very high population size and density.
>
> In all probability, a tropical coastal estuary such as that of the southwest coast is probably the most productive for human exploitation on a hunting-gathering basis. Because of the high stability coupled with great productivity, environmental homogeneity and predictable cycling of resources based on tides, the Southwest Florida coast is an extremely attractive region for human adaptive systems. The sociopolitical response to this adaptation parallels that of agricultural adaptations. (1978 : 136–37)

With the publication of the Goggin and Sturtevant article in 1964 and the later availability of Widmer's thesis, we have excellent interpretive summaries and an explanatory model for the Calusa cultural system. Further "rehashing" of the same data used in their research would not be fruitful, as the available archival and archaeological data have been thoroughly exhausted. What is needed are new data to describe and interpret further the cultural history of the Calusa and to understand how and why their cultural system evolved. These data must be recovered through archival research and problem-oriented archaeological investigation. The various archives containing primary documents pertinent to Spanish colonial Florida almost certainly contain more information regarding southwest Florida, but there has been little research for materials from the post-Jesuit period. And a great deal more information remains in the ground, in archaeological sites. There have been few attempts, for instance, systematically to collect comparative, quantified data regarding either subsistence change or even material culture change through time. An excellent foundation for such studies, however, has been established through the research carried out on the southwest coast to date (e.g., Wing 1965; Cockrell 1970; Widmer 1974, 1978; Fradkin 1976; McMichael 1982).

The modest archaeological investigations on Useppa Island on the southwest Florida coast were undertaken to provide such new data on prehistoric Calusa aboriginal subsistence and settlement patterning as well as to help reconstruct the culture history of Useppa Island. The actual excavations were short-term and limited in scope, but refined analytical techniques were employed and produced significant results. We were able to locate a number of aboriginal shell deposits, most dating between several hundred years B.C. and the historic period. One test (Test B) provided an excellent stratified sample of shellfish and vertebrate faunal remains. Calculation of biomass data from the identified sample shows some changes through time. Overall, however, the picture is one of generalized, intensive fishing along with shellfish collection, especially of clams, oysters, and whelks. Through time, whelks and sharks and rays increased in dietary importance. Mullet, thought by some authorities to have been an important component in the Calusa diet, constituted a negligible portion of the faunal remains.

Technological analysis of the aboriginal ceramics from the same test demonstrates that heterogeneity in ceramic attributes—aplastic constituents, color, and rim form—are indeed present through time. Undecorated, "sand-tempered plain" sherds (as we used to call them) *do* contain cultural and chronological information. Our old practice of simply counting them (and then ignoring them out of frustration, since with the naked eye they all look the same) is no longer the best research strategy.

One small, late Archaic period midden was tested (Test A) and a sample of faunal remains and artifacts recovered. The site, perhaps a short-term camp, appears to have been occupied for the purpose of collecting whelk shells and removing the columellas for use as tools. Such sites have not been recognized previously along the southwest Florida coast.

Perhaps the most important result of the Useppa investigations is that they point out the need for specialized types of analyses and data. In a concluding section, we describe some of the resulting methodological problems encountered in coastal archaeology and offer a minimal research plan for the Calusa region.

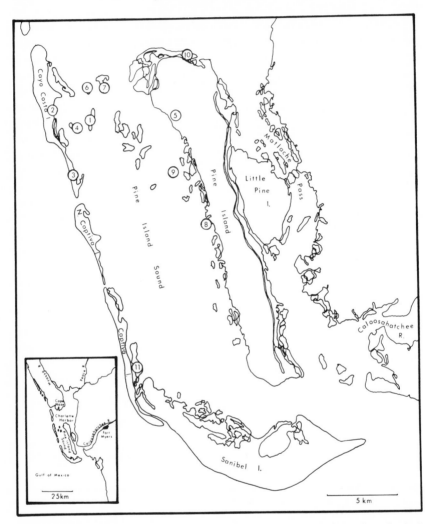

Fig. 11.1. Pine Island Sound, showing locations of selected archaeological sites: (1) Useppa Island; (2) Old Ware Mound; (3) Faulkner Mound; (4) Cabbage Key; (5) Pineland; (6) Mondongo Island; (7) Patricio Island; (8) Demere Key; (9) Joccelyn Key; (10) Howard Mound (11) Buck Key.

Useppa Island and environs

Useppa is located toward the northern end of Pine Island Sound in Lee County (fig. 11.1). The sound itself extends approximately 30 kilometers along the southwest Florida coast from Charlotte Harbor, apparently the northern boundary of the Calusa Indians, southward to the lower portion of Sanibel Island. A barrier island chain consisting of Cayo Costa, North Captiva, Captiva, and Sanibel islands comprises the western boundary of the sound and separates it from the Gulf of Mexico. The eastern boundary is not the southwest Florida mainland, but Pine Island, a large island, 25 kilometers in length. Pine Island, in turn, is separated from the inland by a water passage known as Matlatcha Pass. The Caloosahatchee River empties into San Carlos Bay, which is formed by the south ends of Pine and Sanibel islands and by the mainland. Numerous islands, most with mangrove around them, dot Pine Island Sound.

Some of the islands, e.g., Sanibel (Missimer 1973), were formed in the last several thousand years by depositional processes. Others, like parts of Useppa and Pine Island, apparently were high ground cut off from the mainland by the post-Pleistocene rising waters of the Gulf of Mexico. (This rise in the waters of the sound apparently is ongoing. Profiles cut by mosquito-control ditches through shell mound sites on Buck Key adjacent to Captiva Island have been observed by Milanich; they show that the bases of the shell are as much as 1 meter below the present waterline. Informants on Sanibel have pointed out a field to Milanich in which lime trees were grown in the first quarter of the twentieth century but which today is subject to tidal inundation.) Those portions of Useppa Island believed to have been cut off from the mainland are relatively high, stabilized sand dunes, possibly formed during the Pleistocene when beach conditions were present.

The configuration of the Pine Island Sound region presented the aboriginal inhabitants with at least 100 percent more detailed tidal shoreline than is found in situations where only one linearly positioned barrier island system is present along the coast. The presence of so much saline and brackish mangrove swamp forest along with the nutrients deposited by the Peace and Myakka rivers (which empty into Charlotte Harbor with channels flowing into Pine Island Sound) and the nutrients deposited by the Caloosahatchee make the entire sound an ecologically propitious marine environment for fish and shellfish.

This tropical coastal estuary system, as described by Widmer (1978), apparently did support a relatively large aboriginal population. The distributional density of large shell middens and constructed shell mounds in the sound is extraordinary. If the sites were occupied concurrently by late prehistoric peoples (ancestors of the Calusa Indians), the population density of the 30-by-20-kilometer region (60,000 hectares or about 230 square miles) encompassing the sound, barrier islands, and adjacent mainland may have rivaled that of sections of the lower Mississippi River valley at the same time. Some of these large shell mound sites are (distance is from Useppa Island; see fig. 11.1) Old Ware Mound, 2.4 kilometers west on Cayo Costa (Lacosta); Faulkner Mound, 3.1 kilometers south, also on Cayo Costa; Cabbage Key, 0.7 kilometers west; Pineland, 5.6 kilometers east on Pine Island; Mondongo Island, 0.95 kilometers north; Patricio Island, 1.2 kilometers north; and Demere Key, Joccelyn (Josslyn) Key, sites on North Captiva, and Howard Mound on Bokeelia Island, all within 10 kilometers. Numerous other small middens are found throughout the islands within and bordering the sound (e.g., Buck Key, Sanibel Island, Galt Island) as well as on the mainland. The extraordinary number and size of the sites drew the eye of Frank H. Cushing when he visited the area in 1897:

> Ere passing on to the scene of our long continued and more thorough examination of one of the most ancient and characteristic of these, however, it may be well for me to mention that there were, in Charlotte Harbor, Pine Island Sound, Caloosa Entrance and Matlatcha Bay alone, more than seventy-five of them [shell middens and mounds]. Forty of this number were gigantic, the rest were representative of various stages in the construction of such villages of the reefs. No doubt a more searching exploration of these waters, and of the wide and forbidding mangrove swamps on contiguous shores of Sanybel, and of others of the outer islands, and of Pine Island, as well as of the mainland itself, would reveal many others; but the amount of work represented even by the number I have already named is so enormous and astounding, that it cannot be realized or appreciated by means of mere spoken description or statement. (1897:347)

Fifteen kilometers to the north across Charlotte Harbor are the Cape Haze sites (Bullen and Bullen 1956) and 35 kilometers to the northeast across the harbor is the Aqui Esta site (Luer and Almy 1980b). Charlotte Harbor seems to have constituted a cultural boundary: components at the Cape Haze sites on the harbor's north side apparently share affiliations with the central Gulf coast cultures; Aqui Esta on the east shares similarities with the southwest Florida coastal culture (although Belle Glade Plain pottery is certainly present at some Cape Haze sites and Safety Harbor ceramics are found at Aqui Esta).

Useppa Island itself is about 1.7 kilometers north-south and 0.56 kilometers east-west at its widest point (fig. 11.2). A dune ridge ex-

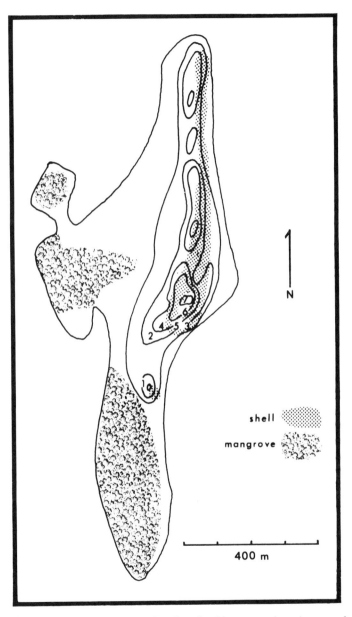

Fig. 11.2. Useppa Island, showing backhoe test locations and shell middens (contour interval 5 feet).

tends along the eastern edge of the island, sloping rapidly to the water on the east. Stands of mangrove are presently found on the southern portion of the island west of higher ground and along the western, lower portion of the island's center. In the Smithsonian Institution Annual Report for 1882, M. H. Simmons described Useppa:

> Less than a mile south is Useppa Key, whose northern extremity is a mud-bank 6 feet in height topped by shells to an equal amount; this widens out into a plateau about 100 yards wide, sloping to the westward. The island is over half a mile in length, and about half way down from the northern end the plateau forks, the eastern arm forming a ridge about 18 feet high facing the channel, the western forming a narrow flat ridge not over 10 feet high. Between and protected by these there is about an acre which is not over 6 feet above mean water, and at the southern extremity of this there is a space about 20 feet square, which is not over 2 feet above water-level, and was probably used by the Indians, as it is now by the Spanish fishermen, as a location for a well. It is protected east and west by a continuation of the ridge and plateau and on the south by a conical mound 15 feet or so in height. Abreast of this mound a boat channel, which runs down from main one, comes close inshore, and probably has always been the landing place, for the ridge, plateau, and mound form a gentle slope to the water's edge; south of this there is another large irregular mound and a high plateau, quite flat, and about 2 acres in extent. (1883:795)

The southernmost "large irregular mound" is apparently a natural dune with shell midden eroding out of the east side in which Test 1, described below, was placed. The "conical mound," the top of which is about 9 meters above mean sea level, is the large midden with ramps, also described below (and referred to here as Collier Mound). Useppa extends southward from this point about 500 meters as a narrow ridge with mangrove along the western side. Apparently, a portion of that mangrove has developed since 1958, when the Bokeelia U.S.G.S. topographic quadrangle map (7½ minute) was first published, and 1972, when that quadrangle map was revised from aerial photographs. The southern ridge is now the location of a grass-covered airstrip. Most of the southern portion of the island may have built up by deposition in the last century; some of the buildup may have been aided by Barron Collier, who contoured much of the southern half of the island for a golf course in the twentieth century.

That the southern ca. 500 meters of the island has appeared in the last century is also suggested by an early-nineteenth-century observer, John Lee Williams, whose 1837 publication refers to the island as Toampe, the home of a Spanish fishing "rancho" operated by the Caldes (Caldez) family:

> Toampe is situated five miles south of Bocca Grande, in the heart of the bay. It is one mile long, from east to west [*sic*], and half a mile wide. It is the seat of the Caldes family. Their village consists of near twenty palmetto houses, and stands on the south west point of the Island. This Island is a high shell bank, covered with large timber. A small portion of the land is under cultivation. The inhabitants living principally on fish, turtle, and coonti; the last, they bring from the main. Here are several cocoanut trees in bearing, orange, lime, papayer, hawey, and hickok plum. They raise cuba corn, peas, mellons, &c. I am told that most of the Islands in this bay, are nearly as fruitful as Toampe. They are innumerable. (1962:33)

Williams evidently switched his east-west and north-south measurements. The "south west point" where the Spanish houses were located may be the "plateau" west of the well area referred to by Simmons. The old well is believed by present inhabitants to be located where a water purification pond was constructed recently.

An excellent article by E. A. Hammond (1973) regarding the Spanish fisheries of Charlotte Harbor provides information on the Caldez family and traces the sale of the island from Caldez to Joseph Ximendez in 1833. Hammond (1973:364n.23), citing documentary evidence, notes that Caldez referred to the island as Josepha's, which was transcribed by a clerk as Tio Sespas. Later, it was Italianized by an inhabitant to Guiseppa, which became Useppa. The romantic notion that Useppa is a corruption of Joseffa, a captive and beautiful wife of the legendary pirate José Gaspar, apparently has no basis in fact. Using Hammond's study as a beginning and key to the historical documents, we should eventually be able to locate more data regarding the material culture of the Spanish fisheries and the subsequent early-nineteenth-century occupations of the island. The history of the later nineteenth century and the twentieth—including the ownership and development of the island by the Barron Collier family—remains to be researched and written.

Prior to the excavations described here, the only modern archaeological work to have been carried out on Useppa was a brief reconnaissance by John Griffin and Hale Smith in 1947 (Griffin 1949b). The ceramic collections recovered from a disturbed shell midden indicated occupations spanning the period ca. 1000 B.C. or earlier (when fiber-tempered pottery was manufactured) into the early nineteenth century. Portions of the "exposed" part of the large midden described by Griffin as west of the tennis court remain today:

> The north and east portions of Useppa Island are covered by an extensive shell deposit, whose highest portion, on the east side of the island, is largely covered by hotels, cottages, a golf course, and other facilities. The exposed section, about 100 feet long, seven feet high at the south end and two feet high at the north end, is located just south and east of the Tarpon Club of America, on the west side of the tennis court. The section was that of a typical shell midden, with shell making up the vast bulk of the volume. (1949b: 92)

Today, scattered shell midden is visible along the eastern dune ridge from the north end of the island down to the older tennis court (more courts have been built; the court built in 1947 is cut into the eastern side of the dune). Except for the immediate vicinity of the tennis court where *in situ* midden remains, most of the shell midden along the eastern dune ridge appears to be very disturbed (although this observation was not substantiated by test excavations). Undecorated pottery with quartz grain temper (often referred to in South Florida by the imprecise term Glades Plain) was collected in May 1979 by Chapman and Milanich from around the tennis court midden along with a *Busycon* shell dipper, a *Strombus* celt, and several fragments of bone, probably all human. William R. Maples of the Florida State Museum identified one *H. sapiens* triquetal bone. Griffin (1949b: 92) reported human skeletal remains from the tennis court midden which were exposed when the court was built. Although the visible shell portion of the midden stops just south of the tennis court (where the dune system is farther from the eastern edge of the island), ditching for utility lines has turned up subsurface shell and pottery.

Farther south, the shell midden again becomes visible, this time forming Collier Mound (the large mound with sloping "ramps" extending north and south parallel to the island's eastern edge). The southern "ramp" connects with the continuation of the midden that was deposited east of the dune system and does not extend above the present ground surface as a mound (but does extend below the ground surface for at least 1.8 meters). Collier Mound and its ramps are clearly shown on the U.S.G.S. quadrangle map of the island. Figure 11.2 shows the distribution of known aboriginal sites and the location of the tests discussed below.

On their initial archaeological reconnaissance of the island in May 1979, Chapman and Milanich used a backhoe to dig a small trench in the southern "ramp" in order to get a profile across the shell feature and to collect samples for radiocarbon dating. This test (Test 6) revealed 1.2 meters of loosely packed fighting conch shells (*Strombus alatus*) overlying a much more densely packed shell midden, evidently the same midden that runs along the eastern dune system and edge of the island. Most likely, the fighting conchs were deposited at two different times, perhaps to make a ramp leading to the high midden. A thin stratum of sea urchin spines and shells separated an upper 30 centimeter-thick layer of fighting conchs from the lower portion. Possibly these urchins were deposited by birds during a period of nonhuman occupation as a result of dropping the sea urchins on the shell to break them open. The backhoe test cut into the midden stratum 0.8 meters and did not reach bottom. Radiocarbon dates from the lower midden and upper ramp shell were obtained on shell samples. The two dates, 1175 ± 75 radiocarbon years: A.D. 775 (UM-1840) from the upper portion of the underlying midden and 1360 ± 65: A.D. 590 (UM-1839) from the lower portion of the "ramp," suggest that the initial layer of fighting conchs was laid down about A.D. 700.

In January 1980, Chapman and Milanich placed a backhoe test (Test 7) in the top of Collier Mound to see if it was constructed purposefully. That test, excavated to a depth of 3 meters, did not reach the bottom of the mound but revealed multiple horizontal shell midden strata, each about 15 centimeters in thickness and characterized by large amounts of fishbone. One such stratum contained large amounts of sand; most did not. Some strata were separated by crushed sea urchin spines and shells. Ash lenses, probably hearths, were present in some strata. These were generally less than 10 centimeters thick and as much as 50 centimeters long. Future work will focus on clearing large horizontal portions of these successive midden strata to see if structures had been present and to collect artifact samples (including faunal) from respective strata.

Backhoe tests (May 1979) were also placed in and adjacent to that portion of the midden south of Collier Mound and the associated ramps (and east of the dunes). Test 3, dug into the midden near the edge of the island, showed 1.8 meters of loosely packed shell midden above a layer of much more densely packed shell midden 0.8 meters thick that was deposited on sterile, white, probably beach sand. Undecorated quartz-tempered pottery was taken from both the upper and the lower portions of the profile. Radiocarbon dates of 1845 ± 90 radiocarbon years: A.D. 105 (UM-1837) and 2260 ± 75: 310 B.C. (UM-1838) were obtained from shell samples taken from the lower, packed midden stratum.

Another backhoe test (Test 5) was placed in the same midden 20 meters to the west (toward the dune ridge). The profile showed several discrete midden strata of shell and of shell and sand. The underlying sterile sand was reached 1.4 meters below the ground surface; a radiocarbon date of 1700 ± 75: A.D. 250 (UM-1841) was obtained from shell brought from the lowest midden stratum. Later a hand-dug test (Test B) was placed adjacent to this backhoe cut.

A third backhoe test (Test 4) was dug about 20 meters farther west at the edge of the dune system. No midden or other evidence of human occupation was encountered, indicating that the shell midden along the edge of the island at that point was less than about 45 meters wide.

Two other backhoe tests were also excavated in May 1979. Test 2 was positioned on the dune system southwest of Test 3–5 in an area believed to have been an old tee or green of the golf course. As expected, the upper 60 centimeters had been disturbed by the course's construction. What was not expected was the buried shell midden that was encountered; evidently landscaping activities, i.e., leveling the natural dune, had deposited 60 centimeters of thin, horizontal strata over an old humus that had been scraped clean before the upper sand was added. Fifteen to 20 centimeters under the top of this scraped humus was a shell midden 15–20 centimeters thick. No pottery was found in the midden, but a large number of *Busycon* shells and columella were observed. Two radiocarbon dates on shell confirmed that the midden was deposited during the preceramic Archaic period. The two dates, 4935 ± 100 radiocarbon years: 2985 B.C. (UM-1836) and 5625 ± 100: 3675 B.C., are the earliest thus far obtained on the southwest Florida coast. One large piece of sandstone (14 by 15 by 3 centimeters) and a smaller piece of a siltstone (4.5 by 2 by 1.5 centimeters) were recovered. Test A, described below, was later hand excavated in this midden.

Test 1, also dug with a backhoe, was placed in what is believed to be the "irregular mound" observed by Simmons. The test confirmed that the mound was a natural dune. On the east side of the mound was a small shell midden that has almost eroded away.

Test A, an Archaic period shell columella tool manufacturing camp

The May 1979 reconnaissance of Useppa Island and the backhoe tests dug at that time indicated that important archaeological data regarding the prehistoric occupants of the island and southwest Florida were present in the extensive middens sampled. We were especially happy to find stratified midden deposits and the Archaic midden since interpreting subsistence change through time is important to understanding Calusa societal development. Further investigation in the form of hand-excavated sampling was certainly warranted, and Chapman and Milanich returned to the island in January 1980 for five days in order to sample more thoroughly the Archaic midden encountered in Test 2 and the later midden in which Test 5 had been placed.

A 3- meter by 3-meter square (Test A) was excavated in the buried Archaic midden. The overburden was removed, and the shell midden stratum was hand excavated with the contents screened initially through window screen. The large amount of small bones and small shell fragments made this process very time consuming (relative to the time available), and a switch was made to a coarser screen (expanded metal hardware cloth with ¾-inch by ⅜-inch diamond-shaped mesh). An 0.5-meter by 0.5-meter "column" was retained and later water-screened through window screen in order to collect all of the midden contents from a measured sample for analysis.

The midden appears to have been deposited by Archaic peoples who camped on the dune for a relatively short period of time while they collected *Busycon* and some *Fasciolaria* shells and removed the columellas from them, presumably for use as tools elsewhere. Shells in the process of having the columellas removed are shown in figure 11.3. The ends were "pecked" to separate the central columella from the outer portions. Evidently the columella "manufacturing" operation was extensive; 133 whole or partial columellas were recovered and many others must have been taken away (fig. 11.4). Three were *Fasciolaria*; the rest were *Busycon*. Ten had one or more sharpened ends; others had battered ends. None showed use as adzes, and the vast majority were unused apparently. Removed columellas ranged in length from 5.9 to 19.5 centimeters.

The method of removing the columellas makes it clear that the columellas themselves were the final product, not cups made from the outer portion. One small piece of columella (3.5 centimeters long) was drilled horizontally at one end.

The pieces of sandstone and siltstone recovered might all have been

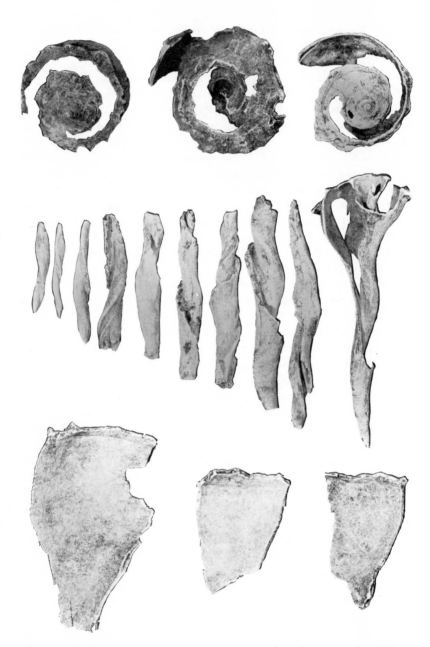

Fig. 11.3. Test A *Busycons. top row*, process of columella removal; *middle row*, columellae; *bottom row*, shell "debitage."

used as saws or smoothing tools (six were recovered in addition to the two mentioned above from Test 2; they ranged in size from 2.5 by 2 by 1 centimeters to 5 by 4 by 3 centimeters). One stemmed projectile point from Test B, a Marion, made from agatized coral, had been thermally altered, giving it a pinkish color. The tip had been broken off and both edges showed heavy use, probably as a hafted knife.

Large *Mercenaria* (clam) shells were distributed throughout the midden. At least seven had abrading along the edge; one had a rectangular section cut out of the edge (fig. 11.3). Thirteen pieces of clam shell were recovered, all heavily rubbed on one or both sides and edges; others were probably discarded before we recognized them as possible tools. All of the stone and clam "tools" were most likely used in the columella manufacturing process as saws or smoothing implements (fig. 11.3).

A large number of pieces of the outer portions of the shells recovered represent debitage from the manufacturing process (fig. 11.3). The best explanation is that the midden represents a short-term occupation by a limited number of people. They evidently camped on the dunes adjacent to the nearby estuary (which was probably quite different from its appearance today, since the barrier islands on the western side of Pine Island Sound were not there). Midden contents include the debitage and expended tools from the columella-removal operation and the remains of foods consumed by the Indians while they camped. The food remains provide data on Archaic period Gulf coastal subsistence, a topic which has received little attention.

As noted, excavation of Test A produced two samples of vertebrate faunal remains, one column sample recovered with window screen (and water screened) and a second sample recovered with large diamond mesh. A total of 2,303 bone fragments was recovered, 2,051 with diamond mesh and 252 from the column sample. It should be noted that the potential cubic volume of the column sample (0.5 meters by 0.5 meters by depth of level) is much less than that of the Test A material recovered through coarser screen. Table 11.1 presents a species list for vertebrates represented in both Test A samples; table 11.2 lists molluscan species.

Greatest diversity exists among bony fish (class Osteichthyes). When the sample is considered as a single unit, a subsistence dependence on fish (55 percent), mammals (33 percent), and sharks and rays (8 percent) is presented (table 11.3). However, if results from the screen sizes are compared, a different picture emerges. Fish (66 percent) increase in importance as do sharks and rays (26 percent) and reptiles

Table 11.1. Identified vertebrate species and common name by test

Taxon	Common name	Test A	Test B
Mammal, large	deer, bear, large cat possibilities		x
Mammal	medium- to small-sized mammals	x	x
Mammal *cf.* Artiodactyla	probably ungulate (deer)	x	x
Mammal *cf. Odocoileus*	probably white-tailed deer		x
Rodentia	rodents		x
Rodentia cf. *Sigmodon*	probably hispid cotton rat		x
Sigmodon hispidus	hispid cotton rat	x	x
Delphinidae	probably porpoise	x	
Procyon lotor	raccoon	x	x
Artiodactyla *cf. Odocoileus*	ungulate, probably white-tailed deer	x	
Odocoileus virginianus	white-tailed deer	x	x
Aves	birds	x	x
Aves *cf.* Passeriformes	songbirds		x
Gavia immer	loon		x
Podicipedidae	grebes		x
Phalacrocorax auritus	double-crested cormorant		x
Casmerodius albus	great egret		x
Anatidae	ducks		x
Aythya sp.	scaups		x
Florida caerula	little blue heron		x
Reptilia cf. Serpentes	reptiles, probably snakes	x	x
Reptilia cf. *Anolis*	reptiles, probably chameleons		x
Testudines	turtles: sea, freshwater, and terrestrial	x	x
Kinosternidae *cf. Sternotherus*	mud and musk turtles		x
Terrapene carolina	eastern box turtle		x
Deirochelys reticularia	chicken turtle	x	
Gopherus polyphemus	gopher tortoise		x
Cheloniidae	sea turtles		x
Anura	frogs and turtles		x
Chondrichthyes	cartilaginous fishes	x	x
Chondrichthyes *cf.* Carcharhinidae	probably requiem sharks		x
Chondrichthyes *cf. Mustela*	probably dogfish or smoothhound		x
Carcharhinidae	requiem sharks		x
Ginglymostoma cirratum	nurse sharks		x
Carcharhinus sp.	requiem sharks		x
Galeocerdo cuvieri	tiger shark	x	x
Sphyrna sp.	hammerhead shark		x
Rhizoprionodon terranovae	sharpnose shark		x
Rajiformes	skates and rays	x	x
Dasyatidae	stingrays	x	x
Dasyatus sp.	stingray		x
Osteichthyes	bony fish	x	x
Osteichthyes *cf.* Sparidae or *Pogonias*	bony fish: porgies or black drum		x
Lepisosteus sp.	gars	x	
Elops saurus	ladyfish		x
Megalops atlanticus	tarpon		x
Clupeidae	herrings	x	x
Ariidae	sea catfishes	x	x
Arius felis	sea catfish	x	x
Bagre marinus	gafftopsail catfish	x	x

(*continued*)

Table 11.1—*continued*

Taxon	Common name	Test A	Test B
Centropomus sp.	snook		x
Epinephelus sp.	groupers	x	x
Carangidae	jacks and pompanos	x	x
Caranx sp.	jack	x	x
Sciaenidae	drums		x
Sciaenidae cf. *Sciaenops*	probably red drum		x
Bairdiella sp.	croaker or perch	x	x
Cynoscion sp.	sea trout	x	x
Pogonias cromis	black drum		x
Sciaenops ocellata	red drum		x
Sparidae	porgies		x
Sparidae cf. *Archosargus*	porgies, probably sheepshead	x	x
Archosargus sp.	sheepshead	x	x
Lagodon rhomboides	pinfish		x
Mugil sp.	mullet	x	x
Bothidae	left-eye flounders		x
Paralichthys sp.	flounder	x	x
Ephippidae	spadefishes		x
Chaetodipterus faber	atlantic spadefish		x
Opsanus sp.	toadfish		x
Diodontidae	porcupinefishes	x	x
unidentified vertebrate	vertebrate remains	x	x
Decapoda	crabs		x
Menippes mercenaria	stone crab		x

Table 11.2. Molluscan species

Species	Test A	Test B
Crassostrea virginica	x	x
Busycon contrarium	x	x
Busycon spiratum		x
Mercenaria campechiensis	x	x
Petaloconchus sp.	x	x
Melongena corona	x	x
Pleuroploca gigantea	x	x
Pectinidae	x	x
Argopectin sp.		
Marocallista nimbosa	x	x
Euglandina rosea	x	x
Spisula solidissima	x	x
Murex pomum	x	x
Fasciolaria tulipa	x	x
Cantharus tinctus	x	
Carditamera floridana	x	x
Cerithium floridanum	x	
Levcozonia nassa	x	
Penidae		x
Neotia ponderosa		x
Strombus pugilis		x
Chione cancellata		x
Conus sp.		x

(*continued*)

Table 11.2—*continued*

Species	Test A	Test B
Polinices duplicatus		x
Crepidula fornicata		x
Dinocardium robustum		x
Trachycardium sp.		x
Vermicularia sp.		x
Polygyra sp.		x
Lucapina sp.		x
Echinochama		x
Fiscus communis		x
Mennipe mercenaria		x
Anthozoa		x
Cancellaria reticulata		x
Batillaria minima		x

Table 11.3. Relative faunal abundances by class, Test A

Class	N fragments	%	MNI	%	Weight in grams	%	Biomass in kilograms	%
Mammals	58	2.51	3	4.48	91.2	31.00	1.8560	33.09
Birds	3	0.13	1	1.49	0.3	0.10	0.0068	0.12
Reptiles	66	2.86	2	2.99	8.0	2.72	0.1735	3.09
Bony fishes	2,120	92.05	59	88.06	173.3	58.92	3.1106	54.47
Sharks and rays	12	0.52	2	2.99	3.6	1.22	0.4604	8.21
Unidentified vertebrate	44	1.91	—	—	17.7	6.01	—	—
Total	2,303	99.98	67	100.01	294.1	99.97	5.6073	99.98

(6 percent). Mammals and birds are not represented in the column sample (table 11.4).

Caution is urged when using column sample materials to reconstruct faunal subsistence patterns. Bias against mammals, whose archaeological fragments tend to be large, may be introduced by selection of a small area (column) for sampling. Comparison with a general sample recovered with a coarser screen is suggested. In a site such as Useppa, recovery of fish remains is increased greatly when a fine screen size is introduced. The results, however, are mixed. In some cases, greater diversity may result; in others, the amount of unidentified fish (Osteichthyes category) may be increased because of the minute size of recovered remains.

Included in the Test A faunal remains were 41 fragments of altered bone, of which 35 were burned (the majority bony fish). Six fragments, all metapodial splinters (Artiodactyla, probably deer), were smoothed, but none was a discernible tool.

This picture of Archaic subsistence is made fuller by the total recovery of molluscs from the Test A column sample. Until recently, limited data have been available on which to base extrapolations of edible meat from molluscs. However, largely through the work by S. Hale and S. Scudder of the Florida State Museum Zooarchaeology Laboratory (under the direction of Elizabeth Wing), values now exist that permit comparison of vertebrate and molluscan fauna. This comparison may be done through calculation of biomass (an attempt to project edible meat using allometric scaling formulae). For Test A, when vertebrate and molluscan remains are compared, slightly less than half of the biomass value is produced by molluscs (table 11.5). These values point out the very real contribution of molluscan fauna to the food base. Test A is consistent with the Archaic subsistence pattern that features reliance on molluscan remains and exploration of a wide range of biotopes to procure the vertebrate dietary constituents. It is interesting to note that clams, oysters, and *Busycon contrarium* together account for more than 98 percent of the total molluscan biomass.

Table 11.4. Relative faunal abundances by class and screen size, Test A

Class	N fragments	%	MNI	%	Weight in grams	%	Biomass in kilograms	%
			Diamond mesh (¾″ by ⅜″)					
Mammals	58	2.82	3	5.26	91.2	33.00	1.8560	35.86
Birds	3	0.14	1	1.75	0.3	0.10	0.0068	0.13
Reptiles	61	2.97	2	3.50	7.1	2.56	0.1441	2.78
Bony fishes	1,883	91.80	49	85.96	159.7	57.79	2.8232	54.54
Sharks and rays	6	0.29	2	3.50	2.7	0.97	0.3455	6.67
Unidentified vertebrate	40	1.95	—	—	15.3	5.53	—	—
Total	2,051	99.97	57	99.97	276.3	99.95	5.1756	99.98
			Column sample, window screen					
Mammals	—	—	—	—	—	—	—	—
Birds	—	—	—	—	—	—	—	—
Reptiles	5	1.98	1	8.33	0.9	5.05	0.0294	6.81
Bony fishes	237	94.04	10	83.33	13.6	76.40	0.2874	66.57
Sharks and rays	6	2.38	1	8.33	0.9	5.05	0.1149	26.61
Unidentified vertebrate	4	1.58	—	—	2.4	13.48	—	—
Total	252	99.98	12	99.99	17.8	99.98	0.4317	99.99

Table 11.5. Vertebrate and molluscan biomass values, Test A

Class	Biomass in kilograms	% of vertebrate	% of invertebrate	% of total
Mammals	1.8560	33.70		17.12
Birds	0.0068	0.12		0.06
Reptiles	0.1735	3.15		1.60
Bony fishes	3.0091	54.65		27.75
Sharks and rays	0.4604	8.36		4.25
Total vertebrate	5.5058	99.98		50.78
Clam	0.7090		13.28	6.54
Oyster	3.6900		69.14	34.03
Busycon contrarium	0.8660		16.22	7.99
All other molluscs	0.0720		1.34	0.66
Total molluscan	5.3370		99.98	49.22
Total	10.8428			100.00

Test B, a stratigraphic cut into shell midden a (ca. A.D. 250 to historic period)

As noted, Tests 3 and 5 had intersected a deep, stratified shell midden that ran along the eastern side of the island south of Collier Mound. When Chapman and Milanich returned to the island in January 1980, they excavated a 2-meter by 2-meter square (Test B) adjacent to back-hoe Test 5. Like Test A, most of the midden contents were screened through expanded metal hardware cloth (at times a ¼-inch mesh screen was also used); also like Test A, an 0.5-meter by 0.5-meter column was retained and later water-screened through window screen, and the total sample of vertebrate and molluscan remains was retained. Profiles obtained from Test 5 had indicated the presence of nine distinct strata in the midden at that point (seven of them shell midden deposits). During the hand excavation of Test B, each of the seven shell strata was removed individually (Zones I at the top to Zone VIB at the bottom). The column was also removed in this fashion. As a result, the contents of each of the strata (including the total sample of shell and faunal remains as well as other artifacts) could be analyzed as a unit and changes through time described.

The various strata (zones) are shown and described in figures 11.4 and 11.5, the profile of the north wall of Test B. Zone II could have been separated into two strata, a layer of yellowish-brown dune sand which seems to have accumulated over a deposit of shell midden with a high frequency of *Busycon* and clam shells. Almost no artifacts were present in the dune sand. Zone VIB is midden deposited in depres-

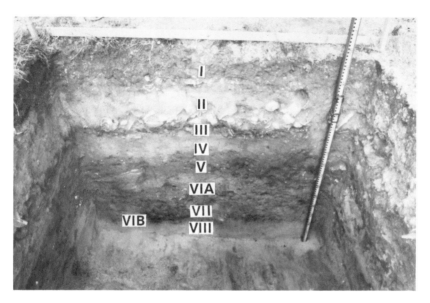

Fig. 11.4. Test B profile.

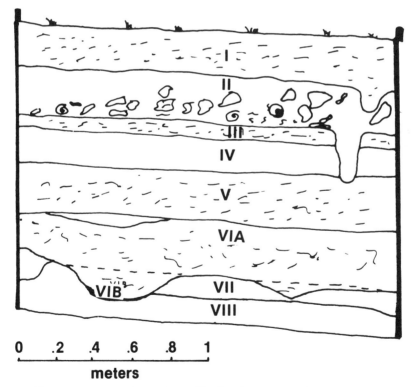

Fig. 11.5. Test B schematic profile showing strata referred to in text.

Table 11.6. Frequencies of major artifact classes, Test B

Zone	Total aboriginal sherds[a]	Other aboriginal artifacts	Nonaboriginal artifacts	Eligible aboriginal sherds used in analysis	Sample size for analysis
I	126/6	3 pieces of sandstone 1 chert drill 1 *Busycon* columella[b]	1 blue-on-white transfer ware cup base 5 pieces of heavily patinated bottle glass 19 green bottle glass 1 blue bottle glass from perfume (?) decanter 1 honey-glazed redware 1 olive jar sherd 1 aquamarine-on-white majolica sherd 14 redware roof tile fragments 1 blue glass bead 1 metal button 1 nail 1 nail	39/5	10/2
II	91/6	1 piece chert debitage		41/4	10/0
III	92/4	1 piece chert debitage		38/2	10/1
IV	25/1	1 piece chert debitage		12/1	10/1
V	113/5	1 piece sandstone 4 pieces siltstone		67/3	10/0
VIA	91/9	1 utilized chert flake 1 broken bone needle 1 *Busycon* cup 2 *Busycon* columellas 1 piece limestone			
VIB	178/4	1 piece chert debitage 1 expended chert core, reused 1 broken, ground limestone bannerstone (?) 1 sandstone smoothing tool 1 *Busycon* shell pick with hafting holes 1 *Busycon* columella		33/5 82/5	10/1 10/0

a. The numbers on the right of the slash marks indicate rim sherds *included* in the left side totals.
b. All columella included in table exhibited battering on one end.

sions in the top of Zone VII. Zone VII was very hummocky on the top and sloped northeast, toward the nearby water. The depressions appear to have been both natural and intentionally shaped; one contained a lens of crushed wood charcoal in the bottom and was probably used as a fire pit. The Zone VIB midden could have been combined with Zone VIA in table 11.6; both represent the same accumulation. However, the VIB portion of the midden was deposited first and allows a convenient separation of the same stratum into two temporally successive units. The radiocarbon date of A.D. 250 (UM-1841) obtained from adjacent Test 5 came from this lowest midden zone.

Deposits of aragonite crystals, appearing as minute needles, were present in all of the shell strata. These crystals result from the natural precipitation of calcium carbonate out of the shells, especially clam shells.

Zone I (see table 11.6) contained a number of Spanish and other artifacts believed to date from the first third of the nineteenth century, the period of the Spanish fisheries; some of the Spanish materials, including the very heavily patinated glass, may have an earlier date. Consequently, the midden appears to date from about A.D. 250 into the early nineteenth century. Table 11.6 lists nonfaunal artifacts recovered from Zone I–VIB. A detailed analysis of the ceramics was undertaken. Results follow the section on analysis of the faunal remains.

Test B faunal analysis

Test B produced 10,364 + vertebrate bone fragments gathered with three screen sizes: coarse diamond mesh, ¼-inch hardware cloth, and window screen. In this discussion a plus sign (+) beside a quantity indicates that the data are from the window-screened column samples. Some such proveniences were not counted entirely since the fragments were minute and the time requirement prohibitive. The reader should note that the relative numbers of fragments are biased, but weights and biomass are comparable.

Test B produced 21 proveniences from seven zones (Zones I through VIB). Zone I may relate to historic period Spanish and Calusa Indian activities while Zones II–VIB represent their prehistoric predecessors. The lowest zone dates from about A.D. 250.

Table 11.1 lists the species identified from the various Test B samples. As shown, diversity in every class is greater than in Test A. Table 11.7 lists the combined results of the vertebrate analysis from

Table 11.7. Relative faunal abundances by class, Test B

Class	N frag-ments	%	MNI	%	Weight in grams	%	Biomass in kilo-grams	%
Mammals	107	1.03	4	1.87	126.6	5.49	3.0773	7.97
Birds	34	0.32	7	3.28	26.1	1.13	0.4989	1.29
Reptiles	41	0.39	3	1.40	32.5	1.41	0.6519	1.69
Amphibians	2	0.01	1	0.46	0.1	0.00	0.0013	0.00
Bony fish	10,008+	96.56	190	89.20	2050.1	88.96	30.9975	80.36
Sharks and rays	99	0.95	6	2.81	27.1	1.17	3.3450	8.67
Unidentified vertebrate	64	0.61	—	—	26.1	1.13	—	—
Crabs	9	0.08	2	0.93	15.7	0.68	—	—
Total	10,634+	99.95	213	99.95	2304.3	99.97	38.5719	99.98

Table 11.8. Osteichthyes: relative abundance of families, Tests A and B

Family	Test A				Test B			
	N frag-ments	%	Biomass in kilo-grams	%	N frag-ments	%	Biomass in kilo-grams	%
Lepisostidae gars	18	0.84	0.0253	0.84	—	—	—	—
Elopidae ladyfish tarpon	—	—	—	—	12	0.11	0.1843	0.59
Clupeidae herrings	7	0.33	0.0101	0.33	560	5.59	0.1018	0.32
Ariidae catfishes	254	11.98	0.5997	19.92	1,567	15.65	5.1464	16.60
Centropomidae snooks	—	—	—	—	3	0.02	0.0560	0.18
Serranidae groupers	3	0.14	0.0103	0.34	12	0.11	0.2227	0.71
Carangidae jacks	33	1.55	0.8713	28.95	74	0.73	3.3355	10.76
Scianenidae drums	7	0.33	0.0754	2.50	97	0.96	1.4412	4.64
Sparidae porgies	83	3.91	0.2723	9.04	686	6.85	4.2715	13.78
Mugilidae mullet	16	0.75	0.0669	2.22	179	1.78	0.8814	2.84
Bothidae flounders	2	0.09	0.0140	0.46	25	0.24	0.1155	0.37
Eppihidae spadefish	—	—	—	—	2	0.01	0.0712	0.22
Batricoididae toadfish	—	—	—	—	7	0.06	0.0406	0.13
Diodontidae porcupine fish	18	0.84	0.0295	0.98	39	0.38	0.5351	1.72
Unidentified fish	1,679	79.19	1.0343	34.37	6,745+	67.39	14.5943	47.08
Total	2,120	99.95	3.0091	99.95	10,008+	99.88	30.9975	99.94

Table 11.9. Relative biomass contribution of selected fish by zone,
Test B

Fish	Zone I	Zone II	Zone III	Zone IV	Zone V	Zone VI	Zone VII
Ariidae catfishes	1.4132	0.1902	0.3644	0.0769	0.4519	1.5073	2.0291
Carangidae jacks	1.6695	0.2637	—	0.0901	0.3473	0.5705	0.3944
Archosargus sp. sheepshead	0.2775	0.1206	0.1491	0.0212	0.3692	1.5485	1.6103
Mugil sp. mullet	0.0455	0.0125	—	—	0.0557	0.2863	0.4814

Test B. The importance of bony fishes is at once obvious (80 percent) with mammals (7 percent) and sharks and rays (8 percent) of much lesser importance.

Significant in this sample is the distribution of usage within the class Osteichthyes. For example, table 11.8 breaks down the families and indicates the percentage of biomass generated by each. Jacks (Carangidae, 10 percent), Sheepshead (Sparidae and *Archosargus*, 13 percent), and catfishes (Ariidae, 16 percent) are the primary contributors.

Overall, the sample reveals a decreasing dependence on vertebrate resources, particularly bony fish, and an increasing dependence on molluscs through time (Zone VIB to Zone I). Figure 11.6 illustrates these trends using biomass values (the only comparable category) and gives percentages for each zone. Molluscan values are included. Together, clams, oysters, and *Busycon contrarium* (whelks) comprise 90 percent or more of the total molluscan biomas sample. In Zone I, molluscan usage falls off markedly with a concomitant rise in fish resources. This latter situation may reflect either Spanish or Calusa fishing practices (or both) at this site. A further consideration in explaining these trends may be the geological-environment events in the Useppa locality.

Because Goggin and Sturtevant (1964:207) have suggested that Calusa society evolved and persisted from a rich fishing resource base utilizing netting of mullet, contention that mullet may have been a major food source was examined. In table 11.8, mullet (Mugilidae) contributed only 2.84 percent of the total fish biomass. Table 11.9 breaks down the contribution of mullet and selected fish for comparison.

Assuming that the upper levels of Test B are Calusa, the faunal samples from Useppa do not support the notion of a mullet fishery as a mainstay of the subsistence system. Rather, the sample suggests that

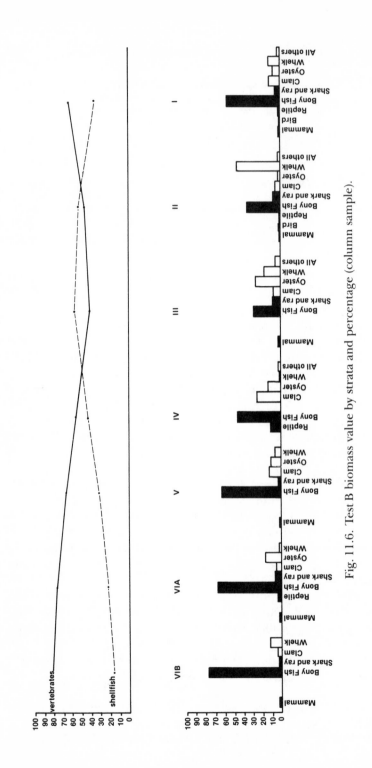

Fig. 11.6. Test B biomass value by strata and percentage (column sample).

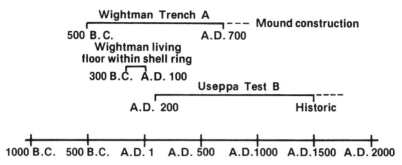

Fig. 11.7. Chronological comparison of Useppa Island and Sanibel Island tests.

an intensive fishing economy did exist but was based on reef and estuarine fishes that required a variety of technological devices for capture—spearing, hooks or gorges, weirs, etc. The emphasis is a generalized one, focusing on some preferred fishes, but not specialized. A small contribution is made to the food base by fishes requiring netting (mullet and herrings).

The Test B sample also included 247 fragments of altered bone, of which 239 were burned (215 of these were bony fish). Eight fragments showed modification for tools. Notably, a ray spine, possibly used as a sawing tool, was recovered. A box turtle coracoid (shoulder girdle area) having a single drilled hole was identified. The sample of worked bone is small and unremarkable.

Faunal collections having a comparable time range do not exist. However, two collections from Sanibel Island (the Wightman site, 8-L-54; Fradkin 1976, n.d.) overlap the Useppa Island samples. Figure 11.7 illustrates chronological overlap of the two Wightman site proveniences with Test B from Useppa. Table 11.10 lists the faunal classes and gives values for all three collections.

Wightman Test A compares favorably with Useppa Test B in terms of total biomass produced (i.e., 38.5719 kilograms for Test B Useppa and 38.3287 kilograms for Wightman Test A). However, the relative importance of sharks and rays is much greater for Wightman (47.47 percent for Wightman, 8.67 percent for Useppa). Additionally, the living floor sample from Wightman is heavily shark-ray dependent (82.02 percent), suggesting that there may have been differences in local availability (the excavation may have intersected such a specialized activity area) or a real dietary difference may be present. More samples from the Sanibel-Useppa area are needed to evaluate seasonal rounds, prehistoric resource distribution, and so forth.

Table 11.10. Comparative faunal abundances by class, Sanibel and Useppa islands

Class	N frag-ments	%	Weight in grams	%	Biomass in kilograms	%
			Useppa, Test B			
Mammals	107	1.03	126.6	5.49	3.0773	7.97
Birds	34	0.32	26.1	1.13	0.4989	1.29
Reptiles	41	0.39	32.5	1.41	0.6519	1.69
Amphibians	2	0.01	0.1	0.00	0.0013	0.00
Bony fishes	10,008+	96.56	2.050.1	88.96	30.9975	80.36
Sharks and rays	99	0.95	27.1	1.17	3.3450	8.67
Unidentified vertebrates	64	0.61	26.1	1.13	—	—
Crabs	9	0.08	15.7	0.68	—	—
Total	10,364+	99.95	2,304.3	99.97	38.5719	99.98
			Sanibel-Wightman, living floor within shell ring (identified by Fradkin)			
Mammals	305	7.22	693.7	22.75	12.3094	10.16
Birds	76	1.79	86.0	2.82	1.3960	1.15
Reptiles	47	1.11	125.8	4.12	1.5420	1.27
Bony fishes	354	8.38	321.4	10.54	6.5175	5.38
Sharks and rays	3,245	76.82	1,672.4	54.86	99.3211	82.02
Unidentified			139.5	4.57		
vertebrates	191	4.52	9.6	0.31	—	—
Crabs	6	0.14	3,048.4	99.97	—	—
Total	4,224	99.98			121.0860	99.98
			Sanibel-Wightman, Test A (analyzed by R. Marrinan, 1975–76)			
Mammals	135	1.97	150.5	9.06	3.3193	8.66
Birds	18	0.26	7.8	0.46	0.1567	0.40
Reptiles	188	2.74	105.6	6.36	1.4975	3.90
Bony fishes	5,632	82.20	864.5	52.05	15.1600	39.55
Sharks and rays	666	9.72	210.2	12.66	18.1952	47.47
Unidentified vertebrate	113	1.64	74.2	4.47	—	—
Crabs	99	1.44	247.1	14.88	—	—
Total	6,851	99.97	1,659.9	99.94	38.3287	99.98

Overall, the Useppa collections (from Tests A and B) represent the continuity of a subsistence system practiced from Archaic times until the demise of aboriginal populations on the southwest Florida Gulf coast. To some extent, it was continued by European successors in the area. An intensive fishing and collecting economy, augmented by hunting of mammals, has been present on Useppa since ca. 2500 B.C.

In the immediate protohistoric period, its latest practitioners would have been the Calusa. In contrast to Goggin and Sturtevant's suggestion (1964:207) that a specialized fishery (in this case the netting of mullet) would provide a subsistence base adequate to support a socially complex polity, the data from Useppa indicate a generalized, intensive fishery requiring a variety of technological items and skills and exploiting a range of maritime biotopes. Mullet do not appear in quantities large enough to be considered major contributors to the food base.

In view of the large number of *Busycon contrarium* shells present in large shell mound sites in the Pine Island Sound–Charlotte Harbor locale, it is tempting to hypothesize that the relative increase in *Busycon* biomass beginning in Zone III of the Useppa Test B sample reflects its increased dietary importance. Future research along the lower Gulf Coast can examine the speculation that evolution of Calusa societal complexity was at least partially based on intensive shark and whelk "sea farming." Milanich guessed that Zone III dates about A.D. 700.

In terms of archaeological methods, the Useppa excavations demonstrate that subsistence reconstruction, to be accurate, requires the use of several screen sizes (see table 11.4, Test A results). A fine-screened column sample provides for quantification of molluscan remains and retrieval of minute skeletal elements, thus enhancing recovery of certain groups (fish, rodents, etc.). A coarse screen size is preferable in field situations where time or personnel, or both, is limited. Coarse screen samples are useful as a check against the bias inherent in small volume samples.

Test B ceramic analysis

A limited ceramic technological analysis was carried out on a sample of 70 sherds recovered from Test B in order to ascertain and document differences that could be useful as temporal indicators in future excavations. The properties or variables measured or observed included surface and core colors, sherd thickness, rim forms, and type, relative frequency, and size of aplastic paste constituents. Sherd surfaces were also examined to determine methods of surface finishing.

Measurement or observation of sherd thickness and rim form attributes has proven useful for construction of relative chronologies in the southwest Florida coast area, in the absence of more traditionally considered decorated ceramics (cf. Luer and Almy 1980a). The other properties listed have not been considered previously in any detail. They were chosen for analysis, in addition to thickness and rim form, in order to examine their potential for documenting changes through time and to provide a larger and more varied body of comparative data for future studies in the area.

The population of sherds available for study is shown in table 11.6. The sample was defined with respect to a sherd size requirement posed by the technological analysis. Sherds needed to be "large" enough so that pieces could be broken off for analysis without destroying the whole sherd. In order to satisfy this size requirement, each sherd from Test B was dropped into a container with a diameter opening of 2.0 centimeters. The sherds that did not pass through this opening were considered eligible for sampling. The number of eligible sherds per stratum is also presented in table 11.6. Random samples of ten sherds from each of the seven strata (I-VIB) were then selected for analysis.

A fresh break from each sampled sherd was examined with a binocular microscope at 70× magnification to obtain type, relative frequency, and relative size of aplastic inclusions. Relative size of inclusions was measured (microscope was equipped with an eyepiece micrometer) with reference to Wentworth's Size Classification (Shepard 1976:118). Relative frequencies of aplastics were rated subjectively as none, rare, occasional, common, or abundant (or combinations such as occasional-to-common).

For determination of color, the entire sample of 70 sherds was handsorted into broad categories of exterior surface color, interior surface color, and core color representing the observed gross range of color variations. Samples of five sherds representing each color category were selected for more precise measurements and description (under consistent lighting conditions) using Munsell Soil Color Charts.

Sherd thickness was measured with sliding metric calipers. Measurements of body or vessel wall, rim, and basal (when applicable) thicknesses were made.

The analysis of rim forms considered all of the excavated rims (n = 39) from each stratum ("ineligible" as well as "eligible" rim sherds). A contour gauge was used to obtain accurate drawings of rim profiles or shapes. Vessel wall orientation of these sherds was determined when possible. Method of surface finishing exhibited by sherds in the sample was hypothesized with reference to Shepard's discussion of surface-finishing technology (Shepard 1976:186–93).

Data pertaining to type, relative frequency, and size of aplastic inclusions were obtained in order to sort the 70 sherds into paste categories that may reflect the range of clay resources utilized for manufacture and may have chronological significance. Two principal aplastic paste constituents were observed in the sample: quartz sand (ranging in size from very fine to very coarse) and sponge spicules (diameters and lengths of which fall within the lower limits of the very fine size category). A third type, identified tentatively as siderite nodules, will be discussed with quartz sand paste categories.

The presence of sponge spicules in Florida pottery is a characteristic of St. Johns or "chalky ware" pottery (Thanz-Borremans and Shaak 1977). But the Useppa spiculite sherds do not resemble chalky pottery; only one of the sherds examined could be considered even remotely "chalky." The frequency of spicules observed in the Useppa sample is generally lower than that observed in chalky ware; size of the spicules is also generally smaller than those observed in chalky pottery.

The presence of sponge spicules is considered a significant criterion for differentiation of paste-resource categories or types. In order to obtain a more accurate estimate of the proportion of spicule-bearing sherds recovered from this test excavation, the unsampled eligible (size criterion) sherds were also examined with the binocular microscope to determine presence and relative frequency of sponge spicules. This procedure was not time-consuming and could usefully be made a routine initial step in the cataloging of specimens prior to sampling for more intensive study. Relative frequency of spicules was determined from sherd surfaces as spicules in the paste often were obscured from observation by the generally laminated paste textures, making it difficult to obtain accurate observations from examination of the paste.

A relative frequency histogram, depicting the percentage of eligible spiculite sherds observed in each occupation zone (I–VIB), was constructed (fig. 11.8) to examine temporal differences. The histogram indicates that the use of pottery made of spiculite materials was low in the lowest, or earliest, occupation levels. A gradual increase through time in use of spiculite pottery is also evident; their increase is followed by a marked leap in Zone IV, in which 100 percent of the sherds examined contained sponge spicules. (This zone is represented, however, by the fewest cases; see table 11.6.) The use of spiculite pottery drops sharply in the stratum directly above it (III) and continues to decrease gradually through time to the historic occupation zone (I), in which only about 38 percent of the pottery examined was made of spiculite resources.

The extent to which the observed changes in relative frequencies of

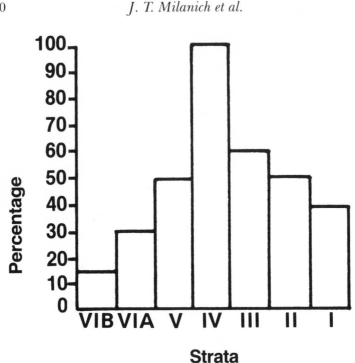

Fig. 11.8. Sherds containing sponge spicules vs. strata.

spiculite sherds could be "artifacts" of the sampling procedures is difficult to ascertain without microscopic examination of some of the "ineligible" sherds (those which passed through the 2-centimeter opening). If, for example, spiculite sherds were more fragile, hence more
"breakable" (through being "sandier" or thinner or "more poorly"
fired) than nonspiculite sherds, then relative frequencies in the sampling population could be skewed—increased, if the greater number
of small sherds (caused by breakability) were still large enough to have
not been eliminated by the sorting procedure, or decreased, if most of
the "small" sherds were eliminated by the sorting procedure. Intui-
tively, the sampling population seems to be representative of the true,
unknown proportions of spiculite and nonspiculite sherds in the
Useppa collection. When sorted into "large" and "small" size categories ("large" defined as sherds greater than 3–4 centimeters in some
dimension), the proportions of large versus small sizes for eligible
spiculite and nonspiculite sherds are overall, and individually for
most strata, quite comparable (see table 11.11).

Table 11.11. Spiculite paste in relation to sherd size, by strata,
in percentages

Paste category	Strata							All strata
	I	II	III	IV	V	VIA	VIB	
Spiculite								
"large"	40	65	73	50	66	50	58	60
"small"	60	35	27	50	34	50	42	40
Nonspiculite								
"large"	30	76	44	—	59	74	56	58
"small"	70	24	56	—	41	26	44	42

Table 11.12. Relative spiculite frequency, by strata

	Spiculite sherds			Relative occurrence of spicules (in percentages)							
			rare	rare/ occa- sional	occa- sional	occa- sional/ com- mon	com- mon	com- mon/ abun- dant	< occa- sional	occa- sional	> occa- sional
Stratum	N	%									
I	15	38.5	26.7	20.0	26.7	13.3	13.3	—	46.7	26.7	26.7
II	20	48.8	22.2	22.2	44.4	11.1	—	—	44.4	44.4	11.2
III	22	57.9	13.6	4.5	36.4	31.8	13.6	—	18.1	36.4	45.4
IV	12	100.0	8.3	—	50.0	16.7	25.0	—	8.3	50.0	41.7
V	32	47.8	3.1	3.1	50.0	18.8	15.6	9.4	6.2	50.0	43.8
VIA	10	30.3	20.0	—	40.0	—	20.0	20.0	20.0	40.0	40.0
VIB	12	14.6	16.7	—	25.0	—	50.0	8.3	16.7	25.0	58.3

Table 11.12 presents a breakdown per occupation level of the relative frequency of spicules observed in the sample of eligible sherds.
These data indicate that spiculite pottery used early in the site's occupation had a higher sponge spicule content than that found in later
levels. Nearly 60 percent of the spiculite sherds in the earliest stratum
(Zone VIB) exhibit relative frequencies that are greater than occasional (occasional-to-common through common-to-abundant). The
proportion of spiculite sherds containing greater-than-occasional
spicules decreases to about 40 percent in the next level (Zone VIA)
and remains more or less unchanged through time until the latest or
most recent two levels (I and II), in which an average of only about
19 percent of the spiculite sherds exhibit a high spicule content.

The percentage of sherds containing "occasional" relative occurrence of spicules increases early in the site's history and remains about
the same through time (40 to 50 percent) until the historic occupation

Table 11.13. Additional characteristics of spiculite and nonspiculite sherds

Nonspiculite categories		Spiculite categories — Relative occurrence of sponge spicules (all also contain quartz sand)				
Quartz sand	Quartz sand and siderite	Rare	Rare-occasional	Occasional-common	Common	Common-abundant
						7 n=1 occas fine occas-com medium mean=6mm lt surfaces dk core
						8 n=1 abund fine mean=10mm dk surfaces dk core
				4 n=3 com-abund fine mean=12mm dk surfaces dk cores		
				5 n=22 com-abund fine occas-com medium mean=10mm dk ext. surfaces lt int. surfaces dk cores		
					6 n=1 abund fine occas medium-coarse rare very-coarse mean=12mm dk surfaces dk core	
			2 n=8 abund fine occas-com medium rare-occas coarse mean=8.5mm dk ext. surfaces lt int. surfaces			
A n=1 abund fine mean=7mm dk surfaces dk core						
B n=2 abund fine occas-com medium mean=7mm dk surfaces dk cores						
C n=6 abund fine common medium rare-occas coarse none-rare very coarse mean=9mm						

dk surfaces
dk cores

dk cores

D   n=9
abund fine
common medium
occas-com coarse
mean=11mm
dk ext. surfaces
dk and lt int. surfaces
lt cores

3   n=3
com-abund fine
occas-com medium
occas-com coarse
mean=9mm
dk ext. surfaces
lt int. surfaces
lt cores

E   n=6
occas-com very fine
abund fine
occas-common medium
rare-occas- coarse
mean=10mm
dk surfaces
dk cores

G   n=4
occas-com very fine
abund fine
occas medium- very coarse
mean=12mm
lt ext. surfaces
dk int. surfaces
dk cores

1   n=2
occas very fine
abund fine
occas medium
none-rare- coarse
mean=8mm
dk surfaces
dk cores

F   n=1
abund very fine
common fine
mean=7mm
dk surfaces
dk core

NOTE: The relative frequency of information and particle size names listed refer to quartz sand. Mean vessel wall thickness and modal surface and core colors are also listed.

abund = abundant; com = common; occas = occasional; dk = dark; lt = light; ext = exterior; int = interior.

level, where it decreases. The plotted proportion of spiculite sherds containing less-than-occasional spicules shows a general trend of increase through time; i.e., spiculite pottery used more recently contains fewer spicules than that used early in the occupation.

Quartz sand, the other principal paste constituent, was also observed (in generally abundant quantities) in the spiculite sherds. The 41 spicule-bearing sherds (of the 70 sampled) were hand-sorted into eight categories (1–8) based on relative frequency of spicules and relative frequency and size of quartz sand inclusions (see table 11.13).

Table 11.13 indicates that, with one exception (category 6[n = 1]), a wider range of sand sizes (very fine through coarse—principally fine through coarse [categories 1, 2, 3]) occurs only in sherds exhibiting low (rare or rare-to-occasional) sponge spicule content. With one exception (category 6), sherds with greater than or equal to occasional occurrence of spicules (categories 4, 5, 7, 8) exhibit only fine or fine-and-medium sizes (a narrower range, in varying quantities) of quartz sand.

Frequency histograms of each spiculite paste category versus excavated strata (fig. 11.9) generally reflect the distribution evident for relative frequencies of sponge spicules (table 11.12). Paste categories 6, 7, and 8, characterized by common or common-to-abundant sponge spicules, occur only in the early levels. Categories 4 and 5, exhibiting occasional or occasional-to-common spicules, were recovered almost exclusively from middle levels (II–V). Categories exhibiting rare or rare-to-occasional spicules (1, 2, and 3) occur more frequently (7 of 13 cases) in the two latest levels but also occur in middle levels (except for one case, from category 2, which occurs in an earlier level, Zone VIA). Only two of the spiculite paste categories identified from the sample (2 and 5) are, however, represented by more than three cases. As a result, any generalizations or conclusions made here about such small categories should be considered with caution.

Six categories (A–F) of sherds containing only quartz sand inclusions were identified from the sample (n = 25). These categories are described in table 11.13. The descriptions in this table are arranged to show similarities in frequency of quartz sand which cross-cut the sponge spicule-quartz and plain quartz sand dichotomy.

Histograms (fig. 11.10) reveal that sherds characterized by fine or fine-and-medium quartz sand (categories A and B) occur only in early levels of occupation (V and VIA), a distribution fairly similar to spiculite categories (4, 5, 7, and 8) exhibiting the same range of sand sizes.

Categories characterized by fine-through-coarse or very coarse quartz sand (C and D), i.e., a wider range of sand sizes, do occur in late levels (as did spiculite categories with similar range of sand sizes) but occur more frequently (9 of 15 cases) in earlier levels (V–VIB). Another category (E), also characterized by a wide range of sand sizes, occurs exclusively in earlier levels (V–VIB; its spiculite counterpart occurs in levels III and V). Category F, characterized by very fine and fine quartz sand (no corresponding spiculite category was observed) occurs only in the latest, historic occupation zone.

Only three of the plain quartz sand categories identified were represented by more than two cases (categories C [n = 6], D [n = 9], and [n = 6]). Hence, once again, conclusions should be considered with caution.

A subgroup of the quartz sand paste sherds (category G), represented in the sample by four sherds, contains occasional-to-common occurrence of medium to very coarse-sized greyish "lumps." These inclusions are generally spherical in shape and greyish in color; they exhibit a slightly metallic-to-vitreous luster and are sometimes softer than the surrounding matrix. They have been tentatively identified as siderite nodules. Siderite is an iron carbonate ($FeCO_3$) with widespread occurrence. It is often found associated with clays and other sedimentary rocks (Berry and Mason 1959), but it is not commonly found in Florida. Local occurrence can still be postulated, however, since Florida possesses abundant quantities of the component materials (iron in various forms and limestone). This paste category occurs most frequently in an early level of occupation (VIA; one case also occurs in III). It exhibits a quartz sand frequency and size configuration similar to quartz sand paste category E and spiculite category I (also occurring principally in early to middle levels).

From examination of combined quartz sand paste and spiculite paste histograms (fig. 11.11, based on similarities in quartz sand frequencies and sizes), it can be stated that, in general, pottery exhibiting a narrow range of sand sizes (fine and medium sizes specifically) appears to have been used during early and middle occupation phases. Pottery exhibiting a wider range of sand sizes appears to have been used throughout the occupations.

The sample of 70 sherds was sorted into four categories of surface color and six categories of core color or degree of coring. Relative frequencies of these categories and their Munsell color descriptions (based on judgmental samples of five sherds [when possible] from

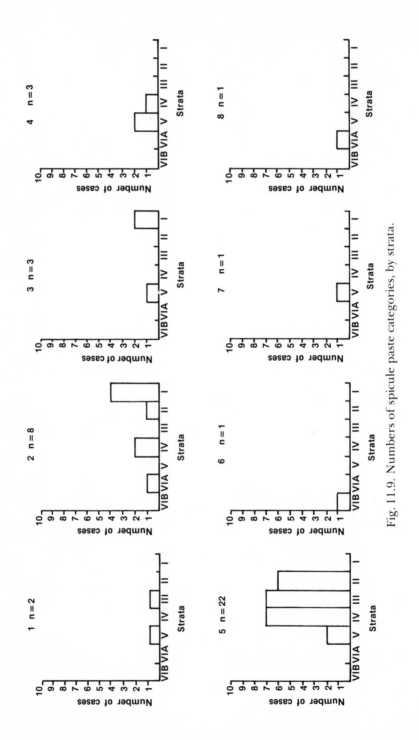

Fig. 11.9. Numbers of spicule paste categories, by strata.

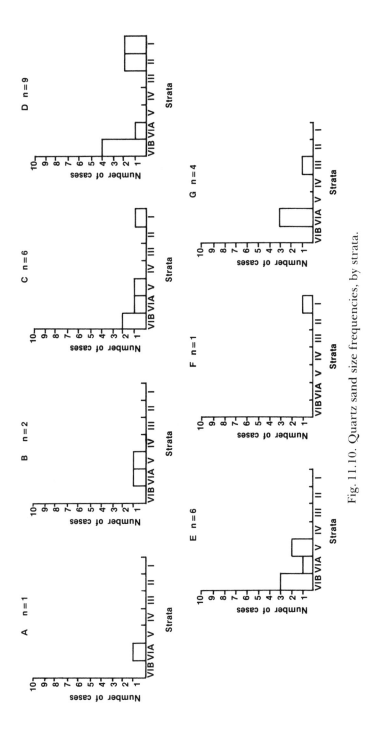

Fig. 11.10. Quartz sand size frequencies, by strata.

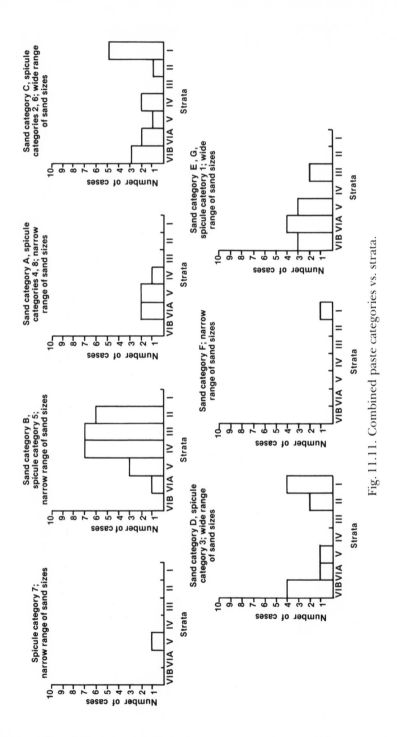

Fig. 11.11. Combined paste categories vs. strata.

Table 11.14. Surface color and core color in the Useppa
ceramic sample

		Surface color categories					
			Exterior		Interior		Core color
Munsell color names		Munsell hue designations	N	%	N	%	N	%

	Munsell color names	Munsell hue designations	Exterior N	Exterior %	Interior N	Interior %	Core color N	Core color %
1	pale browns, browns, yellowish browns	10YR hues	11	17.2	28	41.2	1 23	32.9
2	browns	7.5YR hues (redder than 10YR hues)	0	—	6	8.8	2A 12 2B 19 3 9	17.1 27.1 12.8
3	dark greys	10YR hues	17	26.6	11	16.2	4 4	5.7
4	very dark greys	10YR hues	36	56.2	23	33.8	5 3	4.3

Core color categories

	% coring	Munsell color names of cored zones(s)	Munsell hue designations of cored zones(s)	Color names of oxidized zones	Hue designation
1	100	blacks	10YR, 2.5Y hues	—	—
2A	70	blacks	2.5Y, 5Y hues	reddish browns–strong browns	7.5YR, 5YR hues
2B	70	blacks	10YR, 2.5Y, 5Y hues	browns, yellow-browns	10YR hues
3	30–50	very dark greys, blacks	10YR, 2.5Y hues	browns-dark browns	10YR hues
4	10–30	very dark greys	2.5Y, 5Y hues	reds, reddish browns, yellow-ish reds	2.5YR, 5YR hues
5	0–ca.10	dark greyish browns	10YR hues	browns, yellow-browns	10YR hues

each category) are presented in table 11.14. Frequency histograms of
the color categories versus excavated strata (figs. 11.12–11.14 and
table 11.15) listing percentages of each color category occurring in
levels later and earlier than Zone IV were constructed to document
temporal differences.

Some definite trends are evident from examination of these data.
Pottery exhibiting surface color categories 1 and 2 (lighter, more oxidized colors) occur more frequently in the later or most recent levels.
This trend is more evident for interior surfaces than for vessel exteriors. Pottery exhibiting dark grey to very dark grey surfaces (categories 3 and 4) occurs more frequently in earlier zones. Examination of
core color data indicates that pottery characterized by 100 percent

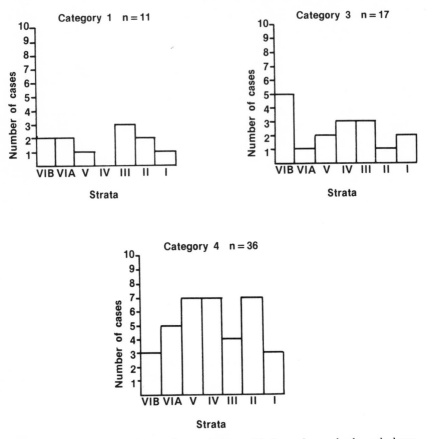

Fig. 11.12. Sherd exterior surface color (n = 64; 6 specimens had eroded surfaces; category 2 had no cases).

dark (very dark grey to black) cores or "coring" occurs more frequently in early levels and that pottery exhibiting no coring or only 30 to 50 percent coring (categories 3–5) is more prominent in later levels. As a group, the categories characterized by about 70 percent coring (2A and 2B) occur slightly more often in later levels. These trends appear to indicate that pottery used later in the site's occupation may have been somewhat better oxidized in firing than earlier pottery.

Table 11.16, listing color categories exhibited by the different paste types, indicates that exterior surfaces of spiculite and nonspiculite categories exhibit about the same proportion of lighter or more oxidized colors (surface color categories 1 and 2, 18.5 percent and 16.2 percent for nonspiculite and spiculite categories, respectively). Spiculite sherds exhibit, however, a greater proportion of more oxidized interior surfaces than do nonspiculite sherds (66.7 percent for spiculite sherds versus 24.1 percent for nonspiculite sherds). Nonspiculite sherds exhibit a somewhat higher proportion of more oxidized cores (categories 3–5, 27.6 percent for nonspiculite sherds versus 19.5 percent for spiculite sherds). While the higher proportion of light interiors exhibited by the spiculite sherds in the sample may indicate somewhat better oxidizing conditions in firing, it does not necessarily mean that spiculite pottery was "better" fired. Hence, it would not necessarily tend to lessen, for example, the "breakability" of spiculite sherds

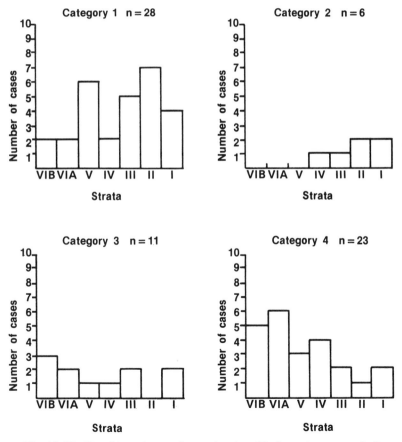

Fig. 11.13. Sherd interior surface color (n =68; 2 specimens eroded).

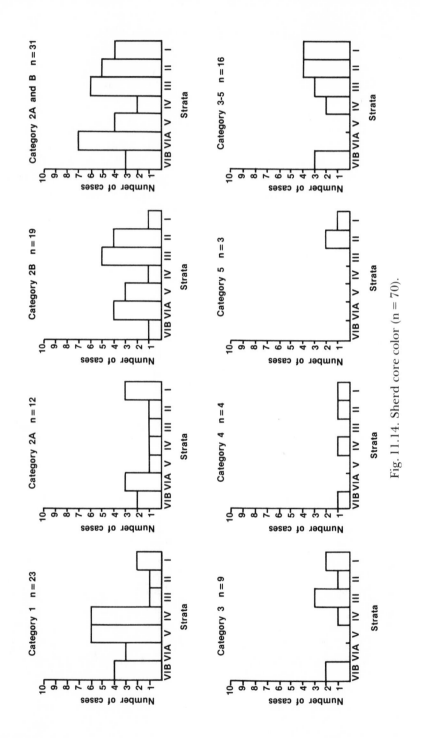

Fig. 11.14. Sherd core color (n = 70).

Table 11.15. Sherd color categories versus excavated strata

| | Color categories | | | | | | | | | | | | |
| | Exteriors | | | | Interiors | | | | Cores | | | | | |
Strata	1	2	3	4	1	2	3	4	1	2A	2B	3	4	5
Earlier than Zone IV	45.4	—	47.1	41.1	35.6	—	54.5	60.9	56.5	50.0	42.1	22.2	25.0	—
Later than Zone IV	54.5	—	35.3	33.3	57.1	83.3	36.4	21.7	17.4	41.7	52.6	66.7	50.0	100.0

Table 11.16. Color categories by paste type

| | Color categories | | | | | | | | | | | | | | | | |
| | Exteriors | | | | | Interiors | | | | | Cores | | | | | |
	1	2	3	4	NA	1	2	3	4	NA	1	2A	2B	3	4	5
Spiculite paste categories																
1	–	–	–	2	–	1	–	–	1	–	2	–	–	–	–	–
2	–	–	2	4	2	4	1	–	3	–	3	3	2	–	–	–
3	–	–	1	1	1	2	1	–	–	–	–	1	–	–	–	2
4	–	–	2	1	–	1	–	–	2	–	1	–	1	1	–	–
5	5	–	5	12	–	12	3	2	3	2	7	2	8	3	2	–
6	–	–	1	–	–	–	–	1	–	–	–	1	–	–	–	–
7	1	–	–	–	–	1	–	–	–	–	–	–	1	–	–	–
8	–	–	–	–	1	–	–	–	1	–	–	1	–	–	–	–
Nonspiculite paste categories																
A	–	–	–	1	–	–	–	–	1	–	1	–	–	–	–	–
B	–	–	–	2	–	–	–	–	2	–	2	–	–	–	–	–
C	1	–	4	1	–	1	–	3	2	–	1	2	2	1	–	–
D	2	–	1	5	1	3	1	2	3	–	–	–	3	3	2	1
E	–	–	1	5	–	1	–	2	3	–	4	–	2	–	–	–
F	–	–	–	1	–	–	–	–	1	–	1	–	–	–	–	–
G	2	–	–	1	1	1	–	1	2	–	1	2	–	1	–	–

| | Exteriors | | | | Interiors | | | | Cores | | | |
| | "Light" (1, 2) | | "Dark" (3, 4) | | "Light" (1, 2) | | "Dark" (3, 4) | | "Light" (3–5) | | "Dark" (1–2B) | |
	N	%	N	%	N	%	N	%	N	%	N	%
Total												
Spiculite	6	16.2	31	83.8	26	66.7	13	33.3	8	19.5	33	80.5
Nonspiculite	5	18.5	22	81.5	7	24.1	22	75.9	8	27.6	21	72.4

NA: not applicable; extremely eroded surfaces were not categorized as to color.

Table 11.17. Sherd thickness, by strata

	Strata						
	I	II	III	IV	V	VIA	VIB
Vessel wall thickness							
Mean (mm)	9	10	10	11	10	10	10
Range (mm)	6–19	5–13	5–15	6–14	6–14	5–16	6–18
% 8mm	43.6	19.5	31.6	8.3	17.9	36.4	19.0
% 10mm	41.0	58.5	52.6	75.0	62.7	48.5	50.6
Rim thickness							
mean (mm)	7	8	11	6	9	8	9
range (mm)	4–9	6–11	9–12	6	8–10	5–10	7–11
N rims	6	6	4	1	5	9	8

(which could have had the potential to skew the observed proportions of spiculite versus nonspiculite sherds).

Thickness of vessel walls has been measured on other southwest Florida coast pottery from stratified sites (Luer and Almy 1980a). The trend observed in other collections was one of general decrease through time in thick-walled vessels. Measurement of vessel wall thickness in this study produced mixed results.

Sherd thickness was recorded for all eligible sherds to obtain a more accurate estimate of mean body thickness from each level for the Useppa collection. The calculated mean values (rounded to the nearest millimeter) are plotted against the excavated strata in figure 11.15. Means and ranges of recorded measurements are listed in table 11.17.

It was found that the lowest mean measurement (ca. 9 millimeters; this value was calculated excluding an extreme value [23 millimeters] which appeared to come from a basal sherd) does correspond to the latest, most recent occupation level, as might be expected. The highest mean value fell, however, in a middle level (Zone IV; $\bar{x} = 11$ millimeters, and means for the remaining levels are all approximately the same (10 millimeters).

Relative frequency histograms were constructed to examine the distribution through time of the proportion of sherds with thicknesses of less than or equal to 8 millimeters (rounded to nearest millimeter) and greater than or equal to 10 millimeters (fig. 11.15). These percentages are listed also in table 11.17. These histograms indicate that later levels do have a higher proportion of thinner-walled pottery than earlier levels as a group. An early level (VIA) does exhibit, however, a relatively high proportion of "thin" pottery. The histogram of the per-

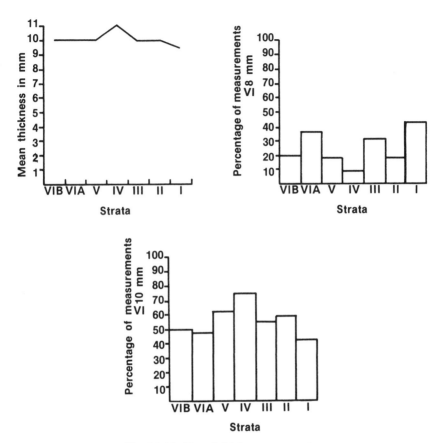

Fig. 11.15. Sherd thickness vs. strata.

centage of "thick-walled" pottery (greater than or equal to 10 millimeters) suggests a gradual increase, followed by a gradual decrease
through time in the use of thick-walled pottery. While there are differences in vessel thickness between and within spiculite and nonspiculite paste categories (see table 11.13), the spiculite sherds as a
group (of all eligible spiculite sherds) are not appreciably thinner or
thicker than the eligible nonspiculite sherds.

Thirty-nine rim sherds were recovered from Test B excavations.
Rim thickness was recorded in order to document any temporal
trends. Table 11.17 lists number of rim sherds, mean rim thickness,
and range of recorded measurements (rounded to nearest millimeter)
per excavated stratum. Mean values are plotted against the excavated

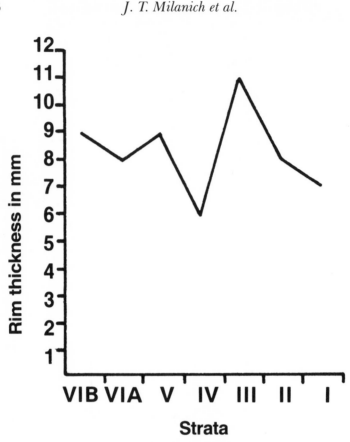

Fig. 11.16. Rim thickness vs. strata.

strata in figure 11.16. These data indicate, in general, that vessel rims are somewhat thicker in earlier occupation levels (V–VIB) than later ones (I and II), but that the thickest vessel rims occur during a middle occupation phase (III). The exception to this trend is middle occupation Zone IV, which yielded the lowest mean value (6 millimeters). This "mean" is, however, based on only one measurement, as only one rim sherd was recovered from this level.

Rim form or shape and vessel wall orientation (e.g., restricted versus unrestricted) have been examined at other stratified southwest Florida coast sites (Luer and Almy 1980a). Temporal trends noted for other collections conclude that higher proportions of unrestricted vessels and a wider range of rim or lip forms or shapes are observed in late occupation levels. These trends were also observed in this study.

Table 11.18. Vessel form, by strata

Strata	No. rims	Restricted forms		Unrestricted forms		Range of rim forms
		N	%	N	%	
I	6	2	33.3	4	66.7	4
II	6	2	33.3	4	66.7	4
III	4	2	50.0	2	50.0	4
IV	1	1	100.0	–	–	1
V	5	3	60.0	2	40.0	3
VIA[a]	9	5	62.5[a]	3	37.5[a]	3
VIB	8	7	87.5	1	12.5	2

a. A case unidentified as to orientation was excluded from calculation of percentages.

The 39 rims were sorted into two general categories of vessel wall orientation, restricted and unrestricted (one rim from Zone VIA could not be identified even tentatively as to orientation), and seven categories of rim or lip shape. The number and percentage of restricted and unrestricted rims and range of shapes per excavated strata are presented in table 11.18. The seven lip and rim forms are presented in figure 11.17. Relative frequency histograms of the proportions of restricted and unrestricted forms in the sample and a frequency histogram of range of lip shapes are shown in figure 11.18. These data suggest that, in general, the proportion of restricted vessels decreases through time, while the range of rim shapes increases. The relatively small number of cases representing each stratum, however, requires that these generalizations be considered only tentative. Zone IV should be deleted altogether from consideration, as it is represented by only one case. It should also be noted that many of the cases from Zone VIB (rounded rims, restricted orientations) appear to belong to a single vessel and that two cases from Zone 1 (rounded rims, restricted orientation) do, in fact, belong to a single vessel.

Surface finish refers to surface characteristics resulting from the manner in which a vessel was smoothed and evened during and subsequent to the shaping process. Surface finishes are often difficult to identify with certainty. The ability to recognize the manner by which a particular surface finish was produced depends on familiarity with how the raw material behaves in different conditions or states of plasticity or dryness when treated or finished with different kinds or classes of tools (e.g., scraping tools or hard and yielding rubbing tools; Shepard 1976: 187).

Exterior and interior surfaces of each of the 70 sherds in the sample were examined to evaluate the chronological significance of particular

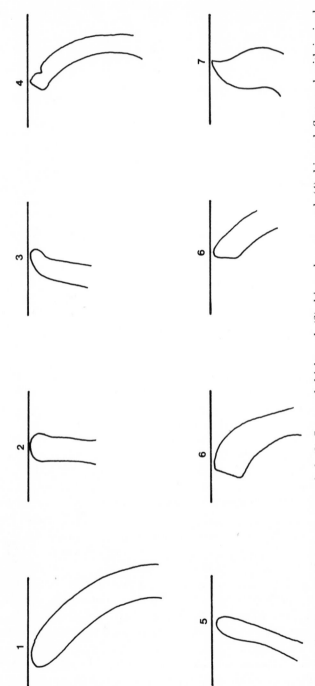

Fig. 11.17. Rim or lip forms: (1) rounded; (2) flattened-thickened; (3) thinned or tapered; (4) thinned, flattened, with incised line; (5) rounded-thickened; (6) beveled-squared; (7) beveled-rounded.

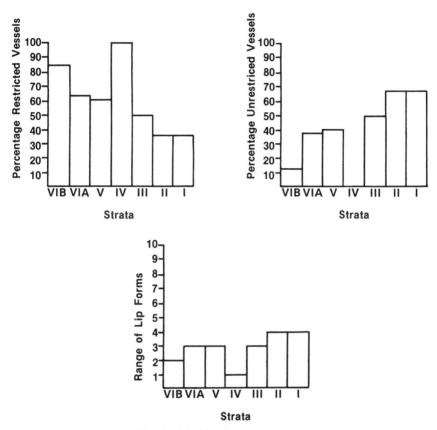

Fig. 11.18. Rim forms vs. strata.

kinds of finishes. Observations were made with reference to Shepard's discussion of surface finishing technology (1976: 186–93).

Five categories of surface finish were observed in the sample; they are described in table 11.19. Table 11.20 presents the breakdown of these categories by excavated stratum. The results of observation are difficult to interpret, as one or both surfaces of many of the sherds examined were eroded to the degree that determination of surface finish was impossible. The trend evident from the recorded observations is that there appears to have been little change through time in surface-finishing technology. Another trend is that interior surfaces exhibit a higher proportion of finishes carried out on still somewhat plastic surfaces than do exteriors. This difference indicates that, quite often, vessel interiors were finished before vessel exteriors.

Table 11.19. Surface finish categories

1. rubbed with a yielding tool (probably dampened or wet—e.g., a wet hand) in leatherhard state—sometimes referred to as "floating" the surface.
2. rubbed or wiped in the plastic state with a yielding tool.
3. scraped with an edged scraping tool (shell in one case) in the plastic state.
4. rubbed or burnished with a hard, smooth tool in the plastic to leatherhard state.
5. rubbed or burnished with a hard, smooth tool in the plastic state.

Table 11.20. Surface finish categories, by strata

	Strata												
	I		II		III		IV		V		VIA		VIB	
	N	%	N	%	N	%	N	%	N	%	N	%	N	%
Exteriors														
1	4	80.0	7	100.0	9	100.0	5	83.3	7	87.5	7	100.0	6	85.7
2	–	–	–	–	–	–	1	16.7	1	12.5	–	–	1	14.3
3	–	–	–	–	–	–	–	–	–	–	–	–	–	–
4	1	20.0	–	–	–	–	–	–	–	–	–	–	–	–
5	–	–	–	–	–	–	–	–	–	–	–	–	–	–
Interiors														
1	2	28.6	6	75.0	6	75.0	5	83.3	1	33.3	4	80.0	4	44.4
2	4	57.1	–	–	1	12.5	–	–	2	66.7	–	–	4	44.4
3	–	–	2	25.0	–	–	–	–	–	–	–	–	–	–
4	1	14.3	–	–	–	–	–	–	–	–	1	20.0	–	–
5	–	–	–	–	1	12.5	1	16.7	–	–	–	–	1	11.1

Conclusions of the ceramic technological analysis

A primary goal of this ceramic analysis was to evaluate the potential of certain ceramic attributes for documenting changes through time. It has demonstrated that not-often-considered paste attributes, such as aplastic constituents and color, did exhibit chronologically significant differences, while surface finish attributes did not. Traditionally considered rim form attributes were also found to exhibit significant temporal differences; examination of vessel thickness (also a more traditionally considered attribute) produced mixed results.

   In general, this study demonstrated, at least for the Useppa site, that a wider range of ceramic attributes on undecorated pottery can be profitably studied to document changes through time. It is also significant to note that, while initial "eyeball examination" of the sherds suggested a great deal of homogeneity of paste characteristics in the Useppa collection (most sherds are generally very "sandy"), a more detailed technological study demonstrated that in fact a great deal of heterogeneity existed. These differences were simply not distinguishable with the unaided eye. More specifically, the differences within and between quartz sand and spiculite paste categories could not have been obtained without the aid of a microscope.

This analysis illustrates that the use of microscopy may be essential in future studies of comparable scope in the southwest coastal area. The observation of initial homogeneity might also indicate that some of the observed differences within and between spiculite and non-spiculite paste categories may not reflect the use of very different resources for manufacture; many of these differences may, rather, reflect the utilization through time of variability (e.g., along vertical and horizontal dimensions) exhibited by a single resource type. Comparable examination of local clay resources would be necessary in proving this hypothesis. Such an endeavor also represents another not-often-considered area of ceramic technology that could be profitably undertaken in future research in this region.

Conclusions, apologies, and suggestions

In the preliminary portion of this paper we referred to the Useppa excavations as "modest." Perhaps immodestly, we referred to our analytical techniques applied to some data from those excavations as "refined." The comprehending reader will recall that we made no promises, and we apologize to anyone who, having studied all 21 tables carefully, expected at this point to come to a punchline, perhaps our unlocking of the secrets of the Calusa's past. We simply cannot deliver. What we have accomplished is only one small step, one small attempt to collect and quantify coastal data and demonstrate that many more steps are needed along the same path before we can reach concrete conclusions about the Calusa and their prehistoric ancestors.

The excavations and program of testing on Useppa Island and other recent excavations on Sanibel Island and on Horr's Island farther south in Collier County (McMichael 1979, 1982) point out some of the inconsistencies that are present in the southwest Florida coastal sites. For instance, at the Wightman site on Sanibel Island, several large mounds constructed of redeposited older midden were built on top of a still earlier midden. Collier Mound on Useppa looks almost identical to the large, artificial shell mounds at Wightman but is constructed (at least in its upper 3 meters) of discrete midden strata. Those strata appear quite different from the strata present in Test B. On Horr's Island a large, horseshoe-shaped shell heap is a midden 4 meters thick, composed mostly of shell but in some places a mixture of black, very humic soil and shell. This midden has been well dated (by radiocarbon analysis) to the late portion of the preceramic Archaic period, 2500–2000 B.C. The middens contain very little food bone relative to other middens on Sanibel and Useppa.

Still other heaps of shell in the Pine Island Sound locale seem to be made entirely out of individual *Busycon* shells. A mosquito control ditch cut through one site on Buck Key shows a deposit of *Busycons* several meters thick. It is possible that such *Busycon* heaps are middens, not intentionally built structures. In addition to sites with shell, dirt middens also are present (Widmer 1978: 90).

It is perhaps an understatement to say that the surface appearance of a site may not be a clue to its nature. And we have not even mentioned the problem of specialized areas within shell middens: is midden refuse homogeneous? Another problem, only alluded to, is the occupation dates for the sites. A shell midden from 2500 B.C. looks a lot like one from A.D. 1500, especially when you are trying to outrun a horde of voracious mosquitos. Consequently, before any overall strategy of sampling sites can be worked out, we need to become better acquainted with our sampling population in order to stratify it.

Once an initial, structured, reconnaissance is completed, the sites need to be tested to see what is under their surface. On Useppa Island, Milanich and Chapman employed a backhoe, a method Chapman had used successfully in Tennessee. A backhoe was also used on Horr's Island. The Useppa and Horr's Island cases showed that such tests—ditches dug with the backhoe as deep as it can go—provide a great deal of data. The profiles reveal the nature of the deposits and artifacts, and samples of material for radiocarbon dating can be taken from the walls. We need to develop a method for quickly extracting large column samples (at least 0.5 by 0.5 meters; but as indicated by the Useppa tests, such samples may be biased against larger mammal remains and a 1-meter by 1-meter size may be better). Vertebrate and invertebrate samples can be rough-sorted to provide information and stored for later analysis, if needed.

After the sites are tested in this manner, they can be classed and stratified for whatever further work seems warranted. We suspect that the testing will have produced sufficient artifact samples and information from some sites so that they will not need to be investigated further, at least for a preliminary study. Once we can sample sites with some measure of confidence regarding what we are sampling, questions concerning economics, settlement systems, demography, environmental change, and so on can be intelligently posed and investigated.

We hope that it is clear to anyone who has not had experience digging in coastal shell middens that those field methods employed at inland sites need to be altered. The plan described for research in the Pine Island Sound would entail a major archaeological effort and a major financial commitment. And it would require innovation. Are granting agencies ready for proposals that request a barge and a backhoe, a houseboat, and other strange but essential equipment? Clearly, field strategy needs to be multi-institutional, and major equipment needs to be shared along with other facilities.

But the situation is far from hopeless. We have made a start; we understand the nature of the problem and can describe a plan of attack. And local people in the Pine Island Sound locale have demonstrated an eagerness to aid archaeological research on their islands. Perhaps just as important, they are making successful efforts to protect their archaeological resources from destruction. The Lee County coastal area is the fastest growing in the United States, and the offshore keys of shell present desired environments for development. Although a few catastrophes in the form of bulldozed sites have occurred, local citizens along with various local organizations and county, state, and federal governments have all taken positive steps to preserve and protect sites.

We might best summarize our conclusions by simply observing that the Useppa excavations accomplished three things: they provided information on the culture history and the nature of archaeological deposits on the island; they provided quantified data on subsistence and ceramics, pointing out the necessity for such detailed analysis in future studies in the Pine Island Sound locale; and they have demonstrated beyond a doubt that we still have a long way to go and we need to step lively before we can explore the development and nature of Calusa Indian culture.

Acknowledgments

We are grateful to Garfield Beckstead, president, and members and staff of the Useppa Island Club for their contributions to the Useppa excavations. They provided bed and board in splendid style, along with labor, goodwill, and a backhoe, all necessary for coastal work. We would also like to acknowledge Michael Hansinger and Charles Wilson for their continued support of archaeological investigations and cultural resource preservation along the southwest Florida coast. The University of Florida provided funds for the malacological, zooarchaeological, and ceramic analyses, all of which were carried out at the Florida State Museum.

This report was prepared in committee fashion: Chapman and Milanich, with the Useppa Island Club, carried out the excavations; Ann Cordell was responsible for the ceramic analysis and prepared that section of the report; Stephen Hale identified the malacological sample; the zooarchaeological analysis and preparation of those sections was done by Rochelle Marrinan; Milanich assembled the report using their materials and filling in the blanks. The result is some data and a few passing remarks. The latter will, we hope, introduce the reader to a unique archaeological situation on a little-known portion of the Gulf coast and point out some of the special problems of doing research there.

12

Perspectives on Gulf Coast Cultural History: A Roundtable Discussion

A primary purpose of the Avery Island conference was to explore the utility of viewing the Gulf coast as a cultural region. Toward this end, one session was devoted to a discussion of cultural interaction and parallel adaptations on the Gulf coast during the Woodland and Mississippian periods. In keeping with that aim, the participants focused in large part upon the cultural history of the coast.

Academic roundtable discussions have some inevitable, often frustrating, limitations as a way to convey information. They are somewhat disjointed; much of the information produced is incomplete, and some of it is based upon faulty recollection of the data. Guesses may occasionally be indistinguishable from statements of fact, and casual interpretations may be inextricable from explanations that are grounded in rigorous analysis.

Yet these limitations are overridden by the value of such discussions. A roundtable format often brings to light significant unpublished information—data which, for various reasons, might otherwise remain unavailable to the archaeological community. Roundtable discussions also promote exchange of innovative ideas that may be in their formative stages and may thereby stimulate progress in the field. Finally, in the case of the U.S. Gulf coast, no single scholar possesses the necessary understanding of the data base to produce a real synthesis of regional prehistory. While a roundtable discussion also cannot produce such a synthesis, it is a useful way to confront questions and problems of regional scope.

The results of such a session may be published in a variety of formats. We have elected to present the roundtable as a discussion (rather than as a narrative summary, for example), for two reasons. First, this format makes it easy to identify which individual controls which data. Second, and perhaps most important, the discussion format is a good way to convey to the reader a sense of the strengths and weaknesses of our current understanding of Gulf coast prehistory, as well as the great variety of perspectives that exist among Gulf coast archaeologists. Recognition of weaknesses in the data base, coupled with a diversity of theoretical orientations, can be a valuable prelude to better research.

The discussion was ably moderated by James Griffin. Other participants were Lawrence Aten, David Brose, Ian Brown, Dave Davis, Sherwood Gagliano, Marco Giardino, John Gibson, William Haag, Vernon J. Knight, Jr., Jerald Milanich, Robert Neuman, J. Richard Shenkel, and Stephen Williams. The transcript has been edited when necessary to maintain consistency in themes.

The terminal Archaic and Early Woodland

Fiber-tempered ceramics

Griffin: Some of the first sound evidence that we have of external contacts with the Gulf coast is the appearance, apparently spreading from the coastal Georgia and Florida areas, of ceramic material across the Southeast. What potential routes might that have taken? I don't know of fiber-tempered materials that moved from that area across the coast. Does anyone know of fiber-tempered material in coastal Alabama, Mississippi, or Louisiana?

Davis: There is fiber-tempered material at the Claiborne site (22HA-501) in west coastal Mississippi.

Gibson: It's been found at several sites on the Vermilion River, with decorations that are in the Tchefuncte style. The sites include Ruth Canal (USL16SM9), Olivier (USL16SL2), and Meche (USL16SL25).

Griffin: When you say Tchefuncte style, could you be a little more specific?

Gibson: It has drag-and-jab. . . .

Brose: There are Stallings Island sherds upstream on the Chattahoochee [White 1981]. We really don't know what's downstream.

Griffin: Coming up from the Tombigbee?

Knight: That Norwood material has a very wide distribution. It goes all the way up the Chattahoochee to the fall line [see, e.g., McMichael and Kellar 1960: 63]. There has never been a consensus about what to call the fiber-tempered ceramics of the lower Chattahoochee River. Many sites yielding fiber-tempered pottery, from the fall line to the Florida coast, have produced only plain sherds, with abundant grit inclusions. This material would fit comfortably within Phelps's Norwood series [Phelps 1965]. On the other hand, certain (earlier?) sites in the same geographical range have yielded samples of fiber-tempered ceramics with less grit inclusion, frequently classified as Stallings Island Plain. As Brose points out, at the few sites where decorated fiber-tempered ceramics have been found [e.g., 1LE1 (McMichael and Keller 1960: 222); 1HO22 (Huscher 1964: 14); 1RU58 (Chase 1978)], the decorations are fairly clearly Stallings Island–derived.

Brose: It's up in all the little spring heads, in the bluffs, and. . . .

Knight: There are sporadic occurrences of fiber-tempered sherds in the Mobile area, but as far as I know every one of them is undecorated.

Brose: Phelps's Norwood material [1966a, 1969] found near the coast, is mostly plain. But farther up the Chattahochee, the material really looks like Stallings Island, although it's very rare. We dug three sites on the bluffs near Torreya, where I-10 crosses the Apalachicola, and . . . out of about 150 sherds I think we got one that was decorated [Brose and Scarry n.d.]. It looks like Stallings Island drag-and-jab.

Griffin: Does no one have any sound dates on this material?

Brose: I certainly don't.

Knight: On the Chattahoochee it appears to persist and apparently shows up for some reason all the way into Cartersville, which is Middle Woodland.

Shenkel: Woody, do you have a date on Claiborne?

Gagliano: It's about 3200 B.P.

Knight: I think fiber-tempered lasts that late on the Georgia coast too, doesn't it?

Griffin: How late?

Knight: Up until around A.D. 100.

Milanich: It's found in Deptford contexts on the Georgia coast. Phelps [1966a: 19] got a date of 1012 B.C. ± 120 on the Norwood site.

Griffin: We have two potential routes, one along the coast and the other perhaps from the Savannah River across into Tennessee.

Williams: Is there anything else that ties them together?

Milanich: There are fiber-tempered camp sites from the Georgia coast down and across North Florida to the Gulf coast, as well as all the way down to southwest Florida and Miami.

Late Archaic and Early Woodland lithic materials

Griffin: Do the projectile point styles have any similarity across the coastal area at this time?

Milanich: The ones on the Georgia coast and across North Florida and on the Florida Gulf coast are the Christmas tree–shaped Archaic projectile points. They don't look like Pontchartrain points. On the Georgia coast there are some engraved and plain bone pins. I think there are occasional Poverty Point objects with fiber-tempered material over in northwest Florida.

Williams: What about the red jasper technology?

Milanich: There are some occasional pieces, but not in good context. . . . Many of the stemmed points from Florida actually appear to be knives. They have the characteristic crushing on the edges and were probably hafted.

Griffin: Is there any evidence in this period for trade in lithic materials across the Gulf coast, running from the interior along the Gulf or being spread along the coast?

Gibson: I would say there is in the Vermilion, in a fiber-tempered context. Frank Servello has dug the Meche Mound with fiber-tempered pottery at the base that has yielded novaculite. . . .

Griffin: Certainly one of the things that ought to be looked for in the future is the interchange between the coastal area and the near interior, coming down in flint materials, for example.

Brose: In Mobile Bay most of the tools are made of quartzite that shows up in a big band across the Tombigbee about 45 miles above the delta—Tallahatta quartzite.

Gagliano: That shows up at the mouth of the Pearl River with fiber-tempered pottery as well [Gagliano and Webb 1970: 66], and a little bit of that gets to Poverty Point.

The spread of Early Woodland pottery and shell artifacts

Griffin: What other things might be observed between the period of about 1000 B.C. and the birth of Christ that indicate coastal interchange?

Shenkel: Well, the ideas for the designs on Tchefuncte pottery are all eastern.

Knight: There are Bayou La Batre connections.

Shenkel: Is there any grog-tempered material over on the St. Johns in the east? Is there anything the Tchefuncte could have copied when they adopted pottery?

Milanich: A lot of pottery, even up to 20 percent, at Gulf sites during the Deptford period has sponge spicules in it, as St. Johns pottery often does. I suspect you get freshwater sponge spicules all over the Gulf coast. But because pottery looks like St. Johns does not mean it came from East Florida.

Gibson: Who identified the sponge spicules in the pottery from Poverty Point?

Haag: I did—rather, I had a geologist at LSU examine them under an electron microscope.

Aten: About 12 or 15 years ago, I had a series of about two dozen thin sections made of fiber-tempered pottery from East Florida, South Louisiana, and Texas. The only ones that had sponge spicules were the St. Johns sherds.

Milanich: In Florida there are spiculite clays in a lot of places, but they didn't always use those clays to make pottery. [After the conference, Milanich and Aten corresponded about sponge spicules in fiber-tempered pottery. A series of 10 St. Johns region fiber-tempered sherds was examined; some had sponge spicules and some did not.]

Griffin: So, we have indications of possible trade, exchange, or spread of ideas across the Gulf area and in the interior on the basis of the ceramic material, on the basis of the Poverty Point objects, and on the basis of the microflint industry which comes down and is found in the Pearl delta, maybe in the Mobile, on the West Florida coast, but doesn't seem to go farther east than that; and other than these, there's not much evidence of the spread of ideas across the area.

Gagliano: Jon, which of those elements are present around Lafayette?

Gibson: Biconical Poverty Point objects, the exotic stones, gray-blue flints and novaculite. . . .

Williams: Is there any copper that comes down?

Gibson: Yes, there's copper at Claiborne at the Pearl River mouth.

Williams: And there's a little at Poverty Point.

Griffin: Is there any emphasis upon the production of shell materials that might be represented in coastal exchange?

Aten: In the Texas coastal bend area around Corpus Christi and farther south we do get large conch growing in the estuaries. Of course, there were large conch artifacts found at the George C. Davis site. With a couple of exceptions, I am not aware of them being found at many other places, except for columella beads. The only conch shell industry (other than beads, occasional whorl pendants, adzes, and projectile points) of which there is any evidence on the Texas coast is in the Brownsville area where they were making *Olivella* tinklers and some other triangular-shaped objects in great quantities. This material may have been going down to Mexico, because there is a fair amount of evidence of Huastecan trade or at least Huastecan artifacts in that area [Suhm, Krieger, and Jelks 1954: 130–34]. It's possible that some of the large conch material was coming from the central Texas coast, but there just isn't any hard evidence of where it was obtained or how it was transported.

Gagliano: *Busycon* still occurs in the Mississippi Sound today.

Shenkel: At Big Oak (16OR6) we have *Busycon* adzes and *Strombus* celts. The *Busycon* adzes are cut around the rim and unifacially sharpened. The *Strombus* celts are bifacially bashed and ground down.

Milanich: *Strombus* is not native to the Mississippi delta area.

Griffin: Now, moving west of the Mississippi, the first indication of real connections along the coast is the appearance of "Tchefunctoid" pottery which is known in the lower Sabine, a little bit into Galveston Bay. . . .

Brown: Alexander Incised turns up in the western delta region in Cameron Parish, Louisiana, on the very western side of the chenier plain [Charles Bollich, personal communication].

Griffin: With the punctates and the nodes?

Brown: Yes.

Griffin: So this Alexander pottery could be in the last part of the millenium before Christ. Presumably the "Tchefunctoid" pottery is going west at some earlier period.

Aten: In the Sabine there is a lot of lower Mississippi valley pottery, with not as much variety: a lot of Tchefuncte Plain, no rocker stamping at all, and yet we have sherds from a perfectly fine Tchefuncte

Stamped vessel from the Galveston area. However, there are almost no other types of Louisiana pottery from around Galveston Bay.

Griffin: So that about does it for demonstrable interconnections.

Mounds in the Late Archaic and Early Woodland

Brose: What about mounds themselves?

Neuman: We don't have any Tchefuncte mounds on the Louisiana coast.

Shenkel: We have only two sets of Tchefuncte sites on the coast: Lake Pontchartrain and Weeks Island. The rest are interior Tchefuncte.

Neuman: What Poverty Point mounds have been excavated on the Louisiana coast?

Haag: The Banana Bayou mound (16IB24).

Brown: I'd put that more in the Late Archaic.

Shenkel: The Hornsby site—is that a mound that's Archaic?

Gibson: Yes.

Shenkel: In Poverty Point times that was the coast because that was the north shore of Lake Pontchartrain.

Gagliano: It is a good distance up the Amite River from Lake Maurepas.

Gibson: How strong is the evidence for mounds in Deptford?

Milanich: On the Atlantic coast, David Thomas [Thomas and Larsen 1979] dug some sites on St. Catherine Island that I feel certain are early Deptford. There are little mounds beginning about 400 B.C. that overlie earlier middens. There is an early mound that Ripley Bullen [Bullen, Bullen, and Bryant 1967] dug at Ross Hammock over at Canaveral that was, I would say, 200 B.C. It had a log tomb, but it was quite like those mounds that Dave Thomas dug at St. Catherine. On the Gulf coast there are a couple of Deptford burials [Willey 1949: 38–39; Bunn 1971], but they are not in mounds.

Shenkel: What about the mound at Claiborne?

Gagliano: A small conical mound was associated with the ring at Claiborne, but it was destroyed before it could be investigated. There was also a small mound at Garcia (16OR3Y). Again it was a multicomponent site, and the mound eroded away before anyone looked at it.

Griffin: Could any reasonable person want to put mound appearance back before 500 B.C.?

Milanich: What is Banana Bayou? What are the dates from that site?

Brown: We have only the date that Woody Gagliano got, which puts it back in the third millennium B.C., but I don't accept that. But the materials that I have seen from the lower mantle are Late Archaic. One of the four or five points is a good Pontchartrain Point.

Haag: Of course, we got a date on pure charcoal from the Monte Sano Mound of 4200 B.C.

Middle Woodland

Louisiana and Texas

Griffin: Let's move on to the Marksville period. Of the many Marksville sites recorded in Alan Toth's thesis, I think that 5–10 percent of them have mounds. In the Marksville period there is not much evidence of burial mounds in the Mississippi delta area. Is there much evidence on the coast for burial mounds between the time of Christ and A.D. 300?

Brown: The Veazey site (16VM7,8) on Pecan Island had anywhere from 11 to 20 conical mounds in a sort of circular arrangement. Nine or 10 of them are still out there on the various wings of the chenier.

Griffin: Let's go west first. In the lower Sabine area, from Galveston Bay, is there much evidence of burial mounds?

Aten: None.

Griffin: Then to the east, how about Mobile Bay or the mouth of the Pearl River?

Knight: Just McQuorquodale (1CK25), which is very far up [Wimberly and Tourtelot 1941].

Brose: That is the only one published, but C. B. Moore recorded more than 50 sites up the Tombigbee, above the delta.

Davis: Do Jon and Woody have any consensus on the age of the Gibson mound?

Brown: Gibson has a strong Coles Creek component.

Gibson: There are some "Marksville" sherds, including cross-hatched rims. Richard Weinstein got a date of 1075 ± 60 B.P. (A.D. 875) [Weinstein, Burden, Brooks, and Gagliano 1978].

Davis: Is there any other type of Marksville material besides cross-hatched rims?

Gibson: There were only two or three sherds, and those were in mound fill.

Griffin: Would we be correct in the inference that these mounds along the coast are derived from mound complexes to the north?

Brose: I think so. There don't seem to be any mounds, whether you call them Yent, Green Point, or whatever, that don't have some evidence of northern exchange.

Griffin: Does anyone want to argue about this?

Milanich: I suspect that mounds such as two near Tarpon Springs, Safford (8PI3) [Bullen, Partridge, and Harris 1970], and Hope (8PA12) [Smith 1971] are in that A.D. 200–400 period. They don't necessarily have nonlocal grave furniture in them.

Brose: That's the same kind of pottery that appears in mounds farther north along the coast that have got copper spears, mica, and ear spools.

Griffin: Did some of the Tarpon Springs sites have zoned rocker stamping?

Milanich: I don't think so.

Aten: One comment is pertinent to this point as far as Texas is concerned. Although Tchefuncte pottery gets over as far as Galveston, immediately after the Tchefuncte pottery is gone, at about A.D. 300, we don't see any Louisiana material west of the Sabine until A.D. 950 or 1000.

Gibson: It probably stops at the mouth of the Mermentau, because the Cameron and Vermilion Parish coast does not look anything like our lower valley sequence. [The southwest Louisiana coast, west of the Mermentau River, is ceramically unique. With only a few exceptions on the cheniers, pottery is predominantly plain with fabrics dominated by the natural inclusions found in local clays (i.e., they are "untempered") during all periods. Lower valley–"inspired" designs are rare to nonexistent (cf. Gibson 1975, 1981).]

Williams: What about projectile points? In northern Louisiana, at the Transylvania site, I have seen cross-hatched rims and Snyders Corner–notched that looks like Crescent City chert. Do you get Snyders points on the coast?

Brose: In Florida, it's more of the little Christmas trees again.

Griffin: The farthest south I know for the occurrence of Snyders points is the Bynum mounds. It is abundantly clear that the Ohio Hopewell has little effect on the lower Mississippi valley in any direct way at all. Their primary means of communication was down the Tennessee into the headwaters of the Chattahoochee, but indications of interareal contacts along the coast during the Middle Woodland are primarily in terms of ceramics at the present time.

Aten: Ethnohistorically, there's a lot of discussion about birds being hunted and the feathers being exported out of the coast of Texas—

white bird feathers in particular [Aten 1979]. [This is reflected archaeologically by blunt bone projectile points which were presumably used to kill birds without discoloring the feathers.]

Milanich: What about red-painted pottery?

Voice: You certainly get it by Marksville times.

Gibson: There are seven sherds and one vessel of it at Crooks (16LA3) [Ford and Willey 1940: table 42].

Possible Weeden Island relationships with coastal Louisiana

Williams: Up at Norman, zoned red occurs quite frequently.

Milanich: At Weeden Island sites such as McKeithen (8CO17), the zoned red appears on flat plates [Milanich and Fairbanks 1980: 135]. We went through Willey's type collections, and nearly all of his zoned red comes from such flat oval plates. Some of them appear to have bird effigies on them.

Brose: I think that material is Weeden Island I, because it shows up at Pierce Mound A (8FR19) and at Green Point (8FR11), [Brose 1979], I would say at about A.D. 300–500.

Griffin: And during the period A.D. 300–500, one of the impressive things is how little evidence there is for trade along the coast— interaction, yes, but very little evidence for trade or exchange.

Aten: Texas at this time seems to be rather isolated. There are not only no Louisiana ceramics, but we also lose the large lithics such as dart points and large knives on materials from north and east Texas. We have bone projectile points for awhile, and then the use of bipolar technology to make very small projectile points, microliths, and so on—but nothing external.

Milanich: Some archaeologists have talked about ceramic similarities between Weeden Island and Coles Creek, but I would maintain that classic (early) Weeden Island ceramics are not around after A.D. 700. And when large quantities of Coles Creek and Weeden Island ceramics are compared, they don't look alike at all. There are specific sherds and some rim forms that are similar, but there aren't many.

Davis: But material has been called Coles Creek that covers as much as 700 years, and early Coles Creek is very different from terminal Coles Creek, at least in southeastern Louisiana. It depends upon what part of the period you're considering. In late Coles Creek, my impression is that French Fork drops off radically, red filmed material drops off. . . .

Brown: Not in south-central Louisiana. And although with the Coles

Creek incision the relationships are to the north, with check stamping the relationships are obviously to the east.

Brose: Most of the Weeden Island pottery is plain or check stamped.

Brown: It's the same in coastal Louisiana.

Brose: And all of your multiplicity of varieties, with that one exception, can be duplicated in western Florida.

Milanich: The ties are going to be Weeden Island I–Troyville and. . . .

Brose: The elaborate Weeden Island incised and punctated material disappears quickly, and what is left is the poorer quality Carrabelle, very sloppy Keith Incised, and a lot of check stamped and a lot of plain.

Williams: What Phil Phillips called late Issaquena—what I would prefer to call Troyville—it's in that period that much of the pottery looks like the material from Indian Pass.

Milanich: I sometimes wonder if a lot of that Indian Pass material doesn't come from the lower Mississippi valley.

Brown: Are there any comments or ideas about complicated stamping?

Neuman: The farthest north I've found it is Baptiste, and there's only one sherd from that site, probably associated with the Marksville component. The others I've studied all came from Troyville–Coles Creek contexts, but only a small number of them were excavated.

Davis: It's difficult, given the small amount of excavated materials, to talk precisely about its relative importance from one place to another within Louisiana. But certainly from the Sims and Bowie sites (16SC2 and 16LF17), and from Springer's site Bruly St. Martin (16IB6), complicated stamping comprises a very small amount of the total decorated ceramics, and it is the same in surface collections from Coles Creek sites in the eastern Mississippi River delta. And yet at the Morgan site [Brown, this volume], and evidently in surface collections from sites in Cameron Parish, it's much more important. We would expect it to be dropping off in those western areas.

Brown: Why is there again the same kind of gap in the eastern delta that we see with the Alexander series pottery?

Neuman: The real gap is in Mississippi.

Brown: On the Louisiana coast, most of the complicated stamping seems to occur in early Coles Creek.

Brose: It's early in Weeden Island, and is gone after about A.D. 500 or 600.

Milanich: There are really two kinds of complicated stamping in

Weeden Island contexts. One is what Sears would call Kolomoki Complicated Stamped, which means simply that it's in a band around the pot; the other is Swift Creek Complicated Stamped.

Neuman: A couple of sherds that I identified were shell tempered.

Brown: Was it an integral part of the paste, or only an incidental inclusion? I get shell-tempered, check-stamped pieces in collections of several thousand pieces, but there is shell everywhere you go on the cheniers.

Knight: Complicated stamping is virtually absent in coastal Alabama. There is just a handful of specimens.

Davis: What is the peak importance of complicated stamping as a percentage of decorated ceramics in Weeden Island?

Brose: About 15 percent.

Milanich: But there is also complicated stamping in Leon-Jefferson and Fort Walton, and it appears very late in coastal Georgia.

Brose: On the Florida Gulf coast there is a gap of at least 500 years after A.D. 600 during which there is almost no complicated stamping. Then it returns after A.D. 1200 and is very similar in design to the earlier material, although the temper is different. Some of the designs are different, but you generally need a large sample in order to make any chronological assignment at all.

Middle and Late Woodland burial patterns

Williams: Is there any mortuary evidence of coastal contacts between Louisiana and Florida?

Brose: Florida mortuary is like Ohio Hopewell in that almost every conceivable means of disposing of the dead was used: cremations, flexed, partly articulated; large mounds, small mounds, log tombs, platforms. . . .

Gibson: What about the east or north side caches?

Brose: There are east side caches toward middle Weeden Island, at roughly A.D. 400–600. But earlier, there are ceramics associated with individuals.

Williams: In the lower Mississippi valley, there are probably no more than a total of three burial vessels known from this period.

Brown: In the Mississippi River delta, I can't think of any.

Neuman: On the Grand Chenier, associated with check-stamped pottery, a zoologist excavated a burial in a flexed position. On its chest were six whooping crane bones, beautifully decorated with incised lines, hachures, checks, etc.

Aten: On the Texas coast at this period, I know of only one burial, of one individual, that is accompanied by a significant quantity of grave goods (Burial 2 at Harris County Boys School Cemetery, 41HR80) [Aten, Chandler, Wesolowsky, and Malina 1976: 59]. They include a set of incised and red painted bone dice, three flagellants, some deer ulna awls, and a number of shell beads.

Williams: So how far west are the elaborate Weeden Island burial customs found?

Brose: Possibly in Escambia County if William Sears [1977] is right in expecting such data from the as-yet unexcavated Mitchell site, which is the third in the triad that includes Kolomoki (9EK1) and McKeithen.

Milanich: Farther up in Alabama, aren't there some Weeden Island sites with caches?

Brose: Yes, but they are not very far up in Alabama.

Griffin: (to Milanich). Haven't you been revising your ideas about Weeden Island social organization?

Milanich: I think that from Poverty Point times up into Mississippian, there are no chiefdoms, but rather, segmented tribes. . . . This would explain the anomalous nature and brief duration of such sites as McKeithen.

The Mississippian period

Griffin: Let us move into the Mississippian period. At the time I wrote my article in *Science* [Griffin 1967], one of my main goals was to get away from using ceramic identification for what I regard as large-scale development taking place in the period after A.D. 700 or so which cropped up in several areas either by spread or based upon developments from a common economic-subsistence base. What about the possibility of such a spread on the Gulf coast? Could anything in Louisiana be attributable to something called "Pensacola"?

Pensacola complex

Knight: I think you can talk about something called the Pensacola ceramic complex that extends all the way from the Mississippi River delta to Choctawhatchee Bay; within that there are different stylistic pockets. It occurs first at, I'd guess, about A.D. 1250 in Mobile Bay.

Williams: Are there ceramic shapes that go with it?

Brose: Yes, there are short-necked bottles, cazuela bowls, incurved bowls, beakers, and jars.

Knight: There are also nice burnished plates.

Brose: But those turn up throughout Mississippian.

Williams: No, they don't come down the Mississippi River.

Brose: Well, they're in Tennessee, Alabama, and Georgia.

Griffin: Clearly connected with Moundville.

Brose: So is Mississippian.

Knight: There is a lot of Natchez-like material in later Pensacola. [Particularly in the Hogstown Bayou–Point Washington subarea of northwest Florida, designs on such types as Pensacola Three-Line Incised and Point Washington Incised are clearly related to the style of Fatherland Incised on a protohistoric time level (cf. Willey 1949: 463).]

Williams: What about the shapes?

Knight: On bowls, and certainly not coming out of Moundville.

Brose: Pensacola doesn't come out of Moundville. In fact, there are few Pensacola vessels at Moundville.

Griffin: But I've seen vessels from the coast that must have been made at Moundville.

Brose: They may have been made at Bottle Creek (1BA18) [Bigelow 1853], because a lot of the pottery at Bottle Creek is very like Moundville.

Gagliano: Roger Saucier once plotted the percentage of shell-tempered wares from all of McIntire's [1958] surface collections, and we added the same information for some 50 collections from coastal Mississippi. There was a very patterned falloff from east coastal Mississippi to the western side of the Mississippi River delta. There are sites in coastal Mississippi, for example the Deer Island site, which has as much as 90 percent shell-tempered pottery.

Mississippian subsistence and settlement

Brose: In western Florida, Pensacola is not the earliest material that I would call Mississippian. In the Chattahoochee and Apalachicola valleys, there is a less spectacular Mississippian that appears as early as about A.D. 900. It's not that different from the intrusive material at Macon, or from Obion.

Shenkel: Is it not your impression that during the agricultural fluorescence that accompanies Mississippian there is a population decline in the Louisiana coastal zone compared to Coles Creek?

Davis: I think we have to temper our ideas about this supposed Coles Creek population expansion. It is true that there is a larger number of Coles Creek sites, but components that have been called Coles Creek cover a massive span of time, while Plaquemine is probably a much shorter period. Also, there may have been some consolidation of peoples in Plaquemine times.

Brown: What I'm seeing in south-central Louisiana between Coles Creek and Plaquemine is a settlement pattern shift to the salt domes. . . .

Shenkel: A shift to arable land habitats.

Brown: At least in part, although the marshes were still being exploited.

Gibson: There are real problems with growing corn in deltas.

Knight: Apparently not in Mobile. They were farming the annually flooded delta lands and regularly producing a surplus. The ethnohistory seems clear on that point.

Shenkel: In Louisiana, historical records suggest that the true coastal groups were mainly hunters and fishers.

Gagliano: Because of land subsidence and post-colonial land use, I think we've lost a large part of the settlement pattern picture. For example, a look at Magnolia Mound today suggests that there is very little topography. But at its peak, the site was 10 feet above sea level on a natural levee that was from a quarter to a half mile wide. Many of the other huge sites that were on natural levee crests have been destroyed because those areas were favored for modern construction.

Brose: In late Fort Walton, most of the sites are around Tallahassee, and the settlement system looks very much like the one inferred for Moundville. That is, there are one or two large ceremonial centers, then scattered out from those at eight- to nine-mile intervals are smaller single-mound or two-mound sites, then a series of little hamlets. This begins around A.D. 1250 or 1300. But this is not coastal. On the coast, there is very little Fort Walton east of Apalachicola. There are some little sites as far east as the Aucilla River. West of the Apalachicola River, we really only have the Fort Walton Mound (8OK1) and a number of small domestic sites that Lazarus and Hawkins [1976] have described the ceramics for. All of these, including the Fort Walton Mound, have admixtures of as much as 25 percent or so of Pensacola-like ceramics. East of the Apalachicola, Pensacola disappears. I believe that the Pensacola ceramics are quite late, that is, after A.D. 1250 or 1300, and that Fort Walton ceramics appear earlier in the area and are followed by a Pensacola stylistic spread from the west. The Fort Walton ceramics are also related to Moundville but only in a very tenuous way.

Other aspects of coastal interaction during the Mississippian

Williams: Are there any similarities to the Alabama River phase?

Brose: Half the Alabama River phase pottery has been called Fort Walton by one person or another and the rest has been called Pensacola.

Griffin: So, while there are similar adaptations along the coast and some very minor trade, most of the similarities indicating adoption of new ideas are coming down rivers from the north.

Brose: Other than connections between Fort Walton and Safety Harbor, that is certainly true.

Giardino: But our protohistoric material from the Sims site is much more similar even to Safety Harbor than to things upriver.

Gagliano: At the Buras Mounds (16PL13), which may be the southernmost Indian site on the Mississippi River, the pottery is a complete mixture of Pensacola-like material and more "traditional" lower valley Mississippian ceramics [Gagliano 1979]. It almost defies classification. I suspect that throughout Louisiana and elsewhere at the distal ends of distributaries we'll find quite a lot of admixture.

Gibson: I wonder what kinds of social or ethnic boundaries are indicated by these ceramics differences along the coast—within the Pensacola complex, for example.

Knight: It transcends a lot. The Pensacola ceramic complex almost certainly crosscuts a number of distinct cultural systems; among these, some appear to have been significantly more complex than others, reflecting different adaptations.

Haag: At times—and we're at such a time—we really have to first work out a good framework for culture history.

Griffin: We do have to recognize these regional variants in terms of their persistence through time.

Brose: There is no question of that. But once you've identified a reasonable block of space and time, there's not much justification for making a lot of assumptions about the affiliations of the groups within that block.

Giardino: We have no model that relates human behavior to the potsherd. We don't have the bridge. . . .

Brose: There is no bridge.

Milanich: If you're going to talk about change through time, then you have to know about time, but. . . .

Knight: Change in what through time?

Brose: One question is, do we see anything really different after A.D. 1000, or is it just. . . .

Griffin: Not really different. The amount of demonstrable interaction along the coastal strip is not very great. We can see that similar things were going on in these different places, so the assumption is that there must have been interaction that we don't recognize.

Shenkel: Would you say that from the early Woodland to the Mississippian each one of the systems that you delineated set out its own series of adaptive evolutions, with each system representing one persisting group of people, each neighboring system borrowing applicable ideas as they might be used in their own system?

Griffin: I would say that that is true, at least to the extent that they are sharing a relatively common environment.

Williams: Would you say that this coastal strip is not a very innovative area?

Knight: I would say that they are economically conservative. . . .

Brose: In terms of ceramics, I think that they are innovative.

Gibson: There are numerous "dynamic habitat" models, but we are missing the "dynamic people" models.

Brown: Does anyone think that migrations did not occur?

Griffin: I can't think of any migrations that would be demonstrable on the coast.

Brown: It's too unpopular to think in those terms now. I can't think of any either.

Brose: Even the differences among ceramic complexes are less overwhelming than the initial indications would have led one to believe. When we were first looking at this material and had two sites that were separated by 500 years, they looked very different; but when we got 15 sites that fell in that gap, they didn't look that different anymore.

Giardino: A large migration of people would be a very peculiar historical event.

Knight: I think we have to take these historically documented migrations and see exactly what they look like in the ground.

Neuman: The only good evidence we have for real population movements are the Sioux moving onto the Plains after 1750, and there they changed so radically that you could not recognize them archaeologically.

Brose: People 50 years ago were looking at a constellation of stratified societies, intensive agriculture, mound building, shell-tempered pottery, particular vessel shapes, common designs. And when you wanted to find it all at once, you looked at the place where it occurred earliest, then you found it later somewhere else. What we have seen in the last 30 years is that these traits came together at different times at different places and had different developmental histories.

Knight: Before, we had population intrusion as an explanation, and now we simply have no explanation.

Brose: The migration alternative simply doesn't work.

Knight: Some of these traits clearly are spreading from one area to another. But we lack the kinds of models that would allow us to account for both short- and long-term stylistic concurrences across large spans of the coastal zone.

References

Adams, Grey L., and Lazarus, William C.
  1960 Two Skulls from a Fort Walton Period Cemetery Site (OK-35), Okaloosa County, Florida. *Florida Anthropologist* 13:92–99.
Albrecht, Andrew C.
  1945 The Origin and Early Settlement of Baton Rouge, Louisiana. *Louisiana Historical Quarterly* 28(1):5–68.
Altschul, J. H.
  1978 *The Houma-Terrebonne Archaeological Project.* New World Research, Report of Investigations 10.
Ambler, Richard J.
  1973 *The Lost River Phase of the Lower Trinity River Delta.* Austin: Texas Archaeological Survey, University of Texas.
Anderson, David G.
  1979 Prehistoric Selection for Intentional Thermal Alteration. *Midcontinental Journal of Archaeology* 4(2):221–54.
Anonymous
  1974 Archaeological Finds in Tallahassee. *Archives and History News* 5(5):2. Tallahassee: Division of Archives, History, and Records Management, Florida Department of State.
Aten, Lawrence E.
  1966a Late Quaternary Surface Geology of the Lower Trinity River Area, Southeastern Texas. Manuscript, Geology Department, University of Houston.
  1966b Late Quaternary Alluvial History of the Lower Trinity River, Texas: A Preliminary Report. In *An Archaeological Survey of Wallisville Reservoir, Chambers County, Texas,* edited by Harry J. Shater. Texas Archaeological Salvage Project, Survey Report 2. Austin: University of Texas.
  1967 *Excavations at the Jamison Site (41LB2), Liberty County, Texas.* Houston Archaeological Society Report 1.
  1971 *Archaeological Excavations at the Dow-Cleaver Site, Brazoria County, Texas.* Texas Archaeological Salvage Project, Technical Bulletin 1. Austin: University of Texas.
  1972 *An Assessment of the Archaeological Resources to be Affected by the Taylors Bayou Drainage and Flood Control Project, Texas.* Texas Archaeological Salvage Project, Research Report 7. Austin: University of Texas.

1979 Indians of the Upper Texas Coast: Ethnohistoric and Archaeological Frameworks. Ph.D. dissertation, University of Texas at Austin.

1981 Determining Seasonality of *Rangia Cuneata* from Gulf Coast Shell Middens. *Texas Archaeological Society Bulletin* 52:179–200.

1983a *Indians of the Upper Texas Coast.* New York: Academic Press.

1983b Analysis of Discrete Habitation Units in the Trinity River Delta, Upper Texas Coast. Texas Archaeological Research Laboratory Occasional Papers No. 2.

Aten, Lawrence E., and Bollich, Charles N.
1969 A Preliminary Report on the Development of a Ceramic Chronology for the Sabine Lake Area of Texas and Louisiana. *Texas Archaeological Society Bulletin* 40:241–58.

Aten, Lawrence E.; Chandler, Charles K.; Wesolowsky, A. B.; and Malina, Robert
1976 *Excavations at the Harris County Boys School Cemetery: Analysis of Galveston Bay Area Mortuary Practices.* Texas Archaeological Society, Special Publication 3.

Baerreis, David A., and Bryson, Reid A.
1965 Climatic Episodes and the Dating of the Mississippi Cultures. *Wisconsin Archaeologist* 46:203–20.

Baerreis, David A.; Bryson, Reid; and Kutzbach, Joan
1976 Climate and Culture in the Western Great Lakes Region. *Midcontinental Journal of Archaeology* 1(1):39–58.

Bandelier, A. F.
1905 *The Journey of Alvar Nuñez Cabeza de Vaca.* New York: A. S. Barnes and Company.

Barth, Frederik, editor
1969 *Ethnic Groups and Boundaries: The Social Organization of Cultural Differences.* London: George Allen and Unwin.

Beavers, Richard C.
1978 *An Archaeological Reconnaissance and Assessment of the Sabine River, North Shore of Sabine Lake to the Gulf Intracoastal Waterway: Cameron, Calcasieu Parishes, Louisiana and Orange County, Texas.* University of New Orleans Archaeological and Cultural Research Program Research Report 1.

Beers, William, (editor)
1911 Early Census of Louisiana. *Louisiana Historical Quarterly* 5.

Bell, Robert E.
1958 *Guide to the Identification of Certain American Indian Projectile Points.* Oklahoma Anthropological Society, Special Bulletin 1.

1960 *Guide to the Identification of Certain American Indian Projectile Points.* Oklahoma Anthropological Society, Special Bulletin 2.

Belmont, John S.
1967 The Culture Sequence at the Greenhouse Site, Louisiana. *Southeastern Archaeological Conference Bulletin* 6:27–34.

Belovich, Stephanie; Brose, David; and Weisman, Russell; with contributions by Nancy White
1982 Archaeology at Lake Seminole: Final Report on the Cultural Resources Survey and Evaluation of Lake Seminole, Alabama, Georgia, and Florida. Submitted to the U.S. Army Corps of Engineers, Mobile District.

Bense, Judith A.
1978 Preliminary Report on the McFadden Site (8By104): A Norwood/Early Deptford and Ft. Walton Village in the St. Andrews Bay Drainage System of Northwest Florida. Paper presented at the 30th Annual Meeting of the Florida Anthropological Society, Fort Walton Beach.

Bernabo, J. C., and Webb, Thomas III
1977 Changing Patterns in the Holocene Pollen Record of Northeastern North America: A Mapped Summary. *Quaternary Research* 8(2):64–96.

Bernard, H. A., and LeBlanc, R. J.
1965 Resumé of the Quaternary Geology of the Northwestern Gulf of Mexico. In

The Quaternary History of the United States, edited by H. G. Wright, Jr., and D. G. Frey, pp. 132–86. Princeton: Princeton University Press.

Bernard, H. A.; Major, C. F.; Parrott, B. S.; and LeBlanc, R. J., Sr.
1970   *Recent Sediments of Southeast Texas: A Field Guide to the Brazos Alluvial and Deltaic Plains and the Galveston Barrier Island Complex.* University of Texas Bureau of Economic Geology, Guidebook 2.

Berry, L. G., and Mason, Brian
1959   *Mineralogy.* San Francisco: W. H. Freeman and Company.

Bienville, Jean Baptist, and Le Moyne, Sieur De
n.d.   The Indians of Louisiana, Their Population and Trading That Can Be Done with Them. *In* A Miscellany of Louisiana Historical Records, Works Progress Administration Survey of Federal Archives of Louisiana. Typescript, Howard-Tilton Library, Tulane University.

Bigelow, Andrew
1853   Observations on Some Mounds on the Tensaw River. *American Journal of Science* 65: 186–92.

Bonnin, Jack C., and Weinstein, Richard A.
1975   The Strohe Site. *Louisiana Archaeological Society Newsletter* 2(1): 8.
1978   The Strohe Site (16JD10), Jefferson Davis Parish, Louisiana. Paper presented at the 4th Annual Meeting of the Louisiana Archaeological Society, Baton Rouge.

Boone, P. A.
1974   Geology of Coastal Alabama. In *The Environment of Offshore and Estuarine Alabama.* Geological Survey of Alabama, Information Series 51.

Boyd, Mark F.
1958   *Historic Sites in and around the Jim Woodruff Reservoir Area, Florida–Georgia.* In River Basin Surveys Papers no. 13, Bureau of American Ethnology Bulletin 169: 195–314. Washington: Smithsonian Institution.

Boyd, Mark; Smith, Hale G.; and Griffin, John W.
1951   *Here They Once Stood: The Story of the Spanish Missions in Northern Florida.* Gainesville: University of Florida Press.

Brain, Jeffrey P.
1969   Winterville: A Case Study of Prehistoric Culture Contact in the Lower Mississippi Valley. Ph.D. dissertation, Yale University.
1977   *On the Tunica Trail.* Louisiana Archaeological Survey and Antiquities Commission, Anthropology Study 1. Baton Rouge.
1979   *Tunica Treasure.* Papers of the Peabody Museum of Archaeology and Ethnology 71. Cambridge: Harvard University.

Brannon, Peter A.
1909   Aboriginal Remains in the Middle Chattahoochee Valley of Alabama and Georgia. *American Anthropologist* 9(2): 186–98.

Brooks, C. E. P.
1949   *Climate through The Ages: A Study of Climatic Factors and Their Variations.* 2d rev. ed. London: E. Benn.

Brose, David S.
1974   A Proposal to the National Science Foundation for Support of Research on Systematic Relationships of Diffusion, Demography, and Cultural Ecology in Prehistory: Archaeological Analysis of Mississippian Origins in Northwest Florida as a Test of Alternative Models. Manuscript, Department of Anthropology, Case Western Reserve University, Cleveland.
1975   Case Western Reserve University Contributions to the 1973 Excavations at the Cayson Site and the Yon Site. Manuscript, Division of Archives, History, and Records Management, Florida Department of State, Tallahassee.
1979   An Interpretation of the Hopewellian Traits in Florida. In *Hopewell Archaeology: The Chillocothe Conference,* edited by David S. Brose and N'omi Greber, pp. 141–49. Kent, Ohio: Kent State University Press.

1980a   Coe's Landing (8Ja137), Jackson County, Florida: A Fort Walton Campsite on
        the Apalachicola River. *Bulletin* 6: 1–31. Tallahassee: Bureau of Historic Sites
        and Properties, Florida Department of State.
1980b   Time Zones and Prehistory in the Lower Chattahoochee/Flint/Apalachicola
        River Valleys. Paper presented at the 37th Annual Meeting of the South-
        eastern Archaeological Conference, New Orleans.
Brose, David S., and Percy, George W.
1974a   Weeden Island Settlement—Subsistence and Ceremonialism: A Reappraisal
        in Systemic Terms. Paper presented at the 39th Annual Meeting of the Society
        for American Archaeology, Washington.
1974b   Fort Walton Settlement. Paper presented at the 39th Annual Meeting of the
        Society for American Archaeology, Washington.
1978   Fort Walton Settlement Patterns. In *Mississippian Settlement Patterns*, edited by
        Bruce D. Smith, pp. 81–108. New York: Academic Press.
Brose, David S., and Scarry, John F.
n.d.   Report to the Florida Division of Archives, History, and Records Management
        on the 1975 Archaeological Investigations of Three Upland Lake Archaic
        Sites (8Gd 14, 15, and 16) along the East Bank Apalachicola River I-10 R/W
        Bridge Project, Gadsden County, Florida. Division of Archives, History, and
        Records and Management, Florida Department of State, Tallahassee.
Brose, David S., and Wilkie, Duncan C.
1980   A Fort Walton Campsite (8Ja201) at the Scholz Steam Plant Parking Lot, Jack-
        son County, Florida. *Florida Anthropologist* 33(4): 172–206.
Brose, David S.; Essenpreis, Patricia; Scarry, John; Bluestone, Helga; and Forsythe,
    Anne
1976   Contributions to the Archaeology of Northwest Florida: Investigations of
        Early Fort Walton Sites in the Middle Apalachicola River Valley. Report of the
        Cleveland Museum of Natural History and Case Western Reserve University
        to Division of Archives, History, and Records Management, Florida Depart-
        ment of State, Tallahassee.
Brown, Calvin S.
1926   *Archaeology of Mississippi.* Mississippi Geological Survey, University of Mis-
        sissippi.
Brown, Clair A.
1936   The Vegetation of the Indian Mounds, Middens and Marshes in Plaquemines
        and St. Bernard Parishes in the Lower Mississippi River Delta. In *Reports on
        the Geology of Plaquemines and St. Bernard Parishes*, pp. 423–40. New Orleans:
        Louisiana Department of Conservation.
1938   The Flora of Pleistocene Deposits in Western Florida Parishes, Western Feli-
        ciana Parish, and East Baton Rouge Parish, Louisiana. *Louisiana Department of
        Conservation Geological Survey Bulletin* 12: 59–96, 121–29.
Brown, Ian W.
1976   A Reexamination of the Houses of the Bayou Goula Site, Iberville Parish,
        Louisiana. *Louisiana Archaeology* 3: 193–205.
1978a   Archaeological Investigations on Avery Island, Louisiana, 1977–78. Paper
        presented at the 35th Annual Meeting of the Southeastern Archaeological
        Conference, Knoxville.
1978b   Archaeology on Avery Island, 1978. *Louisiana Archaeological Society Newsletter*
        5(4): 9–11.
1979a   *Archaeological Investigations at Salt Mine Valley (35-I-5).* Lower Mississippi
        Survey, Petite Anse Project Research Notes 8. Peabody Museum, Harvard
        University.
1979b   Certain Coastal Settlement Pattern Changes in the Petite Anse Region of
        Southwest Louisiana. Paper presented at the 36th Annual Meeting of the
        Southeastern Archaeological Conference, Atlanta.

1979c   A Late Mississippian Component in Southwest Louisiana: Ceramics from the Salt Mine Valley Site. Paper presented at the 36th Annual Meeting of the Southeastern Archaeological Conference, Atlanta.

1980a   Archaeological Investigations on Avery Island, Louisiana, 1977–78. *Southeastern Archaeological Conference Bulletin* 22:110–18.

1980b   *Archaeological Investigations at the Morgan Site (34-G-2), a Coles Creek Mound Complex on Pecan Island, Vermilion Parish, Louisiana.* Lower Mississippi Survey, Petite Anse Project Research Notes 12. Peabody Museum, Harvard University.

1980–81   The Morgan Site: An Important Coles Creek Mound Complex on the Chenier Plain of Southwest Louisiana. *North American Archaeologist* 2:207–37.

1981   *A Preliminary Investigation of Check Stamped Pottery in the Petite Anse Region.* Lower Mississippi Survey, Petite Anse Project Research Notes 9. Peabody Museum, Harvard University.

n.d.   *Archaeological Investigations in the Petite Anse Region, Southwest Louisiana, 1977–79.* Lower Mississippi Survey Bulletin. Peabody Museum, Harvard University.

Brown, Ian W., and Lambert-Brown, Nancy

1978a   Lower Mississippi Survey, Petite Anse Project Research Notes 1. Peabody Museum, Harvard University.

1978b   Lower Mississippi Survey, Petite Anse Project Research Notes 2. Peabody Museum, Harvard University.

1978c   *Plow Strip Survey.* Lower Mississippi Survey, Petite Anse Project Research Notes 3. Peabody Museum, Harvard University.

1978d   *Pepper Field Survey.* Lower Mississippi Survey, Petite Anse Project Research Notes 4. Peabody Museum, Harvard University.

1978e   *Archaeological Investigations at the Banana Bayou Mound (33-I-6).* Lower Mississippi Survey, Petite Anse Project Research Notes 5. Peabody Museum, Harvard University.

1978f   *1978 Excavations at Avery Island: Summary of the Current Petite Anse Project Research.* Lower Mississippi Survey, Petite Anse Project Research Notes 6. Peabody Museum, Harvard University.

1978g   *Archaeological Investigations at Hayes Pond Ridge (33-I-8), Vaughn's Clearing (33-I-12), and Middle Gate Bottom (33-I-33).* Lower Mississippi Survey, Petite Anse Project Research Notes 7. Peabody Museum, Harvard University.

1979   *The Mississippian Ceramics from Salt Mine Valley (33-I-5).* Lower Mississippi Survey, Petite Anse Project Research Notes 10. Peabody Museum, Harvard University.

Brown, Ian W.; Fuller, Richard S.; and Lambert-Brown, Nancy

1979   *Site Survey in the Petite Anse Region, Southwest Coast, Louisiana.* Lower Mississippi Survey, Petite Anse Project Research Notes 11. Peabody Museum, Harvard University.

Broyles, Bettye J.

1963   A Lamar Period Site in Southwest Georgia. In *Survey of Archaeological Sites in Clay and Quitman Counties, Georgia,* by A. R. Kelly, Richard Nonas, Bettye Broyles, Clemens De Baillou, David W. Chase, and Frank T. Schnell, Jr., pp. 29–35. University of Georgia Laboratory of Archaeology, Report 5. Athens.

Bryson, Reid, and Baerreis, David A.

1968   Climatic Change and the Mill Creek Culture of Iowa. *Iowa Archaeological Society Journal* 15(1):1–34.

Bryson, Reid, and Murray, Thomas

1977   *Climates of Hunger.* Madison: University of Wisconsin Press.

Bryson, Reid, and Wendland, Wayne M.

1967   Tentative Climatic Patterns for Some Late Glacial and Post Glacial Episodes in Central North America. In *Life, Land and Water,* edited by W. J. Mayer-Oakes, pp. 271–98. Winnipeg: University of Manitoba Press.

Bullen, Ripley P.
 1949 Indian Sites at Florida Caverns State Park. *Florida Anthropologist* 2(1): 1–9.
 1950 An Archaeological Survey of the Chattahoochee River Valley in Florida. *Journal of the Washington Academy of Sciences* 40: 101–25.
 1952 *Eleven Archaeological Sites in Hillsborough County, Florida.* Florida Geological Survey, Report of Investigations 8. Tallahassee.
 1958 *Six Sites near the Chattahoochee River in the Jim Woodruff Reservoir Area, Florida.* River Basin Surveys Papers, no. 14. Bureau of American Ethnology Bulletin 169: 315–57. Washington: Smithsonian Institution.
 1968 Report of the Florida-South Georgia Group. *Southeastern Archaeological Conference Bulletin* 8: 7–10.
 1971 Some Variations in Settlement Patterns in Peninsular Florida. *Southeast Archaeological Conference Bulletin* 13: 10–19.
 1974 The Origins of the Gulf Tradition as Seen from Florida. *Florida Anthropologist* 27(2): 77–88.
 1975 *A Guide to the Identification of Florida Projectile Points.* Rev. ed. Gainesville: Kendall Books.
Bullen, Ripley P., and Bullen, Adelaide K.
 1956 *Excavations on Cape Haze Peninsula, Florida.* Contributions of the Florida State Museum, Social Sciences 1. Gainesville.
Bullen, Ripley P.; Bullen, Adelaide K.; and Bryant, William J.
 1967 *Archaeological Investigations at the Ross Hammock Site, Florida.* The William J. Bryant Foundation, American Studies, Report 7. Orlando.
Bullen, Ripley P.; Partridge, William L.; and Harris, Donald A.
 1970 The Safford Burial Mound, Tarpon Springs, Florida. *Florida Anthropologist* 23(3): 81–118.
Bunn, Jennings W., Jr.
 1971 Excavation of a Deptford Midden Burial, Destin, Florida. *Florida Anthropologist* 24(4): 169–72.
Bushnell, David I., Jr.
 1917 The Chitimacha Indians of Bayou LaFourche, Louisiana. *Journal of the Washington Academy of Science* 7(10): 301–7.
Butler, Ruth (editor and translator)
 1934 *Journal of Paul DuRu.* Chicago: The Caxton Club.
Butson, Keith
 1962 *Climates of the States: Florida.* U.S. Department of Commerce, Environment Data SVC: Climatography of the United States 60-8.
Butzer, Karl W.
 1971 *Environment and Archaeology.* Chicago: Aldine.
Byrd, Kathleen Mary
 1974 Tchefuncte Subsistence Patterns: Morton Shell Mound, Iberia Parish, Louisiana. Master's thesis, Louisiana State University.
 1976a Brackish Water Clam (*Rangia cuneata*): Prehistoric "Staff of Life" or a Minor Food Resource? *Louisiana Archaeology* 3: 23–31.
 1976b Tchefuncte Subsistence: Information Obtained from the Excavation of the Morton Shell Mound, Iberia Parish, Louisiana. *Southeastern Archaeological Conference Bulletin* 19: 70–75.
Caldwell, Joseph Ralston
 1948 Palachacolas Town, Hampton County, South Carolina. *Journal of the Washington Academy of Sciences* 38: 321–24.
 1955 Investigations at Rood's Landing, Stewart County, Georgia. *Early Georgia* 2(1): 22–49.
 1958 *Trend and Tradition in the Prehistory of the Eastern United States.* American Anthropological Association, Memoir 88.
 1962 Eastern North America. In *Courses toward Urban Life*, edited by Robert J.

Braidwood and Gordon R. Willey, pp. 288–308. Viking Fund Publications in Anthropology 32.

n.d. Archaeological Research in the Jim Woodruff Reservoir. Manuscript, University of Georgia, Athens.

Caldwell, Joseph R., and McCann, Catherine
1941 *Irene Mound Site, Chatham County, Georgia.* Athens: University of Georgia Press.

Caldwell, Joseph R., and Smith, Betty A.
1978 Report of the Excavations at Fairchild's Landing and Hare's Landing, Seminole County, Georgia. Manuscript, collated and edited by Betty A. Smith.

Caldwell, Joseph R., and Waring, Antonio J., Jr.
1939 Pottery Types. *Southeastern Archaeological Conference Newsletter* 1 (5–6).

Caldwell, Joseph R.; Thompson, Charles E.; and Caldwell, Sheila K.
1952 The Booger Bottom Mound: A Forsyth Period Site in Hall County, Georgia. *American Antiquity* 17(4): 319–28.

Campbell, T. N.
1959 Choctaw Subsistence: Ethnographic Notes from the Lincecum Manuscript. *Florida Anthropologist* 12(1): 9–24.

Carr, A., and Giwa, C. J.
1955 *Guide to the Reptiles, Amphibians, and Fresh Water Fishes of Florida.* Gainesville: Biological Division, Florida State Museum.

Catesby, Mark
1731–43 *The Natural History of Carolina, Florida, and The Bahama Islands.* 2 vol. London.

Cathcart, James L.
1945 Southern Louisiana and Southern Alabama in 1819: The Journal of James Leander Cathcart, edited by Walter Pritchard, Fred B. Kniffen, and Clair A. Brown. *Louisiana Historical Quarterly* 28: 735–892.

Chamberlain, Edward, Jr.
1960 *Florida Waterfowl Populations, Habitats, and Management.* Florida Game and Freshwater Fish Commission Technical Bulletin 7. Tallahassee.

Charlevoix, Pierre F. X. De
1923 *Journal of a Voyage to North America,* vols. 1 and 2, edited by L. P. Kellogg. Chicago: Caxton Club.
1977 *Charlevoix's Louisiana: Selections from the History and the Journal,* edited by C. E. O'Neill. Baton Rouge: Louisiana State University Press.

Chase, David W.
1959 *The Averett Culture.* Coweta Memorial Association Papers 1.
1962 A Definition of Lamar in Western Georgia. *Southeastern Archaeological Conference Newsletter* 8: 70–74.
1963 A Reappraisal of the Averett Complex. *Journal of Alabama Archaeology* 9(2): 49–61.
1968 Pottery Typology Committee for Central Alabama. *Southeastern Archaeological Conference Bulletin* 8: 11–22.
1978 Uchee Creek Site 4:1Ru58. *Journal of Alabama Archaeology* 24(1): 53–59.

Chorley, Richard J., and Kennedy, Barbara A.
1971 *Physical Geography: A Systems Approach.* London: Prentice-Hall International Inc.

Claiborne, J. F. H.
1880 *Mississippi as a Province, Territory and State,* vol. 1. Jackson, Mississippi: Power and Bardsdale.

Clark, John
1977 *Coastal Ecosystem Management: A Technical Manual for the Conservation of Coastal Zone Resources.* New York: John Wiley and Sons.

Clausen, C. J.; Cohen, A. D.; Emiliani, C.; Homan, J. H.; and Stipp, J. J.
1979 Little Salt Spring, Florida: A Unique Underwater Site. *Science* 203(4381): 609–14.

Clench, William J., and Turner, Ruth D.
1958 *Freshwater Mollusks of Alabama, Georgia, and Florida from the Escambia to the Suwanee River.* Florida State Museum, Biological Sciences Bulletin 1(3).

Clewell, A. F.
1971 Vegetation of the Apalachicola National Forest: An Ecological Perspective. Report, Office of the Forest Supervisor, U.S.D.A. Forest Service, Tallahassee.

Clouse, Roger A.
1978 *Man's Intervention in the Post-Wisconsin Vegetational Succession of the Great Plains.* University of Kansas, Department of Geography and Meteorology, Occasional Paper 4.

Coastal Environments, Inc.
1977 Cultural Resources Evaluation of the North Gulf of Mexico Continental Shelf. Vols. 1–3. Cultural Resources Management Study. Report for Interagency Archaeological Services, Office of Historic Preservation, National Park Services, U.S. Department of the Interior, Washington.

Cockrell, Wilbur A.
1970 Glades I and Pre-Glades Settlement and Subsistence Patterns on Marco Island (Collier County, Florida). Master's thesis, Florida State University.

Collins, Henry B.
1927a Potsherds from Choctaw Village Sites in Mississippi. *Journal of the Washington Academy of Sciences* 17(10): 259–63.
1927b *Archaeological Work in Louisiana and Mississippi.* Smithsonian Miscellaneous Collections 78(7): 200–207.
1932 Excavations at a Prehistoric Indian Village in Mississippi. *Proceedings of the United States National Museum* 79(32).
1941 Relationships of an Early Indian Cranial Series from Louisiana. *Journal of the Washington Academy of Science* 31(4): 145–55.

Comeaux, Malcolm (editor)
1976 An Early View of the Atchafalaya: The Lt. Enoch Humphrey Expedition of 1805. *Attakoin Gazette* 4.

Cook, T. G.
1976 Broad Point Culture, Phase Horizon, Tradition or Knife? *Journal of Anthropological Research* 32(4): 337–57.

Cooke, C. Wythe
1926 The Cenozoic Formations. In *Geology of Alabama.* Geological Survey of Alabama, Information Series 51.
1939 *Scenery of Florida.* The State Geological Survey, Bulletin 17.

Corthell, E. L.
1880 *A History of the Jetties at the Mouths of the Mississippi River.* New York: John Wiley and Sons.

Cottier, John
1968 Archaeological Salvage Investigations in the Miller's Ferry Lock and Dam Reservoir, Alabama. Report to the National Park Service, Atlanta.

Cox, Isaac Joslin
1905 *The Journeys of Rene Robert Cavalier, Sieur De La Salle.* Vols. 1 and 2. New York: Allerton Book Company.

Craig, A. J.
1969 Vegetational History of the Shenandoah Valley, Virginia. *Geological Society of America, Special Papers* 123: 283–96.

Crocker, T. C., Jr.
1963 Challenge of the Branch Bottoms in the Longleaf Forests of South Alabama. *Journal of the Alabama Academy of Science* 34: 138–39.

1969   Ecology of an Ideal Forest Community in the Longleaf–Slash Pine Region. In *The Ecology of Southern Forests*, edited by N. E. Linnartz. Baton Rouge: Louisiana State University Press.

Crosby, A. W.
1972   *The Columbian Exchange: Biological and Cultural Consequences of 1492.* Westport: Greenwood Press.

Cruzat, Heloise H.
1925   Documents Concerning the Sale of the Chouachas Plantation in Louisiana, 1737–38. *Louisiana Historical Quarterly* 8(4):594–646.
1940   Louisiana in 1724. Banet's Report to the Company of the Indies, Paris: December 20, 1724. *Louisiana Historical Quarterly* 23(2):120–63.

Cummings, William P.
1958   *The Southeast in Early Maps.* Princeton: Princeton University Press.

Curren, C. B., Jr.
1971   A Progress Report Conducted through an Agreement between the University of South Alabama Archaeological Research Program and the Archaeological Research Association of Alabama, Inc. Manuscript, University of South Alabama, Mobile.
1976   Prehistoric and Early Historic Occupation of the Mobile Bay and Mobile Delta Area of Alabama with an Emphasis on Subsistence. *Journal of Alabama Archaeology* 22(1):61–84.
1978   The Zooarchaeology of the D'Olive Creek Site (1Ba196), Baldwin County, Alabama. *Journal of Alabama Archaeology* 24(1):33–51.

Curry, Jan
1979   A History of the Houma Indians and Their Story of Federal Nonrecognition. *American Indian Journal* 5(2):9–28.

Cushing, Frank H.
1897   Explorations of Ancient Key Dwellers' Remains on the Gulf Coast of Florida. *Proceedings of the American Philosophical Society* 35(153):329–448.

Czajkowski, J. Richard
1934   Preliminary Report of Archaeological Excavations in Orleans Parish. *Louisiana Conservation Review* 4(3):12–18.

Darby, William
1816   A Geographical Description of the State of Louisiana . . . with an Account of the Character and Manners of the Inhabitants. Being an Accompaniment to the Map of Louisiana. Philadelphia: John Melish.

Daugherty, S. J.; Martin, J. R.; and Phelps, D. S.
1971   Florida State University Radiocarbon Dates IV. *Radiocarbon* 13(1):19–25.

Davis, Dave D.
1981   Ceramic Classification and Temporal Discrimination: A Consideration of Later Prehistoric Ceramic Change in the Mississippi River Delta. *Midcontinental Journal of Archaeology* 6(1):55–89.

Davis, Dave D., and Giardino, M. J.
1980   Some Notes Concerning Mississippian Period Ceramics in the Mississippi River Delta. *Louisiana Archaeology* 7:53–66.

Dean, Jeffrey S., and Robinson, William J.
1976   Dendro Climatic Variability in the American Southwest A.D. 680 to A.D. 1969. Report to the National Park Service, Laboratory of Tree-Ring Research, University of Arizona, Tucson.

Deetz, James
1965   *The Dynamics of Stylistic Change in Arikara Ceramics.* Illinois Studies in Anthropology 4. Urbana: University of Illinois Press.

DeJarnette, David L.
1952   Alabama Archaeology: A Summary. In *Archeology of Eastern United States*, edited by James B. Griffin, pp. 272–84. Chicago: University of Chicago Press.
1976   Highway Salvage Excavations at Two French Colonial Period Indian Sites on

Mobile Bay, Alabama. University of Alabama Museums. Manuscript, Mound State Monument, Moundville, Alabama.

DeJarnette, David L. (editor)

1975 *Archaeological Salvage in the Walter F. George Basin of the Chattahoochee River in Alabama.* University: University of Alabama Press.

DeJarnette, David L., and Wimberly, Steve B.

1941 *The Bessemer Site: Excavation of Three Mounds and Surrounding Village Areas Near Bessemer, Alabama.* Geological Survey of Alabama, Museum Paper 17.

DeJarnette, David L.; Anderson, H. V.; and Wimberly, S. B.

1941 Report on a Gulf State Park Shell Bank, 1Ba81, in Baldwin County, Alabama. Manuscript, Mound State Monument, Moundville, Alabama.

DeJarnette, David L.; Walthall, John A.; and Wimberly, Steve B.

1975a Archaeological Investigations in the Buttahatchee River Valley, Lamar County, Alabama. *Journal of Alabama Archaeology* 21(1):1–37.

1975b Archaeological Investigations in the Buttahatchee River Valley II: Excavations at Stuck's Bluff Rock Shelter. *Journal of Alabama Archaeology* 21(2): 99–119.

Delcourt, Hazel R., and Delcourt, Paul A.

1977 Presettlement Magnolia-Beech Climax of the Gulf Coastal Plain. Qualitative Evidence from the Apalachicola River Bluffs, North-Central Florida. *Ecology* 58:1085–93.

Delcourt, Paul A.

1978 Quaternary Vegetation History of the Gulf Coastal Plain. Ph.D. dissertation, University of Minnesota.

Delcourt, Paul A., and Delcourt, Hazel R.

1978a *Late Pleistocene and Holocene Distributional History of the Deciduous Forest in the Southeastern U.S.* Center for Quaternary Studies of the Southeastern U.S., Contribution 12. Oak Ridge: Oak Ridge National Laboratory.

1978b *Goshen Springs: A Late Quaternary Vegetation Record for Southern Alabama.* Center for Quaternary Studies of the Southeastern U.S., Contribution 10. Oak Ridge: Oak Ridge National Laboratory.

DeLeon, M. F.

1976 The Geographic Setting of Mobile Bay. *In* Highway Salvage Excavations at Two French Colonial Period Indian Sites on Mobile Bay, Alabama, edited by David L. DeJarnette. University of Alabama Museums. Manuscript, Mound State Monument, Moundville, Alabama.

DeLisle, Guillaume

1701 Carte des environs du Missisipi. Par G. de L'Isle Geogr. Donné par M. d'Iberville en 1701. Photocopy, Library of Congress.

1702 Carte de la Riviere de Mississippi. Sur le memoirs de M. Le Sueur qui en aupris avec la boussola tous les tours et detours depuis la mer jusque la Riviere St. Pierre et apris le hauteur du pole en plusiurs endroits. Louisiana State University Map Library.

Denten, G. H., and Karlen, W.

1973 Holocene Climatic Variations, Their Pattern and Possible Cause. *Quaternary Research* 13(2):155–205.

Dillehay, Tom D.

1974 Late Quaternary Bison Population Changes on the Southern Plains. *Plains Anthropologist* 19:180–96.

1975 *Prehistoric Subsistence Exploitation in the Lower Trinity River Delta, Texas.* Texas Archaeological Survey Research Report 51. Austin: University of Texas.

Diron d'Artaquiette

1916 1722–1723 Journal of Diron d'Artaquiette. In *Travels in the American Colonies*, edited by N. D. Mereness. New York: Macmillan.

Dobyns, H. F.
   1966   Estimating Aboriginal Population: An Appraisal of Techniques with a New
          Hemisphere Estimate. *Current Anthropologist* 7:395–416.
Dolan, Robert; Hayden, Bruce; and Lins, Harry
   1980   Barrier Islands. *American Scientist* 68:16–25.
Doran, J. E., and Hodson, F. R.
   1975   *Mathematics and Computers in Archaeology*. Cambridge: Harvard University
          Press.
DuBow, J. D. B.
   1847   The Mississippi, its Sources, Mouth, and Valley. *DuBows Review* 3:423–37.
Duhe, Brian J.
   1979   A Critical Analysis of the Paddle Stamp Tradition in Coastal Louisiana. Paper
          presented at the 5th Annual Meeting of the Louisiana Archaeological Society,
          Lake Charles.
   1981   A Study of Prehistoric Coles Creek–Plaquemine Cultural Technological
          Adaptations in the Upper Barataria Basin. *Southeastern Archaeological Confer-
          ence Bulletin* 24:34–37.
Dumont de Montigny, Louis Francis Benjamin
   1753   *Memories Historiques sur la Louisiane*. Vols. 1 and 2. Paris: J. B. Bauche.
DuPratz, Antoine Simon LePage
   1757   Carte de la Louisiane et Colonie Francaise avec le Cours du Fleuve St. Louis,
          Par M. LePage DuPratz, 1757. Louisiana State University Map Library.
   1758   *Histoire de la Louisiane*. Tomes I–III. De Bure, Paris.
   1774   *The History of Louisiana or of the Western Parts of Virginia and Carolina, Containing
          a Description of the Counties that Lie on Both Sides of the River Mississippi, with
          an Account of the Settlements, Inhabitants, Soil, Climate and Products*. London:
          T. Becker.
Dyer, J. O.
   1917   *The Lake Charles Attakapas (Cannibals): Period of 1817–1820*. Galveston: pri-
          vately printed.
Eggan, Fred
   1937   Historical Changes in Choctaw Kinship System. *American Anthropologist* 29:
          34–52.
Evans-Pritchard, E. E.
   1965   *Theories of Primitive Religions*. New York: Oxford University Press.
Fairbanks, Charles H.
   1952   Creek and Pre-Creek. In *Archeology of the Eastern United States*, edited by
          James B. Griffin, pp. 285–300. Chicago: University of Chicago Press.
   1955   The Abercrombie Mound, Russell County, Alabama. *Early Georgia* 2(1):
          13–19.
   1956   An Historic Check Stamped Pottery. In *Prehistoric Pottery of the Eastern United
          States*, assembled by James B. Griffin. Ann Arbor: University of Michigan.
   1958   Some Problems of the Origins of Creek Pottery. *Florida Anthropologist* 11(2):
          53–63.
   1960   Excavations at the Fort Walton Temple Mound. Report to the City of Fort
          Walton Beach, Florida.
   1964   The Early Occupations of Northwestern Florida. *Southeastern Archaeological
          Conference Bulletin* 1:27–30.
   1965a Excavations at the Fort Walton Temple Mound, 1960. *Florida Anthropologist*
          18(4):239–64.
   1965b Gulf Complex Subsistence Economy. *Southeastern Archaeological Conference
          Bulletin* 3:57–62.
   1971a Comments. In *Red, White and Black*, edited by C. Hudson, pp. 67–75. Ath-
          ens: University of Georgia Press.

1971b   The Apalachicola River Area of Florida. *Southeastern Archaeological Conference Newsletter* 10(2):38−40.

Ferguson, Vera M.
1951   *Chronology at South Indian Field, Florida.* Yale University Publications in Anthropology 45. New Haven.

Fewkes, J. Walter
1924   *Preliminary Archaeological Explorations at Weeden Island, Florida.* Smithsonian Miscellaneous Collections 73(13):1−26. Washington.

Fewkes, V. J.
1944   Catawba Pottery-Making with Notes on Paimunkey Pottery-Making, Cherokee Pottery-Making, and Coiling. *Proceedings of the American Philosophical Society* 88:69−125.

Fisher, W. L.; McGowen, J. H.; Brown, L. F., Jr.; and Groat, C. G.
1972   *Environmental Geologic Atlas of the Texas Coastal Zone: Galveston-Houston Area.* Austin: Bureau of Economic Geology, University of Texas.

Fisk, H. N.
1938a   Pleistocene Exposures in Western Florida Parishes. *Louisiana Department of Conservation Geological Survey Bulletin* 12:3−25.
1938b   Geology of Grant and LaSalle Parishes. *Louisiana Department of Conservation Geological Survey Bulletin* 10:1−146.
1944   *Geological Investigation of the Alluvial Valley of the Lower Mississippi River.* Vicksburg: U.S. Army Corps of Engineers and the Mississippi River Commission.
1959   Padre Island and Laguna Madre Flats, Coastal South Texas. In *Second Coastal Geography Conference,* pp. 103−51. Baton Rouge: Coastal Studies Institute, Louisiana State University.

Florida Division of State Planning
1974   *The Florida General Soils Atlas for Regional Planning Districts I and II.* Tallahassee.

Ford, James A.
1935   *Ceramic Decoration Sequence at an Old Indian Village Site Near Sicily Island, Louisiana.* Department of Conservation, Louisiana Geological Survey, Anthropological Study 1.
1936   *Analysis of Indian Village Site Collections from Louisiana and Mississippi.* Department of Conservation, Louisiana Geological Survey, Anthropological Study 2.
1951   *Greenhouse: A Troyville−Coles Creek Period Site in Avoyelles Parish, Louisiana.* Anthropological Papers of the American Museum of Natural History 44(1).
1952   *Measurements of Some Prehistoric Design Developments in the Southeastern States.* Anthropological Papers of the American Museum of Natural History 44(3).
1969   *A Comparison of Formative Cultures in the Americas, Diffusion or the Psychic Unity of Man.* Smithsonian Contributions to Anthropology 11.

Ford, James A., and Quimby, George I., Jr.
1945   *The Tchefuncte Culture, an Early Occupation of the Lower Mississippi Valley.* Society for American Archaeology Memoir 2.

Ford, James A., and Webb, Clarence H.
1956   *Poverty Point, a Late Archaic Site in Louisiana.* Anthropological Papers of the American Museum of Natural History 46(1).

Ford, James A., and Willey, Gordon
1940   *Crooks Site, a Marksville Period Burial Mound in LaSalle Parish, Louisiana.* Department of Conservation, Louisiana Geological Survey, Anthropological Study 3.

Ford, J. A.; Phillips, Philip; and Haag, W. G.
1955   *The Jaketown Site in West-Central Mississippi.* Anthropological Papers of the American Museum of Natural History 45(1).

Fortier, Alcee
1904   *A History of Louisiana.* Vol. 1, *Early Explorers and the Domination of the French, 1512−1768.* New York: Manze, Joyant and Co.

Fradkin, Arlene
1976 The Wightman Site: A Study of Prehistoric Culture and Environment on Sanibel Island, Lee County, Florida. Master's thesis, University of Florida.
n.d. Revised Species List from the Wightman Site. Manuscript, Zooarchaeology Range, Florida State Museum, Gainesville.
Frazier, David E.
1967 Recent Deltaic Deposits of the Mississippi: Their Development and Chronology. *Gulf Coast Association of Geological Societies Transactions*. San Antonio.
French, Benjamin Franklin (editor)
1846 *Historical Collections of Louisiana, Embracing Many Rare and Valuable Documents Relating to the Natural, Civil and Political History of that State*. New York: New Series.
1875 *Historical Collections of Louisiana and Florida, Including Translations of Original Manuscripts Relating to their Discovery and Settlement*. Vol. 1. New York: Wiley and Putnam.
Frey, David G.
1953 Regional Aspects of the Late-Glacial and Post-Glacial Pollen Succession of Southeastern North Carolina. *Ecological Monographs* 23:289–313.
Fryman, Frank B., Jr.
1971 Highway Salvage Archaeology in Florida. *Archives and History News* 2(1):1–4. Tallahassee: Division of Archives, History, and Records Management, Florida Department of State.
Futch, Robin S.
1979 Prehistoric Human Ecology at the Morton Shell Mound (16Ib3), Iberia Parish, Louisiana. Master's thesis, Louisiana State University.
Gagliano, Sherwood M.
1963 A Survey of Prehistoric Occupations in Portions of South Louisiana and South Mississippi. *Florida Anthropologist* 16(4):105–32.
1964 An Archaeological Survey of Avery Island. Report, Louisiana State University Coastal Studies Institute, Baton Rouge.
1967 *Occupation Sequence at Avery Island*. Coastal Studies Series 22. Baton Rouge: Louisiana State University Press.
1979 A Cultural Resource Survey of the Empire to Gulf of Mexico Waterway. Manuscript prepared for U.S. Army Corps of Engineers, New Orleans District.
Gagliano, S. M., and Saucier, Roger T.
1963 Poverty Point Sites in Southeastern Louisiana. *American Antiquity* 28(3):320–27.
Gagliano, Sherwood M., and Webb, Clarence H.
1970 Archaic-Poverty Point Transition at the Pearl River Mouth. In *The Poverty Point Culture*, edited by Bettye J. Broyles and Clarence H. Webb. *Southeastern Archaeological Conference Bulletin* 12:47–72.
Gagliano, Sherwood M.; Weinstein, R.; and Burden, K.
1975 Investigations along the Gulf Intracoastal Waterway. Coastal Louisiana Area. Report prepared for U.S. Army Corps of Engineers, New Orleans District.
Gagliano, S. M.; Fulgham, S.; Rader, B.; and Wiseman, D. E.
1979 Cultural Resources Studies in the Pearl River Mouth Area, Louisiana-Mississippi. Report prepared by Coastal Environments, Inc., for New Orleans District Corps of Engineers, Contract No. DACW-29-77-D-9262
Gagliano, S. M.; Pearson, C. E.; Weinstein, R. A.; Wiseman, D. E.; and McClendon, C. M.
1982 Sedimentary Studies of Prehistoric Archaeological Sites: Criteria for Identification of Submerged Archaeological Sites of the Northern Gulf of Mexico Continental Shelf. Report, Preservation Planning Series. U.S. Department of the Interior. National Park Service, Division of State Plans and Grants.
Gagliano, S. M.; Weinstein, R. A.; Burden, E. K.; Glander, W. P.; and Brooks, K. L.
1980 Cultural Resources Survey of the Barataria, Segnette, and Rigaud Waterways,

Jefferson Parish, Louisiana. 2 vols. Report prepared by Coastal Environments, Inc., for U.S. Army Corps of Engineers, New Orleans District.

Gardner, William A.
1966　The Waddells Mill Pond Site. *Florida Anthropologist* 19(2): 43–64.
1969　An Example of the Association of Archaeological Complexes with Tribal and Linguistic Groupings: The Fort Walton Complex of Northwest Florida. *Florida Anthropologist* 22(1): 1–11.
1971　Fort Walton in Inland Florida. *Southeastern Archaeological Conference Newsletter* 10(2): 48–50.

Gatschet, Albert Samuel
1883　The Shetimasha Indians of St. Mary's Parish, South Louisiana. *Anthropological Society of Washington, Transactions* 2: 148–58.
1884　*A Migration Legend of the Creek Indians.* Vol. 1. Philadelphia: Brinton's Library of Aboriginal American Literature.
1891　*The Karankawa Indians.* Peabody Museum of American Archaeology and Ethnology, Manual 2. Cambridge.

Gibson, Jon L.
1968　Russell Landing: A North Louisiana Phase of the Tchefuncte Period. Master's thesis, Louisiana State University.
1973　Social systems at Poverty Point: An Analysis of Intersite and Intrasite Variability. Ph.D. dissertation, Southern Methodist University.
1974a　Aboriginal Warfare in the Protohistoric Southeast: An Alternative Perspective. *American Antiquity* 39(1): 130–33.
1974b　Poverty Point: The First North American Chiefdom. *Archaeology* 27(2): 97–105.
1974c　*The Rise and Decline of Poverty Point.* Louisiana Archaeology 1.
1975　The Prehistory of Acadiana. In *The Culture of Acadiana: Tradition and Change in South Louisiana,* edited by S. L. Del Sesto and J. L. Gibson, pp. 16–40. Lafayette: University of Southwestern Louisiana.
1976a　*Archaeological Survey of Bayou Teche, Vermilion River, and Freshwater Bayou, South-Central Louisiana.* The University of Southwestern Louisiana, Center for Archaeological Studies, Report 2. Lafayette.
1976b　*An Archaeological Survey of the Mermentau River and Bayous Nezpique and Des Cannes, Southwestern Louisiana.* The University of Southwestern Louisiana, Center for Archaeological Studies, Report 1. Lafayette.
1978　*Archaeological Survey of the Lower Atchafalaya Region, South Central Louisiana.* The University of Southwestern Louisiana, Center for Archaeological Studies, Report 5. Lafayette.
1980　Cultural Assessment of the Chattahoochee and Apalachicola River Valleys in Georgia, Alabama, and Florida: Archaeology, History. Manuscript.
1981　Archaeological Survey along the Eastern Shore of Calcasieu Lake, Western Coastal Louisiana. Manuscript, U.S. Soil Conservation Service, Alexandria, Louisiana.
1982　Archaeology and Ethnology on the Edges of the Atchafalaya Basin, a Cultural Resources Survey of the Atchafalaya Protection Levees. Report prepared for the U.S. Army Corps of Engineers, New Orleans District, by the Center for Archaeological Studies, University of Southwestern Louisiana, Lafayette.

Gilmore, Kathleen
1974　*Cultural Variation on the Texas Coast: Analysis of an Aboriginal Shell Midden, Wallisville Reservoir, Texas.* Texas Archaeological Survey Research Report 44. Austin: University of Texas.

Giraud, Marcel
1974　*A History of French Louisiana.* Vol. 1, *The Reign of Louis XIV.* Baton Rouge: Louisiana State University Press.

Gladfelter, Bruce G.
  1977   Geoarchaeology: The Geomorphologist and Archaeology. *American Antiquity*
         42(4):519–38.
Goggin, John M.
  1947   A Preliminary Definition of Archaeological Areas and Periods in Florida.
         American Antiquity 13(3):114–27.
  1949   Cultural Traditions in Florida Prehistory. In *The Florida Indian and His Neigh-*
         bors, edited by John W. Griffin, pp. 13–44. Winter Park, Florida: Rollins Col-
         lege Inter-American Center.
Goggin, John M., and Sturtevant, William C.
  1964   The Calusa: A Stratified, Nonagricultural Society (with Notes on Sibling Mar-
         riage). In *Explorations in Cultural Anthropology: Essays in Honor of George Peter*
         Murdock, edited by Ward H. Goodenough, pp. 179–219. New York: McGraw-
         Hill.
Goggin, John M. (editor)
  1971   Dispersal of Mississippi Culture. *Southeastern Archaeological Conference Newslet-*
         ter 10(2):35–53.
Golley, Frank B.
  1962   *The Mammals of Georgia.* Athens: University of Georgia Press.
Goodyear, A. C., and Warren, L. O.
  1972   Further Observations on the Submarine Oyster Shell Deposits of Tampa Bay.
         Florida Anthropologist 25(2):52–66.
Goodyear, A. C.; Upchurch, S. B.; and Brooks, M. J.
  1980   Turtlecrawl Point: An Inundated Early Holocene Archaeological Site on the
         West Coast of Florida. In *Holocene Geology and Man in Pinellas and Hillsborough*
         Counties, Florida, compiled by S. B. Upchurch. Tallahassee: Southeastern Geo-
         logical Society.
Greenwell, Dale
  1968   *Twelve Flags, Triumphs and Tragedies* 1. Kingsport, Tennessee: Kingsport Press.
Griffin, James B.
  1937   The Archaeological Remains of the Chiwere Sioux. *American Antiquity* 2(3):
         180–81.
  1960   Climatic Change: A Contributory Cause of the Growth and Decline of North-
         ern Hopewell Culture. *Wisconsin Archaeologist* 41(2):21–33.
  1961   Some Correlations of Climatic and Cultural Change in Eastern North Ameri-
         can Prehistory. *Annals of the New York Academy of Science* 95(1):710–17.
  1966   *The Fort Ancient Aspect: Its Cultural and Chronological Position in Mississippi Valley*
         Archaeology. University of Michigan Museum of Anthropology Papers 28.
  1967   Eastern North American Archaeology: A Summary. *Science* 156:175–91.
  1979   An Overview of the Chillicothe Conference. In *Hopewell Archaeology: The*
         Chillicothe Conference, edited by David S. Brose and N'omi Greber, pp. 266–70.
         Kent, Ohio: Kent State University Press.
Griffin, John W.
  1949a The Historical Archaeology of Florida. In *The Florida Indian and His Neigh-*
         bors, edited by John W. Griffin, pp. 45–54. Winter Park: Rollins College Inter-
         American Center.
  1949b Notes on the Archaeology of Useppa Island. *Florida Anthropologist* 2(3–4):
         92–93.
  1950   Test Excavations at the Lake Jackson Site. *American Antiquity* 16(2):99–112.
Griffin, John W., and Bullen, R. P.
  1950   *The Safety Harbor Site, Pinellas County, Florida.* Florida Anthropological Society
         Publications 2. Gainesville: University of Florida Press.
Gunn, Joel, and Mahula, Royce
  1977   *Hop Hill: Culture and Climatic Change in Central Texas.* Center for Archaeologi-
         cal Research, Special Paper 5:1–295. Austin: University of Texas.

Gunn, Joel; Muto, Guy; Toms, Alston; and Whitehead, Donald
 n.d. Climatic Reconstructions. In *First Annual Project Progress Report to the U.S. Army Corps of Engineers, Mobile District, and to the Inter-Agency Archaeological Services—Atlanta on the Early Man and Environment Study: Tennessee-Tombigbee Waterway, Mississippi and Alabama.* Vols. 1–3. Oklahoma City: Blenham, Blair and Affiliates.

Haag, William G.
 1939 Pottery Types. *Southeastern Archaeological Conference Newsletter* 1(1).
 1962 The Bering Strait Land Bridge. *Scientific American* 206(1): 112–23.
 1971 *Louisiana in North American Prehistory.* Melanges 1. Baton Rouge: Louisiana State University.

Haas, Mary Rosamond
 1939 Natchez and Chitimacha Clans and Kinship Terminology. *American Anthropologist* 41(4): 597–610.

Haggett, Peter; Cliff, Andrew D.; and Frey, Allen
 1977 *Locational Analysis in Human Geography: Models and Methods.* Vols. 1 and 2. New York: John Wiley and Sons.

Hall, Grant D.
 1981 *Allen Creek: A Study in the Cultural Prehistory of the Lower Brazos River Valley, Texas.* Texas Archaeological Survey, Research Report 61. Austin: University of Texas.

Hally, David J.
 1971 The Archaeology of European Indian Contact in the Southeast. In *Red, White and Black*, edited by Charles Hudson, pp. 155–66. Athens: University of Georgia Press.

Hamilton, P. J.
 1910 *Colonial Mobile.* New York: Houghton Mifflin Company.

Hammel, E. A.; McDaniel, C. K.; and Wachter, K. W.
 1979 Demographic Consequences of Incest Taboo: A Microsimulation Analysis. *Science* 205: 972–77.

Hammond, E. A.
 1973 The Spanish Fisheries of Charlotte Harbor. *Florida Historical Quarterly* 51(4): 355–80.

Hardin-Friedrich, Margaret
 1970 Design Structure and Social Interaction: Archaeological Implications of Ethnographic Analysis. *American Antiquity* 35(4): 332–43.
 1979 Comparative Stylistic Analysis of Lubbub-Moundville Ceramics. Manuscript incorporated in the University of Michigan Museum of Anthropology Proposal to Interagency Archaeological Services—Atlanta.
 1980 Design/Motif Analyses of a Prehistoric Ceramic "School" at Moundville, Alabama. Paper presented at the 37th Annual Meeting of the Southeastern Archaeological Conference, New Orleans.

Harlow, Richard F.
 1959 *Evaluation of White-tailed Deer Habitat in Florida.* Florida Game and Freshwater Fish Commission Technical Bulletin 5. Tallahassee.

Harper, R. M.
 1914 Geography and Vegetation of Northern Florida. *Florida State Geological Survey Annual Report* 6: 163–437. Tallahassee.

Harris, D. A.
 1969 Fort Condé, a Problem in Salvage Archaeology. Master's thesis, University of Florida.
 1970 An Archaeological Survey of Fort Louis de la Mobile. Manuscript, Mobile Historical Development Commission, Mobile, Alabama.

Hassan, Fekri A.
 1979 Geoarchaeology: The Geologist and Archaeology. *American Antiquity* 44(2): 267–70.

Haury, E. W.; Rands, R. L; Spaulding, A. C.; Taylor, W. W.; Thompson, R. T.; Wauchope, R.; and White, M. E.
  1956   An Archaeological Approach to the Study of Cultural Stability. Society for American Archaeology, Memoir 11, pp. 31–57.
Hawkins, Benjamin
  1848   A Sketch of the Creek Country in 1798 and 1799. Georgia Historical Society Collections 3(1):1–88.
Hedlund, A., and Knight, H. A.
  1969   Hardwood Distribution Maps for the Southeast. U.S.D.A. Forest Service Resource Bulletin SO-19. New Orleans: Southern Forest Experimental Station.
Hendry, Charles W., Jr., and Yon, William J., Jr.
  1958   Geology of the Area in and around the Jim Woodruff Reservoir. Florida Geological Survey Miscellaneous Studies, Report of Investigations 16. Tallahassee.
Higginbotham, Jay (editor)
  1969   The Journal of Sauvole: Historical Journal of the Establishment of the French in Louisiana by M. de Sauvole. Mobile, Alabama: Colonial Books.
  1977   Old Mobile: Fort Louis de la Louisiane, 1702–1711. Mobile, Alabama: Museum of the City of Mobile.
Hill, James N.
  1968   Broken K. Pueblo: Patterns of Form and Function. In New Perspectives in Archaeology, edited by S. Binford and L. Binford, pp. 103–42. Chicago: Aldine Press.
Hodder, Ian
  1978   The Spatial Organization of Culture. London: Duckworth.
  1979   Economic and Social Stress and Material Culture Patterning. American Antiquity 44(3):446–54.
Holmes, N. H., Jr.
  1963   The Site on Bottle Creek. Journal of Alabama Archaeology 9(1):16–17.
Holmes, N. H., and Trickey, E. B.
  1974   Late Holocene Sea-Level Oscillations in Mobile Bay. American Antiquity 39(1): 122–24.
Holmes, William H.
  1903   Aboriginal Pottery of the Eastern United States. Bureau of American Ethnology Annual Report 20:1–237. Washington: Smithsonian Institution.
Hornbeck Tanner, Helen
  1980   The Land and Water Commission System of the Southeastern Indians. Paper presented at the 37th Annual Meeting of the Southeastern Archaeological Conference, New Orleans.
Howe, Henry V.; Russell, Richard J.; McGuirt, James H.; Craft, Benjamin C.; and Stephenson, Morton B.
  1935   Reports on the Geology of Cameron and Vermilion Parishes. Louisiana Department of Conservation Geological Survey Bulletin 6.
Hrdlička, Ales
  1917   Preliminary Report on Finds of Supposedly Ancient Remains at Vero, Florida. Journal of Geology 25:43–51.
  1918   Recent Discoveries Attributed to Early Man in America. Bureau of American Ethnology Bulletin 64. Washington: Smithsonian Institution.
  1940   Catalog of Human Crania in the United States National Museum Collections: Indians of the Gulf States. Proceedings of the United States National Museum, vol. 87. Washington.
Hubbell, T. H.; Laessle, A. M.; and Dickinson, J. C.
  1956   The Flint-Chattahoochee-Apalachicola Region and Its Environments. Florida State Museum, Biological Sciences Bulletin 1:1–72.
Hudson, Charles
  1976   The Southeastern Indians. Knoxville: University of Tennessee Press.

Hunter, Donald G.
    1975   Functional Analysis of Clay Objects. *Florida Anthropologist 28(2): 57–71.*
Hurt, Wesley R., Jr.
    1947   An Archaeological Survey, Chattahoochee Valley, Alabama. Manuscript, Alabama Museum of Natural History.
Huscher, Harold A.
    1959   *Appraisal of the Archaeological Resources of the Walter F. George Reservoir, Chattahoochee River, Alabama and Georgia.* River Basin Surveys Papers. Washington: Smithsonian Institution.
    1964   The Standing Boy Flint Industry. *Southern Indian Studies* 16: 3–20.
    1971   Two Mississippian Mound Sites in Quitman County, Georgia. *Southeastern Archaeological Conference Newsletter* 10(2): 35–38.
Jenkins, Ned J.
    1976   An Inventory and Evaluation of Archaeological Resources in and around the Proposed Alabama Enrichment Plant Site in Houston County, Alabama. Manuscript, Office of Archaeological Research, Moundville, Alabama.
    1978   Prehistoric Chronology of the Lower Chattahoochee Valley. *Journal of Alabama Archaeology* 24(2): 73–91.
    1979   Gainesville Reservoir Ceramic Description and Chronology. In *Archaeological Investigations in the Gainesville Reservoir of the Tennessee-Tombigbee Waterway,* vol. 2. University of Alabama, O.A.R. Report of Investigations 12.
Jennings, Jesse D.
    1941   Chickasaw and Earlier Indian Cultures of North Eastern Mississippi. *Journal of Mississippi History* 3(3): 155–226.
    1974   *Prehistory of North America.* 2d ed. New York: McGraw-Hill.
Jennings, Jesse D., and Fairbanks, Charles H.
    1939   Pottery Types. *Southeastern Archaeological Conference Newsletter* 1(2).
Jeter, Marvin D.
    1977   Late Woodland Chronology and Change in Central Alabama. *Journal of Alabama Archaeology* 23(2): 112–36.
Jones, B. Calvin
    1971   Division Archaeologist Active Throughout Florida. *Archives and History News* 4: 1–2. Tallahassee: Division of Archives, History, and Records Management, Florida Department of State.
    1982   Southern Cult Manifestations at the Lake Jackson Site, Leon County, Florida: Salvage Excavation at Mound 3. *Midcontinental Journal of Archaeology* 7(1): 3–44.
Jones, B. Calvin, and Penman, John T.
    1973   Winewood: An Inland Fort Walton Site in Tallahassee. *Bulletin* 3: 65–90. Tallahassee: Bureau of Historic Sites and Properties, Florida Department of State.
Jordan, D. C.; Evermann, B. W.; and Clark, H. W.
    1930   Checklist of the Fishes and Fish-like Vertebrates of North and Middle America North of Venezuela and Colombia. *U.S. Department of Commerce, Report of the U.S. Commission of Fisheries for the Year 1928.* 1962 reprint. Ashton, Maryland.
Keesing, Roger M.
    1975   *Kin Groups and Social Structure.* New York: Holt, Rinehart, and Winston.
Kelly, Arthur R.
    1938   *A Preliminary Report on Archaeological Explorations at Macon, Georgia.* Bureau of American Ethnology Bulletin 119. Washington: Smithsonian Institution.
    1950   Survey of the Lower Flint and Chattahoochee Rivers. *Early Georgia* 1: 27–33.
    1960   *A Weeden Island Burial Mound in Decatur County, Georgia: The Lake Douglas Mound, 9Dr21.* University of Georgia Laboratory of Archaeology Series, Report No. 1. Athens.

n.d.   Notes on the Hornsby's Bluff Site, 9Se7 (now 9Dr22). Manuscript, University of Georgia Laboratory of Archaeology, Athens.

Kelly, Arthur A., and Smith, Betty
1975   The Swift Creek Site. Report to the National Park Service, Southeast Regional Center, Atlanta.

Kenner, W. E.; Hampton, E. R.; and Conover, C. S.
1969   Average Flow of Major Streams in Florida. Report prepared by the United States Geological Survey in Cooperation with the Division of Geology. Tallahassee: Florida Department of Natural Resources.

Kenner, W. E.; Pride, R. W.; and Conover, C. S.
1967   Drainage Basins in Florida. Report prepared by the United States Geological Survey in Cooperation with the Division of Geology. Tallahassee: Florida Board of Conservation.

King, J. E., and Allen, W. H., Jr.
1977   A Holocene Vegetation Record from the Mississippi River Valley, S. E. Missouri. *Quaternary Research* 87:307–23.

Kniffen, F. B.
1936   Preliminary Report on the Indian Mounds and Middens of Plaquemines and St. Bernard Parishes. In *Reports on the Geology of Plaquemines and St. Bernard Parishes*, Louisiana Department of Conservation. Geological Survey Bulletin 8:407–22.

Knight, Vernon J., Jr.
1979   Ceramic Stratigraphy at the Singer-Moyer Site, 9Sw2. *Journal of Alabama Archaeology* 25:138–51.
1980a   Comments on Brose and Percy, "Fort Walton Settlement Patterns." *Florida Journal of Anthropology* 5:20–25.
1980b   Interregional Relationships and the Study of Fort Walton Mississippian Ceramic Style. Paper presented at the 37th Annual Meeting of the Southeastern Archaeological Conference, New Orleans.

Knight, Vernon J., Jr., and Adams, S.
n.d.   A Voyage to the Mobile and Tomeh in 1700, with notes on the Interior Regions of Alabama. Manuscript.

Knight, Vernon J., Jr., and Schnell, Frank T.
1977   Archaeological Assessment of the East Bank of the Chattahoochee River between Channel Mile 105.3 and 107 and Immediate Vicinity, Steward County, Georgia. Manuscript, Columbus Museum of Arts and Sciences, Columbus, Georgia.

Knudsen, Gary D.
1979   *Partial Cultural Resource Inventory of Tyndall A.F.B., Bay County, Florida.* Florida State University Archaeological Research Report 7:1–119. Tallahassee.

Kohler, Timothy
1978   The Social and Chronological Dimensions of Village Occupation at a North Florida Weeden Island Site. Ph.D. dissertation, University of Florida.

Kolb, C. R., and Van Lopick, Jack
1958   *Geology of the Mississippi River Deltaic Plain, Southeastern Louisiana.* U.S. Army Corps of Engineers Waterway Experiment Station, Technical Report, pp. 3–438. Vicksburg, Mississippi.

Komarek, Roy (editor)
1962   *Proceedings of the Annual Tall Timbers Fire Ecology Conference.* Tallahassee, Florida: Tall Timbers Research Station.

Krieger, A. D.
1945   An Inquiry into Supposed Mexican Influence on a Prehistoric "Cult" in the Southern United States. *American Anthropologist* 47(3):483–515.
1951   Review of *Archeology of the Florida Gulf Coast*, by G. R. Willey. *American Antiquity* 17(1):62–64.

Kroeber, A. L.
1939 *Cultural and Natural Areas of Native North America.* University of California Publications in American Archaeology and Ethnology 38.
LaHarpe, J. B. Benard de
1971 *The Historical Journal of the Establishment of the French in Louisiana* by J. B. Benard de LaHarpe. Translated by Joan Cain and Virginia Doenig. Edited and annotated by Glenn R. Conrad. University of Southwestern Louisiana History Series 3. Lafayette: University of Southwestern Louisiana, Center for Louisiana Studies.
LaMarche, Valmore C., Jr.
1974 Paleoclimatic Inferences from Long Tree Ring Records. *Science* 183(4129): 1043–48.
Lamb, H. H.
1966 *Our Changing Climate.* London: Methuen.
Landreth, John
1819 The Journal of John Landreth, edited by Dennis Gibson. *Attaka Gazette* 14(3): 1979.
Larson, Lewis H.
1980 *Aboriginal Subsistence Technology on the Southeastern Coastal Plain during the Late Prehistoric Period.* Ripley P. Bullen Monographs in Anthropology and History 2. Gainesville: University Presses of Florida.
Lazarus, William C.
1960 Human Figurines from the Coast of Northwest Florida. *Florida Anthropologist* 13(2–3): 61–70.
1961 Ten Middens on the Navy Live Oak Reservation. *Florida Anthropologist* 14(3–4): 49–64.
1964a The 16th-Century Spanish Coin from a Fort Walton Burial. *Florida Anthropologist* 17(2): 134–38.
1964b The Postl's Lake II Site, Eglin AFB, Florida (80K71). *Florida Anthropologist* 17(1): 1–16.
1971 The Fort Walton Culture West of the Apalachicola River. *Southeastern Archaeological Conference Newsletter* 10(2): 40–48.
Lazarus, Yulee W., and Fornaro, Robert J.
1975 Fort Walton Temple Mound (80K6M): Further Test Excavations, DePauw 1973. *Florida Anthropologist* 28(4): 159–77.
Lazarus, Yulee W., and Hawkins, Carolyn B.
1976 *Pottery of the Fort Walton Period.* Fort Walton Beach, Florida: Temple Mound Museum.
Lazarus, Yulee W.; Lazarus, W. C.; and Sharon, Donald W.
1967 The Navy Live Oak Reservation Cemetery Site (8Sa36). *Florida Anthropologist* 20(3–4): 103.
Leach, Edmund
1954 *Political Systems of Highland Burma.* Cambridge: Harvard University Press.
LeBlanc, Rufus J., and Hodgson, W. D.
1959 Origin and Development of the Texas Shoreline. In *Second Coastal Geography Conference, April 6–9, 1959,* edited by Richard J. Russell, pp. 87–102. Baton Rouge: Coastal Studies Institute, Louisiana State University.
Lee, Richard B.
1979 *The Kung San.* London: Cambridge University Press.
LeMaire, F.
1716 Carte Nouvelle de la Louisiane et Pays Circonvoison Dressée sur les Lieux pour etre Presentee a Sa Majeste Tres Chretienne par F. LeMaire Prestre Parisien et Missionnaire apostolique. Louisiana State University Map Library.
n.d. Documents Concerning Indians of the Eastern Region of Louisiana. *In* A Mis-

cellany of Louisiana Historical Records, Works Progress Administration Survey of Federal Archives of Louisiana. Typescript, Howard-Tilton Library, Tulane University, New Orleans.

Lemon, Paul C.
1967   Effect of Fire on Herbs of the Southeastern United States. In *Proceedings of the Tall Timbers Fire Ecology Conference* (1962), edited by R. Komarek, pp. 113–30. Tallahassee, Florida: Tall Timbers Research Stations.

Lewis, Clifford M.
1978   The Calusa. In *Tacachale: Essays on the Indians of Florida and Southeastern Georgia during the Historic Period*, edited by J. T. Milanich and Samuel Proctor, pp. 19–49. Ripley P. Bullen Monographs in Anthropology and History 1. Gainesville: University Presses of Florida.

Lewis, Thomas M. N.
1931   A Florida Burial Mound. *Wisconsin Archaeologist* 10(4): 123–28.
1943   Late Horizons in the Southeast. *Proceedings of the American Philosophical Society* 86: 304–12.

Lincecum, G.
1904   Choctaw Traditions about Their Settlement in Mississippi and the Origin of the Mounds. *Publications of the Mississippi Historical Society* 8: 521–42.

Linduska, Joseph P. (editor)
1964   *Waterfowl Tomorrow*. Washington: U.S. Department of the Interior, Bureau of Fish and Wildlife.

Longacre, William A.
1964   Sociological Implications of the Ceramic Analysis. In *Chapters in the Prehistory of Eastern Arizona II. Fieldiana Anthropology* 55: 155–170.
1968   Some Aspects of Prehistoric Society in East Central Arizona. In *New Perspectives in Archaeology*, edited by S. Binford and L. Binford, pp. 89–102. Chicago: Aldine Press.

Louisiana Indian Miscellany
1937–38 Works Progress Administration Survey of Federal Archives of Louisiana. Typescript, Howard-Tilton Library, Tulane University, New Orleans.

Luer, George M., and Almy, Marion M.
1980a   The Development of Some Aboriginal Pottery on the Central Peninsular Gulf Coast of Florida. *Florida Anthropologist* 33: 207–25.
1980b   The Aqui Esta Site at Charlotte Harbor: A Safety Harbor–Influenced Prehistoric Aboriginal Site. Paper presented at the Annual Meeting of the Florida Anthropological Society, Winter Park.

McCane-O'Conner, Mallory
1979   A Comparative Study of Design Motifs found on Weeden Island and Fort Walton Ceramics. Fort Walton Beach, Florida: Temple Mound Museum.

McHarg, Ian
1969   *Design with Nature*. Garden City: Doubleday/Natural History Press.

McIntire, William G.
1958   *Prehistoric Indian Settlements of the Changing Mississippi River Delta*. Coastal Studies Series 1. Baton Rouge: Louisiana State University Press.
1959   Methods of Correlating Cultural Remains with States of Coastal Development. In *Second Coastal Geography Conference*, edited by R. J. Russell, pp. 341–59. Baton Rouge: Coastal Studies Institute, Louisiana State University.

McMichael, Alan E.
1979   Archaeological Research on the Southwest Florida Coast: The Florida State Museum Horr's Island Survey. Paper presented at the 36th Annual Meeting of the Southeastern Archaeological Conference, Atlanta.
1982   A Cultural Resource Assessment of Horrs Island, Collier County, Florida. Master's thesis, University of Florida.

McMichael, Edward V., and Kellar, James H.
  1960 *Archaeological Salvage in the Oliver Basin.* University of Georgia Laboratory of Archaeology Series 2. Athens.
McWilliams, R. (editor)
  1953 *Fleur de Lis and Calumet: Being the Penicaut Narrative of French Adventure in Louisiana.* Baton Rouge: Louisiana State University Press.
Maduell, Charles, Jr.
  1972 *The Census Tables of the French Colony of Louisiana, 1699–1732.* Baltimore: Genealogical Publishing Company.
Margry, Pierre (compiler and editor)
  1879–88 *Découvertes et Etablissements des Français dans l'Ouest de dans le Sud de l'Amérique Septentrionale (1614–1754).* 6 vols. Paris: Imprimerie D. Jouaust.
Marsh, W. M.
  1978 *Environmental Analysis for Land Use and Site Planning.* New York: McGraw Hill.
Matson, Frederick R. (editor)
  1965 *Ceramics & Man.* Viking Fund Publications in Anthropology 41. Chicago: Aldine Publishing Company.
Mereness, Newton D. (editor)
  1916 *Travels in the American Colonies.* New York: Antiquarian Press Ltd.
Milanich, Jerald T.
  1969 The Alachua Tradition: Extensions of Wilmington-Savannah Peoples into Central Florida. *Florida Anthropologist* 22(1–4): 17–23.
  1971 The Deptford Phase: An Archaeological Reconstruction. Ph.D. dissertation, University of Florida, Gainesville.
  1974 Life in a 9th-Century Indian Household, A Weeden Island Fall-Winter Site on the Upper Apalachicola River, Florida. *Bulletin* 4: 1–44. Tallahassee: Bureau of Historic Sites and Properties, Florida Department of State.
  1980 Weeden Island Studies—Past and Present. *Southeastern Archaeological Conference Bulletin* 22: 11–18.
Milanich, Jerald T., and Fairbanks, Charles H.
  1980 *Florida Archaeology.* New York: Academic Press.
Miller, Carl
  n.d. Notes and Correspondence Concerning Archaeological Investigations in the Jim Woodruff Reservoir. Manuscript, Anthropological Archives, Smithsonian Institution, Washington.
Milner, G. R.
  1980 Epidemic Disease in the Postcontact Southeast. *Midcontinental Journal of Archaeology* 5(1): 39–56.
Minet
  1685a Carte de la Louisiane–A. Embouchure de la Rivierre (*sic*) comme Consieur de la Salle le Marque dans la Carte. B. Costes et Lacs part la Hauteur de la Riviere, comme nous les Avons Trouvez. Louisiana State University Map Library.
  1685b Extrait de la Carte de la Louisiane, part Minet, Mai 1685. Louisiana State University Map Library.
Missimer, Thomas M.
  1973 The Depositional History of Sanibel Island, Florida. Master's thesis, Florida State University.
Mitchell, Robert S.
  1963 Phytogeography and Floristic Survey of a Relic Area in the Marianna Lowlands, Florida. *American Midland Naturalist* 69: 328–66.
Moll, Herman
  1701 Northern America and the Artick Countries, the Isle of California, New Mexico, Louisiana. The River Mississippi and the Lakes of Canada. Herman Moll Fecit. In *A System of Geography*, by H. Moll. London.

1715   A Map of the West Indies or the Islands of America. University of Orleans, Louisiana Collection.

Mooney, J.
1928   *The Aboriginal Population of America North of Mexico.* Smithsonian Miscellaneous Collections 80(7).

Moore, Clarence B.
1901   Certain Aboriginal Remains of the Northwest Florida Coast, Part 1. *Journal of the Academy of Natural Sciences* 11:42–97.
1902   Certain Aboriginal Remains of the Northwest Florida Coast, Part 2. *Journal of the Academy of Natural Sciences* 12:127–355.
1903   Certain Aboriginal Mounds of the Apalachicola River. *Journal of the Academy of Natural Sciences* 12:437–92.
1905a   Certain Aboriginal Remains of the Lower Tombigbee River. *Journal of the Academy of Natural Sciences* 13:245–78.
1905b   Certain Aboriginal Remains of Mobile Bay and on Mississippi Sound. *Journal of the Academy of Natural Sciences* 13:279–97.
1905c   A Form of Urn-burial on Mobile Bay. *American Anthropologist* 7(1):167–68.
1905d   Miscellaneous Investigations in Florida. *Journal of the Academy of Natural Sciences* 13:298–325.
1907   Mounds of the Lower Chattahoochee and Lower Flint Rivers. *Journal of the Academy of Natural Sciences* 13:426–56.
1918   The Northwestern Florida Coast Revisited. *Journal of the Academy of Natural Sciences* 16:513–79.

Morgan, D. J.
1977   The Mississippi River Delta: Legal, Geomorphologic Evaluation of Historic Shoreline Changes. In *Geoscience and Man* 16. Baton Rouge.

Morse, Dan, Jr., and Morse, Phyllis A. (editors)
1976   *A Preliminary Report of the Zebree Project: 1975.* Arkansas Archaeological Survey Research Report 8. Fayetteville.

Mutch, Robert W.
1970   Wildland Fires and Ecosystems: An Hypothesis. *Ecology* 51:1046–51.

Nance, Roger C.
1976   *The Archaeological Sequence at Durant Bend, Dallas County, Alabama.* Alabama Archaeological Society, Special Publication 2.

Neitzel, Robert S.
1965   *Archaeology of the Fatherland Site: The Grand Village of the Natchez.* Anthropological Papers 51, part 1. New York: The American Museum of Natural History.

Neuman, Robert W.
1961   Domesticated Corn from a Fort Walton Mound Site in Houston County, Alabama. *Florida Anthropologist* 14(3–4):75–80.
1972   Archaeological Investigations at the Morton Shell Mound, Weeks Island, Iberia Parish, Louisiana. Report Submitted to the National Science Foundation, Washington.
1976   Archaeological Techniques in the Louisiana Coastal Region. *Louisiana Archaeology* 3:1–21.
1977   An Archaeological Assessment of Coastal Louisiana. Melanges 11. Museum of Geoscience, Louisiana State University, Baton Rouge.
1981   Complicated Stamped Pottery in Louisiana: Its Spatial Distribution and Chronology. *Geoscience and Man* 22:71–76.

Newell, H. Perry, and Krieger, Alex D.
1949   *The George C. Davis Site, Cherokee County, Texas.* Society for American Archaeology Memoir 5.

Odum, E. P.
1971   *Fundamentals of Ecology.* 3d ed. Philadelphia: W. B. Saunders Co.

Ottens, Reinier, and Ottens, Josua
  1730   Stoel des Oorogs en America Waar in Vertoont Werden alle Desself Voor Naamste Eylande Nieuruelychs Uytgeven Doos. Louisiana State University Map Library.
Otvos, Ervin G., Jr.
  1978   New Orleans–South Hancock Holocene Barrier Trends and Origins of Lake Pontchartrain. *Gulf Coast Association of Geological Societies Transactions* 28:337–55. San Antonio.
Paullin, Charles O.
  1932   *Atlas of the Historical Geography of the United States.* Edited by John K. Wright. Carnegie Institution of Washington, Publication 401.
Payne, Claudine
  1980   A Preliminary Investigation of Fort Walton Settlement Patterns in the Tallahassee Red Hills. Paper presented at the 37th Annual Meeting of the Southeastern Archaeological Conference, New Orleans.
Peebles, Christopher
  1970   Moundville: The Analysis of a Prehistoric Culture. Ph.D. dissertation, University of California; Santa Barbara.
  1971   Moundville and Surrounding Sites: Some Structural Considerations of Mortuary Practices II. In *Approaches to the Social Dimensions of Mortuary Practices,* edited by James A. Brown. Society for American Archaeology, Memoir 25: 68–91.
Penman, John T.
  1976   The Lamar Phase in Central Georgia. *Southeastern Archaeological Conference Bulletin* 19:18–21.
Percy, George W.
  1971   Preliminary Report to the Division of Recreation and Parks, Department of Natural Resources, State of Florida, on Archaeological Work in Torreya State Park during the year 1971 by the Department of Anthropology at Florida State University. Manuscript, Florida Division of Archives, History, and Records Management, Tallahassee.
  1972a   Current Research, Florida. *Southeastern Archaeological Conference Newsletter* 16(1):3–6.
  1972b   Current Research, Florida. *Southeastern Archaeological Conference Newsletter* 16(2):9–10.
  1972c   Preliminary Report on Recent Archaeological Investigations in Torreya State Park, Liberty County, Florida. Manuscript, Division of Archives, History, and Records Management, Florida Department of State, Tallahassee. Paper presented at the 24th Annual Meeting of the Florida Anthropological Society, Winter Park.
  1974   Review of Evidence for Prehistoric Indian Use of Animals in Northwest Florida. *Bulletin* 4:65–93. Tallahassee: Bureau of Historic Sites and Properties, Florida Department of State.
  1976   *Salvage Investigations at the Scholz Steam Plant Site (8Ja104), A Middle Weeden Island Habitation Site in Jackson County, Florida.* Bureau of Historic Sites and Properties, Miscellaneous Project Report Series 35. Tallahassee: Division of Archives, History, and Records Management, Florida Department of State.
Percy, George W., and Brose, David S.
  1974   Weeden Island Ecology, Subsistence, and Village Life in Northwest Florida. Outline of paper presented at the 39th Annual Meeting of the Society for American Archaeology, Washington.
Percy, George W., and Jones, M. Katherine
  1976   An Archaeological Survey of Upland Locales in Gadsden and Liberty Counties, Florida. *Florida Anthropologist* 29(3):105–25.

Perino, Gregory
    1968   *Guide to the Identification of Certain American Indian Projectile Points.* Oklahoma Anthropological Society, Special Bulletin 3.
    1971   *Guide to the Identification of Certain American Indian Projectile Points.* Oklahoma Anthropological Society, Special Bulletin 4.
Phelps, David S.
    1965   The Norwood Series of Fiber-Tempered Ceramics. *Southeastern Archaeological Conference Bulletin* 2:65–69.
    1966a   Early and Late Components of the Tucker Site. *Florida Anthropologist* 19(1): 11–38.
    1966b   Prehistory of North Central Florida, Final Report. Manuscript, Department of Anthropology, Florida State University, Tallahassee.
    1969   Swift Creek and Santa Rosa in Northwest Florida. *Institute of Archaeology and Anthropology, Notebook* 1(6–9):14–24.
    n.d.   Investigation of Two Prehistoric Ceremonial Sites, Final Report. Manuscript, Department of Anthropology, Florida State University, Tallahassee.
Phillips, Philip
    1970   *Archaeological Survey in the Lower Yazoo Basin, Mississippi, 1949–1955.* Papers of the Peabody Museum of Archaeology and Ethnology 60. Cambridge: Harvard University.
Phillips, Philip; Ford, J. A.; and Griffin, J. B.
    1951   *Archaeological Survey in the Lower Mississippi Alluvial Valley, 1940–1947.* Papers of the Peabody Museum of Archaeology and Ethnology 25. Cambridge: Harvard University.
Pierce, J.
    1825   Notices of the Agriculture, Scenery, Geology and Animal, Vegetable and Mineral Productions of the Floridas, and the Indian Tribes, Made During a Recent Tour in these Counties. *American Journal of Science* 9:119–136.
Post, L. C.
    1962   Some Notes on the Attakapas Indians of Southwest Louisiana. *Louisiana History* 3:221–42.
Priestley, Herbert I. (editor)
    1928   *The Luna Papers.* Vols. 1 and 2. Deland: Florida State Historical Society.
Puri, Harbans S., and Vernon, Robert O.
    1964   *Summary of the Geology of Florida and a Guidebook to the Classic Exposures.* Florida Geological Survey Special Publication 5 (rev.). Tallahassee.
Quarterman, E., and Keever, K.
    1962   Southern Mixed Hardwood Forest: Climax in the Southeastern Coastal Plain, U.S.A. *Ecological Monographs* 226(2):167–85.
Quimby, George I., Jr.
    1957   The Bayou Goula Site, Iberville Parish, Louisiana. *Fieldiana Anthropology* 47(2):97–170.
Rapp, George, and Gifford, John A.
    1982   Archaeological Geology. *American Scientist* 70:45–53.
Read, William A.
    1928   Indian Place Names in Louisiana. *Louisiana Historical Quarterly* 11(4):445–62.
Riis, Maurice
    1936   The Mississippi Fort Called Fort de la Boulaye, 1700–1715. *Louisiana Historical Quarterly* 19(4):829–99.
Rivet, Phillip G.
    1973   Tchefuncte Ceramic Typology: A Reappraisal. Master's thesis, Louisiana State University.
Robbins, Louise M.
    1976   Analysis of Human Skeletal Material from Morton Shell Mound (16IB3),

Iberia Parish, Louisiana. Manuscript, Department of Geography and Anthropology, Louisiana State University, Baton Rouge.

Robin, C. C.
1805   *Voyage to Louisiana by C. C. Robin, 1803–1804.* Abridged translation by Stuart Landry. New Orleans: Pelican Press, 1976.

Romans, Bernard
1776   A General Map of the Southern British Colonies in America. Copy on file, PKY121, P. K. Yonge Library of Florida History, University of Florida, Gainesville.

Ross, John
1775   *Course of the River Mississippi from the Balize to Fort Chartres, Taken on an Expedition to the Illinois in the Latter End of the Year 1765 by Lieutenant Ross of the 31st Regiment Improved from the Surveys of that River made by the French.* 2d ed. London: Robert Sayer, Publisher. Copy, University of New Orleans, Louisiana Collection.

Rouse, Irving
1951   *A Survey of Indian River Archaeology, Florida.* Yale University Publications in Anthropology 44.
1972   *Introduction to Prehistory, a Systematic Approach.* New York: McGraw-Hill.

Rowland, Dunbar, and Sanders, Alfred G. (editors)
1929   *Mississippi Provincial Archives, 1701–1729, French Dominion.* Vols. 2–3. Jackson: Mississippi Department of Archives and History.

Russell, Richard J.
1936   Lower Mississippi River Delta. In *Reports on the Geology of Plaquemines and St. Bernard Parishes.* Louisiana Department of Conservation Geological Survey Bulletin 8:3–199.

Sanchez, W. A., and Kutzbach, J. E.
1974   Climate of the American Tropics and Subtropics in the 1960s and Possible Comparisons with Climatic Variations of the Last Millenium. *Quaternary Research* 4(2):128–35.

Saucier, Roger T.
1963   *Recent Geomorphic History of the Pontchartrain Basin.* Louisiana State University Studies, Coastal Studies Series 9.
1974   *Quaternary Geology of the Lower Mississippi Valley.* Arkansas Archaeological Survey Research Series 6.
1981   Current Thinking on Riverine Processes and Geologic History as Related to Human Settlement in the Southeast. In *Traces of Prehistory: Papers in Honor of W. G. Haag,* edited by F. H. West and R. W. Neuman. *Geoscience and Man* 22:7–18.

Scarry, John F.
1979a   The Chronology of Fort Walton Development in the Upper Apalachicola Valley, Florida. Paper presented at the 36th Annual Meeting of the Southeastern Archaeological Conference, Atlanta.
1979b   The Development of Mississippian Chiefdoms in Northwest Florida: Fort Walton in the Upper Apalachicola River Valley. A preliminary report submitted to the National Science Foundation (1 March 1979) re: Grant No. 742-8270 to David S. Brose, Case Western Reserve University, Cleveland.
1980a   Fort Walton Cultures: A Redefinition. Paper presented at the 37th Annual Meeting of the Southeastern Archaeological Conference, New Orleans.
1980b   Subsistence Costs and Information: A Preliminary Model of Fort Walton Development. Paper presented at the 37th Annual Meeting of the Southeastern Archaeological Conference, New Orleans.
1983   The Development of Mississippian Chiefdoms in Northwest Florida: Fort Walton in the Upper Apalachicola River Valley. Ph.D. Dissertation, Case Western Reserve University.

Schnell, Frank T., Jr.
  1970   A Comparative Study of Some Lower Creek Sites. *Southeastern Archaeological Conference Bulletin* 13:133–36.
  1973   A Preliminary Assessment of Archaeological Resources Remaining in the Walter F. George Lake Area. Manuscript, Columbus Museum of Arts and Sciences, Columbus, Georgia.
  1975a   An Archaeological Survey of Lake Blackshear. *Southeastern Archaeological Conference Bulletin* 18:117–22.
  1975b   The Woodland Period South of the Fall Line. *Early Georgia* 3(1).
  1978   Weeden Island–Swift Creek Affinities in the Middle Chattahoochee Valley. *Journal of Alabama Archaeology* 24(1):60–64.
  1980   Late Prehistoric Ceramic Chronology of the Lower Chattahoochee Valley. Paper presented at the 37th Annual Meeting of the Southeastern Archaeological Conference, New Orleans.
  n.d.   Cultural Change among the Lower Creeks as Reflected in the Archaeological Record. Manuscript, Columbus Museum of Arts and Sciences, Columbus.
Schnell, Frank T., Jr., and Knight, Vernon J., Jr.
  1978   Rood and Cemochechobee: A Chattahoochee Perspective of Fort Walton. Paper presented at the Annual Meeting of the Florida Anthropological Society, Fort Walton, 1978.
Schnell, Frank T.; Knight, Vernon J., Jr.; and Schnell, Gail S.
  1979   *Cemochechobee: Archaeological Investigations at the Walter F. George Dam Mound Site, (9Cla62), Clay County, Georgia.* Columbus, Georgia: Columbus Museum of Arts and Sciences, Inc.
  1981   *Cemochechobee: Archaeology of a Mississippian Ceremonial Center on the Chattahoochee River.* Ripley P. Bullen Monographs in Anthropology and History 3. Gainesville: University Presses of Florida.
Schnell, Gail
  1980   A Preliminary Political Model for the Roods Phase. Paper presented at the 27th Annual Meeting of the Southeastern Archaeological Conference, New Orleans.
Schoolcraft, Henry R.
  1849   *Notices of Some Antique Earthen Vessels Found in the Low Tumuli of Florida and in the Caves and Burial Places of the Indian Tribes North of those Latitudes.* New York: William Van Norden, Printer.
Sears, William H.
  1953   *Excavations at Kolomoki: Seasons III and IV, Mound D.* University of Georgia Series in Anthropology 4. Athens.
  1954   The Sociopolitical Organization of Pre-Columbian Cultures on the Gulf Coastal Plain. *American Anthropologist* 56(3):339–46.
  1956   *Excavations at Kolomoki: Final Report.* University of Georgia Series in Anthropology 5. Athens.
  1958   Burial Mounds in the Gulf Coastal Plain. *American Antiquity* 23(3):274–84.
  1961   The Study of Social and Religious Systems in North American Archaeology. *Current Anthropology* 2(3):223–46.
  1962a   The State in Certain Areas and Periods of the Prehistoric Southeastern United States. *Ethnohistory* 9(5):109–25.
  1962b   An Investigation of Prehistoric Processes on the Gulf Coastal Plain. NSF G-5019. Manuscript, National Science Foundation.
  1963   *The Tucker Site on Alligator Harbor, Franklin County, Florida.* Contributions of the Florida State Museum, Social Sciences 9. Gainesville.
  1964   The Southeastern United States. In *Prehistoric Man in the New World*, edited by J. D. Jennings and E. Norbeck, pp. 259–90. Chicago: University of Chicago Press.
  1967   The Tierra Verde Burial Mound. *Florida Anthropologist* 20(1–2):25–74.

1968   The State and Settlement Patterns in the New World. In *Settlement Archae-
        ology*, edited by K. C. Chang, pp. 134–53. Palo Alto, California: National
        Press.
1973   The Sacred and the Secular in Prehistoric Ceramics. In *Variations in Anthropol-
        ogy: Essays in Honor of John C. McGregor*, edited by D. Lathrup and J. Douglas,
        pp. 31–42. Urbana: Illinois Archaeological Survey.
1977   Prehistoric Culture Areas and Culture Change on the Gulf Coastal Plain. In
        For the Director: Research Essays in Honor of James B. Griffin, edited by C. E. Cle-
        land, pp. 152–84. Anthropological Papers, Museum of Anthropology, Uni-
        versity of Michigan 61. Ann Arbor.
Sellards, E. H.
1912   The Soils and Other Surface Residual Materials of Florida. *Florida Geological
        Survey, Fourth Annual Report*, pp. 8–79. Tallahassee.
1916   Human Remains and Associated Fossils from the Pleistocene of Florida. *Flor-
        ida Geological Survey, Eighth Annual Report*, pp. 121–60. Tallahassee.
1917   On the Association of Human Remains and Extinct Vertebrates at Vero, Flor-
        ida. *Journal of Geology* 25:4–24.
1940   Pleistocene Artifacts and Associated Fossils from Bee County, Texas. *Bulletin
        of the Geological Society of America* 51:1627–58.
Sellards, E. H., and Gunter, H.
1918   Geology between the Apalachicola and Ocklocknee Rivers in Florida. *Florida
        Geological Survey, Tenth Annual Report*, pp. 11–55. Tallahassee.
Service, Elman R.
1971   *Primitive Social Organization*. 2d ed. New York: Random House.
Setzler, Frank M., and Jennings, Jesse D.
1941   *Peachtree Mound and Village Site, Cherokee County, North Carolina*. Bureau of
        American Ethnology Bulletin 131. Washington: Smithsonian Institution.
Shafer, Harry J.
1966   *An Archaeological Survey of Wallisville Reservoir, Chambers County, Texas*. Texas
        Archaeological Salvage Project Survey Reports 2. Austin: University of Texas.
1975   Comments on Woodland Cultures of East Texas. *Bulletin of the Texas Archaeo-
        logical Society* 46:249–54.
Shea, John Gilmary (editor)
1861   *Early Voyages Up and Down the Mississippi by Cavelier, St. Cosme, Le Sueur, Gravier
        and Guignas*. Albany: Joel Munsell.
Sheldon, Craig T., Jr.
1974   The Mississippian-Historic Transition in Central Alabama. Ph.D. Disserta-
        tion, University of Oregon.
Sheldon, Elizabeth, and Cameron, Marguerita L.
1976   Reconstruction of Prehistoric Environments: The Warm Mineral Springs
        Project. *Southeastern Archaeological Conference Bulletin* 19:68–69.
Shelford, Victor E.
1963   *The Ecology of North America*. Urbana: University of Illinois Press.
Shelley, Steven D.
1981   The Coles Creek Period Settlement System of Louisiana's Chenier Coastal
        Plain. *Southeastern Archaeological Conference Bulletin* 24:41–43.
Shenkel, J. Richard
1974   Big Oak and Little Oak Islands: Excavations and Interpretation. *Louisiana Ar-
        chaeology Bulletin* 1:37–65.
1976   Ceramics of the Tchefuncte Period. Paper presented at the 33d Annual Meet-
        ing of the Southeastern Archaeological Conference, Tuscaloosa.
1979   Tchefuncte Site Specialization. Paper presented at the 36th Annual Meeting
        of the Southeastern Archaeological Conference, Atlanta.
1980   Oak Island Archaeology: Prehistoric Estuarine Adaptations in the Mississippi
        River Delta. Manuscript, University of New Orleans.

1984   An Early Marksville Ossuary in Coastal Louisiana. *Midcontinental Journal of Archaeology* 9. In press.

n.d.   Oak Island Archaeology Prehistoric Estuarine Adaptations in the Mississippi River Delta. Manuscript prepared for the Jean Lafitte Historical Park, National Park Service, through the Archaeological and Cultural Research Program, University of New Orleans.

Shenkel, J. Richard, and Gibson, John L.
1974   Big Oak Island: An Historical Perspective of Changing Site Function. *Louisiana Studies* 8(2): 173–86.

Shenkel, J. Richard, with Holley, George
1975   A Tchefuncte House. *Southeastern Archaeological Conference Bulletin* 18: 226–42.

Shepard, Anna O.
1976   *Ceramics for the Archaeologist*. Carnegie Institution of Washington Publication 609.

Shepard, F. P., and Wanless, H. R.
1971   *Our Changing Coastlines*. New York: McGraw-Hill.

Sherman, Harley B.
1952   A History and Bibliography of the Mammals of Florida, Living and Extinct. *Quarterly Journal of Academic Sciences* 15(2): 86–126.

Sibley, John
1806   Historical Sketches of the Indian Tribes in Louisiana, South of the Arkansas River. *American State Papers, 9th Congress and Session*, pp. 1076–88.

Simmons, M. H.
1883   Shell-heaps of Charlotte Harbor, Florida. In *Annual Report of the Smithsonian Institution for 1882*, pp. 794–96. Washington.

Smith, Betty A.
1975   The Relationship between Deptford and Swift Creek Ceramics as Evidenced at the Mandeville Site 9Cla1. *Southeastern Archaeological Conference Bulletin* 18: 195–200.

1977   Southwest Georgia Prehistory: An Overview. *Early Georgia* 5(1–2): 61–72.

Smith, Bruce D.
1978   Variation in Mississippian Settlement Patterns. In *Mississippian Settlement Patterns*, edited by Bruce Smith, pp. 479–504. New York: Academic Press.

Smith, Bruce D. (editor)
1978   *Mississippian Settlement Patterns*. New York: Academic Press.

Smith, Buckingham (translator)
1968   *Narratives of de Soto in the Conquest of Florida*. Facsimile of the 1866 Bradford Club edition. Gainesville: Palmetto Books.

Smith, Hale G.
1948   Two Historic Archaeological Periods in Florida. *American Antiquity* 13(4): 313–19.

1951   The Influence of European Cultural Contact upon Aboriginal Cultures of North Florida. Ph.D. dissertation, University of Michigan.

1957   A Fort Walton Shellfish Collecting Station, Wakulla County, Florida. In *Tidal Marshes of the Gulf and Atlantic Coasts of Northern Florida and Charleston, S.C.*, edited by Herman Kurz and Kenneth Wagner, pp. 105–8. Florida State University Studies 24. Tallahassee.

Smith, Samuel D.
1971   Excavations at the Hope Mound, with an Addendum to the Safford Mound Report. *Florida Anthropologist* 24(3): 107–34.

Snow, Charles E.
1945   Tchefuncte Skeletal Remains. In *The Tchefuncte Culture, An Early Occupation of the Lower Mississippi Valley*, edited by James A. Ford and George I. Quimby, Jr. Society for American Archaeology, Memoir 2.

Sokal, R., and Sneath, P. H. A.
 1963 *Principals of Numerical Taxonomy*. San Francisco: Freeman.
Spellman, C. H.
 1948 The Agriculture of the Early North Florida Indians. *Florida Anthropologist* 1(3–4):37–48.
Springer, James W.
 1973 The Prehistory and Cultural Geography of Coastal Louisiana. Ph.D. dissertation, Yale University.
 1974 The Bruly St. Martin Site and its Implications for Coastal Settlement in Louisiana. *Louisiana Archaeology* 1:75–82.
 1976 A Ceramic Sequence from Southern Louisiana and its Implications for Type Frequency Seriation. *Louisiana Archaeology* 3:123–91.
 1979 Excavations at the Pierre Clement Site, Cameron Parish, Louisiana. *Louisiana Archaeology* 4:53–90.
 1980 An Analysis of Prehistoric Food Remains from the Bruly St. Martin Site, Louisiana, with a Comparative Discussion of Mississippi Valley Faunal Studies. *Midcontinental Journal of Archaeology* 5(2):193–223.
Stafford, Malinda
 1979 Preliminary Design Attribute Analysis of Weeden Island Ceramics. Temple Mound Museum, Fort Walton Beach, Florida.
Steinen, Karl
 1977 Weeden Island in Southwest Georgia. *Early Georgia* 5(1–2):13–21.
Steponaitis, Vincas P.
 1976 Plaquemine Ceramic Chronology in the Natchez Region. Paper presented at the 33d Annual Meeting of the Southeastern Archaeological Conference, Tuscaloosa.
 1978 Some Preliminary Chronological and Technological Notes on Moundville Pottery. Paper presented at the 35th Annual Meeting of the Southeastern Archaeological Conference, Knoxville.
 1980a Some Preliminary Chronological and Technological Notes on Moundville Pottery. *Southeastern Archaeological Conference Bulletin* 22:46–51.
 1980b Ceramics, Chronology and Community Patterns at Moundville, Late Prehistoric Site in Alabama. Vols. 1 and 2. Ph.D. dissertation, University of Michigan.
Sternberg, G. M.
 1876 Indian Burial Mounds and Shellheaps near Pensacola, Florida. *American Association for the Advancement of Science Proceedings* 24:282–92.
Stevenson, Henry M.
 1960 *A Key to Florida Birds*. Tallahassee: Peninsular Publishers.
Steward, Julian
 1955 *Theory of Culture Change: The Methodology of Multilineal Evolution*. Urbana: University of Illinois Press.
Stockdale, Mabel K., and Bryenton, Sally E.
 1978 Indian Plant Foods of the Florida Panhandle. *Florida Anthropologist* 31(3):109–16.
Stoltman, J. B.
 1978 Temporal Models in Prehistory: An Example from Eastern North America. *Current Anthropology* 19(4):703–46.
Strong, W. D.
 1935 *An Introduction to Nebraska Archaeology*. Smithsonian Miscellaneous Collections 93(10).
Suhm, Dee Ann; Krieger, Alex D.; and Jelks, Edward B.
 1954 *An Introductory Handbook of Texas Archaeology*. Bulletin of the Texas Archaeological Society 25.

Swanton, John R.
1911   *Indian Tribes of the Lower Mississippi Valley and Adjacent Coast of the Gulf of Mexico.* Bureau of American Ethnology Bulletin 43. Washington: Smithsonian Institution.
1917   Unclassified Languages of the Southeast. *International Journal of American Linguistics* 1(1): 47–49.
1922   *Early History of the Creek Indians and Their Neighbors.* Bureau of American Ethnology Bulletin 73. Washington: Smithsonian Institution.
1928a   Aboriginal Culture of the Southeast. *Bureau of American Ethnology, 42d Annual Report, 1924–25,* pp. 673–726. Washington: Smithsonian Institution.
1928b   Social Organization and Social Usages of the Indians of the Creek Confederacy. *Bureau of American Ethnology, 42d Annual Report, 1924–25,* pp. 23–472. Washington: Smithsonian Institution.
1928c   The Interpretation of Aboriginal Mounds by Means of Creek Customs. *Smithsonian Institution Annual Report for 1927,* pp. 495–506. Washington.
1931   Indian Language Studies in Louisiana. *Explorations and Fieldwork of the Smithsonian Institution in 1930,* pp. 195–200. Washington.
1932   Choctaw Societies. *American Anthropologist* 34: 357.
1935   Notes on the Cultural Province of the Southeast. *American Anthropologist* 37: 373–385.
1939   *Final Report of the United States De Soto Expedition Commission.* House Document 71, 76th Congress, 1st sess. Washington.
1946   *The Indians of the Southeastern United States.* Bureau of American Ethnology Bulletin 137. Washington: Smithsonian Institution.
1952   *The Indian Tribes of North America.* Bureau of American Ethnology Bulletin 145. Washington: Smithsonian Institution.
Tesar, Louis
1973   *Archaeological Survey of the Proposed Gulf Islands National Recreation Area, Alabama, Florida, and Mississippi.* Vols. 1 and 2. Report to the National Park Service, Atlanta.
1979   *The Leon County Bicentennial Survey Project: An Archaeological Survey of Selected Portions of Leon County, Florida.* Bureau of Historic Sites and Properties Miscellaneous Project Report Series 49. Tallahassee: Division of Archives, History, and Records Management, Florida Department of State.
1980   The De Soto Entrada and Fort Walton Chronology in the Tallahassee Red Hills. Paper presented at the 37th Annual Meeting of the Southeastern Archaeological Conference, New Orleans.
Thanz-Borremans, Nina, and Shaak, Graig D.
1977   Significance of a Sponge Spicule Temper in Florida Chalky Paste Pottery. Paper presented at the Florida Anthropological Society Annual Meeting, Tampa.
Thomas, David H., and Larsen, Clark S.
1979   *The Anthropology of St. Catherine's Island 2: The Refuge-Deptford Mortuary Complex.* Anthropological Papers of the American Museum of Natural History 56(1). New York.
Thwaites, Reuben Gold (editor)
1896–1901   *The Jesuit Relations and Allied Documents: Travel and Exploration of the Jesuit Missionaries in New France, 1610–1791: The Original French, Latin, and Italian Texts, with English Translations and Notes.* 73 vols. Cleveland: The Burrows Brothers Company.
Toth, Alan
1974   *Archaeology and Ceramics at the Marksville Site.* University of Michigan Anthropological Papers 56. Ann Arbor.

1977   Early Marksville Phases in the Lower Mississippi Valley: A Study of Culture
        Contact Dynamics. Ph.D. dissertation, Harvard University.
Trickey, E. B.
    1958   A Chronological Framework for the Mobile Bay Region. *American Antiquity*
            23:388–96.
Trickey, E. B., and Holmes, N. H.
    1967   The Mobile Bay Chronology. *Southeastern Archaeological Conference Bulletin*
            6:23–26.
    1971   A Chronological Framework for the Mobile Bay Region. *Journal of Alabama
            Archaeology* 17(1):115–28.
Turnbaugh, William A.
    1978   Floods and Archaeology. *American Antiquity* 43(4):593–607.
Ubelaker, D. H.
    1974   *Reconstruction of Demographic Profiles from Ossuary Skeletal Samples.* Smithsonian
            Contributions to Anthropology 18. Washington.
Upchurch, Sam B.
    1980   Chert Origins and Availability, Pinellas and Hillsborough Counties, Florida.
            In *Holocene Geology and Man in Pinellas and Hillsborough Counties, Florida*, com-
            piled by S. B. Upchurch, pp. 48–55. Tampa: Southeastern Geological Society.
Walker, S. T.
    1885   Mounds and Shell Heaps on the West Coast of Florida. *Smithsonian Institution,
            Annual Report for 1883*, pp. 854–68. Washington.
Walthall, John A.
    1980   *Prehistoric Indians of the Southeast: Archaeology of Alabama and the Middle South.*
            University: University of Alabama Press.
Walthall, John A., and Jenkins, Ned J.
    1976   The Gulf Formational Stage in Southeastern Prehistory. *Southeastern Archaeo-
            logical Conference Bulletin* 19:43–49.
Waring, Antonio J.
    1968   The Southern Cult and Muskhogean Ceremonial. In *The Waring Papers, the
            Collected Works of Antonio J. Waring, Jr.*, edited by Stephen Williams, pp. 30–69.
            Papers of the Peabody Museum of Archaeology and Ethnology 58. Cam-
            bridge: Harvard University.
Waring, Antonio J., and Holder, Preston
    1945   A Prehistoric Ceremonial Complex in the Southeastern United States. *Ameri-
            can Anthropologist* 47(1):1–34.
Watts, W. A.
    1969   A Pollen Diagram from Mud Lake, Marion County, Florida. *Geological Society
            of America Bulletin* 80:631–42.
    1971   Post-glacial and Inter-glacial Vegetation History of Southern Georgia and
            Central Florida. *Ecology* 52:676–90.
    1980   Late Quaternary Vegetation History at White Pond on the Inner Coastal Plain
            of South Carolina. *Quaternary Research* 13:187–99.
Wauchope, Robert
    1947   Notes on Little Pecan Island, Louisiana. *American Antiquity* 12(3):186–88.
    1948   The Ceramic Sequence in the Etowah Drainage, Northwest Georgia. *American
            Antiquity* 13(3):201–9.
    1966   *Archaeological Survey of Northern Georgia, with a Test of some Cultural Hypotheses.*
            Memoirs of the Society for American Archaeology 21.
Webb, Clarence H.
    1968   Evidences of Prepottery Cultures in Louisiana. *American Antiquity* 33(3):
            297–321.
    1970   Intrasite Distribution of Artifacts at the Poverty Point Site, with Special Refer-
            ence to Women's and Men's Activities. In *The Poverty Point Culture, Southeast
            Archaeological Conference Bulletin* 12:21–36.

1977   The Poverty Point Culture. *Geoscience and Man* 17. Baton Rouge.

Wedel, W. R.
1938   Hopewellian Remains Near Kansas City, Missouri. *Proceedings: United States National Museum* 86.

Weigel, Robert D.
1962   *Fossil Vertebrates of Vero, Florida.* Florida Geological Survey, Special Publications 10.

Weinstein, Richard A.
1981   Meandering Rivers and Shifting Villages: A Prehistoric Settlement Model in the Upper Steele Bayou Basin. *Southeastern Archaeological Conference Bulletin* 24:34–37.

Weinstein, Richard A., and Rivet, Phillip G.
1978   *Beau Mire: A Late Tchula Period Site of the Tchefuncte Culture, Ascension Parish, Louisiana.* Louisiana Archaeological Survey and Antiquities Commission Anthropological Report 1. Baton Rouge: Department of Culture, Recreation, and Tourism.

Weinstein, Richard A.; Burden, Eileen, K.; and Gagliano, Sherwood M.
1977   Archaeological Phases—Coastal Louisiana. Paper presented at the 3d Annual Meeting of the Louisiana Archaeological Society, New Orleans.

Weinstein, Richard A.; Burden, Eileen K.; Brooks, Katherine L.; and Gagliano, Sherwood M.
1978   Cultural Resource Survey of the Proposed Relocation Route of U.S. 90 (LA 3052), Assumption, St. Mary, and Terrebonne Parishes, Louisiana. Manuscript, Coastal Environments, Inc., Baton Rouge.

Weinstein, Richard A.; Wiseman, Diane E.; Landry, Laura A.; and Glander, Wayne P.
1979   Environment and Settlement on the Southwestern Louisiana Prairies: A Cultural Resources Survey in the Bayou Mallet Watershed. Coastal Environments, Inc., Baton Rouge.

Weinstein, R. A.; Glander, W. P.; Gagliano, S. M.; Burden, E. K.; and McCloskey, K. G.
1979   Cultural Resources Survey of the Upper Steele Bayou Basin, West Central Mississippi. Report prepared by Coastal Environments, Inc., for U.S. Army Corps of Engineers, Vicksburg District, Contract No. DACW-38-78C-0030.

Wendland, Wayne M., and Bryson, Reid A.
1974   Dating Climatic Episodes of the Holocene. *Quaternary Research* 4(1):9–24.

White, Nancy M.
1980   Fort Walton Development in the Upper Apalachicola–Lower Chattahoochee Valley. Paper presented at the 37th Annual Meeting of the Southeastern Archaeological Conference, New Orleans.
1981   The Curlee Site (85a7) and Fort Walton Development in the Upper Apalachicola–Lower Chattahoochee Valley. Ph.D. dissertation, Case Western Reserve University.

White, Nancy M.; Brose, David D.; Belovich, Stephanie; and Wiseman, Russell
1981   Archaeology at Lake Seminole. Final Report on the Cultural Resources Survey and Evaluation of Lake Seminole, Alabama, Georgia and Florida. Report in progress, to be submitted to the U.S. Army Corps of Engineers, Mobile District.

Whitehead, Donald R.
1972   Developmental and Environmental History of the Dismal Swamp. *Ecological Monographs* 43:301–15.

Widmer, Randolph J.
1974   *A Survey and Assessment of Archaeological Resources on Marco Island, Collier County, Florida.* Bureau of Historic Sites and Properties, Miscellaneous Project Report Series 19. Tallahassee: Division of Archives, History, and Records Management, Florida Department of State.

1978   The Structure of Late Prehistoric Adaptation on the Southwest Florida Coast.
        Master's thesis, Pennsylvania State University.

Willey, Gordon R.
1945   The Weeden Island Culture: A Preliminary Definition. *American Antiquity*
        10(3):225–54.
1948   Culture Sequence in the Manatee Region of West Florida. *American Antiquity*
        13(3):209–18.
1949   *Archeology of the Florida Gulf Coast.* Smithsonian Miscellaneous Collections 113.
        Washington.
1960   *New World Prehistory.* Smithsonian Report. Washington.

Willey, Gordon R., and Phillips, Philip
1958   *Method and Theory in American Archaeology.* Chicago: University of Chicago
        Press.

Willey, Gordon, and Woodbury, Richard
1942   A Chronological Outline for the Northwest Florida Coast. *American Antiquity*
        7(3):232–54.

Williams, John Lee
1962   *The Territory of Florida: Or, Sketches of the Topography, Civil and Natural History of
        the Country, the Climate, and the Indian Tribes from the First Discovery to the Present
        Time.* Facsimile of the original 1837 edition. Gainesville: University of Florida
        Press.

Williams, Stephen (editor)
1971   Round Table on the Definition of Mississippian Culture. *Southeastern Archaeo-
        logical Conference Newsletter* 10(2):1–19.

Williams, Stephen, and Brain, Jeffrey P.
n.d.   *Excavations at Lake George, Yazoo County, Mississippi, 1958–1960.* Papers of the
        Peabody Museum of Archaeology and Ethnology, in press.

Williams, Stephen, and Stoltman, James B.
1965   An Outline of Southeastern United States Prehistory with Particular Empha-
        sis on the Paleo-Indian Era. In *The Quaternary of the United States,* edited by
        N. E. Wright and D. G. Frey, pp. 669–83. Princeton: Princeton University
        Press.

Williams, Stephen; Kean, W.; and Toth, Alan
1966   *The Archaeology of the Upper Tensas Basin.* Lower Mississippi Survey Bulletin 1.
        Peabody Museum, Harvard University.

Wimberly, Stephen B.
1953a   McLeod Deptford Pottery Series. In *Prehistoric Pottery of the Eastern United
        States,* edited by J. B. Griffin. Ann Arbor: Museum of Anthropology, Univer-
        sity of Michigan.
1953b   Bayou La Batre Tchefuncte Series. In *Prehistoric Pottery of the Eastern United
        States,* edited by J. B. Griffin. Ann Arbor: Museum of Anthropology, Univer-
        sity of Michigan.
1960   *Indian Pottery from Clarke County and Mobile County, Southern Alabama.* Alabama
        Museum of Natural History, Museum Paper 36.

Wimberly, Stephen B., and Tourtelot, Harry A.
1941   *The McQuorquodale Mound: A Manifestation of the Hopewellian Phase in South Ala-
        bama.* Geological Survey of Alabama, Museum Paper 19.

Wing, Elizabeth S.
1965   Animal Bones Associated with Two Indian Sites on Marco Island, Florida.
        Florida Anthropologist 18(1):21–28.
1977   Subsistence Systems in the Southeast. *Florida Anthropologist* 30(2):81–87.

Wiseman, Diane E.; Weinstein, Richard A.; and McCloskey, Kathleen G.
1979   Cultural Resources Survey of the Mississippi River–Gulf Outlet, Orleans and
        St. Bernard Parishes, Louisiana. Coastal Environments, Inc., Baton Rouge.

Wood, Roland, and Fernald, Edward A.
  1974 *The New Florida Atlas: Patterns of the Sunshine State.* Tallahassee: Trend
        Publishers.
Wright, Herbert E., Jr.
  1976 The Dynamic Nature of Holocene Vegetation: A Problem in Paleoclimatol-
        ogy, Biogeography and Stratigraphic Nomenclature. *Quaternary Research*
        6:581–96.
Yesner, D. R.
  1980 Maritime Hunter-Gatherers: Ecology and Prehistory. *Current Anthropology*
        21(6):727–50.
Zubillaga, Felix (editor)
  1946 Monumenta Antiquae Floridae (1566–1572). *Monumenta Historica Societatis
        Iesu* 69, *Monumenta Missionum Societatis Iesu* 3. Rome.

Index

An italic page number indicates that the reference is to a table or illustration on that page.